THE MAN WHO WAS NEVER SHAKESPEARE

The Theft of
William Shakspere's Identity

1. The Sanders Portrait of William Shakspere?
By permission of the owner, Lloyd Sullivan, Canada.

THE MAN WHO WAS
NEVER SHAKESPEARE

The Theft of
William Shakspere's Identity

by

A. J. Pointon

Also published by Parapress:
Dating Shakespeare's Plays, ed. Kevin Gilvary, 2010
The Knocknobbler by Bernard Cartwright, 2007
*Great Oxford: Essays on the Life and Works of Edward de Vere,
17th Earl of Oxford*, ed. Richard Malim, 2004

ISBN: 978-1-898594-88-8

First published in the UK by
PARAPRESS
9 Frant Road
Tunbridge Wells
Kent TN2 5SD
www.parapress.co.uk

Typeset in Aldine by Helm Information
amandahelm@helm-information.co.uk
www.helm-information.co.uk

Print management by Sutherland Eve Production
guyeve@theeves.fsnet.co.uk

Cover Illustration by Helm Information: the Warwickshire Avon flows
past Stratford's Holy Trinity Church, where William Shakspere and
his son Hamnet Shakspere were both baptised and buried. Detail of a
painting, courtesy of *Postcards of the Past* (www.oldstratforduponavon.
com). Inset is the original (1623) bust in the Church, showing William
Shakspere holding a sack of goods.

Printed and bound in Great Britain
by Berforts Group, Stevenage, SG1 2BH
www.berforts.co.uk

Contents

Illustrations

Acknowledgements

In writing this book, the Roman principle has been applied – "who can run [to the Forum] can read". For writing a book on the great poet-playwright Shakespeare and William Shakspere of Stratford requires trawling through, and acknowledging, the work of a ghostly army of scholars and researchers who, stretching back into four centuries, have discovered and analysed more relevant (and irrelevant) material than could ever have been imagined when the marvellous plays and poems first appeared. Many would find things not only unexpected but also unwanted, and one must be grateful, though temptation must at times have been great, that there seem to have been few cases where inconvenient documents relevant to the Shakespeare authorship question were destroyed. On a more personal level, I would wish to thank those who have discussed the content of this text (particularly Elizabeth Imlay, my publisher; Amanda Helm, editor; Hugh Mason of Portsmouth; Diana Price of Cleveland, Ohio, Robin Williams of Santa Fé, and Kevin Gilvary of Titchfield), and the University of Portsmouth Library, the Portsmouth City Library and the British Library. I would also like to thank David Gregory of Postcards of the Past (www.oldstratforduponavon.com) for providing the cover image.

I thank Shakespeare's Globe, London, for the splendour of its presentations of Shakespeare's works and the wonder that it actually exists.

All views, arguments and opinions advanced in this book are at the sole responsibility of the author.

References and Notes

Main Bibliographic References

Chambers, E. K., *Shakespeare: a Study of Facts and
Problems*, (1930)   – *EKC*
Oxford Companion to Shakespeare, (2000)   – *OCS*
Schoenbaum, S. *Shakespeare: A Documentary Life* (1975)   – *SDL*
—, *Shakespeare: A Concise Documentary Life* (1987)   – *SCDL*
Oxford Dictionary of National Biography (2004)   – *ODNB*
Oxford Companion to English Literature (2000)   – *OCEL*

A Note on Spelling

In dealing with variant spellings in the records for the player William Shakspere and the writer William Shakespeare, those two will be used as generic names; specific spellings will be used when occasion demands. Shakspere's grandson was baptised "Shaksper": that will be used for the record but he will be "Shakspere" in general. A poem written for the writer as "Will. Shake-speare" will be referred to as being for Shakespeare. And we will be noting that Shakspere and Shakespeare never used each others' names.

The spelling and punctuation has been modernised except where it is better left as in the original. The purpose is to avoid misleading anyone, and it is hoped the spellings as printed are as we intended, given the spell-checker's tendency to "correct" us.

A Note on Elizabethan Prices

As we are bound to mention money, costs and values in this book, and we need to realise that William Shakspere would have been a millionaire in today's money, we need to have a conversion factor for inflation since 1616. Fortunately, it is pretty accurate to take the rise in prices to be by a factor 600 which is fairly easy to handle. We also need to note that British currency in 1600, and right up to 1971, had 240 pence or 240d to £1; 20 shillings or 20s to £1, and 12d to 1s. (A sum of money like one pound ten shillings would be written as £1..10s..0d or just £1..10..0, while a guinea was 21 shillings or £1..1..0. The price of a sixpenny or 6d Quarto edition of a play would equate to £15 today; a 2d chicken to £5 now; the First Folio unbound at 15s would be £0.75 then and some £450 now; Jonson's Crown pension of 100 marks would be £40,000 (as 1 mark = 2/3 of £1 = 13s..4d = 160d) and Shakspere's Chapel Lane house at £80 would be £48,000 which would be cheap today. (Most books work on too low a figure, possibly because it seems hard to believe inflation since World War Two has been well over 30 times.)

THE WORKS OF SHAKESPEARE

First Folio Plays

All is True (or *Henry VIII*)	*Julius Caesar*	*Richard II*
All's Well that Ends Well	*King John*	*Richard III*
Antony and Cleopatra	*King Lear*	*Romeo and Juliet*
As You Like it	*Love's Labour's Lost*	*The Taming of the Shrew*
The Comedy of Errors	*Macbeth*	*The Tempest*
Coriolanus	*Measure for Measure*	*Timon of Athens*
Cymbeline	*The Merchant of Venice*	*Titus Andronicus*
Hamlet	*The Merry Wives of Windsor*	*Troilus and Cressida*
Henry IV (Parts *I* and 2)	*A Midsummer Night's Dream*	*Twelfth Night*
Henry V	*Much Ado About Nothing*	*The Two Gentlemen of Verona*
Henry VI (Parts *1, 2, & 3*)	*Othello*	*The Winter's Tale*

Added to Third Folio: *Pericles*

Poems

The Rape of Lucrece   *The Sonnets*
Venus and Adonis

Doubtful Poems

A Lover's Complaint
The Phoenix and the Turtle

Sure he that made us with such large discourse,
Looking before and after, gave us not
That capability and God-like reason
To fust in us unus'd.

Hamlet

"We will probably never know what Shakespeare looked like."
Searching for Shakespeare,
National Portrait Gallery, London (2006)

"We probably already know what both William Shakspere of Stratford and William Shakespeare the poet-playwright looked like."
A. J. Pointon, Lecture, Ontario Shakespeare Festival (2007)

CHAPTER 1

The Problem in a Nutshell

"Our plot was as good a plot as ever was laid."
Henry IV Part I

It is not surprising that it takes most people a long time to realise that the name William Shakespeare, invented for himself in 1593 by the writer of the poem *Venus and Adonis,* was a pseudonym – and some may never get it. All pseudonyms can be difficult to penetrate, even when the real writers take only the simplest precautions; however, in this case it was made far worse. When this writer's collected plays were published thirty years later, in 1623, in what would become known as Shakespeare's "First Folio", someone had the idea, not entirely original, of setting up a decoy for him, with hints that the pseudonym hid some other known real person. This strategy, most probably originating with those who planned the publication of this great book, cleverly used as decoy an actor-businessman from Stratford-upon-Avon with a name similar to "Shakespeare" – William Shakspere – who, being dead, was not in a position to object.

Their aim, of course, was to continue to protect the identity of the real author at a time when writing dramatic fiction was thought unbecoming for some (as it remained to the twentieth century) and possibly dangerous. Writers who touched on political, religious or even personal issues could be at risk – like when Ben Jonson and others went to prison for poking fun at Scotsmen who had come to London with James I – and so might their families. The sleight of hand used to switch the identity of this William Shakspere to the writer Shakespeare is dealt with in detail in Chapter 13; the way the deception developed after that is discussed in Chapter 14; and, in Chapter 15, it is shown how we know William Shakspere was never Shakespeare, and was never thought to be so during his lifetime.

Today, the Shakespeare substitution, based on the theft of an innocent man's identity and helped along by generations of scholars, has led to the

1

widespread myth that Stratford's William Shakspere was actually named "Shakespeare", which he was not; and that he wrote magnificent plays and poems under his own name, when he was not writing at all. Now, after several centuries spent bolstering this "orthodox" view of Shakespeare, the result is that many people find it hard to accept that they might have fallen victim to a clever confidence trick.

For those who do accept, or deduce, that there is a "Shakespeare authorship problem" – and that is not too difficult when the facts are laid out – it is natural to want to know who the real Shakespeare was. Yet that question has to come later. Before one seeks the real writer to take on the mantle that was thrust on the unsuspecting Shakspere – whether one wants to choose Christopher Marlowe or Francis Bacon or even someone yet unknown – one has to show first that there really has been a Shakespeare deception. It is no use just asserting that Shakespeare was not William Shakspere. Relying on assertion is how the Shakspere myth – or the "orthodox" Shakespeare theory – got where it is now. Instead, we must show what actually happened to Shakspere's identity in 1623 and what has happened to it since; and hope in the process to restore to him, as far as possible, his own identity and his real family name. In doing that, we will find William Shakspere of Stratford, though very different from the person who wrote as "Shakespeare", was actually of interest in his own right, and that no apology is needed on his behalf for him not being Shakespeare.

It is not difficult to work out what happened when William Shakspere was credited with the works of Shakespeare. This was a very different kind of theft from those that were attempted after Charlotte Brontë and Marian Evans had written under the pen-names of Currer Bell and George Eliot in the 1800s. During their lifetimes these two women had to contend with men who deliberately put themselves forward as the writers behind those pseudonyms with the intention of stealing the income and credit that went with their works. William Shakspere, on the contrary, had no part in any deception. He was long dead when hints appeared, as if from nowhere, that he was the writer Shakespeare. No benefits from those hints, or from the works so strangely attributed to him, accrued to him or to his family. Instead, he lost his identity, his character and the true story of his life, while his family lost its proper name.

It never occurred to the present writer, a Midlands boy whose background was comparable to William Shakspere's – even earning money by curing rabbit skins for gloves and going to work early – that a tradesman's son from Stratford could not have written superb plays and poems given the opportunities, abilities, experiences, resources and the inclination. Indeed, no one can deny Shakspere had abilities, even if he did employ them in directions very different from those of the writer Shakespeare. The first difficulty in accepting the "Shakspere was Shakespeare" nonsense is that the real facts of William Shakspere's life (as opposed to the many inventions used to distort it) are totally at odds with what would be required of any candidate put forward to be the writer Shakespeare. History Professor Blair Worden expressed it with admirable precision in 1992 when he wrote of the playwright Shakespeare, believing him to be William Shakspere of Stratford:

> The relationship between an artist's biography and his writing is always a difficult subject, but there can be no other important writer since the invention of printing for whom we are unable to demonstrate any relationship at all.

If Worden had accepted that the actor-businessman from Stratford and the man writing as Shakespeare were two quite different individuals, the problem he thought he was facing would have simply evaporated.

Now, unlike various books that approach the Shakspere myth by setting out to find a writer better fitted than Shakspere to be the real Shakespeare, this one is dedicated primarily to Shakspere himself, seeking to give him back his true identity, as far as we can, and to understand the reality of the life he must have led in Stratford and London. This will naturally involve showing why (and how) someone used him as a decoy, or a shield, to hide the real Shakespeare, thereby creating the myth that he was a writer, and also how that myth was nurtured over nearly four hundred years. Once that is done, it may be possible for the genuine evidence about Shakespeare to be shared by scholars who differ about who the real writer really was.

This process should also allow the removal of the distortions which have been introduced into the character of the writer Shakespeare to try to maintain the illusion that he was Shakspere; and also allow the disposal of the fictitious portraits of Shakespeare that have been foisted on public, publishers, and public art galleries alike. We may even find that we already know what both William Shakspere and the real William Shakespeare looked like.

For ease of cross-reference by the reader when we are talking of our William Shakspere, some 150 salient facts about him and his family are given in Appendix I. The nature of these facts is so different from what one would expect from the lifetime of a top writer that they must recall Schoenbaum's words at the end of his book *Shakespeare's Lives* (1970):

> Perhaps we should despair of ever bridging the vertiginous expanse between the sublimity of the subject [i.e. Shakespeare] and the mundane inconsequence of the documentary record [of Shakspere].

There is no "perhaps" about it. The man for whom we have the mundane documentary record was not Schoenbaum's sublime subject: he is yet to be uncovered. In addition, we can quote examples of other scholars and writers who, sometimes unintentionally, have identified the same problem which they too should have seen simply as a matter of identities confused through the use of a pseudonym.

Margaret Drabble (editor of the fifth edition of the *Oxford Companion to English Literature*):

> I feel [Shakespeare] did not want us to know him.

Thomas Hardy:

> Bright baffling soul.

Ian Wilson:

> Although Jonson's remarks as recorded by Drummond [a Scots poet] actually include brief mention of Shakespeare, these are mere criticisms of his work, rather than comments about the man.

Harold Bloom:

> There are no great biographies of Shakespeare, not because we do not know enough, but because there is not enough to know.

Charles Dickens:

> The life of Shakespeare is a fine mystery, and I tremble every day that something should turn up.

C. M. Ingleby (Founder Trustee of the Shakespeare Birthplace Trust):

> It is plain, for one thing, that the bard of our imagination was unknown to the men of that age.

Germaine Greer:

> All biographies of Shakespeare are houses built of straw.

Hugh Trevor Roper (Regius Professor of History):

> Armies of scholars, formidably equipped, have examined all the documents which could possibly contain mention of [Shakespeare's] name. One hundredth part of this labour applied to one of his insignificant contemporaries would be sufficient to produce a substantial biography.

A Note on "Orthodoxy" and "Unorthodoxy"

Those who believe the writer William Shakespeare was William Shakspere of Stratford can be called "orthodox", because they share the same views as those who control mainstream Shakespeare, and often mainstream English, scholarship. Sometimes they are termed "Stratfordians", because they identify their interests with that town, though they could be called "Shakspereans" as they believe the author was a man who was really named Shakspere, although they rarely, if ever, admit it in public.

Those who believe Shakespeare was not Shakspere are often called unorthodox. They are sometimes called heretics – or worse – but that will change.

The orthodox position can be well expressed by a quote from R. C. Churchill (1959):

> That William Shakespeare of Stratford wrote the plays and poems attributed to him is not a theory at the present time, it is a fact at the present time – and will continue to be a fact until it is definitely proved wrong.

Here we take up that challenge, which is a good starting point even if it is a quite unscholarly assertion. We will show Churchill's supposed "fact" is a misapprehension, just as there never was a William Shakespeare of Stratford. This may seem to imply there has been complicity among orthodox scholars in sustaining the Shakspere myth over many years, but if readers look in books and articles on "Shakespeare", and note how many of them hide, overlook or disregard the fact that William Shakspere and his brothers and sisters and children were all baptised as Shakspere, and that – as Bill Bryson (1990) has pointed out – he never used the name Shakespeare in his life, they may start to wonder about it for themselves. Oddly, one will often hear it asked whether it matters how Shakspere spelt his name: well, it certainly does, or orthodox scholars would not be so keen to change it. The myth about this name is very strong: generations have been brought up on it and fortunes and reputations built on it.

5

CHAPTER 2

How the Theft of Shakspere's Identity Began

When he died in 1616, the actor-businessman William Shakspere of Stratford was one of the richest men in his home town, if not *the* richest. In spite of that, he would never have thought of being long remembered after his death, and certainly not of being remembered four hundred years later as one of the most famous and important men in the history of the world. He made no arrangements for a memorial in his will. He left no personal written records of himself or his life, and neither did his family. Yet, for reasons that will be – or at least will become – obvious, more official records have been uncovered for him than for any of his contemporaries of similar standing. This is not a tribute to Shakspere himself, for those records are of no great intrinsic interest; it is rather a tribute to those researchers who have directed their efforts, often for many years at a stretch – and always unsuccessfully – to the discovery of any record that might show this William Shakspere was the writer Shakespeare.

Although the researchers found absolutely nothing to support that myth, they did unearth in the process numerous official documents which would normally have been left undisturbed; but these we can now use to build up an outline of Shakspere's real life, even if it does not fit with him having been a writer of any description.

Shakspere held no public offices in his home town and none in London where he worked on and off for perhaps ten or fifteen years. He left no great bequests or great works that would have moved his fellow citizens to honour him, nor any mementoes that would recall him to their minds. It is actually not known, even now, in spite of what might be claimed, whether his real grave lies inside or outside Holy Trinity Church, his parish church in Stratford where his burial was recorded on 25th April 1616. For seven-and-a-half years after Shakspere's death, there was absolutely no indication that he would be remembered at all;

6

and those years are just one of three blank periods which together would form his "lost years" as they are called: the thirty years or so out of the fifty-nine between his birth and his sudden fame in 1623 which left no records found to date.

Then, in November 1623, the deafening silence of those seven plus years ended (or so it was made to appear). A magnificent book of thirty-six plays was published in London with clever but ambiguous hints that our William Shakspere had all the time been a playwright and, by implication, a poet. Not just any playwright, mind you, but the writer of plays published as by "William Shakespeare", a pseudonym first made famous with the appearance of the best-selling erotic poem *Venus and Adonis* in 1593. That name, Shakespeare, belonging to no known writer, was printed at the end of the author's dedication of that poem which was to the nineteen-year-old third Earl of Southampton. And it was identified as a pseudonym within a year when the poem itself was parodied by an equally erotic one, *Oenone and Paris*, by a "T.H.", with its dedication parodied by one pointing to a "hiding" and a "lurking" author. The hints of November 1623 were thus suggesting (ambiguously) that the dead Shakspere had been the writer hidden behind the pseudonym Shakespeare, whose masterpieces such as *Love's Labour's Lost*, *Richard the Third*, *The Merry Wives of Windsor* and *Hamlet* had been presented to the public in theatre performances and small books called "quartos".

That 1623 book, with its 900-plus pages and thirty-six plays, was impressive. It is now known familiarly as the Shakespeare "First Folio"; "Folio" because of its large folio-sized pages (13 inches by 8 inches or 33 cms by 20 cms) and "First" because it ran to second, third and fourth full-sized folio editions (the third edition even running to a revised reprint with additional material, as we will discuss later). Its actual title was *William Shakespeare's Comedies, Histories, and Tragedies*, and the world had seen nothing to compare with it.

The hints that were inserted into the introduction to the First Folio in order to suggest William Shakspere was its author – hints that will be discussed in Chapter 13 – were backed up by the hasty erection of a monument in Stratford's Holy Trinity Church. This, a complex memorial to Shakspere put up by persons who themselves remained anonymous, carried additional ambiguous hints about him. These suggested he had been something very different from what people who had known him had thought him to be, though these hints did not make precisely clear what that different something actually was.

It is perhaps not surprising that the implications of the hints in the First Folio, and on the Monument, that William Shakspere of Stratford was the writer Shakespeare did not immediately take root with the townsfolk of Stratford. The reasons for that will become clear as we go

7

through the story. Yet, by the end of the eighteenth century, dozens of invented "facts" had been created, designed to reinforce those hints, or even replace them. For example, locations in Shakespeare's plays were "discovered" to be near Stratford – though they were not. Friends and relatives were discovered for him whom he would never have known, but who were chosen because they might be of use, with a little sleight of hand, to help his identification as Shakespeare. Denizens of Stratford were dubiously put forward as models for characters in the plays. Real people whom Shakspere might actually have known had their relationships to him exaggerated; and, if there was any chance the relationship might be used in an anecdote that suggested he was a writer, it would be firmed up by assertion and invention into an intimate friendship.

Circular arguments were developed to confirm the First Folio hints about Shakspere. A typical such fallacious argument was created, for example, from the fact that the writer Shakespeare – whoever he was – had dedicated his 1593 poem *Venus and Adonis* to the third Earl of Southampton. From this, although there was no evidence to support them, stories were invented that this aristocratic young Earl had not only known the actor-businessman William Shakspere, but had also acted as a patron and supporter for him as a writer, and had possibly been his lover. From such unfounded stories about these two men, a whole history grew up about their supposed relationship though it was a complete fiction. The truth is that decades of intense research failed, and still fail, to find a single record of any meeting or correspondence or any other real connection between Shakspere and Southampton. Moreover, the Earl of Southampton was only one among a number of fictional firm friends who would be invented for Shakspere, along with fictional biographies of their close and even intimate friendships.

Because intensive searches in the archives and elsewhere turned up none of the documents that would have been expected if Shakspere had been Shakespeare, hundreds of forgeries were created to fill the gap, some by top scholars (see Lee, 1916). Some of the most famous libraries were infiltrated: Shakspere's name and initials were added to manuscripts, documents and books – and it is still not certain that all these deceptions have been discovered and eliminated. At the same time, if any actual annotations were found in books or on documents, and they were of a kind that might possibly have been made by Shakespeare, they would have to be attributed, at least by some, to Shakspere.

Scholars who believed Shakspere was Shakespeare often took delight in using circular arguments to "prove" he was educated enough to write the plays and poems of Shakespeare. One example is that readers would be told that they knew Shakspere must have gone to Stratford Grammar School because, if he had not, he could never have become the great

Shakespeare. Another is that Shakespeare was only able to refer to schools, schoolboys, schoolmasters and boys going to school in his plays because, as Shakspere, he had gone to Stratford Grammar School. Of course, all that these circular arguments tell us is that some people have been sufficiently desperate to believe that Shakspere was or could have been Shakespeare, to overlook or ignore the fallacy in their reasoning. All they are saying is that, if Shakspere was Shakespeare, he must have gone to school. Totally missing from their arguments is evidence that Shakspere went to school at all (as we discuss below).

Attempts have been made to strengthen claims that Shakspere went to school by picking out teachers among the characters in Shakespeare's plays – like Holofernes in *Love's Labour's Lost*, or Evans in *The Merry Wives of Windsor* – and then asserting they were based on teachers who were employed at Stratford's Grammar School while Shakspere was a boy. Yet nothing relevant is known of the characters of those Stratford teachers to allow such comparisons to be made. All that is being done is to assume that, if Shakspere had gone to school and grown up to be the writer Shakespeare, he might have used Stratford teachers as models for teachers in plays, but there is no evidence he did any of these things.

Now these assertions are used in a sort of game in which anyone doubting Shakspere wrote the plays is called a snob, because, it is claimed, they are denying that a grammar school boy could have written them. However, orthodox scholars have never been able to prove Shakspere was even literate, let alone went to grammar school.

It has been recognised by scholars for over two centuries that the clever hints in the First Folio about Shakespeare being Shakspere involved a deception orchestrated by Ben Jonson. It is clear, for instance, that he wrote a poem for inclusion in the First Folio to bestow fictional praise on a fictional portrait of the author. Also, as will be discussed in Chapter 13, it is clear that Jonson wrote pieces which he then had printed over other people's names – those of John Heminges and Henry Condell – because these two were former colleagues of Shakspere. When the problems over Jonson's hints in the First Folio were exposed, it seems most orthodox scholars who were aware stopped using them as best evidence for their theory that William Shakspere was Shakespeare. Instead, they turned to so-called traditions, or anecdotal evidence, which on examination actually prove to be nothing but collections of inventions and legends that grew up around Shakspere over the centuries because he was thought to be Shakespeare. Yet those "traditions" and anecdotes would never have come into being without the spurious hints about him in the First Folio; and still new invented stories about him are added to the collection all the time.

The most effective of all the deceptions that were introduced to try to convince ordinary fans of Shakespeare that he was definitely our William Shakspere, namely the change to his name, became entrenched around 1916, the tercentenary of Shakspere's death. It was then that orthodox scholars and even individuals and organisations involved in what had become the lucrative "Shakespeare business", began to have the name "Shakspere" air-brushed out of existence. In all new publications it would be replaced by Shakespeare, while every Shakspere family tree published became the Shakespeare family tree. By this technique, people would eventually believe the Shaksperes of Stratford were really called Shakespeare and doubts about this would be met with astonishment and incomprehension. For example, the normally sober Lee (1916) actually wrote of the name Shakspere that its

> first recorded holder is William Shakespeare or 'Sakspere', who was convicted of robbery and hanged in 1248.

With this bold approach, anyone who ever had a name vaguely like Shakspere would eventually be converted by orthodox scholars to a "Shakespeare", and our William Shakspere would disappear as a man in his own right.

This airbrushing of Shakspere's name was a good trick. It allowed students and the general public to be told that nobody could doubt that "Shakespeare" wrote the plays of "Shakespeare", and it allowed anybody who apparently raised a doubt about the authorship of Shakespeare's plays, however reputable a scholar he or she might be, to be treated as a moron who thought that "Shakespeare" did not write his own plays. Such is the power of brain-washing.

In the next chapter, it will be shown this deliberate changing of William Shakspere's real name was, and continues to be, total disinformation. For example, if today one types "Shakspere" into a computer with English or American as its language, it will be shown as a spelling mistake or automatically "corrected" to Shakespeare. Yet, the name Shakspere seems to have been a well-loved family name. The assertion some still make that few people in Elizabethan times including Shakespeare and other learned writers could spell their own names consistently is an exaggeration used to bolster the claim that Shakespeare was the true name of our William Shakspere – when it was not. Of course spelling was not as well codified then as it is today, but it was not the random mess that orthodox scholars feel they must say it was. Readers who have believed them may be quite amazed by what they find in the next chapter.

CHAPTER 3

Shakspere – A Well-Loved Family Name

Separated by fifty-two years almost to the day, two related entries appeared in the registers of Holy Trinity Church, Stratford. The first was on 26th April 1564, when the baptismal register recorded the arrival of the subject of this book as

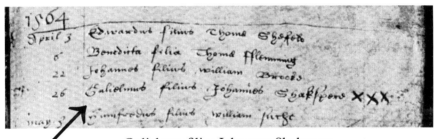

Gulielmus filius Johannes Shakspere

or, translated from the Latin, William son of John Shakspere. Here was the first son and third child of John and Mary Shakspere.

Much less cheerfully, there was an entry in the burial register on 25th April 1616, possibly written by a less educated clerk than the one at the baptism, for it announced in plain English that our subject had departed this life as

Will. Shakspere, gent.

The title or dignity of "gent." added to his name in that entry was short for Gentleman and indicated our William Shakspere had proudly gained for himself and his family a higher social status and a coat of arms. More importantly, this entry shows that those close to our William Shakspere used his father's family name for him faithfully, right up to his death (as he did himself).

Some biographers will tell their readers that those entries both called him "Shakespeare", which they did not. Dr Germaine Greer, for example, stated in the many editions of her popular book, *Shakespeare,* that the baptismal entry was "Gulielmus filius Johannes Shakespeare". Given that the main argument for Shakspere being Shakespeare is that this was his name, it may have been thought best not to confuse readers by printing what was actually written.

Of course, it is well known that spelling in Elizabethan times was not fixed as it is today. A person's name was likely to be spelled in many different ways by other people, especially when someone, a clerk for instance, wrote down a name phonetically: it happens frequently enough today, especially over the telephone, while the semi-literate might sometimes mis-spell their own names. But this is really no excuse for scholars and biographers to pretend that this is what happened in the records of the Shakspere family. Some people have claimed to have found twenty spellings of the name Shakspere around Stratford, with as many as eighty-three being claimed by going further afield – and one joker actually published a list of four thousand variants of the name Shakspere, finishing up with the French "Jacques père". For some reason, this is supposed to make it easier to give the Shakspere family the name "Shakespeare", when in fact we will see the opposite is the case. A list of the family Shakspere entries in the records, with references, is given at the end of this chapter, and the conclusion is obvious: Shakspere was Shakspere. Some may query how an illiterate family might keep their name consistently spelt, but it is well known that people who can read almost nothing else can recognise their own name when it is written down for them.

We want to begin, though, by considering an outline history of William's immediate family and the way the name Shakspere runs through it. To start with, it seems John Shakspere must have been born around 1530, though we have no record of his actual baptism. This educated guess would mean that when his first son, William, was born in 1564, his father would have been about thirty-four. We can arrive at this estimate of his age because he must have been at least twenty-one in 1552 when, as a tenant or (less likely) owner of a house in Henley Street, he was fined as "John Shakspere" for having an illegal dung-heap – not the only one in the area – outside it. It appears he must have married his wife, Mary Arden, in or about 1557 because their first child, a girl, was baptised in 1558, and, according to the will of his father-in-law Robert Arden, Mary was still single in 1556.

The house in which William was born is unknown, nor is it known where John and Mary were living at the time. Today, however, so as not to disappoint visitors, an Elizabethan house has been reconstructed on one of several sites John Shakspere is known to have owned later, and it is cheerfully called "The Shakespeare Birthplace". It has been furnished in an appropriate Elizabethan country-town style so that visitors can have some idea of what the writer William Shakespeare's early life would have been like, if only he had been William Shakspere.

By the time of William's birth, John and his wife Mary had already shared the joy of the birth of two daughters, Joan in 1558 and Margaret in 1562, both of whom were baptised as Shakspere. Sadly, John and Mary had also shared the sorrow of losing both of them in infancy. That was not such a rare thing then, and, as parents often did in such cases, John and Mary were to name another child in memory of their first. The second Joan, born in 1569 (also baptised as Shakspere), kept the memory of the deceased Joan alive. Indeed, she survived to be the longest lived of all John and Mary's children, outliving her eldest brother, William, by thirty years. Their other daughter who survived beyond infancy was baptised as Anne Shakspere but lived only seven-and-a-half years from her birth in 1571. Besides his two surviving sisters, William had three younger brothers who were all baptised as Shakspere and who all predeceased him: Gilbert (1566–1612), Richard (1574–1613) and Edmund (1580–1607). See the family tree in Appendix J.

William was the only Shakspere son to get married and to attempt to carry on the family name, at least legitimately, but, before he married, a period of eighteen years was to elapse after his baptism during which nothing was heard of him in any record or anywhere else. This gap would be the first and longest of his "lost years".

Then, in November 1582, there was a flurry of activity. Urgent preparations were made for William to be married before the start of the Christmas season on 3rd December, which that year was the date after which weddings – and even the reading of the banns that had to precede weddings – would not be allowed.

William's bride was to be a young woman, Anne Hathaway, from nearby Shottery, and the urgency was because she was four months pregnant with her teenage bridegroom's child. Anne was twenty-five, and her family would have been desperate to establish both her security and her respectability. William, being only eighteen, was still a minor. In a period of fifty years, he was the only Stratford man who married under the age of twenty, and out of necessity. Moreover, because he was a minor, Anne's family were required to lodge a bond with the Bishop of Worcester as a guarantee in case any complaint of irregularity might come to light later. The bond was for £40 (around £24,000 in today's money), a sum so large that it certainly must have been refundable in the event of there being no later problems – and the plain evidence is that there were not.

There was some confusion over the marriage or over its registration, or both. William's name may have been misheard, for it appeared as

"Shagspere" on the certificate that was issued by a clerk at Worcester on 28th November 1582 giving permission for him to marry Anne Hathaway of Shottery. Yet this is a trivial problem for the biographer compared with what had happened only the day before, on 27th November. On that day another certificate had been issued at Worcester that was made out for William to marry an Anne Whateley of Temple Grafton, and this time his name was spelt "Shaxper". Of course, both those spellings of his family name are consistent with it being told to the clerks uniformly as "Shakspere", and not "Shakespeare"; we discuss the difference in pronunciation below.

Because so little is really known about the people involved in this confusion, the possible speculations that can be created about William Shakspere and the two Annes are unlimited. There has also been no limit on the speculation about where the marriage took place. Stratford, Shottery, Luddington and Temple Grafton have all been proposed, all being within three miles of Stratford, but there is simply no surviving record of it. Those who wish to think that Shakspere was Catholic, favour Temple Grafton: but we will look at the religious question in a later chapter. One thing is certain, however: the marriage did take place and Anne Hathaway became Anne Shakspere. Another is that, contrary to what is sometimes said, she was not at all old for marrying at that time: it was William who was unusually young. Anne was obviously sexually attractive to the teenager and she was to outlive him by over seven years.

The outcome of the pre-marital liaison that must have occurred between William and Anne in the summer of 1582 and precipitated their marriage was a little girl who was baptised as Susanna Shakspere, daughter of William Shakspere, on 26th May 1583. For some reason her baptism record has been specially picked out by some and claimed to be in the name "Shakespeare", yet the entry clearly reads Shakspere with no medial "e" and no "a" in the last syllable. This girl was to be her father's favourite; and she would certainly have done him proud when, in 1607, and in spite of her rich father giving her no education, she married Dr John Hall, the local physician. Although the bridegroom was well known as a Puritan, the marriage certificate shows the wedding took place in the parish church – there was no real alternative – with the bride as Susanna Shaxspere, another obvious phonetic spelling of "Shakspere".

In May 1584, a year after the birth of Susanna, Anne was pregnant again, this time with different-sex twins. On 2nd February 1585, in the parish church, the boy would be baptised as Hamnet Shakspere and the girl as Judith Shakspere. It appears they were named, respectively, after Hamnet and Judith Sadler who were the Shakspere's neighbours and, if that was so, it implies that these two probably stood at the font in Stratford's Holy Trinity Church as joint godparents for both of the infants in a standard Protestant baptism. Hamnet Sadler's name would appear thus twenty-one years later as witness (as well as legatee) to Shakspere's will, though, as we will note later, at some time the "Hamnet" in the body of the will would be altered to "Hamlett" to make a (false) link with the writer Shakespeare.

The adherence of Shakspere to his family name was amazingly consistent. When William's only son died aged a mere eleven-and-a-half years, he was buried on 11th August 1596 as *"Hamnet filius William Shakspere"*. The boy had been the hope of both his grandfather John Shakspere and father William Shakspere to carry on the family name in direct line from his great-grandfather Richard Shakspere who had lived at nearby Snittering. That death must have been a particularly bitter blow for both John and William. It occurred when the family fortunes were showing improvement after some difficult times, and William was about to revive an application for a coat of arms which his father had first made twenty years previously (see Chapter 9). Responsibility for the continuance of the family name passed to the three younger Shakspere brothers – Gilbert, Richard and Edmund – but all were to pre-decease their elder brother and die leaving no descendants. Anne was only twenty-seven or twenty-eight when she had the twins, but, as appears to have been fairly common at the time, the birth of twins may have ended her ability to have children, as she had no more.

William's daughter Judith did try to keep the family name going when she was married (and quickly got pregnant) just before her father's death in 1616. Her first child, a boy, was baptised with the name spelled Shaksper Quiney (though he was buried as Shakspere). Judith's wedding (as Shakspere) to Thomas Quiney of Stratford on 10th February 1616 had been hurried. It took place within the period of Lent, the time of fasting, a circumstance that required the bridegroom to obtain a special licence, and he did not. As a result, Thomas Quiney was temporarily excommunicated from the Anglican Church.

The need for the marriage to happen urgently could not have been due to Judith's pregnancy as her son was baptised on 23rd November, nine months and thirteen days from the wedding. The hurry was clearly the result of a much less pleasant cause (see Chapter 11). Shakspere Quiney's baptism would have been almost exactly seven months to the day after his grandfather's death, which must have been on or very near 23rd April 1616. It must have been sad for Judith that her father did not live to see his first grandson baptised in the family name, even if only as a Christian name. It is pretty certain Judith's mother, Anne Shakspere, would have been happily present at the birth and the baptism of her first grandson, who, especially with his baptismal name, might have been some consolation for the earlier loss of her husband: yet the joy must have turned to added grief when the child died and was buried as Shakspere the following May, less than six months old.

William Shakspere's parents did not live to see the birth of Shakspere Quiney either. His father had been buried in 1601 as simple *"John Shakspeare"*. He sadly could not be entered in the burial register as "Gent.", the title he had so long coveted, because the coat of arms he had first applied for twenty-five years previously had not quite been granted. William's mother was buried as *"Mayry Shaxspere"* in September 1608, and she had lived to see the birth of her first grandchild, Elizabeth Hall, who was baptised in the February of the same year.

The second member of William Shakspere's family who could have been buried as Shakspere but was not – that is if we accept his mother's "Shaxs" stood for "Shaks" – was his brother Edmund. His burial was registered on 31st December 1607 in London as "Shakespeare", being given the better known spelling of the name with the medial "e"; and this London burial was the only time in the context of family matters that the spelling Shakespeare was used. Incidentally, Edmund's burial is the only one in the family of which we have some details. He is recorded as being buried as a player and with the main bell tolling, at a cost of 20 shillings, in the parish church that is now Southwark Cathedral. It is naturally assumed, though without evidence, that the arrangements were made by his brother William. Edmund's name has been put on a stone in the Cathedral choir, but it is of late date and the location is too grand for a player.

Edmund did have a baby son, but he died in infancy and was buried in London with his name recorded as Edward "Shackspeere" on 12th August 1607. However, the child was illegitimate and would have had no right to carry on the Shakspere Arms.

The Stratford burial of the last of William's brothers, Richard, occurred in February 1613 and was recorded as "Shakspeare".

In the only known record of the spelling of the married name of William's wife before his death, she was described as *"Anne Shaxpere, wife unto Wyllyam Shaxpere"*. This was in the 1601 will of her father's shepherd, Thomas Whittington; in the absence of banks, he seems to have entrusted to her safe-keeping a sum of 40 shillings (over £1200 today) which his will left to the parish.

Though William Shakspere used his family name to the end of his life, it was in the face of great difficulties. When he got to London (see Chapter 6) and began his rise in the theatre world, mainly as a manager and shareholder but also as a player, the first time his name was written into any record it was as "Shakespeare". The occasion, on 15th March 1595, was when £20 was paid for a Christmas (or rather St Stephen's Day) performance before Queen Elizabeth at Greenwich in 1594. The payment was made to three managers of the Lord Chamberlain's Men, our Shakspere, Richard Burbage and William Kempe. Some scholars, puzzled to find there were two performances that could have involved the Lord Chamberlain's Men on the same day, one at Greenwich and one at the Inns of Court, have suggested this record was a rogue entry in the ledger, possibly inserted by someone trying to pocket cash by making a fraudulent claim. Yet, whether that was so or not, it seems it was the Stratford man to whom the ledger entry referred. It would, of course, have been made in the absence of the parties and at a time when the person making the entry would have been familiar with the name "Shakespeare", now famous from its appearance on two erotic poems much read by young literate males, *Venus and Adonis* and *The Rape of Lucrece*.

On a few, perhaps six, occasions the Shakspere name was spelt as "Shakespeare" by people in and around Stratford, but nothing like the number of times it was written that way in London by literate clerks who would have known those poems. William Shakspere suffered the fate of all those of us whose names have a better known alternative spelling. In 1612, when he made a witness statement in what is known as the Bellot–Mountjoy case (see Chapter 8), the lawyer who took down his deposition wrote his name five times in the body of the document with the famous spelling "Shakespeare": yet, when Shakspere gave his oath to his name when it was written on the document in the place where his signature would have been, it was nothing like Shakespeare. It was badly written (see Chapter 10) but it clearly looks as though it was intended for "Shakspere", being normally read as just "Shakp" or "Shaxp".

There are actually six instances we know of when there was a requirement for Shakspere's name to be written on legal documents to signify his assent to them, and in no case did he affirm to Shakespeare. There were three on his last will and testament where, even though his name was written differently in the body of the document – twice as Shackspeare and once as Shackspere – it reads as a badly made Shakspere for each of the three so-called "signatures" (see Chapter 10). It seems William Shakspere had a proprietal interest if not a pride in his name and wished to use no other. Even when he was having problems getting his coat of arms because he was only a player, and it would have helped his case if he had identified himself as the poet William Shakespeare, he did not do so (see Chapter 9).

The move by orthodox scholars to take Shakspere's name from him and his family, either deliberately or through sloppy scholarship, even changing Shaksper Quiney's name to Shakespeare, seems to have started seriously after 1916. Up to then, many orthodox scholars acknowledged their candidate for the authorship was named Shakspere. This spelling was happily used in the text of books and in their titles, showing that

17

Shakspere was thought to have done the writing but not under his real name. Ingleby wrote his *Shakspere Allusion Books* in 1874, Coleridge his *Lectures and Notes on Shakspere* in 1883, and Boas his *Shakspere and his Predecessors* in 1895. The "New Shakspere Society" was founded by orthodox scholars in 1873, but their use of the proper spelling for Shakspere of Stratford had to give way to twentieth-century pressure: its name was changed to "New Shakespeare Society". A *Shakspere Concordance* appeared in 1875. The *Shakspere Quarto Facsimiles* (reproductions of the small-sized copies of the Shakespeare plays) were published in 1891. But the name was vanishing. One major publication did use the Stratford man's name in 1923 (*The Bibliographical Study of Shakspere*), and *Shakspere's Small Latin and Less Greek* by Baldwin, possibly the last, came in 1944. Thus Shakspere's name was taken from him, along with his true identity, by those holding the centre, so-called orthodox, ground of Shakespeare scholarship.

The trigger for killing off Shakspere's true name seems to have been the three-pronged attack on the orthodox theory of Shakespeare that occurred around and just after the tercentenary of Shakspere's death in 1916. The first prong was a growth of support among senior legal and literary figures for the old theory that Francis Bacon was Shakespeare. The second was the growth of scepticism about the idea that William Shakspere had ever been Shakespeare, encouraged by the publication of Mark Twain's *Is Shakespeare Dead?* in 1909. The third attack came from the publication around 1920 of two forceful claims, one for William Stanley, 6th Earl of Derby, the other for Edward de Vere, 17th Earl of Oxford, that each was the writer Shakespeare, adding to claims already made for Marlowe and Bacon (see Chapter 16).

To be generous, to orthodox scholars who thought Shakespeare was Shakspere, one might suppose they thought it best to use the same name for both, and avoid confusion. But that still would not excuse them denying that two different names were used, one for the writer and one for the Shakspere family, and using that denial to argue that they were the same man.

As pointed out in the previous chapter, it was of great advantage to the orthodox theory to pretend William Shakspere's name had really been "Shakespeare" as it made possible arguments such as "Nobody ever doubted William Shakespeare wrote the plays that were published under his name." The mistreatment of Shakspere's name is now so well embedded that most new biographies of "Shakespeare" – and that includes the 30,000 word article about "William Shakespeare" in the prestigious 2004 *Oxford Dictionary of National Biography* – will nowhere alert their readers to the most basic fact regarding the Stratford man about whom they think they are reading: that he used the name Shakspere, his baptismal, burial and family name, and never used "Shakespeare". It is like omitting the information that George Eliot was, in fact, a woman.

It seems that the only British reference book still to use the proper family name of Shakspere for the actor-businessman from Stratford is the *Oxford English Dictionary*. Yet it does so under pressure. The *OED*'s use of Shakspere has been said to be its *"greatest idiosyncrasy"*. What is idiosyncratic, of course, is how orthodox Shakespeare scholars have managed to mislead the public so long about Shakspere's name. Actually Bryson, the writer who made the above comment about the *OED*, drew attention in his book *Shakespeare* to the fact that Shakspere of Stratford never used the name "Shakespeare".

There is, however, something else that this unilateral changing of someone's name doesn't take into account: it ignores the fact that, however many different ways other people may spell a man's name, that does not stop him knowing how he prefers it spelt. This is very important because whoever wrote under the name Shakespeare was remarkably consistent with the spelling of that pseudonym and never spelt it as Shakspere. This alone in any ordinary investigation would be highly indicative that here were two entirely different people using these two apparently similar but actually different names. If William Shakspere had been the brilliant, intelligent writer he has been claimed to be, it is hard to believe he would have wasted his time and risked confusion by writing his name one way at home, so to speak, and in a similar – but clearly different – way for a writing career in London.

Orthodox scholars may pour scorn on the idea that people like Bacon or the Earl of Oxford might have used a pen-name so different from their own. But they take it for granted that it would not be odd for Shakspere to have taken a pen name so similar to his own as Shakespeare. A trawl through hundreds of authors who used pseudonyms shows almost all of them took names totally different from their own. The odd ones were Addison who used the name "Atticus", Ben Jonson who deliberately and publicly dropped the "h" from his family name to distinguish himself from the hundreds of other "Johnsons", Quincey who raised himself in status to "De Quincey", and Harold Rubin who deliberately anglicised his name to "Harold Robbins". Nobody went for the sort of accidental change that it is claimed happened with Shakespeare. As will become clear, there was somebody who deliberately chose the pseudonym "Shakespeare" and used it rigorously.

When the poem *Venus and Adonis* was published in 1593, its dedication had the name "Shakespeare" spelt the same in all five quarto editions and all eight octavo (half-quarto size) editions. For *The Rape of Lucrece* it was uniformly "Shakespeare" in the one quarto and five octavo editions. There were nineteen of Shakespeare's plays that were published in various quarto editions before the First Folio appeared in 1623. Of these editions, which numbered fifty-two in total, sixteen had no author's name. For the other thirty-six Quartos, all dated between 1598 and 1622, the author's name appeared thirty-nine times, three of which were in the announcements of the registration of particular Quartos. On nineteen of those thirty-nine occasions, the name was given as "Shakespeare" and on fifteen it was "Shake-speare" with a hyphen. Of the remaining five, "Shak-speare" occurred twice and "Shakespere" three times. The Sonnets' author's name was given as "Shake-speare", as was the author of the odd (and originally untitled) *The Phoenix and the Turtle*. With this consistency – the playwright-poet's name being spelt Shakespeare or Shake-speare 92 percent of the time, and never Shakspere – it is nonsense to suppose the writer was someone who did not know how to spell his name, or that the consistency of its spelling on the plays was some enormous statistical aberration. Even less could one think the writer was a William Shakspere, who never used the name Shakespeare in his life, even when others were using it in writing about him, and it would have been advantageous for him to do the same.

Some scholars, perhaps because they realised that Abraham Lincoln's rule – about not being able to fool all the people all of the time – would one day catch up with them, have tried a bold bluff about how William Shakspere's name got changed to Shakespeare. They (and that "they" includes some senior scholars) have a story that it had to be changed because of a problem at the printers. Readers are told that, when typesetters first came to put the letters "k" and "s" in Shakspere's name next to each other in an Italianate form of italic type, they found that the forward tail or curlicue on the "k" in that type would break the backward tail that occurs on the "s"; and so (they say) in order to avoid that problem, the printers had to put an "e" in between those two letters so giving the central "kes" of Shakespeare instead of the "ks" of Shakspere. Unfortunately, as any Shakespeare scholar may observe, the first printings of the name "Shakespeare" were on the *Venus and Adonis* and *The Rape of Lucrece* dedications and neither used Italianate script at all: they used a Roman typeface which had no tails or curlicues and in which the "k" and "s" could not possibly overlap (see Figure 3). Such an invented explanation indicates the problem orthodox scholars have with the differences in spelling and their need to distract readers from them. Figures 4a-d show how Shakespeare's name was typeset on various quarto editions, and it is obvious that typefaces could have been chosen so that the "k" and "s" never overlapped

A minor point in this discussion is the different pronunciations of "Shakspere and "Shakespeare". Some orthodox scholars have tried to argue that they must have sounded the same, possibly hoping to explain

20

TO THE RIGHT HONORABLE
Henrie VVriothefley, Earle of Southampton,
and Baron of Titchfield.

Ight Honourable, I know not how I shall offend in dedicating my vnpolisht lines to your Lordship, nor how the worlde vvill cenfure mee for choofing fo ftrong a proppe to fupport fo vveake a burthen, onelye if your Honour feeme but pleafed, I account my felfe highly praifed, and vowe to take aduantage of all idle houres, till I haue honoured you vvith fome grauer labour. But if the firft heire of my inuention proue deformed, I fhall be forie it had fo noble a god-father : and neuer after eare fo barren a land, for feare it yeeld me ftill fo bad a harueft, I leaue it to your Honourable furuey, and your Honor to your hearts content, vvhich I wifh may alvvaies anfvvere your ovvne vvifh, and the vvorlds hopefull expeÆation.

Your Honors in all dutie,

William Shakefpeare.

3. Dedication from *Venus and Adonis,* 1593, the earliest example of Shakespeare's name in print.

4a. Detail from the title page of the 1603 Quarto of *Hamlet.*

THE
HISTORY OF
HENRIE THE
FOVRTH;

With the battell at Shrewsburie,
betweene the *King and Lord* Henry
Percy, *surnamed* Henry Hotspur of the North.

VV ith the humorous conceits of Sir
Iohn Falstalffe.

Newly corrected by *W. Shake-speare.*

4b. Detail from the title page of the 1599 Quarto of *Henry IV Pt 1*.

Written by William Shakespeare.

4c. Detail from the title page of the 1600 Quarto of *Henry IV Pt II*.

As it hath beene diuerse times acted at the
Globe, and at the Black-Friers, by
his Maiesties Seruants.

Written by VVilliam Shakespeare.

4d. Detail from the title page of the 1622 Quarto of *Othello*.

why those who did not know how Shakspere spelt his name might have preferred to use the form Shakespeare. Yet that is counter-productive as it would accentuate how determined the Stratford man and the poet-playwright must have been, one to use Shakspere, the other Shakespeare. From what is known of Midlands pronunciation in the nineteenth century, and the way it carried through from Anglo-Saxon, the short flat "a" of, say, "hat" and the drawn out "a" of, say, "date" (sounding almost "dirt") were quite different. So it seems impossible "Shak" and "Shake" ever sounded the same. We can still usefully distinguish the two names and the two men by using the modern different pronunciations.

The orthodox theory about Shakspere being Shakespeare or Shake-speare faces another major problem in having to explain why Shakspere, who never had his name hyphenated, might, if he had been the writer, have hyphenated "Shake-speare" on so many of the Quartos, as well as the Sonnets. Some have tried to get round this problem by saying that the printers or publishers would have inserted hyphens in names on their own whims. Yet that has to assume the gritty Shakspere – as the great writer – would not know what was happening or was happy for his name to be messed about on a regular basis; it did not happen for others. It is more convincing to say that printers might have preferred the form Shake-speare if they knew it was a pseudonym.

During what is known as the Martin Marprelate or Mar-Prelate controversy around 1589, hyphenated pseudonyms were thick on the ground. In addition to Marprelate itself, other pseudonyms that were so treated were Mar-Martin, Mar-ton, Mar-tother, Trouble-knave, Signior Some-body, Tom Tell-truth and – this one being known to have hidden Thomas Nashe – Cuthbert Curry-knave. Shake-speare looks to fit into that pseudonymous class very well. Moreover, Pallas Athena, warrior goddess of the Arts, praised as the tenth muse in Shakespeare's Sonnet 38, was a spear-shaker, and William was a standard nickname for a poet – used, for example, for Philip Sidney. So the name William Shake-speare adopted by a poet who was noted by Jonson to "shake a lance ... at ignorance" looks too good to be coincidental. In a period when the use of pseudonyms as an alternative to straight anonymity was taken for granted, this would have been a good one for a poet-playwright. The hyphenation of the name alone would not prove "Shake-speare" was a pseudonym, but it is entirely consistent with all the other evidence that it was; and there is more to come.

The truth is that, whatever protests orthodox scholars may make, there would be nothing odd about an Elizabethan writer hiding behind a pseudonym. As the research of Taylor and Mosher showed, the sixteenth and seventeenth centuries were the golden age for pseudonyms.

This discussion of the different names used by the Stratford man and the writer is very important. The false claim that those names were the same is used as the main, sometimes the only argument for William Shakspere being the great poet-playwright. In effect, the argument goes full circle. It is claimed Shakspere's name was really Shakespeare and then claimed that that is enough to prove he was the writer Shakespeare. But even if Shakspere had been baptised as Shakespeare that would not prove he was the writer. There were lots of Robert Greenes around in Elizabethan times but they were not all the playwright of that name. To prove a given man named Robert Greene was the writer Robert Greene would need rather more evidence than the similarity of name.

There will be further discussion about the pseudonym Shakespeare in Chapter 14, but here, by way of redress for the way William Shakspere's family name has been effectively airbrushed out of history as part of the theft of his identity, a list has been drawn up of official entries for the Shakspere family, as well as a proper family tree for them at Appendix J.

Shakspere family records with sources.

C = Christening, B = Burial, M = Marriage.

C **Joan** (1st): *"Jone Shakspere daughter of John Shakspere"*; 15 September 1558
C **Margaret**: *"Margareta filia Johannis Shakspere"*; 2 December 1562
B *"* *"Margareta filia Johannes Shakspere"*; 30 April 1563
C **William**: *"Gulielmus filius Johannes Shakspere"*; 26 April 1564
B *"* *"Will. Shakspere, gent."*; 25 April 1616
C **Gilbert**: *"Gilbertus Filius Johannis Shakspere"*; 13 October 1566
B *"* *"Gilbert Shakspere adolescens"*; 3 December 1612 (1)
C **Joan** (2nd): *"Jone the daughter of John Shakspere"*; 15 April 1569
C **Anne**: *"Anna filia magistri Shakspere"*; 28 September 1571
B *"* *"Anne daughter of Mr John Shakspere"*; 4 April 1579
C **Richard**: *"Richard Sonne to Mr John Shakspere"*; 4 April 1574
B *"* *"Rich. Shakspeare"*: 4 February 1613
C **Edmund**: *"Edmund Sonne to John Shakspere"*; 3 August 1580
B *"* *"Edmund Shakespeare a player"*; 31 December 1607 (2)
M **William**: Licence entry for *"Willellmum Shaxpere and Annam Whately"*; 27 November 1582
M *"* Bond of Sureties Entry for *"William Shagspere on thone partie and Anne Hathwey"*; 28 November 1582
C **Susanna**: *"Susanna daughter to William Shakspere"*; 26 May 1583 (3)
C **Twins**: *"Hamnet and Judeth sonne and daughter to William Shakspere"*; 2 February 1585
B **Hamnet**: *"Hamnet filius William Shakspere"*; 11 August 1596
B **Father**: *"Mr Johannes Shakspeare"*; 8 September 1601
M **Susanna**: *"M. Hall gentleman & Susanna Shaxspere"*; 5 June 1607
B **Edward**: *"Edward, sonne of Edward [mistake for Edmund] Shackspeere player, base-borne"*: 12 August 1607 (4)
B **Mother**: *"Mayry Shaxspere, wydowe"*; 9 July 1608
M **Judith**: *"Tho Queeny tow Judith Shakspere"*; 20 February 1616
C **Shaksper**: *"Shaksper fillius Thomas Quyny"*; 23 November 1616
B *"* *"Shakspere fillius Tho. Quyny"*; 8 May 1617

(1) adolecens = unmarried; (2) Registered in London; (3) Chambers and many others give Susanna as "Shakespear", but the register is clearly "Shakspere". (4) Registered in London: father should be Edmund.

Sources: these details are all given in Chambers *EKC* in plain type and all but one spelt as in the records (note (3) above). They are in Schoenbaum *SDL* in facsimile, with eleven of the twenty-six in his more accessible *SCDL*, including Susanna.

CHAPTER 4

Young William Shakspere in Stratford

The Stratford-upon-Avon where our William Shakspere was born was a modest market town – "undistinguished", said Schoenbaum unkindly in *SDL*. It was one of a dozen Stratfords (meaning "street ford") in the country. Some orthodox biographers make out there was some cultural advantage in being born in Stratford, Warwickshire, and they may use a well-known painting of Queen Elizabeth standing on a map of England, with her feet naturally planted somewhere in the Midlands, to "prove" it. However, a glance at Fuller's *Worthies of England* will show Warwickshire was way down the list of English counties for its number of celebrities. The two nearest towns to Stratford-upon-Avon lay to its north – Warwick and Kenilworth – both having castles, both bigger, but comparable with Stratford in size, and both needed more than a day's travelling for a visit. To south, east and west there were no other "towns" within the county's borders. Stratford, with fields, woods and six rivers or substantial brooks in the vicinity would, however, have been a good place to grow up for a youngster with three brothers, two sisters and a bevy of aunts – as long as Father could avoid getting the family tangled with the various and dreaded systems of Tudor poor relief. And, in William's case, Father John did so even when times were fraught.

It would naturally be helpful if we had some records of the young William Shakspere for use in writing a biography of his early life, but we have nothing of the sort. It is disappointing, but wholly consistent with his growing up to be a businessman and minor actor. Yet that gap in our knowledge of him is not for want of looking. Researchers have turned up a number of official records relevant to his father from the time of William's childhood, but none for him. It would probably have been different if the young Shakspere had grown up to be a great writer as is often claimed, but he did not, and the numerous anecdotes told about him are never traceable to people who actually knew him. The result is that all attempts to get an idea of William's early years must draw partly on what we know of his later life, partly on what we know of his father's situation at different times during his son's youth and partly on what is known generally of the lives of boys of his status and situation in the late sixteenth century.

John Shakspere's official occupation was glover or glove-maker, a trade for which he would have had to serve a seven-year apprenticeship and then be accepted for registration as a master craftsman. He would have had to become a member of his relevant guild or "mystery", to which he would have paid annual dues, as did several of his fellow townsmen. It was not an uncommon occupation. There were, at the time John was working, no fewer that twelve glovers in Stratford, including neighbour Gilbert Bradley, the probable godfather of his second son, Gilbert. Stratford may only have been a moderate-sized country town, with its population of less than two thousand, but its market day – when craftsmen would sell their wares – would have catered for all the villages within a three-mile radius or even more.

The records show that John had a subsidiary activity related to his glove-making, namely as a whittawer: that is as a cleaner, curer and whitener of the skins needed for his trade, an activity that apparently did not need registering in any way. There are anecdotes about him also carrying on the trade of butcher, with William as his apprentice. Yet those are likely to be untrue, not least because the hygiene rules required butchers to have a licence which John did not have, and there was one licensed butcher in Stratford already. Also, the "butcher" anecdotes only surfaced at a time when stories about William Shakspere were in great demand, after hints in the First Folio had suggested he was its author.

John Shakspere had two additional commercial activities, both of which required capital and both of which ran him into trouble with the law. One of these was wool-trading, which the Government kept under close control because it was not only crucial to the English economy but was also fundamental to the collection of revenue. The other was moneylending, an occupation or service that was a necessary adjunct to trade, because moneylenders made cash available to ordinary people at a time when there were no banks to support commercial ventures or to tide them over bad patches or periods when they were simply short of ready cash. Yet moneylending or usury (the use of money to make money) tended to be frowned upon in a hypocritical way, as it still is, particularly by those with loans to repay. It could also cause problems to the lender (or usurer), either when a borrower failed to make repayment or when the lender was judged to have set his level of interest too high, which John was recorded as doing.

Given his activities, it is not surprising that many of the records that have been found concerning John Shakspere relate to his involvement with the law, either as defendant or plaintiff. We find him being reported for misdemeanours, but also seeking the court's protection when he was threatened by those he had offended. As examples of his troubles, he was fined 40 shillings in 1570 for usury (£1200 in today's money), and £40 in 1580 for illegal wool-trading.

Of course, legal records will generally show their subjects in a poor light; they rarely waste time on the good things people do. On the other hand, between 1556 and 1577, John was noted in the Stratford records as holding a variety of positions in the corporate life of his town. These ranged from "Taster of Bread and Ale" (those being staple parts of the people's diets and liable to adulteration or dilution), to Alderman and even town Bailiff, the latter being the most senior post an ordinary citizen could hold. Some scholars write of these posts as though they would have carried the pageantry of a Bristol or Norwich or London where the wealth that the cities and their guilds amassed from trade and fees could sustain expensive costumes and pageantry, but that would hardly have been so at Stratford. A chain of office and a black gown was likely to be the maximum adornment of a Stratford bailiff. However, although it is obviously to his credit that John Shakspere carried out his civic duties, service to the corporation was not entirely voluntary and elective. Payment could be levied on someone who sought to avoid such service. Dr John Hall, the Puritan who became William Shakspere's son-in-law, later preferred to pay a fine rather than accept a knighthood.

While William Shakspere was growing to adulthood unnoticed by the records, his father's business affairs were erratic. It is possible they improved when he got away with his marginally illegal trading activities and worsened when he was caught and fined. In 1575, when William was eleven, John Shakspere bought an extra house in Henley Street. In 1576 he lodged an application for a coat of arms. In 1577, he had ceased to attend the meetings of the Stratford council, the stated reason being his debts: yet there cannot have been many of John's fellow townsmen rushing to take his place as he was not replaced in his position of Alderman until ten years later. The following year, 1578, he sold off part of his properties and he was also sued for the repayment of a loan of £30. That same year, he mortgaged property at Wilmcot, 3 miles from Stratford, which was part of the dowry that his wife Mary had brought to her marriage in (probably) 1557, twenty-one years before. The loan he got for that mortgage from his brother-in-law Edmund Lambert was only £40, probably much less than the real value of the property. Then, when the time came in 1580 for the mortgage to be redeemed, John could not repay all the loans he had had from Lambert; so the latter refused to give up the mortgaged property (which was possibly his only surety). This bitter loss led to a dispute with Lambert, whom John and Mary Shakspere felt to have improperly foreclosed on them; and, when he died in 1587, they engaged in a ten-year court case against his heir, John Lambert, without success. In 1585 William was joined as co-applicant in case both his parents died before completion. As they did not die, he would never have been called on to play an active role, even as a witness. The year following the mortgage, 1579, John raised more money by selling off one-ninth of Mary's remaining property.

As we have already mentioned, there is no record of our William Shakspere between his baptism in 1564 and his marriage in 1582. This suggests he neither got into trouble in that time nor attracted attention for any outstanding achievement or activity. There are some anecdotes about Shakspere's youth that have come down to us through the notes of the diarist John Aubrey compiled about a century after William's marriage, but all these seem to have originated long after William had had posthumous fame thrust upon him in 1623, and so became anecdote-worthy. These anecdotes are – like Aubrey himself – uniformly unreliable, like the one he passed down about William being apprenticed to a butcher which gave rise to a story mentioned above. Other Aubrey offerings include one about Shakspere going to London aged eighteen to escape from his master – the butcher – though that was just when he was begetting a daughter and getting married to Anne Hathaway. Aubrey built up his tale of William's flight from Stratford to make it the reason he became an actor, which seems no more than an invented fiction to explain one of the real facts we know about him, namely that he did become involved with the London theatre. With Aubrey as catalyst, stories grew up about William and the local squire, Sir Thomas Lucy, though nothing supported them.

Our starting point for reconstructing Shakspere's boyhood, in the absence of reliable personal information, has to be the question, "What would have been the normal experience of a boy in his position?" Well, first of all, there was no compulsory education. That would not come for three centuries. The opportunity for a boy to try to get into a school, like the Stratford Grammar School, would depend on three things. One was the ability of the parents to give the boy the rudiments of education by age five to make him acceptable for entry to a dame school or "petty" – meaning little – school. If he got to such an establishment, he would learn more of the basics he would need to be accepted into the grammar school at age seven, ready to cope with Latin from day one. The second thing was the ability of the parents to meet the cost of sending him to the dame school and of keeping him in food and clothes. Finally, the parents would need to have the motivation to put him through the dame school at all when that would mean them paying to keep him there and losing his input to the domestic economy into the bargain.

If the boy did get to the point where he could try for entrance to the grammar school, he still faced obstacles. He might not succeed in getting in when the number of places available was smaller than the number of potential pupils, as there was only one master and one usher for all ten years. If accepted, he could only go if his parents were willing to continue to forego his earning capacity while keeping, clothing and feeding him for an extended period. Moreover, besides this, it is most likely they would have had to find money to pay fees to the school, since it seems few grammar schools were fully funded. Even if the basics were paid for, there would be extras for which fees would be charged. The budget of £20 per annum allocated to the school-master of Stratford Grammar School (£12,000) today) would barely give him a labourer's wage after he had met the other expenses required of him, such as the salary for the "usher" to teach the juniors and the cost of maintaining the school and the school-house. It has been boasted by some that the Stratford schoolmaster's budget was twice that of the headmaster of Eton at the time, who got £10 per annum: but rather this suggests that, at Eton, the headmaster could command higher fees from the parents.

The obstacles identified here explain the relatively low uptake of schooling at the time, and that would be particularly so in the case of Stratford where there are no records of scholarships being available for the boys as there were at other schools, like Westminster School of which Ben Jonson left us an account. Greenblatt has stated that there were scholarships for boys to go from Stratford to university but, if there were, nobody made use of them during Shakspere's youth. It is sometimes said, off-handedly, that John Shakspere would have had a right to send his sons to the Grammar School because he was an officer of the corporation, but there is no evidence he would have had more rights than other fathers. There is also no evidence that William's brothers attended the school, and they would have had the same rights as he had. In any case, rights were not the problem: this lay in the willingness to let the children go to school and to forego the value of their labour, and the ability to prepare them and pay for them to go to petty school in the first place. If a boy had the necessary basic education from his family, he would, in principle but not necessarily in practice, be able to go, but no one in William's family was literate. Although biographies often call the Stratford Grammar School a "Free School" or refer to it as a King Edward VI Grammar School, it seems that, in 1568, when William was four, the school was taken over by the corporation because it had lost its endowment, and was given the name of "The King's New School" – see *SDL*. Ackroyd estimated that the fee may have been £5 per annum, but that seems high and may have been based on those of more prestigious schools than Stratford's.

Though it is not really relevant to William Shakspere's education, one has to note the peculiar claim made about Stratford's Grammar School: that it provided a level of education comparable, some have said superior, to that of a university. There is no evidence, however, of any boy from that Grammar School during William's youth going on to university. The rapid turnover of teachers after 1566 – eight in sixteen years – does not argue for a stable regime of education in the town. The sole Stratford boy of that time to leave a record of going on to higher education, one William Smith, only did so after he had been sent away to Winchester College following home tutoring by the local parson.

Appleton Morgan, who reviewed the education available at the Stratford Grammar School, concluded it was not well provided with teachers or teaching aids. He quoted Elizabethan Thomas Tusser that the most common aid in a school was probably the birch rod. Tusser's comments were consistent with the views expressed on the general level of schooling by John Milton and Roger Ascham. Henry Peacham, in a treatise on education, described English schools as poor and cruel; he compared them badly with Dutch schools that he knew, saying poor teaching was

> a general plague and complaint of the whole land; for one discrete and able teacher you shall find twenty ignorant and careless.

It seems those who have "discovered" a high-level curriculum for Stratford have actually taken it in detail from one that Peacham described as being used in educating the sons of nobility and landed gentry. Bate (2008) used the curriculum of the King Edward Grammar School at Lincoln to try to make a case for a high standard at Stratford; yet Lincoln was one of the major and most prosperous cities in England, and had its own College at Oxford. In addition to these remarks on education levels, one can estimate, from the physical size of the King's New School, from its average complement (reckoned to be twelve to twenty-four), and the Stratford population, that fewer than one-tenth of the boys in the town were pupils there, possibly as few as one in twenty.

Too late for Shakspere, even if he had gone to school, the education in Stratford seems to have improved after 1582, the year of his marriage, with the appointment of one Alexander Aspinall. He, of whom more later, was there for forty-two years and did have pupils who went on to Oxford University.

At the crucial point in William's life, when he was five in 1569 and might have started petty school if he had been taught the basics, the Shakspere family had three children to be kept, fed and looked after – Joan, Gilbert and William himself. As the eldest, William would have been looked to for simple assistance at home. His mother was not only busy with new baby Joan but she was likely to be a missing economic factor in her husband's business; so William would have been expected to do simple jobs for his father. Daniel Defoe, a hundred years later, would note that he found no child in the wool industry over the age of four that could not earn its own living, while children of similar age worked down mines, swept chimneys and worked in the fields. It would have been the natural expectation that a boy in William's position would be set to work at an early age rather than go to school, and that situation would last into the time of Charles Dickens.

Honan (1998) wrote that *"A grammar school boy was part of an elite"*, a small proportion of the population. They were such an elite, and their skills so rare, that men who could read Latin could avoid execution for murder by claiming "benefit of clergy", which meant they were qualified to go into or work for the church. Ben Jonson did just that when he was found guilty of killing a man: he showed he could read a Latin piece from the Bible and escaped with only a brand burned in his thumb with "T" for Tyburn, the place for London hangings.

There was no tradition of education or literacy in the Shakspere family. William had three brothers and there is no more evidence that their father exercised his "right" to send them to the Grammar School than there is for his sending William. It is said that there exists a signature of his brother Gilbert, but since he left no handwriting with which it can be compared that means nothing. It was quite normal at the time for scribes to write someone's name for them on a document and have the person swear to it, as they would to a cross or other mark, and that means one written copy of a name cannot be evidence for anything. If there had been two written copies of Gilbert's name that looked sufficiently alike but had been made on different occasions and in different places, then there might be evidence of him writing – but there is nothing like that.

William's son, Hamnet, left no trace of being at school. His daughter Susanna apparently learnt to make a very laboured signature after she married Dr John Hall since there are two copies of her name written fairly similarly on different documents, yet her inability to read is known from an account left by a Dr James Cooke who visited her in 1642 to look at her deceased husband's books. (And the form of her two signatures actually stressed her illiteracy.) William's daughter Judith could only make a mark. Yet, by the time Shakspere's daughters were teenagers, William was a rich man who could easily have paid for private tutoring, even if only to get them to be able to read, which was then considered a much more useful skill for wives than writing. Their tutoring would have cost Shakspere much less than the money he would pay for his coat of arms, but the evidence is that his daughters had none. If he had been the brilliant writer Shakespeare, who extolled the virtues of learning, and paraded the intellectual abilities of women in his plays – Beatrice, Portia, for example – he could have taught them himself. The first evidence of a literate child in the Shakspere family was William's granddaughter Elizabeth (born 1608) who was probably taught by her father, Dr John Hall.

There is also no evidence that anything out of the ordinary happened in William's young life at Stratford. Consequently, one has to assume he followed the normal pattern for the first-born son in a tradesman's family of middling means. Indeed, because John Shakspere's finances are known to have been erratic, it must be judged particularly unlikely he would have wanted to take on a commitment to educate William, or any of his children, even if he had had the inclination or incentive to do something so unusual.

Because of the intensive though wholly fruitless search that was carried out, particularly around 1900, to find some note or document that might point to our William Shakspere being Shakespeare, there are now available in the records a total of six handwritten copies of his name which are erroneously referred to as his "signatures". These are clearly written by at least four different people on four different documents at those points where he should have signed his name, if he could have done so. The omissions on his part confirm that he did not go to school. These "signatures" are fully discussed in Chapter 10, where we expand on the problem of William Shakspere's illiteracy.

In the absence of schooling, it might have been expected that, when William was old enough, father John would have found him an apprenticeship, just as it seems John's father, Richard Shakspere, had done for him. There is no record, however, of him doing so and William must simply have picked up what knowledge he gained as he assisted his father.

From what we know of William's later career, it looks as though the parts of his father's activities that most matched his abilities and inclinations were trade and speculation (including usury), while he learnt from John Shakspere the technique of sailing close to the legal wind. To these activities, William added investing. The records suggest he learnt not to lay out effort or money where there was no return. He certainly appeared to have adopted the principle that what he did lay out he always looked to get back, with interest.

It seems most likely that William would have taken part in his father's trading, and it is interesting to see how far afield that would have extended. The travelling of ordinary folk was generally very limited at the end of the sixteenth century. Agricultural workers are recorded who never in their lives left the estates on which they were born: working, marrying, raising their families and dying in the same location.

Journeys were neither comfortable nor cheap, nor were they entirely safe. The sword that William Shakspere left in his will was unlikely to have been purely decorative, although (unlike with some of his contemporaries) there is no record of him using it. The roads could be largely impassable in winter and, even in fine weather, a day's journey of twenty miles on horseback would have been good going (see Mountfield, 1976). The trading area around Stratford has been estimated as no more than five miles, and it is no accident that both John Shakspere and his son William married girls from within that radius, while William's sister Joan (the one who survived) and his own daughters all married Stratford residents. Yet it seems John Shakspere's trading could take him much further. He would have attended country fairs to carry out his trade as a brogger – a dealer in wool – weighing the high risks and the high profits it involved. He would, on the side, have bought up skins for his glove-making, while the experiences of other children in similar circumstances suggest that John would have taken along his stock of gloves to the markets and set up his eldest son with a simple stall to sell them while he was trading.

Though there were plenty of sheep in the Cotswolds, not much more than ten miles distant, to produce wool for John's trading, he went much further afield. Among the list of wool transactions collated by Wood (2003), the largest was at the major wool market in the centre of the City of Westminster. It took place when William was eight years old, and it is quite likely John would have taken him along for company and assistance – children were a resource, not a decoration. John might have owned his own horse, and he could have hired one for William from the local carrier to do the trip to London at a cost of 5 shillings. On occasion, they would also have used horses as pack animals. The journey to Westminster identified here is unlikely to have been the only one that John – and possibly his son – made.

William's experiences with his father over the hidden period of his life up to 1582, added to what seems to have been his natural shrewdness, must have formed the basis on which he built his business fortune later. Yet his visit or visits to London may have introduced him to something quite different – the excitement of theatrical performances. There would have been visits of different troupes of players to Stratford – an average of one a year during his youth, according to the records – but they could not have competed for atmosphere and excitement with what he saw in London. At the same time, his vision of the trading opportunities that might have seemed open to him in England's capital – seen, or heard of from his father – would have eclipsed anything that the area around Stratford could have offered to his talents. His later move to London was quite possibly determined during this time purely on business grounds, but the potential excitement of the Metropolis could well have been an added attraction.

Also in the period up to his marriage, William would have been introduced to methods of debt collecting, this being probably the courts' most frequent type of civil case. When his father made application to a court for an order that would enforce repayment of money he had loaned, that would have been drawn up for him by a solicitor's clerk and have had a simple formality; it was a regular occurrence, and William would follow in his footsteps. John also found himself in court for setting his interest rates too high. Once he had asked for the return of £120 for a short-term £100 loan, but, although that may seem excessive now, tracing debtors then was not always easy, and the risks facing the lender had to be taken into account when setting the interest. John had a different kind of problem in the year of William's marriage when, as the debtor in a case, he had to apply to the Queen's Bench court in London for an order preventing four creditors from doing him harm.

William Shakspere's youth can be taken to have ended when he married in 1582, and we will discuss the next stages in his life in Chapters 6 and 7, yet it can again be regretted there is so little to tell about his early days. What we have told here, though, is consistent with his status, consistent with what we know of him and his family, and consistent with the conditions of England at the time. If anyone wants to make out that his life in his younger days was much different from what we have reconstructed here, they would need some convincing facts to go on, and there are none. Indeed, the evidence that we discuss in Chapter 10 will confirm that he was never at school. Stories about him may abound, of course, but no facts, and certainly not the facts we would expect if he had been the brilliant youth who became the brilliant Shakespeare. There are anecdotes about his early life but, as we have said, they only appeared after 1623.

Although no anecdotes have been traced to anyone who knew him, some will be revisited when we deal with their contribution to the myth that Shakspere was Shakespeare. However, one particular fantasy about him, not really built up until the late twentieth century, will be eliminated in the next chapter, where we discuss the religion of the Shakspere family.

Chapter 5

The Religion of William Shakspere's Family

A discussion of Shakspere's family religion could be interesting simply for what one might learn about the conflicts between Protestants and Catholics (and Puritans) that dominated, even haunted, much of sixteenth and seventeenth-century England. It could, but its main interest here comes from the way it has been subjected to fraud, forgery and fantasy in an attempt to turn the Shakspere family into Catholics. As it is obvious, whatever some say, that the author Shakespeare did not write as a Catholic, it is a bit of a two-edged sword to make out that Shakspere was one, even if it is done in a vain effort to try to link him to the aristocratic Ardens of Birmingham. Well, we shall see.

John Shakspere was born while England was still a Roman Catholic country owing religious and even political allegiance to the Pope in Rome. Mary Arden, John's future wife, was probably born a little later, just after Henry VIII, while he remained a Catholic, had begun a process that would turn the country – forcefully, but with a large measure of consent – from a Catholic to a Protestant one. In 1533, while John would still have been an infant, Henry rejected all rights the Pope might have claimed over England and its people. He created a new, "English" Catholic church that was effectively anti-Papal in nature; and, with the agreement of Parliament, he declared himself its head. When Henry died in 1547, the reign of his nine-year-old son Edward VI, bright and mature for his age, saw the state religion become steadily more Protestant and anti-Catholic. Then, when Edward died in 1553, the accession of his Roman Catholic sister, Mary Tudor, saw the "old religion", as it was known, restored. It was during her five-year reign that John and Mary Shakspere were married (c. 1557) in what had to be a Catholic service. In that short reign, the torturing and burning of obstinate Protestants and Puritans helped to create the conditions for the more drastic changes that were to follow, and earned the Queen the title "Bloody Mary". With her death in

1558, her Protestant younger sister Elizabeth ascended the throne. This twenty-five-year-old – who was lucky to have survived, let alone become Queen – began a determined process of trying to unify her country in a single Protestant religion, under a very "English" Anglican Church.

With Elizabeth's reforms, there was almost a total collapse, an implosion, of Catholic organisation in the country. Catholic families in her realm were effectively left with a choice of apathetic acceptance of the change to Protestantism, of feigned acquiescence in public while continuing Catholic practices in private, or of emigration. Former Catholic priests who refused to convert were banned from practising, and some went into exile. Attendance at the new Anglican services was made compulsory, with fines and punishments for absence from church services (or "recusancy" as it was termed). Every adult was required (at least in principle) to take the Oath of Supremacy which acknowledged Elizabeth as the head of the church, and that applied particularly to those taking public office. Because Puritans – extreme Protestants – objected to the retention in the Anglican Church of bishops and other remnants of what they saw as "popish" idolatry, as well as to the idea that anyone merely human could tell them what they should or should not believe, some of them would also get caught up with the recusancy laws, though they were almost always treated more mildly than were the Catholics.

In the atmosphere of religious tension that existed during Elizabeth's reign, pragmatic parents could be expected to raise their children to conform, or to appear to conform, to the new religion, and to keep out of trouble even if they had reservations, whether Catholic or Puritan ones. Certainly John and Mary Shakspere seem to have raised their family with every appearance of being conforming Protestants. All their children, including William, emulated their mother Mary and lived out their lives without attracting notice for either religious devotion or religious deviation.

John Shakspere, as treasurer (or Chamberlain) of Stratford Corporation in 1561, must have taken the Oath of Supremacy. Both Sir Thomas Lucy, the Justice of the Peace from nearby Charlecote, and the Earl of Warwick were noted for their diligent watch for straying Catholics, often sweeping up recalcitrant Puritans in the process. It is likely that any official who tried to dodge the Oath would have attracted their eye and their wrath.

In his new position, John, who was now around thirty years of age, would have administered the finances needed for the removal of the Catholic frescoes from the walls of Stratford's Guild Chapel, for the destruction of the Catholic altar, and for the pulling down of the rood screen and rood loft, besides which he would have had to pay from the town's treasury for the destruction of the classical Catholic copes and vestments. Nothing has ever been found to indicate he impeded that work, though it is suggested his natural frugality would have lead him, in common with many other corporation treasurers, to pay out only for painting over the offending frescoes rather than for their more costly physical destruction.

In spite of his conforming activities, John Shakspere fell foul of the recusancy laws twice in 1592. This was at a time of imminent threat of another invasion from the Spanish, who still apparently hoped to dethrone Elizabeth even after the disastrous fate of their great Armada in 1588. The Government ordered the arrest of all recusants, aiming to forestall any treasonable Catholic activity in support of the Spanish. John Shakspere found himself arrested among a small number who were separated in the records from the block of arrested Catholics. Those with whom John Shakspere was named were not actually treated as religious recusants, but were stated in the record to have absented themselves from church for fear of being "taken for debt" – for a debtor attending church would be in a known place at a known time, making it easy for a creditor to apprehend him. In John Shakspere's case that could certainly have been true, as in the previous ten years he had been pursued for debt on some half-dozen occasions and once had to seek court protection from his creditors. However, in the group of nine in which he was included, three were known Puritans, so it seems the "debt" excuse could equally have been a device to avoid detaining Puritan recusants without the leniency extended to them being too obvious. Such people were certainly not the Government's target in the sweep of recusants because, with their hatred of Catholicism (or "Popery", as they called it), they would have made excellent recruits and recruiting agents if a militia were needed to fight against a Spanish invasion. John was never fined for any of his absences for debt, if that is what they were, and claims that some large but unspecified fines paid by him must have been for recusancy are illogical.

The only member of the Shakspere family other than John to be named for recusancy was William's daughter Susanna, John's granddaughter. She must have sorely tried the patience of the authorities when she missed the most significant of all annual Christian services, the Easter communion, in 1606. The fact that the case against her was simply dropped and that a year later she married the acknowledged Puritan, Dr John Hall, are both clear indications that she was a Puritan recusant rather than a Catholic one. Incidentally, the names of William Shakspere's daughters, Susanna and Judith, both taken from biblical women who protected their purity against male assault, were dear to Puritans. There is no record of John Hall being accused of recusancy: possibly he was excused religious services because of his onerous medical duties which covered a wide area of Warwickshire and Northamptonshire. He may have avoided taking the Oath of Supremacy and recognising the Anglican Church by avoiding public office on the same grounds, at least up to the death of his father-in-law. Hall did, however, record in his notebooks those Catholics – "papists" he called them – who were among his patients, indicating an antipathy to their religion even though he treated them. None of the Shaksperes or Hathaways were entered in his notes under that description.

When Susanna died in 1649, her Puritanism was confirmed by the first four lines of her epitaph:

> *Witty above her sex, but that's not all,*
> *Wise to salvation was good Mistress Hall,*
> *Something of Shakespere was in that, but this*
> *Wholly of him with whom she's now in bliss.*

John Hall – he "with whom she's now in bliss" – was definitely a Puritan. As the words "wit" and "witty" were used then to denote intelligence and wisdom, rather than their modern meanings, those lines cannot be claimed, as is often done, to honour Shakspere in the role of Shakespeare the writer. And, since "wholly" did not have the precision it tends to have today, just as one could then have "several halves", those lines can be read as implying her Puritanism owed something, if not much, to her father. (The alternative is to say that her epitaph unnecessarily insulted him, her progenitor and main benefactor.) That verse makes William Shakspere out to be a Puritan – if not a very serious one. That is consistent with the observations of Greer (2008) that the original Stratford bust of Shakspere (which we will discuss in Chapter 12) had the sort of clothing a Puritan would wear and that Anne Hathaway apparently had Puritan friends, as well as with what we know of John Shakspere's religious activities. It also fits with what we know of William's life in London: for, while three of his close friends – Augustine Phillips, John Heminges and Henry Condell, fellow sharers with him in the Globe – were fully active as Protestants in their respective churches, William went unnoticed as an invisible conforming member of various Anglican congregations.

The facts about John Shakspere's family reviewed above indicate that he and son William were likely to have inclined towards Puritanism, though they mainly behaved as conforming Protestants. That has long been the orthodox view, and it certainly does not harm the case for Shakspere being Shakespeare, a writer whose plays and poems show no partisan religious feeling (see *OCS*). In spite of this, some orthodox scholars have recently pushed the idea of a Catholic Shakespeare hard, possibly hoping to help link Shakspere to the aristocratic Ardens and hence, at some distance, to the Earl of Southampton.

Attempts to make out that Shakespeare was a Catholic go back at least to around 1850, when some Catholics seemed to see advantages in recruiting him to the cause of their Church. Anything in his works that showed Shakespeare had a knowledge of the "old religion", was taken as evidence of Catholic sympathies, even though, whoever the author was, it would have been impossible for him to be ignorant of religious tradition in England. A subtler route has been attempted (see Asquith, 2005) with claims that Shakespeare's plays and poems included hidden messages intended to encourage Catholics to keep the faith. Yet, if these had been detectable by Catholics, they would hardly have escaped Elizabeth's trained anti-Catholic agents. The weak case for Shakespeare being a Catholic fails seriously, for example, with the blatant anti-Papal sentiments found in the play *King John*, or in the phrase "*twenty popish tricks*" in *Titus Andronicus*, or in the passages in *King Lear* which mock the trials of Catholic exorcists. In addition, the "Catholic" case faces the big problem of how Shakespeare treated over a dozen suicides in his plays. Suicide was a "mortal" or irredeemable sin for a Catholic, yet those of Brutus, Romeo, Ophelia, Cleopatra and the rest he represented as noble and dignified, or at least understandable and forgivable.

Wilson (1993) tried to construct a "Catholic" William Shakspere by linking him to the Gunpowder Plot of 1605. He pointed out that, when his daughter Judith got married – eleven years after the Plot – she acquired a brother-in-law whose father-in-law had been married to a lady (long dead when Judith married) who had had nephews who were associated with the Plot. Yet, as anyone will guess, no connection has been found between these plotters and Shakspere. It is just unhelpful whimsy.

The attempts to "convert" William Shakspere into a Catholic, totally contrary to the evidence, depend on invention. Apart from seizing on the recusancy of John Shakspere and Susanna Hall, some scholars have placed uncritical reliance on a note made by a Reverend Richard Davies around 1700 that asserted of William Shakspere "*he died a papist*". Davies must have been repeating in his note stuff he had heard at several removes. For instance, he wrote of there being a Justice Clodpole in a Shakespeare play based on a "*Sir Lucy*" (which there is not). He had clearly picked up a story that Shakspere "*hath a monument on which he lays a heavy curse upon any one who shall remove his bones.*" That curse was not on the Shakspere Monument, of course, but on a stone plaque in the Stratford church with the line "*And curst be he that moves my bones.*" Since everyone of any (or no) religion, might well wish to have their bones left alone, it cannot be assumed the plaque was for a Catholic. If it had borne an obvious Catholic message, it would hardly have been allowed in a Protestant church. However, it should be obvious it had nothing to do with Shakspere. It was only attributed to Shakspere seventy-seven years after his death when a Mr Dowdall got the story from an octogenarian guide who presumably threw the invention in as a tit-bit to increase the size of his tip. The plaque's text was recorded by Sir William Dugdale in 1634, but no one before 1693 said it was Shakspere's. The guide would hardly have been around for Shakspere's burial, and it is amazing that Dowdall, a lawyer, could believe that this poor plaque was what Shakspere's rich heirs had left him. It was crudely formed – the present plaque is a prettied-up copy of the original – and displayed non-original doggerel verse: no date, no name, no epitaph. Neither Davies's comments, nor the use he makes of the curse on the plaque, nor the way some have rushed to believe it, can be evidence of anything much other than human gullibility. Related to the claim that the plaque was Shakspere's memorial, has spread the nonsense that he was a Lay Rector of Holy Trinity Church and, recently, a claim that he failed in his duties (see Appendix H).

A third invention about the family being Catholic is a claim that Mary Arden, William's mother, must have been Catholic because she was related to the aristocratic Catholic Arden family from Park Hall, Birmingham, Warwickshire. Yet this is contrary to the evidence. Stopes (1914) did speculate that Thomas Arden, the great-grandfather of William Shakspere, was the same man as the Thomas Arden who was a distant cousin of Edward Arden, head of the Park Hall Ardens. Yet the only evidence she produced actually showed there were two men of that name with differing financial status. The next paragraph shows clearly that Mary was no Catholic and no relation to those Ardens.

In 1583, Sir John Somerville, a deranged relative of the Park Hall Ardens, went to London with a gun and announced his intention of killing Queen Elizabeth. As a result both he and the head of the family, Edward Arden, were tortured, tried and sentenced to traitors' deaths. As a sequel, the authorities in Warwickshire were ordered to apprehend *"such as shall be in any way kin to all touched, and to search their houses."* In spite of this, and though her name would have drawn immediate attention, neither Mary Arden nor any relative of hers was apprehended or had their houses searched. Her total immunity can only mean she was known not to be related to Somerville or Edward Arden at a time when quite a number of Ardens and other persons related to Somerville were arrested, and some who lived near Stratford, not named Arden, had their houses searched. In addition, when her husband and son William later tried to get the coat of arms of the Park Hall Ardens associated (quartered) with their own, in order to add to the family's prestige, that request was refused, and their claim to be related to them was denied by the Court of Heralds in London – see Chapter 8. How much evidence is enough?

Regarding Mary's supposed Catholicism, it is sometimes pointed out that her father, Robert Arden, left a will with a standard Catholic preamble. Yet that must be put in contextulised: he died in 1556, in the reign of Mary Tudor, when not to write a standard Catholic preamble could have been dangerous for his family. It can be evidence for nothing.

Another attempt to create a prop for the Catholic-Shakspere theory is to claim William's wedding was a Catholic one conducted at Temple Grafton. There is no record that the wedding took place there and none that, if it had, it would have been Catholic. In the absence of a record of the marriage, although it clearly happened, one has to assume it was at Stratford, since the "licence" named both parties as being of that parish.

A more serious and persistent attempt to make out the Shakspheres were Catholic has used a lost fraudulent document, or, rather, one that was used fraudulently. This is usually referred to wrongly (though presumably deliberately) as *"John Shakespeare's Spiritual Testament"*, and one still finds it described as a statement of Catholic faith made by William Shakspere's father. In truth it was just an artefact used in one of the more interesting confidence tricks of a John Jordan of Stratford, the third most famous fabricator and forger in the Shakespeare story. (Jordan's successors in this field were William Henry Ireland – whom Jordan introduced to the game – and John Payne Collier; they were better at it than he, but no more audacious.) As it seems there is no serious account of this attempted deception easily available, an extended discussion of it is given in Appendix A. Scholars who want nothing to do with it ignore it, while those who like it prefer to fabricate their own evidence, even quoting from documents different from Jordan's. Here we give a brief summary of what actually happened with this "Catholic will", which may be enough to show why having nothing to do with it is a sensible response.

Jordan's Fraud against John Shakspere – a Résumé

In 1789, Edmond Malone, a well known lawyer and serious Shakespeare scholar, was given a document that appeared to be a handwritten copy of five pages taken from a six-page Catholic "will" bearing the name John Shakspear [*sic*]. It was clear the front page was missing. John Jordan of Stratford presented the document to Malone, a man he had tricked before (see Schoenbaum, 1970). After he had heard Jordan's story and had investigated the document, Malone concluded it was a copy made somewhere around 1600 of a genuine Catholic text that must have been circulated secretly. He published it as being John Shakspere's, and a most important Shakespearean discovery. For reasons we can guess, the lawyer in Malone developed doubts about this find and made further inquiries. Jordan produced what he said was the missing front page but was clearly a fake. Malone worked out that the five pages he had originally been given were indeed part of a genuine document, but one that had nothing to do with John Shakspere. Although it was unlikely anyone would have challenged his already published conclusion, Malone honourably issued a retraction. It was confirmed that Jordan was conducting a scam when he and those involved with him made no challenge to Malone's retraction, even though it destroyed the value of their document and publicly implied they had all been involved in a fraud. They wisely let the potentially valuable document quietly disappear, never to be seen again.

The real mystery about this Catholic testament is that there are scholars who claim Jordan was a reliable antiquarian; that Malone, a lawyer, did not know what he was doing when he so obviously did, and that he was at fault for destroying the document when it was not his to keep or destroy. But Malone had been obliged to return the document to its owners, who must conveniently have "lost" it once they realised the game was up.

We see from the above discussions that there is good evidence that William Shakspere was a conforming Protestant, or even a Protestant with Puritan leanings, and no evidence that he was not. A conference in Stratford in June 2008 firmly supported that conclusion. However, some seem to think that, if they can get people to believe Shakspere was related to the Catholic Ardens, they can pass him off as related to any number of aristocrats, however distant, and so explain how (if he had been Shakespeare) at least some of his otherwise inexplicable writing activity came about. Deception in this area actually seems to have started in Edward Capell's edition of Shakespeare's plays in 1768, when he converted a messenger named "Somervile" in *Henry VI Part 3* – a character based on a real fifteenth-century person – into "John Somerville", the name of the cousin whose stupidity led to the death of the head of the Catholic Ardens. Even today, Capell's fraud is quoted as if it showed William Shakspere honouring an infamous and mad Arden relative!

A particularly weird use that has been made of Shakspere's supposed Catholicism is an attempt to involve him in a short, inconvenient and pointless visit to Lancashire, and in the adoption of yet another name, "Shakeshafte". Pointless, that is, to any ordinary person, but not perhaps to those who have seen this fiction as a chance to speculate in biographies on how Shakspere filled in some of his "lost years" and got into acting. As this Shakeshafte story is now regularly quoted by biographers to help the case for Shakspere being Shakespeare, or for him being a Catholic (or both) – even when they often seem not to believe it themselves – we will deal with it summarily in Appendix B.

Chapter 6

Shakspere the Player in London

Though there is no firm evidence for how our William Shakspere suddenly materialised in London in 1595 as part of a leading group of players, the Lord Chamberlain's Men, our earlier suggestion that it came about through his known business activities does seem more realistic than other speculations. One story some biographers prefer, though it has nothing to recommend it, involves a troupe of travelling players who had one of their number die on them while they were at Stratford, and then invited Shakspere to step in to take his place. That is not only fanciful but seems totally out of character for Shakspere and wholly out of keeping with the way professional acting troupes recruited. Given how Shakspere treated his business life, carefully judging the outcome of his efforts and getting extraordinarily rich, it seems unlikely he did anything so impetuous as to leave his home and occupation and family without due consideration and without prospect of seeing a satisfactory financial return from his decision.

Another story that has recently gained some popularity, though no credibility (see Appendix B), has Shakspere making a short visit to Lancashire, taking a change of name, receiving a large legacy and joining an acting troupe there. Yet those two examples of moonshine are no better than the old anecdotes of the go-getting Shakspere going to London to hold horses for theatre-patrons, or going to London to get away from a butcher to whom he was apprenticed, or fleeing to London following a run-in with the local Squire, Sir Thomas Lucy, all occurring at just the time he was being sufficiently close to Anne Hathaway to get her pregnant with their daughter Susanna.

Sometimes biographers imply that Shakspere derived a love for the theatre from seeing religious "miracle" or "mystery" plays that were performed at Coventry twenty miles away until 1579 when William was fifteen. Such occasions did attract traders, but that could equally apply to events at the nearer Warwick and Kenilworth. However, the related claim that the plays of Shakespeare show a knowledge of mystery plays because Shakspere went to Coventry is undermined by the fact the material in the plays has been traced to the written texts of the *Chester* mystery plays rather than to the less sophisticated performances at Coventry.

The commonly made suggestion that Shakspere turned his back on Stratford and left for the London theatre in 1587 at the age of twenty-three involves serious problems. There was no tradition of young fathers casually leaving their wives and families, and for him to have left Anne with three small children, one just four years old and the twins just two, is against common sense. The rearing of twins was particularly fraught at the time, feeding being difficult and twin mortality high.

It would have been bad enough if London had actually been only the six-day round trip from Stratford that is usually suggested, but that would have been good going in the best of weathers, with the conditions of the roads as they were at the time. Married couples were expected to live together, and the church courts took action if they did not. In 1584, for instance, Henry Field and his wife, the parents of Richard Field (of whom more will follow), were censored by the court in Stratford for living apart without the sanction of the law. If Shakspere had effectively abandoned his wife and children in the way that some imply, it is unlikely that there would have been no recorded consequences. There is no actual evidence he had even semi-permanent lodgings in London until after 1595 when records show him defaulting on his local taxes in the following two years. If he defaulted on his taxes when he had become rich, it would be surprising if he had left no records of such defaults earlier when he was still making his way.

Some biographers have tried to place Shakspere as lodging in the theatrical area of Shoreditch before 1590, but they have no evidence. They use a phrase from diarist John Aubrey's notes written around 1680 that reads "lived in Shoreditch". Aubrey's notes may be muddled in their detail but they clearly show that the phrase about Shoreditch was written before he started a new section with the name "W Shakespeare". The reference to Shoreditch in the text was better placed to relate to John Fletcher (the writer) or a John Ogilby (a dancing master) than to "Shakespeare". Moreover, there is no indication at all of the date to which Aubrey's note about Shoreditch referred. All this had been made clear by Lee before 1916.

There has been a suggestion that Shakspere went to London in 1588 and stayed there when he attended a court hearing with his parents on their case against a relative, Lambert, who had foreclosed on a mortgage. However, as he was a secondary party to that case, only needed if his parents died, that is most unlikely.

Those who try to establish a scenario in which Shakspere went off to London for the express purpose of becoming an actor or player have a big problem. Writers on the theatre have estimated that, at the time, a player would act in fifty or sixty plays a year, probably with two parts in each of six different plays in a week unless he was one of the leads. Given that Shakspere needed to carry out trading activities in London and Stratford to build up his finances, it is much more likely he had a low profile as an actor, possibly playing part-time, than that he had a full-blown stage career.

The most likely reason for William Shakspere to have left Stratford was that he had seen opportunities for trading in London when he was on a visit there with or for his father, and decided to try to exploit them. He may well have been used by his father as his London agent, since speculative deals often took place without any goods or money actually changing hands except at a final settling up. A dealer, even an unregistered one, could make transactions that way in any commodity, and there were more opportunities in London for him than elsewhere. This is consistent with our William Shakspere's known activities and with the fact that the easiest commodity for him to begin with would have been a cache of money for either personal loans or capital.

It is interesting, in this context, that the earliest date at which any record seems to place Shakspere in London comes from a court case in the year 1600. This referred to a William Shackspere who had made a loan of £7 to a John Clayton of Willington, Bedfordshire in 1592 and now, eight years later, had to sue him for repayment in the Queen's Bench Court. Some scholars question whether this 1600 entry is a reference to our William Shakspere, without giving a reason for their doubt. However, it refers to two activities that are associated with Shakspere: moneylending and suing for repayment; and both the loan and the action to reclaim it took place in London at periods when it is more likely that he was there than anywhere else. The probability that the lender was our Shakspere might have been diminished when a biographer reported that a William Shakespeare of Bedfordshire had been identified. However, this has not been verified, and it has certainly not been explained why the making of the relatively small loan and its reclamation would have taken place in London if both parties were from the same county.

On arrival in London, for whatever reason, Shakspere would have found that one particular professional group in the City whose members were regularly in need of loans consisted of theatrical players and their managers; and the same could be said of their associated playwrights or playmakers. The records of Philip Henslowe, the Elizabethan theatrical impresario and buyer of plays, show that he was a moneylender to his playwrights almost as much as a buyer, tiding them over when money was not forthcoming from patrons, or when they needed to be paid advances on their works. He complains in his diaries of times when authors were late with delivery of their promised plays and when they were slow, indeed reluctant, to pay back loans he had made them. When William became associated with the Lord Chamberlain's Men, including the Burbages who were theatre managers, his role of "sharer" or investor in the troupe may have simply been a refined extension of his lending of money to individuals.

If he did start his relationship with the theatre as financier, the easiest route to envisage for Shakspere getting into small-part acting would be by accident. It would have been normal that, while he was involved in doing business with a theatre or acting troupe, miles from home, he should become interested in the theatrical life of his clients; and it can be imagined that he became engaged in theatrical activities through doing small tasks backstage. This may be speculation, but it fits the lives of apprentice actors at the time – see Holmes (1978) – as well as the ideas reported by Malone in 1790 of Shakspere starting as "a call-boy or prompter's attendant". It is what happened backstage at the Portsmouth Theatre in the 1830s with publican's son Ben Terry, father of Ellen Terry and great-grandfather of Sir John Gielgud, so it would easily account for the level achieved by Shakspere: he would have learned by listening – aural learning – which was much more usual then than it is now, although many actors learn their parts by ear to this day. It has to be stressed that, though he was not Shakespeare, Shakspere was not lacking in ability: the fortune that he made by his dealings is testimony to that.

The development of Shakspere's connections with the theatre as a player could have proceeded gradually to the point where, after becoming a sharer and manager, he began taking minor roles, picking them up by ear and standing in when there was illness or some other problem, and he certainly appears to have been pleased to be referred to as a "player" rather than as a moneylender, even though the former title was itself not exactly prestigious. Officially, players were classed socially along with rogues and vagabonds, though they did have a safer status if they belonged to some aristocrat's acting troupe. This scenario would explain the way Shakspere first appeared in the London records on 15th March 1595: he was in the role of a payee, not of an actor, when, with Richard Burbage and William Kempe, two other sharers in the same troupe, he collected the company's fee of £20 for Christmas (or actually St Stephen's Day) performances the Lord Chamberlain's Men had given at Greenwich in 1594. It would also explain why the only records we have of William's relationships with individuals in the Lord Chamberlain's Men are with Richard Burbage, Henry Condell, John Heminges, William Kempe and

Augustine Phillips, all of whom were, besides being players, leading "sharers" in the company, just as they would be later in the Globe.

The idea we have discussed here of Shakspere becoming a player by a sort of osmosis fits well with the research of Southworth (2000), who showed that it was normal for players, if they were not born to the theatre like Richard Burbage, to enter the profession formally as apprentices at sixteen years or earlier, but never over twenty-one. That professional route would not have been available to the young father from Stratford.

There is no doubt William Shakspere was known as a player, even though some writers have expressed doubts whether the lack of contemporary references to him actually playing any parts might suggest otherwise. He was obviously less important as a player than sharer, but also obviously he was not negligible. He was named as a player during his application for a coat of arms (even though that was possibly not helpful to his case, given the status of players), and he was named as a player who was also a sharer in a legal document by one of the Burbage brothers, as mentioned below.

There is no record of the parts Shakspere played or of anyone seeing him act, which suggests that he was not a player of substantial roles. There are posthumous, very much second-hand, anecdotes about him playing Adam in *As You Like It* and the ghost of Hamlet's father – reasonable and satisfying parts for a minor player – but no evidence.

When Shakspere was given top place in the list of his troupe of players in the First Folio in 1623, this simply echoed the normal practice of putting the sharers and managers above the "mere" players. There is the clear record, for example, of Christopher Beeston, who was briefly a member of Burbage's troupe, putting himself at the head of the Queen's Men in their listings even when he had long given up acting in order to become their full-time manager. A similar situation applied when Shakspere's name was given a high placing in Jonson's works (published 1616): there he was well up the list of the Lord Chamberlain's Men who had played in *Every Man in his Humour* in 1598, while, among those who had acted in his *Sejanus* in 1603, Jonson put Shakspere on the same level as Burbage, who was a lead manager as well as being very much the lead actor of the troupe.

Some scholars – e.g. Southworth, Honan – in an attempt to put flesh on the myth that Shakspere was both player and writer, have tried to argue that, as Shakespeare, he would have written himself good parts. Yet this totally backfires. The better the parts that it is claimed Shakspere wrote for himself, the less likely it must be that, among all those contemporaries who wrote about the theatre, no one would have noted him acting well in his own plays.

Clear evidence that William Shakspere was known as a player (but not as a writer) came in 1635 when Cuthbert Burbage, with whom he had been a joint sharer in the Globe theatre, had to produce a petition to the Lord Chamberlain in a legal case. This Burbage, as part of his petition, named the people who had risked losing their money by investing as sharers in the Globe, and he included "the player Shakspere". As it happened, the then Lord Chamberlain was one of the two dedicatees of Shakespeare's First Folio, Philip Herbert, who had since become Earl of both Pembroke and Montgomery. Had Shakspere been Shakespeare, Cuthbert Burbage would certainly have used this connection in his efforts to get his petition accepted. That was how things were done – but he did not.

Shakspere was clearly recognised as being a Lord Chamberlain's Man when James I issued letters patent to change the troupe to the "King's Players" in 1603. His name was well up the list. Later, nine of the troupe (including Shakspere) were created Grooms of the Chamber, and these nine were each granted four-and-a-half yards of scarlet cloth to make royally red suits suitable for King James's procession to Westminster Abbey for his coronation. The grant for the cloth itself had Shakspere's name at the top, even above top-actor Burbage, possibly indicating he had by then become the senior manager of the King's Men, consistent with his top place in the list of actors in the First Folio.

Now, during the period Shakspere was involved with the theatre, many opportunities occurred when observers could have made a connection between Shakspere the player and Shakespeare the writer, had they been the same person. It is a problem for those who claim everyone knew they were the same person that nobody noted any connection, for instance, when the Globe burnt down during a performance of *Henry VIII* in 1613. The fire was started by a discharge of cannon required by the stage directions: yet nobody – not even the prolific letter writers Henry Wotton and John Chamberlain, who both noted the destruction of the theatre – commented on the irony of a playwright destroying his own property.

There is an earlier example where no connection was made between player and author, one often used to pad out "Shakespeare" biographies. A theatre-going lawyer, John Manningham, noted in his diary for March 1602 a trivial joke about the actors Burbage and Shakspere (to whom he gave the well known spelling Shakespeare). He clearly had to have it explained to him, for he made a note for himself that Shakspere's Christian name was William (the whole point of the joke), but this implied that he did not connect him with the famous author of *Venus and Adonis* and *The Rape of Lucrece*, whose first name he would have known. Within eleven months of this entry, in February 1603, Manningham recorded in his diary that he had seen *Twelfth Night* at the Middle Temple. He could, on that occasion, have noted seeing a play by the subject of that joke, or even seeing him in the cast, but he did not. In such situations, nobody ever noted Shakespeare acting in his own plays, nor linked the actor Shakspere to the author: good indicators that Shakspere was not a notable actor, and that the pseudonym Shakespeare was not associated with him.

A late record exists of Shakspere possibly being involved with one of his fellows in the theatre in 1613, a date well after it is generally assumed he had retired to Stratford. He and Burbage were apparently employed on a task totally different from acting: that of producing an *impresa* for the Sixth Earl of Rutland. This was an emblem or device on a shield, with a motto, design and colour to identify the owner in a tournament which was to celebrate the tenth anniversary of the accession of James I. For obvious reasons, scholars try to give the impression that Shakspere wrote the motto, while the manual work was done by Burbage, who is sometimes put forward as an expert painter on the strength of it. They both received 2 jacobusses (or 44 shillings) for their part in the work. Burbage devised an *impresa* for Rutland later by himself, when Shakspere was dead, and was paid extra, namely 98 shillings. Because the employment of Shakspere or Shakespeare and Burbage on this task seems so strange and late, it is sometimes suggested that the story applies to someone other than our Shakspere and, possibly, another Burbage. However, because it has had an effect on the myth that Shakspere was the writer Shakespeare, it is looked at again in Chapter 10.

Two other late records – 10th and 11th March 1613 – exist for Shakspere's purchase and mortgage of the Blackfriars Gatehouse on the north side of the Thames opposite the Globe, and close by the Blackfriars Theatre in which he was, or at least had been, a sharer. He paid £80 down, and took a £60 mortgage which was paid off before 27 September. In this transaction Shakspere used three trustees, two of whom signed both documents, the third being his fellow sharer and actor, John Heminges. A theory that the use of trustees here was to stop his wife benefitting from it when he died, as some have suggested, will be discussed in Chapter 11. It has also been suggested, most improbably, that the purchase was related to the building's previous association with Catholic activities which had been investigated by Government agents. Those activities had not been mentioned for some years and, anyway, even if Shakspere had been a Catholic, it was a bit late in his life to put himself at risk by getting involved with anti-Catholic forces in London. The purchase looks most like an opportunistic, theatre-related project, since Richard and Cuthbert Burbage were busy buying up property in the Blackfriars area at this time.

Although those late records indicate Shakspere was in London in 1613, many scholars think he had quit both acting and London after 1604. There is no trace of him having lodgings in London after that date.

Jonson noted him being in the King's Men when they played *Sejanus* in 1603, but not in his *Volpone* in 1605, *The Alchemist* in 1610, *Catilene* in 1611, nor in the King's men in the Royal Household "Players of Interludes" in 1607. This is all consistent with the papers in the Belott–Mountjoy case (see Chapter 8) which show that Shakspere had left London before 1612.

We now move to one of the oddest items in the whole Shakespeare–Shakspere mythology: a supposed attack on the writer and the player in a little book generally referred to as "Greene's *Groatsworth*".

Although Shakspere was not mentioned in the context of the London theatre until March 1595, most orthodox Shakespeare scholars seem determined to claim that this muddled little book identified Shakspere as a player in London before 1592 – which it does not – and that it attacks him in the role of the author Shakespeare for writing plays by plagiarising from other authors – which it does not. And these claims about this book, among the most peculiar in the whole of scholarship, are regularly quoted as gospel.

The author of the book as given on the title page is Robert Greene, although he probably did not write it. Greene died in misery in September 1592 and the book was published at the end of the year with the title *Groatsworth of wit bought with a million of repentance*. It is usually talked of as Greene's and referred to with the reverence reserved for sacred texts of the kind everybody quotes but nobody reads, and it is systematically misused.

The book has at its heart an attack on actors who stole the works of playwrights and performed them without permission. Its fame arises because it calls one of the actors a "Shake-scene", and it is asserted without evidence or logic that this had to refer to Shakspere as Shakespeare. Yet around that time, there were references to Shake-bags and Shake-rags, where the word "shake" meant "steal", a sense in which the writer Shakespeare also used it. So the face value of "Shake-scene" is as an insult directed at some actor who steals the scenes he plays – someone like a Richard Burbage or an Edward Alleyn. The name was obviously not meant for a writer, nor a player of no reputation. The punishment proposed by the *Groatsworth* was for the wronged playwrights to withold their new works from the miscreant players. Yet this could hardly have been directed at Shakespeare, since he would benefit from the increased demand for his own plays if other writers withheld theirs.

Probably the worst consequence of the misuse of this little book arises from a phrase in it about an actor-manager being an *"upstart crow"*. This has been falsely hammered into the public consciousness as referring to

Shakespeare the writer, and is often the first thing about him journalists and other devotees of sound-bites think of and trot out for use as a false and insulting descriptor on every possible occasion.

One feature that attracts orthodox scholars to the *Groatsworth* is that it attacks the actor-manager "Shake-scene" as having a *"Tiger's heart wrapped in a player's hide"*, which phrase is, of course, a parody on *"Tiger's heart wrapped in a woman's hide"* from *Henry VI Part 3*. This parody is said to prove that the actor under attack could only be Shakespeare. Yet nobody would parody one of the best known lines from one of the most successful plays of the time if they wanted to denigrate its author as an upstart plagiarist. Clearly, the parodied phrase was used for the impact of what it said, not as an attack against its author.

Given that the *Groatsworth* has been so abused in the struggle to try to make Shakspere into Shakespeare and to fool generations into thinking (to paraphrase Tillyard) that the greatest playwright in history was also the greatest plagiarist (and in the process seriously damaging Shakespearean scholarship), a fuller analysis of it is given in Appendix C.

Because of the *Groatsworth* and the way it has been misused, it has seemed natural for some to find insults against the player Shakspere or the writer Shakespeare, or both, in all sorts of odd places. Some quote an epigram Ben Jonson wrote in 1600 entitled "On Poet-Ape" which attacks a pretended poet for stealing another's work, though it could not have applied to Shakspere or Shakespeare. This and other supposed insults that some seem to think were directed at one or both of these men are discussed in their turn in Appendix H; but it is worth noting here that Jonson, in all his snide remarks about the writer Shakespeare, never accused him of plagiarism, nor once spoke of him as an actor.

Chapter 7

William Shakspere the Successful Businessman

It seems sometimes to be forgotten – sometimes conveniently so – that Shakspere was an active and successful businessman. It might simply be that this detracts somewhat from the myth that he was Shakespeare. Yet the estate that he left in his will in 1616 shows he may have been the richest man in Stratford at his death (see Chapter 11).

The business acumen necessary for the accumulation of that fortune was likely to have been inherited, at least in part, from his mother, Mary Arden. Her father, Robert Arden, William Shakspere's maternal grandfather, was a successful farmer at Wilmcot, three miles north-west from Stratford; and, at his death in 1556, he chose Mary, the youngest of his eight daughters and still single, to be the executrix of his will even though she was probably only in her teens. That argues for her being reliable in business matters and to have had at least basic numeracy – a skill considered then, and a long time afterwards, as much more useful for a farmer's daughter or wife than literacy. At the same time, it is clear that John Shakspere was familiar with business methods in a number of trades, and that he would from time to time test the advantages of, shall we say, deviating from the strict limitations of the law – though he was not always successful at it. There are five known legal records critical of his dealings – in 1570, 1572, 1573, 1578 and 1580 – though there will almost certainly be more as yet undiscovered.

The fortune that their son William left is a good argument for his having learnt well from his parents and their experiences. Its very magnitude argues that he exercised good judgement in taking risks, as well as determination in pursuing through the courts those who had failed to repay even relatively minor debts. Given his undoubted business and financial success, it might appear strange that Shakspere seemed to prefer to be known as a man of the theatre or just as a player (with the modest financial rewards that that could have afforded) than to publicise his main money-making activities. Yet, at that time, the most honest businessman might carry a stigma for being "in trade".

Shakspere's dealings in goods, loans and investments would hardly have been as exciting as investing in the theatre. For such dealings, he would have needed to bargain, to come to agreement, and, where substantial sums were involved or the transaction was risky, to have the agreements documented by a legal clerk. Given that a number of Shakspere's deals led to court cases, it is likely the documents used in evidence were sworn before a notary, the "signatures" normally being a mark or a copy of a person's name which they would swear to. Such documents might well have been held by the clerk and, unless they were used in court proceedings, would have disappeared after a transaction was completed. The only evidence for most of these successful transactions was Shakespere's swelling assets from the profits.

Now, the limited financial rewards from the theatre that were available to someone like Shakspere through acting, or even writing, can be judged from the experience of two of his most famous contemporaries – Richard Burbage and Ben Jonson. The first of these he certainly knew, the second possibly. Burbage was close enough to Shakspere to be left a legacy in his will; both of them were shareholders (or "sharers") in the same troupe of players and joint shareholders in both the Globe and Blackfriars theatres in London. Jonson may have seen Shakspere on stage when his troupe of players, the Lord Chamberlain's Men, acted in Jonson's *Every Man in his Humour* in 1598 and in his *Sejanus* in 1603, but there is no reason why they should have met. Jonson, a great gossip and a great writer, made no mention of any actor by the name of Shakspere (or Shakespeare or any similar name) in any of his records, writings or reported conversations, except when he included him in lists of players and sharers in his published works in 1616.

Richard Burbage, as the lead actor of the Lord Chamberlain's Men, had only one real rival on the Elizabethan and Jacobean stage: Edward Alleyn, lead actor of the Admiral's Men. The Burbage family built and owned the first playhouse in London, namely "the Theatre", which existed at Shoreditch from 1576 until 1599. In that latter year, it was clandestinely dismantled following a dispute with the landlord and transported across the Thames to Southwark where it was rebuilt as the "Globe". The Burbages took a half-share in the Globe project, while Shakspere may have taken one-tenth or one-twelfth, which gave him a proportionate share in the profits. Richard Burbage also inherited the Blackfriars Theatre from his father. Yet, even with all the advantages in the theatre world that Burbage had over Shakspere, none of whose acting parts was important enough to be recorded, he left an estate when he died in 1619 worth only £300: less than one-fifth of that left by Shakspere.

To try to diminish Shakspere's achievement, it is sometimes pointed out – correctly – that fellow actor and sharer Condell left a larger estate than his. In fact, this only emphasises the point, since Condell's fortune was made when he married a widow who owned twelve valuable houses on the Strand in London. Similarly, it may be noted that when Edward Alleyn died in 1626, he left an estate much larger than Shakspere's, but he owed his wealth partly to his marrying the daughter of the impresario and moneylender, Philip Henslowe, in whose business he became a partner, and partly to his wise investment of his eventual inheritance from Henslowe. Shakspere had none of those advantages.

Ben Jonson, a man who gave up attempts at an acting career to become a playwright and poet, fared financially much worse than Burbage. Yet he had, at one time or another, seven patrons for his writing, and received two pensions. One pension was from the Crown for being, in effect if not in name, the poet laureate, and the other was from the third Earl of Pembroke, who provided him with an annual allowance of £20 for books (£12,000 today), and paid him extra when he worked on the Shakespeare First Folio in the years leading up to 1623. Jonson estimated that, during his life, he made less than £200 from all his writing, a figure that fits well with the relatively small amounts recorded as being paid by impresarios like Philip Henslowe and by theatre companies, and the small sums, around £4, that might be paid to a writer by a patron for the dedication of a poem or play. Certainly, when he died, Jonson had debts of £8 that his estate was unable to pay in full. Those figures for Jonson should provide an effective rebuttal to those who argue William Shakspere could have made his fortune from writing: it was not a lucrative profession and it is more usual to hear about writers issuing begging letters than bequests. Michael Drayton, who also had a Crown pension as effective poet laureate, left £25.

In contrast to Burbage and Jonson, both at the top in their chosen careers, Shakspere left an estate worth over £2000. Initially at least, his money must have been built up from his business and trading activities, and it was these that provided the basis for the wise investments he made as his capital grew with the years. His income from his minor acting career would not have been expected to exceed £1 per week, even less when the company was on tour; and that income, if it had been all Shakspere had, would have been easily absorbed by his expenses for the upkeep of himself and his lodgings in London and his family and home in Stratford – and for his commuting between the two. Some biographers have greatly exaggerated Shakspere's income from his work in the theatre as an actor – one crediting him with taking from it no less than £150 per annum (£90,000 today). He has, of course, also been credited with receiving an income – which would have been small – from the writings of Shakespeare, though there is no evidence of anyone with that name (or anything like it) receiving a single penny for any play or poem or from any patron of any description. That absence of payments to a playwright Shakespeare is just what would have been expected if the true author was hiding behind a pseudonym. And he could not have been the financially aware Shakspere, a man who was a dedicated collector of his dues, right down to reclaiming his expenses of 20d (one-twelfth of a pound) from the Stratford Corporation when he (or his wife) gave hospitality to a visiting preacher in his home in 1598, by which time he was a rich man.

The magnitude of Shakspere's business success probably came as a complete surprise to later researchers who found the records for his spending from 1596/97. Yet the fact that he had been able to invest money to become a sharer in the Lord Chamberlain's Men before March 1595 indicates that he had been making steady progress for some years before then. In 1596, he had sufficient wealth, and sufficient reliable wealth, to be confident in renewing his father's application for a coat of arms which, by the time it was fully granted and ready for use, would have cost him around £100. Then, in 1597, he bought the largest domestic house in Stratford, "New Place", together with its substantial estate.

This was a mansion with some thirty main rooms, which needed a complement of servants running to double figures. The money that officially changed hands for this large house was a mere £60, though that could only have been the nominal sum disclosed for the benefit of the tax collector's records. The remainder of the price, a much larger sum, would have been paid privately to avoid the tax and duty that would have been due if the full price had been declared. If we note that, three years after buying New Place, Shakspere paid £80 for a small family house or cottage for his sister Joan in nearby Chapel Lane, and that the largest house in the area, Clopton Manor, went on the market a few years later for £3,700, it is possible to believe that the true price of New Place would have been well over £500. So that they might set that price lower, some biographers have pointed to the evidence that New Place was in need of repair when Shakspere bought it – see Murray (1936). Yet the price quoted here has taken account of the need for repairs, for Shakspere obviously laid out the money necessary to restore it well enough for Queen Henrietta Maria, wife of Charles I, to stay there in 1643.

The wealth demonstrated by Shakspere around 1597 explains why John Shakspere was never again recorded as being in debt: the rich son obviously took care of his parents. Another sign of Shakspere's substantial wealth is that he kept capital by him for moneylending and investment. It was in 1598 that Richard Quiney of Stratford approached him for a loan of £30 (£20,000 today) as though he was sure Shakspere would be able and willing to oblige. He must have known Shakspere regularly made such loans. Indeed, there is a record from 1605 of Shakspere taking a debtor to court for a £20 loan he had made earlier, and these examples will only be a fraction of the loans he made. There is more on aspects of the Richard Quiney loan in Chapter 10.

In the years after 1597 there are records of Shakspere's purchases amounting to some £1100. These included £320 for 127 acres of land near Stratford, £440 for a share in the lease of corporation tithes from another area near to Stratford including Welcome (of which more later), and £140 for the Blackfriars Gatehouse in London. He had shares in the Globe, the Blackfriars theatre and the Lord Chamberlain's Men. Yet, once again, it has to be realised it would be a miracle if the records that have been found of his investments were complete, and if they had not been reduced by sleight of hand in some cases to avoid tax.

The build-up of Shakspere's wealth after 1600 from his investments is difficult to estimate, but a figure of £300 per annum (getting on for £200,000 in today's money) cannot be unreasonable (see *EKC*). And, as we shall see, he had other sources.

One truly remarkable fiction about Shakspere's wealth that has been repeated for 300 years has depended on an anecdote which said he became wealthy in 1596 through a gift of £1000 from the third Earl of Southampton. That canard – which few biographers can resist – appeared in print in 1709 when Nicholas Rowe produced his sketchy biography of Shakespeare based on the little that was then known about Shakspere. Rowe admitted he would have rejected the story as nonsense if he had not been told it originated from a Sir William Davenant. Today, we should be ready to reject it completely. In spite of decades of research and sifting of documents, not a thing has been found to link William Shakspere to the Earl of Southampton. Indeed, the two main books which discuss the relationship between Shakespeare (meaning Shakspere) and Southampton – Stopes (1922) and Ackrigg (1968) – contain not a single fact between them to justify their efforts, only supposition. Those authors began with the pseudonym Shakespeare used on the dedications to Southampton of *Venus and Adonis* and *The Rape of Lucrece*, and that is where they finished. They had no evidence Shakspere knew Southampton.

Of the supposed source of that canard – Poet Laureate Sir William Davenant (born 1606) – the sober Schoenbaum (1970) advised that *"any intelligence transmitted on the authority of Davenant must awaken suspicions in the wary"*. This was not because Davenant was dishonest, but because his name has been used to validate a dozen or more unbelievable stories that have never been traced to him, never been linked to actual events and have never had evidence to support them. Indeed, the rush to misuse Davenant's name to try to give substance to Shakespeare or Shakspere anecdotes itself depends wholly on another unlikely anecdote.

This one says that Davenant openly claimed to be the natural son of Shakspere. That claim requires one to believe not only that his mother, Jane Davenant, risked telling her son he was the product of her adultery, but also to believe that he, a man of ambition, then went round proclaiming himself a by-blow and his mother an adulteress. The story is not only improbable, but naturally lacks any supporting evidence. It looks just what someone might have mischievously built up on the back of an actual claim by Davenant that, as a poet-playwright, he felt himself to be the heir of Shakespeare. Because of the obvious problems with that anecdote about Davenant, some writers have tried to change it by having him claim that Shakspere was his godfather. Unfortunately for this new version, no church record has been found to justify it, and it is unlikely Shakspere would have left money in his will in 1616 to his known godson, eight-year old William Walker, and omitted to do so for the ten-year old William Davenant, whether he was his natural son or just his godson. Also, the anecdote is odd in its assumption that it would have been natural for Shakspere to stay with the Davenants at Oxford while commuting between London and Stratford, when they had six children and a tavern that provided no accommodation – see *SDL*. Anyway, Shakspere's obvious route from Stratford to London would have been via Banbury, Bicester, Aylesbury, Berkhamstead and Watford: this had better and more conveniently placed stops than the longer route through Oxford.

Even if anecdotes that were attributed to Davenant were usually credible and reliable, which they never are, and even if Southampton knew Shakspere, for which there is no evidence, and even if Southampton had a good reason for making a gift of any sort to Shakspere, which is most difficult to imagine, the probability would still have to be negligible that he gave anyone £1000 in 1596 (£600,000 in today's money). One only has to look at the size of that supposed gift to realise its improbability, but there is an additional, very practical, difficulty to accepting that it happened. In that year of 1596, Southampton was in serious financial straits because he had dared to refuse to marry the grand-daughter of his guardian, Lord Burghley. His disobedience had been punished by a fine estimated at a crippling £5000 (£3 million today). Southampton would therefore have had serious difficulties in raising £1000 in cash and has to be ruled out as a benefactor. Some biographers have tried to make the anecdote more acceptable by reducing the sum to £100, as if adding another assumption is a way to get at the truth.

With the fiction of the Southampton gift removed, we are freed up to look seriously at the source of Shakspere's apparent affluence around 1596, recognising that it must have some realistic, fact-based explanation or explanations.

One activity which added to Shakspere's earnings was his trading in grain, the price of which reached in 1596 its highest point during the whole of the sixteenth and seventeenth centuries. Following protests that appear to have been made about people hoarding grain at this period of shortage, and particularly about them converting it into malt for brewing when there was not enough for bread, the Stratford Corporation took an inventory in the winter of 1598. Shakspere was noted as holding grain and malt "at a lean time" to the weight of 10 quarters (of a ton): that made 2.5 tons in total – or 80 bushels for those familiar with old British measures. In that year, the price of grain was about £2 per quarter, having fallen from its peak value of £5..4s in 1596. Shakspere's holding was much more than he could have needed for his domestic use, but there were a few others in Stratford who held more than he, including the school master, Alexander Aspinall. It is not known, though, how much Shakspere originally bought at harvest time and had sold over the subsequent months.

Shakspere obviously continued his trading in grain when the price fell, for he was not only recorded as suing a Mr Rogers over a debt for malt in 1604, but he was depicted with a sack, possibly of grain, with its corners specially tied for lifting, in the original Monument erected for him in 1623. The folk of Stratford would have remembered the Shaksperes, father and son, for this trade, for we know John Shakspere had sued Henry Field – father of Richard Field – over a debt for barley back in 1556. The annual profit from such trading is difficult to estimate, but it was obviously worthwhile to Shakspere and would have provided a regular addition to his income. The same can be said of the rents he must have been getting from the several properties that he owned and had available, and rooms he let in New Place. He could then use his surplus income to make more money.

Another activity of Shakspere's for which we have no indication of the profits, was his moneylending, but that also seems to have been continuous. A return on his capital of ten per cent would not have been unexpected from the records, with probably the same, or even more, for his grain dealing. Though those profits would not have been enormous, they would have been surplus to his requirements, cumulative and continuous.

While he was moneylending, trading and renting, in 1596, Shakspere was also purchasing properties, pursuing his coat of arms, and coping with the death of his son. Some have questioned whether he could have spent any time at all in London over this period. Yet there is evidence that he was involved in some peculiar activity in Southwark in that year. On 29th November, a joint order was sought from the Sheriff of Surrey against Willelmum Shakspere, Francis Langley (a theatre owner), Dorothy Soer and Anne Lee. The Sheriff of Surrey was responsible for the borough of Southwark where Langley's theatre, the Swan, was located, which indicates Shakspere was living in that area at the time, four years before the Globe was transferred across the Thames to the South Bank. The order, requested by a William Wayte, was that the four defendants should *"keep the peace towards him"*. Because we have so few facts about the order, there is plenty of scope for speculation, but it does link Shakspere with three characters whose reputations were not of the highest – Langley (who had already been sued for libel), Wayte (described in a court case as a *"loose person of no reckoning"*) and Wayte's step-father, a shady anti-theatre magistrate, William Gardiner.

As Southwark was the "red-light" district of London, and the connection between theatres and brothels goes back a long way, the association of Shakspere and Langley with two female defendants in the court-order has not reduced speculation. Nevertheless, it is possible that Shakspere just got caught up in a theatre dispute, or even simply as a commercial investor in a brothel owned by Langley, and the order may just have been part of a tit-for-tat dispute. However, in that case, one would have expected Langley, rather than Shakspere, to have been named first in the order. There is known to have been a dispute going on for months, according to an order taken out earlier by Langley against Wayte, who seemed to be acting for the unsavoury Gardiner, but Shakspere's role is still a puzzle. For some of the less outlandish speculation, one can read Schoenbaum (1970) or Wilson (1993), but one cannot escape the fact that the events leading to the order must have involved Shakspere in one more distraction in what had to be a stressful year.

For some reason, there are writers who have actually sought to demean Shakspere's character as a businessman. Duncan Jones (2000), for instance, gave her (orthodox) biography of Shakespeare the title *Ungentle Shakespeare*. In it, all the negative aspects she claimed to have identified for her subject were actually not Shakespeare's but Shakspere's, though, perhaps strangely, she did not mention the affair with Wayte and Langley discussed above. She could have drawn attention to the bawdy in Shakespeare and his invention of well-turned insults; but she did not. Yet there is no real evidence that Shakspere was more (or less) gentle – in the sense of being courteous or benevolent – than the average man of business of his day. It is true he appeared in the legal and tax records for actions that were not too flattering, but, as we have said, such records tend naturally to dwell on matters of dispute, not harmony. The piece of evidence most often produced to show Shakspere was "ungentle" is a statement made in 1614 by the Town Clerk of Stratford, Thomas Greene, a close friend of the Shakspere family, about what is generally called "the Welcome enclosure".

Greene noted that Shakspere would not join in Stratford's fight against the enclosure of surrounding common land, even though it would affect the livelihoods of many of his fellow townsfolk. Instead, Shakspere negotiated an agreement with those seeking the enclosure, the Combe family, so that his own rights would be protected in the event that the townsfolk lost. Picked out in a journalistic manner, it does sound callous. Yet it may just have been an additional precautionary measure, for he had already predicted to Thomas Greene that the Combes would not succeed – and they did not. The play *Bingo* (first performance 1973) is written around this episode, suggesting that Shakspere's action led to rioting, which it did not: the general Warwickshire riots were in 1607, and such action – legal and physical – as was taken by local people in 1614 was directed at the Combe family.

There are a number of records of occasions when William Shakspere had outstanding debts himself. One in 1606 showed him owing £20 to the neighbour, Hubaud, who had sold part of the Old Stratford and Welcome tithes which Shakspere had bought. Others were mainly for small but regular amounts of local taxes he owed in various London parishes where he had lodged. Yet these could simply show him acting as a cautious businessman, protecting his cash flow and his capital by delaying payment on sums which would cost him no interest or penalty until he was put under pressure. Shakspere was a man who used money to make money, and it was better for him if he kept other people's money in his own hands as long as possible, much as the banks do today. There is no good evidence Shakspere ever defaulted on a debt. There is no record of him being sued in court over the rates he owed. Even the 40 shillings we know Shakspere's wife owed to, or held for, her father's shepherd when he died in 1601, may have been properly settled without it being noted down anywhere.

What the various small debts for rates in various London parishes do show, is that Shakspere did not have any settled residence there, and that he appeared to consider Stratford as his permanent home. Even so, he somehow avoided the civic duties in his home town that he might have been required to undertake; and there is no record of him paying fines for such avoidance, as might have been expected, at least in his final years when he was settled. It seems every explanation for Shakspere avoiding such service would have left something in the records, but there is nothing, and no point in speculation.

There is no point either in trying to put a protective gloss on Shakspere's character as a businessman. He did what he did within the customs of his times. Starting with no advantages, in a large illiterate family, marrying and starting his own family early, he made his money where he could by his own effort and ingenuity, and his financial provision for his family exceeded anything that could have been dreamed of when he was born. It is only if one wants to take on the task of fitting this active and successful actor-businessman to some idealised image of the writer Shakespeare that one has problems. It is no use trying to demean Shakspere by claiming, as Greer (2008) seemed to do, that he abandoned his wife, leaving her to protect their children and herself from going on poor relief as best she could while he made his "fame" in London. He went to London to make money, not fame, and it is hardly valid to assume he provided none to his family, or that he was rarely at Stratford with them because he was wasting his time in London writing. When we look at his frequent changes of lodgings in London and the difficulty the authorities apparently had in finding him to get him to pay the tax on his lowly-rated and few possessions, we can see that this is not consistent with him being settled in London or seeing the capital as his main residence. There is nothing to show he left Stratford before 1590, if then, or that, when he did go, it was other than to do the best for his family. One only has to think of the house he managed to buy and the servants he would have had to employ to run it to understand that he was successful and that his family benefitted.

We hope that, at this point, we have led the reader to see that the actor-businesman Shakspere is interesting in his own right. There is more to come.

Chapter 8

The Belott–Mountjoy Case and Shakspere's Memory

A major new light was thrown on William Shakspere in 1909 when documents were discovered which showed he had once been called to give evidence in a London court case. The action was "Belott versus Mountjoy" and it took place in 1612, though it had had its origin eight years earlier. The papers in this case – mainly statements or depositions from people involved on one side or the other – revealed information about Shakspere of a quality only slightly less than when his will was found in 1747 (see Chapter 11). And no single discovery has spawned more inventions to try to link Shakspere to Shakespeare.

The people who found this "Mountjoy" bundle, Dr Charles Wallace and his wife Hulda, two Americans from the University of Nebraska, had spent nearly ten years working through collections of records in London in an attempt to find anything to do with the writer Shakespeare. Then this. It was not their only discovery, but it was probably their most interesting, even if it did, in fact, tell us nothing about Shakespeare.

One thing found from the bundle was unique: an address where Shakspere had lodged in London, with the name and business of a landlord, Christopher Mountjoy to whom he paid his rent. And then, on his deposition of 11 May 1612, was the earliest example of his name on a legal document written where he would have put his signature had he been able to write. The way that name came to be written so oddly, looking like "Willm Shakp", is discussed in Chapter 10, but it immediately tells us something of how Shakspere viewed his name. In writing the deposition, the solicitor had used the better known spelling "Shakespeare" for him several times, yet the name written at the end for him to swear to on oath was certainly not that.

The papers show our Shakspere had lodged with a Huguenot family on the corner of Silver Street and Monkwell (or Mugle) Street, close to St Olave's church in the City of London. His landlord, Mountjoy, had

5. Agas's map of 1558, showing the Mountjoys' house at the junction of Silver Street and Mugle [Monkwell] Street in the City.

his workshop there for making and trading in "tires" – high-class wigs and head-dresses for society ladies. In his statement, Shakspere indicates he was living there from around 1602, since he refers to knowing the Mountjoys for ten years. He was certainly there in 1604 when the problem arose that was the cause of the dispute, and, as we will discuss below, his statement shows he had definitely left London by 1612.

Judging from the papers in the case, Shakspere seems not to have been living in Silver Street in any style, which is consistent with what we know of the low assessments made on his belongings for tax purposes in other London parishes in the years 1596 to 1599. Those never showed him owning goods worth more than £5, enough for basic wearing apparel and personal necessities and implying, as we have said, that his London lodgings were mere transient accommodation.

Mountjoy's family at Silver Street consisted of himself and his wife Marie and their daughter, another Marie. They give every sign of being what today would be called dysfunctional. Also there in 1604, living at the Silver Street premises, was an apprentice, Stephen Belott, whom the Mountjoys wished to persuade to marry their daughter. The statements of various witnesses show the Mountjoys enlisted the aid of our Shakspere as a broker in the affair. He was to mediate negotiations between Belott and themselves to find terms on which the young man would agree to the marriage. He obviously succeeded, as the marriage took place that same year. The dispute that arose from the marriage, and opened this window on Shakspere's life, was Belott's claim that Mountjoy had reneged on the terms of the marriage settlement Shakspere had negotiated for him.

It seems certain that, had she not died in 1606, Mrs Mountjoy would have sided with the newlyweds. She was clearly not on the best of terms with her husband, as there was a record of her visiting the famous physician-magician, Simon Forman, to check if she was pregnant through an extra-marital affair. As Mountjoy was later admonished publicly for getting a servant pregnant, it seems the infidelities were mutual.

Belott claimed in his personal deposition that Shakspere had negotiated a dowry of £60 (£36,000) to be paid immediately on the marriage and a change to Mountjoy's will to provide a legacy of £200 to his daughter Marie on his death. He stated that it was on these terms that Shakspere had brought him to agree to the marriage, and it was on these same terms, he alleged, that Mountjoy had defaulted, though they were never written down.

Belott's testimony was corroborated in some of its details by other witnesses: a Joan Johnson and a Daniel Nicholas, employees of the Mountjoys. They both said Shakspere had negotiated the marriage settlement. Nicholas testified that Shakspere had told him Mountjoy had promised a substantial legacy, a dowry of £50 and a portion of goods, though he forgot whether he was told what value those goods would have.

Another witness in the case was a George Wilkins, owner of a nearby tavern and brothel, who had convictions for illegal trading and grievous bodily harm to women. The Belotts had taken lodgings with him shortly after their wedding. He testified for the Bellots that, when they took up their lodgings, they brought domestic goods given them by Mountjoy which he, George Wilkins, "would not have paid above £5 for". Thus he undermined Mountjoy's claim that he had given the couple goods in lieu of the money. Unfortunately for the Belotts, Shakspere – the prime witness in the case – stated in his deposition that he could not remember the sums which he had negotiated with Mountjoy in persuading Stephen Belott into the marriage.

This information faces orthodox scholars with a dilemma. They can admit it shows he did not have the sort of memory needed to be Shakespeare, as do other lapses we will note later, or they can construct scenarios where, for some reason, he perjured himself, reneged on his duty as honest broker to Belott, and put his reputation, his liberty and even his person at risk. Most either duck the problem or go for the option of dishonesty, inventing excuses for Shakspere's supposed disgraceful behaviour rather than admit what is the simplest explanation. (Just the odd one or two think it plausible that forgetfulness in this situation would be consistent with Shakspere being the Shakespeare who was able to recall at will disparate bits of information from a plethora of sources.)

Let down by Shakspere, Belott was forced to go for arbitration before the elders of the French church in London. He won a settlement there, mainly because those elders distrusted the evidence of Mountjoy, but it was less than he claimed Shakspere had negotiated.

The time lapse between his negotiations and the dispute going to court may have been eight years, but Shakspere must have been reminded of them as soon as the Belotts realised Mountjoy had reneged on the deal; and anyone with a reasonable memory would have good recall in that situation. It was not as if Shakspere negotiated marriages every day, or that he only heard of this one second hand: as key mover in an interesting human process the outcomes should have been imprinted on his mind.

Because it is so unlikely Shakspere, if he was Shakespeare, would have failed to recall the details of such a matter, some biographers have preferred to think he lied in his evidence, and was possibly bribed to do so. Nicholl (2005) suggested he might have felt it was risky to give evidence in a lawsuit, though he must have done it in a number of actions for debt. One can see why some may feel it is better to have Shakspere lying than forgetting, but no reasons put forward for him doing so seem sufficient for him to break his trust in such a solemn matter, harming two young people and risking a spell in the stocks for it (or worse). The other witnesses seem to have had no difficulty, even those who worked for Mountjoy. It has been claimed Shakspere must have had a good memory for his business dealings but, as discussed earlier, those would have relied on short-term memory and notes of sums that would be destroyed on completion of a transaction. Suggestions that illness had affected his memory in 1612 must fail, because two years later he was sent to London with his son-in-law, John Hall, in a two-man delegation on Stratford business. His mental acuity must have been good, it is his long-term memory that is in question.

Now, it is natural for scholars to have scoured the Belott–Mountjoy documents for something to link Shakspere and Shakespeare, yet the result has been a quantity of suppositions unhelpful to the orthodox cause. One was that Shakespeare got the name "Montjoy", the title of a French herald in *Henry V*, from living with the Mountjoys. Yet that play was written well before Shakspere moved into Silver Street about 1602 and, anyway, what Shakespeare wrote about the herald Montjoy was available in his historical sources. Another claim was that Shakspere learnt the French he needed to write as Shakespeare from the Mountjoys, though French and French sources were used in the plays much earlier than 1602. A third theory based on those documents was that Shakespeare (as Shakspere) could only have written about "tires" or head-dresses in his plays from seeing Mountjoy make them in his workshop: yet such items of dress also appeared in his plays much earlier. A fourth was that the reluctant husband in *All's Well that Ends Well* was inspired by Stephen Belott, yet the cases were totally different. Shakespeare's source was wholly Boccacio, and the play was written well before any problem with Belott had occurred.

A fifth, and more recent attempt to link Shakspere to Shakespeare through Mountjoy is a claim that it was only because he saw Mountjoy prepare coloured silk yarn from raw silk for his tires that he could, as the writer Shakespeare, make allusions in some of his plays to raw silk and silk-spinning. Yet Shakespeare's plays mentioned raw silk and silk spinning before Shakspere lodged with Mountjoy. This idea of Nicholl's also suffers from the fact that the first silk mill in England was not founded until 1721 after Sir Thomas Lombe had pirated from Italy the carefully guarded specialised processes of preparing the silk for dyeing, dyeing it, and spinning it. Shakespeare's knowledge of silk processing probably came, as did much of the detail he put in his plays on Italy, from visiting that country which, with France, shared a virtual monopoly for the production of silk yarns in Western Europe. Even if Mountjoy had obtained those Italian secrets by 1604, he would hardly have set up and staffed workshops to prepare, dye and spin the small amounts of coloured silk yarns he needed. Still less would he, as Nicholl suggested, have got his daughter Marie to do it in a spare room in her lodgings using a second-hand spinning wheel.

Finally, it is noted that, in his statement, William Shakspere, Gent. was recorded as a resident of Stratford-upon-Avon, indicating he had quit London. However, as we have pointed out, he had dropped off the radar as far as acting went as long ago as 1604.

The Mountjoy Case and *Pericles*

An adventurous off-shoot from the Mountjoy case is an attempt to link Shakspere with Shakespeare through the play *Pericles* (possibly his most popular at the time). This relies on the claims that a minor writer George Wilkins was also the witness George Wilkins (not proven) and a friend of Shakspere's (not proven) and collaborated with Shakespeare on the play (not proven) and that this is evidence for Shakspere being Shakespeare. Those four steps have become more strongly urged, the more it has looked necessary to find a real connection between Shakspere and Shakespeare, though they were not mentioned, for example in the books of the thorough and orthodox Samuel Schoenbaum in the 1970s, and were given little attention by many other orthodox scholars. It is easy for biographers, writing like journalists, now to give the impression, without having to argue the case, that the link between Shakspere and Shakespeare through this composite "George Wilkins" is almost proven. Yet it is unlikely *Pericles* was a collaboration and illogical to suppose that, if there was a collaborator, it was this "Wilkins".

It is true the play had problems. It was first printed in a quarto edition in 1609 with Shakespeare's name alone on it, but in a state which showed it had been pirated by two different people who had written down the text as they recalled it from performances. One had made an absolute mess of the first two acts so that they were garbled, being almost incoherent in parts and, although the other pirate made an acceptable job of the last three acts, it had to be left out of the First Folio of Shakespeare's works. A common theory is that the two garbled acts were written by an inferior writer, while the ungarbled three were Shakespeare's. Editors of *Pericles* (e.g. Edwards) have shown, however, that the first two acts can be amended to get a play which looks wholly Shakespeare's. Moreover, there are more reasons than that for rejecting the notion that Wilkins (whoever he was) collaborated with Shakespeare on the play, and those will be discussed more fully in Appendix D.

It is fascinating how much the supposed Shakespeare–Wilkins collaborative relationship has been firmed up as the Shakspere myth has increasingly needed support. At first it was said that someone had started *Pericles* with two poor acts and Shakespeare added three good ones. Then it became a collaboration between Shakespeare and a poor author. Then the collaborator became the writer Wilkins who finished up as Wilkins the brothel-keeper and a friend of Shakspere. As a conclusion to all this, Wells (2006) wrote of *Pericles* that: *"there is little doubt that [Shakespeare and Wilkins] worked closely on it together"*. But see Appendix D.

To Sum Up

We have shown that the documents in the "Mountjoy" case discovered in 1909 might have pointed up problems with Shakspere's memory. They also emphasise the temporary conditions he lived in in London and his departure from London before 1612. But it is clearly not acceptable to hold that the documents reveal sure evidence of Shakspere's dishonesty, or that they prove that Shakespeare the writer was a friend of the criminal George Wilkins, as put forward in Duncan-Jones's treatment of the Shakspere–Mountjoy–Wilkins relationship in her book, *Ungentle Shakespeare*.

We have discussed failed attempts to use the Belott–Moutjoy documents to connect Shakspere to Shakespeare – through the play *All's Well that Ends Well*; through Mountjoy being French; through use of the title "Montjoy" in *Henry V*; through references in the plays to "tires" and to silk-spinning; and through a Wilkins being a collaborator on the play *Pericles*. However, before moving to the main areas of invention and disinformation that have characterised the Shakspere myth, we will look in the next four chapters at other subjects relevant to the real Shakspere as well as the myth – his coat of arms, his literacy, his will and his appearance and portraits.

Chapter 9

The Shakspere Coat of Arms

Nowhere is the family pride of John Shakspere and his son William better illustrated than in the way they worked to get themselves a coat of arms. If successful, their efforts would be rewarded with the title "Gentleman" being conferred on them and their successors, thereby raising the social status of the family both in and beyond the township of Stratford. The end result was success, but it was only achieved with difficulty and disappointment.

John Shakspere's first application for a coat of arms was made to the College of Heralds in 1576 but the arms were not awarded until some time after 1601, over twenty-five years later. In the meantime, son William had suffered two major bereavements. His father, for whom he had worked so hard to bring the application to fruition, died in 1601. Even before that loss and worse in its way, the death of William's son Hamnet in 1596 robbed him of the heir he would have been expecting to carry on both his family name and his family coat of arms for posterity. One cannot help but feel sadness for a man who, even as he renewed the family application after Hamnet's death, could see that any eventual success might have been rendered hollow.

The long delay in the award of the Shakspere arms had several causes, the most serious being the collapse of John Shakspere's fortunes straight after he had made the first application in 1576. This coincided with him being forced to withdraw from meetings of the Stratford Council, apparently because he feared being taken for debt if he appeared there. He had to ask to be excused from the "poor" tax; he had to sell or mortgage some of his and his wife's property, and so on. All this caused Rowe (1709) to assume he would have had to take son William out of school in 1577 when he was thirteen, unable to afford to keep him there (though that was on the assumption William had gone to school in the first place). What is certain is that John was not able to pay to the College of Heralds the additional money needed to keep his application for the coat of arms alive. So it lapsed – for twenty years – and John would have forfeited the up-front £30 application fee he would have already paid (nearly £20,000 in today's money).

The second delay in the award of the Shakspere arms came shortly after the application was renewed in 1596. It was now William who was managing the application, and it is obvious he was confident he could not only find the application fee, but could also meet the various additional payments the College of Arms would require at every stage, from the sketching (or tricking out) of the arms to its delivery in the final form, totalling about £100.

Dated 20th October 1596, a sketch or "trick" of the Shaksperes' arms was prepared and a draft for the award was drawn up by one of the Heralds, Sir William Dethick. However, the grant of the arms must have been delayed when the words "Non, Sanz Droict" – Norman-French for "No, without right" were written on the sketch. At this point, William's own name was coupled with his father's and even superseded it as the application proceeded. Indeed, this association of William's name with his father's may in part explain the second delay. It seems that some general questions were raised in the College of Arms about the suitability of a number of the people who had lodged applications with them, and the Shaksperes got caught up in the dispute that followed. William's lowly rated status as a player, technically ranked with rogues and vagabonds, would not have been helpful. There are signs he had to expend some considerable effort (and possibly money) to get over the difficulties. The detailed ramifications that attended the Shakspere application are discussed in Lee (1916) and *EKC* but below we will outline the basics. There is detailed and enlightening research by Duncan-Jones in her book *Ungentle Shakespeare*, but her attempts to link the award of the Shakspere arms to both the writer Shakespeare and the Earl of Southampton are not very helpful. If there had been a real writer applying for his arms under the name Shakespeare, and he had been supported by the high-ranking Southampton as his patron, he would have easily achieved his coat of arms, just as the poet Michael Drayton did with none of the quibbles and hurdles that troubled the Shaksperes.

When the lapsed Shakspere application was renewed in 1596, a note was attached to it in the College of Heralds showing that, back in 1576, John Shakspere had claimed the right to the status of Gentleman and a coat of arms on three grounds.

He had been a senior officer of the town of Stratford-upon-Avon.
He had married "a daughter and heir of Arden, a gent. of worship".
He had "lands and tenements of good wealth and £500 of substance".

Of these three grounds, the first one was completely true. The second was true only in so far as Mary Shakspere was the daughter of Robert Arden: there is no record of her father having the title "gent." For the third claim there is no evidence whatsoever, and it has been suggested it was simply the sort of invention often added at the time as make-weights in this type of application. The false claim had never been tested because, as explained above, John did not pursue the 1576 application in spite of having laid out a substantial sum to lodge it.

It appears the Shakspères tried to enhance their application in 1596 by producing an extra claim to the effect that John Shakspere's forebears had given service to Henry VII for which they had received gifts of land. No evidence has been found, either in the records or through the deeds of John Shakspere's possessions, to substantiate either aspect of that claim.

Various sketches were made of the proposed coat of arms, all being similar to that which was put on the top of the monument in the wall of Stratford's Holy Trinity Church around 1623 (Figure 11). Basically, they showed a shield bearing a diagonal band along which lay a spear, an object that could act as a rebus or pun for the "spere" part of the Shakspere name. Then, on the top of the shield, stood a bird holding another spear. This bird has been claimed by some to be an eagle, apparently in an attempt to raise the status of the Shakspere family. Others have claimed it to be a shag (a bird that would provide another rebus or pun, this time to make the family name "Shagspere"). In fact, in the College of Arms description of the sketches, it is simply called a falcon.

Contrary to what is often asserted, it is clear the arms were only sketched or "tricked" in 1596 and not granted until later. Besides the words "Non, Sanz Droict," there was a dispute some time after 1596 about a claim that the proposed Shakspere arms were invalid, being too like those of three other families – the Manley arms, the Harly arms and the Ferrers arms. The record shows the dispute was resolved in the Shakspères' favour, but that may not have been until 1602.

John Shakspere was buried in Stratford church on 8th September 1601 without the title "Gent." after his name in the register, which means the arms had not been awarded by then. It has been suggested the title's omission was a clerical error, but it would have been a careless family who let that happen after all their effort to get it. The third reason for accepting that the arms were awarded late is that there were protests in the College of Arms, particularly from the member with the title "York Herald". These were objections to proposals to award Arms to "undeserving people". Near the top of York Herald's list of undeserving people was "Shakespear the player" along with two of his fellow players in the Lord Chamberlain's Men.

Finally, among the causes of the delay of the award, was the rejection

71

6. Stages in the sketching of the Shakspere Coat of Arms, 1596–1602.

of the application after the arms had been sketched by Sir William Dethick, Garter King of Arms in 1596 with the phrase "Non, Sanz Droict", repeated on the sketch twice more, the last in capital letters. William Shakspere must have been persistent and persuasive to obtain his arms in the face of all those setbacks.

The date the arms were finally awarded is not known. It seems to have been 1602, because, in that year, William Shakspere was referred to as *"generoso"* – indicating "arms-bearing" – in the warrant for the final stage of the purchase of New Place. It was certainly before 1612, because reference was made to him as a "Gentleman" in the witness statement prepared for him in the case of Belott–*v.*–Mountjoy (see Chapter 8): it would have been too risky to claim a false title in a legal document. Later, on 25th April 1616, the Stratford burial register recorded the interment of *"Will. Shakspere Gent."* The evidence that the arms were actually awarded is being stressed because there exists no record that the finalized form of them was ever delivered over to William Shakspere himself.

There are interesting side issues that arise from the Shaksperes' coat of arms and the problems it faced. Most important is that the placing of the arms on the monument raised in Stratford church in 1623 absolutely defined it as William Shakspere's. The inscription on the monument did not make that point at all clearly, but it would have been illegal to use the arms for someone other than a member of the Stratford Shakspere family.

Also important is the delay that occurred in 1599 when John Shakspere – or possibly William – tried to enhance their status by requesting permission to add "Arden" arms to their own. The Heralds had obviously assumed, and the Shaksperes may have intended, that they should be those of the aristocratic Ardens of Park Hall, Birmingham, and a provisional sketch exists showing those coupled with the Shakspere arms. However, the Heralds obviously realised the Catholic Park Hall Ardens were a totally different family because they crossed that sketch out. Moreover, it appears searches were made for other Arden families with arms so that, if they were related to Mary Arden, they could be joined with those of the Shaksperes. In the end, the Shakspere Arms had to stand alone.

When we noted above how the coat of arms on the Stratford Monument legally identified it as Shakspere's, this also had implications for the authorship of the plays in the First Folio. If Shakspere had written them, it would have been normal for his arms to be printed on the book's title page to establish the fact clearly. This omission has to be a warning for anyone wishing to believe the First Folio contained thirty-six plays written by Shakspere of Stratford. To try to get round that problem, a claim has been made that their omission from the First Folio showed the arms had not been awarded by 1623. Yet, given the evidence cited above, that claim rather becomes an admission that the absence of the arms from the First Folio presents difficulties for the orthodox theory. If the publishers really believed the unlikely Shakspere was its author, they must have added his arms as proof, just as they were on the Stratford Monument – this was one of the major uses of arms.

As if the above complexities were not enough, the Shakspere coat of arms has been the source of one of the oddest quirks of Shakespeare scholarship. It seems that, at some point, it was realised no one would have written "Non, sanz droict" on Shakspere's application and rejected it if they thought he was the poet-playwright Shakespeare. It seems someone spotted an opportunity to get round that problem by taking advantage of the fact that the third writing of the rejection "Non, sanz droict" on Dethick's sketch had the comma missing, so they could claim the meaning had been totally changed to "Not without right".

This requires one to believe that, in something as formalised as Heraldry, where commas are generally eschewed to avoid ambiguity, rejection could be turned into approval simply by removing one. This foolishness has gone further, perhaps because it was then realised that the simple dropping of the comma would not do. A claim was then made that the phrase "Non sanz droict" on the third instance was Shakspere's idea for a family motto, thus diverting attention from the two clearer rejections. For this final twist, one is asked to believe he chose a motto which could be read two ways, both of which could be made fun of. Also, one has to believe the motto was inserted by the Herald on the early drafts of the arms, when it was not an official part of them, and then left it off in the later exemplifications when it was. It is obvious it was not a motto: mottos were not written on the drafts, and it appeared on none of the three occasions when the arms were used for members of the Shakspere family – William himself, daughter Susanna, and son-in-law John Hall.

Still, imagination appears to be uninhibited when it comes to the Shakspere myth. Today, one will often find in Shakespeare biographies the claim that, in his play *Every Man Out Of His Humour*, Jonson insulted Shakspere through a character Sogliado to whom he gave a coat of arms with a cooked boar's head and had it suggested to him he should use the motto *"Not Without Mustard"*. Yet, when that play was written in 1599, Shakspere's arms had not been issued, and, when they were seen in public, no motto was attached. The phrase "Not without mustard" was actually part of a joke in Thomas Nashe's 1592 *Pierce Penilesse*.

It has to be odd that this canard about Shakspere's arms is so often repeated. Scholars obviously recognise that the supposed motto, "Non Sanz Droict", is open to ridicule in any translation; and one would have to think Shakspere very thick – *"thick as Tewkesbury mustard"* as Shakespeare had it – to have used it after Jonson had mocked "Not Without Mustard" in a play which was first acted by the troupe of which he was a member. In any case, the Arms of the troupe's leading actor had an actual boar's head – Richard Burbage.

It is not known who it was that decided to convert the rejection of the Shakspere arms into a motto, though the idea had certainly been seized on by the end of the nineteenth century and used to invent a pretended insult against Shakespeare. However, since there were those who added to and altered documents in attempts to influence people's thoughts about Shakespeare and Shakspere – Ireland, Collier, Halliwell-Phillips and others – one might wonder if a comma was not actually erased in the case of one of the sketches of the arms.

In 1950, to make up for the fact that no final, definitive, issued form of the Shakspere arms has ever come to light, one was published semi-officially with the spear magically turned into a steel pen and, for the very first time, the words "NON SANZ DROICT" were boldly printed as if they were an official motto. Today if one puts the term "Shakespeare coat of arms" (Shakspere is not recognised) into a search engine on the web, you will be directed to several sites, most of which illustrate the arms complete with "Non Sanz Droict" as the motto, often with the spear turned into a pen.

It seems very clear that the objections to and the delay in the award of the Shakspere coat of arms, its rejection, and its use on the Monument but not on the First Folio, are only consistent with Shakspere the player-businessman not being Shakespeare the poet-playwright. Sadly, one will not easily find an orthodox account of the Shakspere coat of arms which tells the full story.

Chapter 10

Shakspere's Literacy and his "Signatures"

The improbability of a boy such as William Shakspere of Stratford going to school has been discussed in Chapter 3, along with the lack of evidence that he, or any member of his immediate family, was literate. This situation would have been normal and not something to be ashamed of. It fits our knowledge of illiteracy in the country at the time; and it must be seriously improbable for all members of a family except one to be illiterate through four generations and for that exception to rank among the most literate persons who ever lived.

It has been claimed that John Shakspere must have been able to write to be a burgess, but two-thirds of his colleagues at least could not write. It has been suggested they might have been able to write but chose to affirm to documents with a cross or other mark, but Cressy's research showed that to be most unlikely: people who did not write their signatures would not write anything else either. Assertions are now being made that others in William Shakspere's immediate family could write, but they are only supported by wishful thinking – see below. Of course, anyone who assumes our Shakspere was the poet-playwright Shakespeare has also to assume he could read and write well – and not only in English – but assumption is not enough. Proof that Shakspere had literacy of any kind would be helpful to the orthodox cause: even though it would not remove all the other problems facing his candidacy for being Shakespeare, it would be a start.

Another piece of evidence against Shakspere being literate, one also related to his family, is that there are no records or even hints of letters ever being sent or received by him. This would be strong negative evidence for anyone but it is much stronger in the case of Shakspere, a man who carried out business in two locations several days' journey apart and spent substantial periods separated from his home and family. This lack of correspondence would be a puzzle even for a man of only moderate literacy, but almost impossible to imagine if the man had been the great writer Shakespeare. One could think of inventing a theory that Shakspere, or someone near him, destroyed or lost every letter he received and every document he possessed in his own handwriting, but one would then have to invent another theory that everyone who had received anything from him in his handwriting also destroyed it as a matter of course, however important it might have been. George Eliot and Charles Dickens, for example, are both known to have made bonfires of letters written to them, but the letters they wrote to other people were saved almost religiously.

Even if one could believe a theory that Shakspere could write and that everything he wrote disappeared, there is the problem of other people who kept diaries and left records and who could have referred to the receipt of correspondence from Shakspere. The Burbages were literate, as were some other people associated with the theatres, and their communications have been noted or preserved. There was also the carrier Greenway who operated between Stratford and London at the time when Shakspere was commuting between those two towns. He left records of messages and letters he had carried between members of other families who spent time in London, and it is hard to believe he selectively destroyed his records to do with Shakspere. Shapiro (2005), perhaps in desperation, invented for his readers examples of the sort of letter a literate Shakspere must have sent via Greenway: he could not have seen the irony of what he was doing – identifying what Shakspere must have done if he had been Shakespeare, but actually didn't do.

In their efforts to try to find something, anything, to "prove" Shakspere was literate, some turn to notes the diarist John Aubrey made on conversations he had with people around 1680. The first extract that they try to use from those notes for this purpose is a set of phrases Aubrey got at second or third-hand, supposedly from some of Shakspere's acting colleagues via people who never knew him. Aubrey's editors have published these as: *"he was not a company keeper, lived in Shoreditch, wouldn't be debauched, and if invited to writ; he was in pain"*.

The last part of that selection – *"if invited to writ; he was in pain"* – is a statement that Shakspere hid his inability to write by making an excuse (a well know device for the illiterate). However, some scholars have tried to remove the problem that that poses by making changes to turn it into evidence that Shakspere could write! (They will also join the phrases "if invited to writ" and "wouldn't be debauched" together though they were more probably unrelated.)

Honan (1998) edited Aubrey's notes to give: *'he "wouldn't be debauched, and if invited to writ that he was in pain." '*. Thus, with only a comma and a semicolon removed and the word "that" inserted, Honan changed the sense of Aubrey's words to the exact opposite of their obvious meaning; of course, no one who believed Shakspere was Shakespeare could accept the suggestion by Aubrey that the author could not write: he would feel Aubrey's notes were wrong and must be changed.

Schoenbaum, another top orthodox scholar, felt the phrases should be changed in a different way in *SCDL* to make out Shakspere could write. His version was: *'he "wouldn't be debauched" excusing himself when approached ("and if invited to, writ: he was in pain").'* Such a complicated change might disguise the real meaning of the words – comma added, colon for semicolon, words added – but it should really startle even the most acquiescent reader.

There is a second quotation extracted from Aubrey that some scholars treat cavalierly. This reads: *"in his younger days he was a schoolmaster in the country"*. It will be said the "he" in that statement had to be Shakspere. Yet, as Schoenbaum pointed out, it is not at all clear that this phrase in Aubrey's notes applied to him rather than to someone else. Aubrey did make rough notes containing references to Shakspere, but the "schoolmaster" quote occurred at a point where he was obtaining information about, or from, a person called "Beeston". This man is said to be a William Beeston, born 1608, but the notes indicate Aubrey's or Beeston's source was a player, John Lacy, born 1615. Aubrey was writing a century after Shakspere's younger days and one cannot really trust speculative interpretations of his muddled notes against the hard evidence. His "diary" – often used as a major source of information on Shakespeare – is known for its unreliability: his patron landed in prison for libel after relying on him, and called him *"maggoty headed"* while another who suffered said he was ready for a lunatic asylum, *"Bedlam"*. His notes that are clearly about Shakspere contain no fewer than eight errors of fact. With all that, one might simply ignore that "schoolmaster" phrase without anything else, but it is still given credence in biographies. It is worth noting no record exists of Shakspere being granted the licence he would have needed for such a post (see Honan, 1998). Similarly, if young William Shakspere of Stratford had had the literary and Latin abilities necessary to be a schoolmaster, let alone to be Shakespeare, his teachers would have had to notify the Bishop of Worcester that he was a pupil suitable for a career in the church: there is no record of such notification. To get round the problems, it has been suggested the quotation could possibly apply to Shakspere if he had taken a post as a private tutor not needing a licence. In that case, though, he would not have been called a "schoolmaster", a job which then had very specific status and duties different from a tutor; not only that, but when Shakspere was seventeen, penalties were introduced for unlicensed teaching even in private houses.

In view of the above analysis, it is strange that the *OCEL* refers to the "schoolmaster" story as *the best-authenticated tradition* about Shakspere: this simply confirms how bad the rest must be. But this anecdote holds another problem since, if Shakspere had been one of the Stratford elite – a reader and writer who had been to grammar school – it would be expected he would have been put to work there in a profession that used his skills – the church, legal profession, personal secretary if he did not go to university – and yet he was not even found an apprenticeship.

The discussion so far should be sufficient to show Shakspere could not write, and the changing of available information to try to make it fit the myth that he was Shakespeare is not helpful. Yet the most telling evidence against him being literate comes from a strange quarter, namely the six very different handwritten copies of his name we mentioned in Chapter 3 that are usually referred to incorrectly as "signatures". These, as we discuss below, were obviously not all written by the same person, and are nobody's signatures. They are simply copies of what may be called Shakspere's "sworn name", written for him by other people, probably legal clerks, at the points on legal documents where he would have signed his name if he could write. Once his name had been written for him – on his instructions – Shakspere would have touched the "signature" and sworn on oath before notaries or other qualified persons that the name written was his. This was, at the time, a standard way for a person to affirm a name on a document as opposed to affirming his or her mark or seal or even a personal signature.

The six copies of Shakspere's "sworn name" – or so-called "signature" – are shown in Figure 7. They are numbered in date order, with details of the purpose for which they were written. They are difficult to reproduce well, but it is clear they have a variety of spellings with different forms for both "William" and "Shakspere". Just as important or even more so, is that no two examples of a given letter in the six copies of his name can be matched against each other – no two "a"s match each other, no two "e"s, no two "h"s, and so on. One can see this is true without being able to read the standard Elizabethan script in which they were written – a hand which was known as the "Secretary Script" because it was common among legal clerks such as would have written Shakspere's name for him. One only has to compare each of the copies of his name against the other five to see how differently they were written. The difficulty of getting a match between them has nothing to do with the Secretary Script, it is due to the way the name has been written out by different hands or, in the case of the last three, by a single hand trying out the name for the first time. We are not, of course, asking whether any of the "signatures" might belong to the great writer Shakespeare. None of them has that spelling. Our question is whether they could have all been the signatures of a single, competently literate, individual.

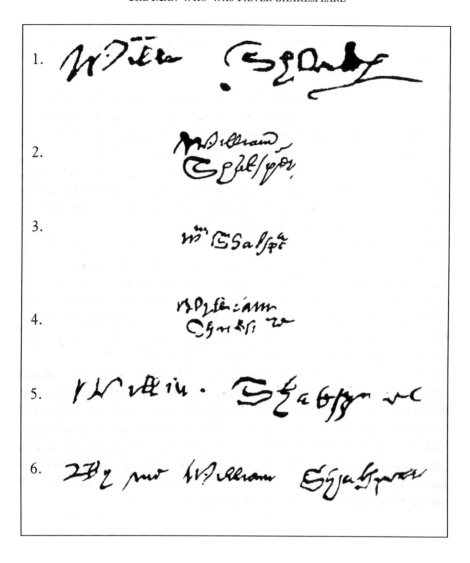

7. The six substitute Shakspere "signatures":

1. From the Belott–Mountjoy deposition, 11th May 1612.
2. From the Blackfriars Gatehouse conveyance, 10th March 1613.
3. From the Blackfriars Gatehouse mortgage, 11th March 1613.
4. From page 1 of Shakspere's will, 25th March 1616.
5. From page 2 of the will.
6. From the final page of the will.

Some people assert that "experts" have certified or validated these six copies of Shakspere's name as all being written by the same person. This is pure bluff. The most quoted "expert", Sir Maunde Thompson, is on record as saying that, if the last three "signatures" (Nos 4, 5 and 6) had not all been on the Shakspere will, he would have judged them as being written by three different hands. The Shakespeare scholar Malone, who was also a lawyer, had made a similar observation when he saw the will in the eighteenth century, and *Shakespeare's England*, Vol. I (1916) noted that Shakespeare scholars admitted the differences in the "signatures" were *"almost beyond explanation"* (though only, of course, if one refuses to accept the obvious). It defies belief to say Thompson, a former Director of the British Museum, could see that the three "signatures" on Shakspere's will appeared to have been by different hands but not see the other three Shakspere "signatures" (Nos 1, 2 and 3) made over three years earlier, were even more clearly not by the same hand.

The second most quoted "expert" on the signatures, Charles Hamilton, claimed to show, from an examination of the "signatures" and of the variations in the way the will was written, that Shakspere wrote it himself, though it will be hard to find anybody who agrees with him. Anyway, the writing in the will has been identified as being that of someone who worked in the office of Francis Collins, Shakspere's solicitor (Lee, 1916).

One finds, on examination, that the supposed authentication of the six "signatures" was nothing to do with the actual handwriting. It relied on the same fallacious argument used by Maunde Thompson and quoted above, that if they were on Shakspere's will, for example, they had to have been written by Shakespeare. The first step in the "authentication" process would be to find "experts" who accepted Shakespeare was Shakspere: most people did and no expert would be trusted who did not. That meant they could not doubt Shakspere's literacy or they would think they were saying Shakespeare was illiterate. With that mind-set, they had to accept that Shakspere's name written on a document where a literate man would have signed his name had to be a proper autograph or signature. This process, which rather reminds one of the story of the Emperor's new clothes, only left the "experts" to argue over the reason why Shakspere might have written six incompatible "signatures".

To make the problem simple for "non-experts", one needs only look at copies Nos 2 and 3 of Shakspere's "signature" in Figure 7. It must be clear no genuine expert, unless such a person had been preconditioned, would put their hand to a statement that both those signatures were written by the same man. A teenager on a store checkout or in a bank would very likely lose their job if they accepted a cheque with the signature written like copy No 2 when the identification used to support it had the signature written as copy No 3. Yet those two so-called "signatures" were actually written less than thirty-six hours apart.

"Experts" who believe the "signatures" were all by Shakespeare, however great their dissimilarity, then have had to accept a theory that Shakspere must have been suffering from one or more of the many illnesses proposed for him by scholars – from scrivener's palsy (writer's cramp) to cholera to gonorrhoea to senility to syphilis to *delirium tremens* to typhus to typhoid and so on – though, in fact, the only reason for thinking him ill in the first place is the need to explain away the inexplicably different "signatures". Apparently, the first scholar to remark on the three "sworn names" on the will looking to be by different hands was Malone in 1776, and it was he who came up with the idea that Shakspere might have been too ill in his last days to write properly. He, of course, had never seen the three earlier signatures (Nos 1, 2 and 3), but, when those were studied years later, Malone's "illness" theory based on the "signatures" on the will was, however unreasonably, adopted to explain the state of all of them, and it has been cheerfully repeated ever since. Hamilton (1985) took another tack. He said there were famous people, like Napoleon, who left "signatures" more varied than those attributed to Shakspere. But it is known Napoleon would dictate several letters at a time, and whoever wrote the letter also wrote his name, a common practice for the inordinately busy.

Two other unlikely explanations have been proposed for the variations between signatures Nos 1, 2 and 3. One is that conditions in the solicitors' offices where they were made were all so bad that no one could have written their name properly. The second is that the "signatures" were distorted by being written to fit a supposed limited space. Yet both those fail on the same two points. First, they do not explain the differences in the spellings as well as the handwritings. Second, the two other witnesses who in 1613 put their names on the same two documents as Shakspere in the same two offices at the same times, did so perfectly. If we showed the two copies of the signature of a William Johnson, one on each of the 1613 documents, they would simply look like two copies of the same one. The same is true of the signatures of a John Jackson, except one is slightly faded. They are available in *SDL* for anyone to see, and they discredit the orthodox theory at a blow, especially as they were not made by men in learned occupations. In the case of the terrible 1612 "signature", nothing in the signatures of other witnesses in the Bellot–Mountjoy case indicates a problem with the solicitor's office or methods either.

Some people might feel that the idea of experts letting themselves be misled in the way described here is fanciful; yet the Eysencks, in their 1981 book *Mindwatching*, quoted cases which showed how easily experts could be misled if given false information they have no reason to doubt. For example, in a 1999 finger-print case – the "Shirley McKie case" – a process of "collective manipulation" as it was called, cost the Scottish Police Force dearly when expert evidence that two finger prints were identical was thrown out once copies of them were examined side-by-side by non-experts – a method offered here for the Shakspere "signatures".

In this situation, one would expect that, of all the handwriting experts available, those most eager to show the six Shakspere "signatures" were authentic would be those employed at the Public Records Office in London, the body that owns four of them. Yet, in a 1985 booklet called *Shakespeare in the Public Records*, they (particularly Jane Cox) concluded the six "signatures" were definitely not all written by the same person. They then explained how disparate copies of the written name of a given person would have occurred on legal documents at that time (see Jenkinson, 1922). They pointed to many instances where, instead of affirming to a mark or seal on a document, a person who could not write had had their name written for them by the clerk who had written out the document to be "signed". The clerk would normally have used a disguised hand for the fabricated "signature" to distinguish it from the writing of the general text and so give it "verisimilitude". The person whose name had been written would then swear to the "signature" in the same way that they would have sworn to their mark or seal – hence the term "sworn name" that we have used. When this explanation, namely that the "signature" was written by the person who wrote the document, was first put forward – for example by a German expert, Thumm-Kintzel, in 1909 – it was naturally dismissed, even though it was then (and still is) the only one that made any sense.

It is particularly interesting how the suggestion from the Public Records Office so easily explains the appearance of the last three instances of Shakspere's "sworn name", those on the will. The clerk writing that will would have written Shakspere's name at the point where his mark or signature would have gone, either as it appeared written by someone else on a piece of paper that Shakspere carried, or as Shakspere told it to him. Since the clerk was not used to writing Shakspere's name, he could have done it somewhat differently each time he tried it.

In respect of the will, it is interesting to note that the scribe initially thought Shakspere had a seal that he would have sworn to and so wrote for him "*I have hereunto put my seal*". He then crossed out "seal" and changed the wording to "*put my hand*". It is sometimes claimed that shows Shakspere could write, but this is not so. If the scribe thought he could write and had a seal he would have written "*put my hand and seal*", just as one says a document is "signed and sealed". An illiterate person who had a seal would just use that. The will therefore tells us Shakspere could not sign his name, and that the clerk, finding Shakspere had no seal, had to change "seal" to "hand" or "mark". In the event Shakspere would touch his name when it was written for him and swear it was his.

If one looks at the third "signature" on the will – No.6 in Figure 7 – it is delightfully easy to see how nearly 400 years ago the clerk slipped up in writing it, so that the very last Shakspere "signature" would contain the best and the worst writing in the six. Relieved at getting to the end of his task, the clerk forgot he was supposed to be disguising the "signature" and wrote the formal words "By me William" in his best legal hand. At that point, he obviously realised his mistake and wrote the surname much as he had done in the disguised hand of the previous two examples. What is most peculiar about those three words mistakenly written by the clerk in his own handwriting, making them totally different from anything else in the six "signatures", is how they have been used by some orthodox scholars to claim that they show Shakspere had been taught to write in a good Elizabethan legal script, and even that he had worked in a good Elizabethan legal office. However, while that was true for the clerk who actually wrote those three words, it was not so for Shakspere.

What also takes one aback about the first three words in "signature" No 6 is that biographers who do choose to show their readers a specimen of Shakspere's "signatures" (almost invariably only one) nearly always pick this last one on the will, the one that is so clearly in two completely different styles of handwriting.

It is worthwhile, in the context of the Public Record Office's explanation, to note that "signatures" Nos 1, 2 and 3 finish with totally different endings: the first with a stroke under the "p" that was a typical legal abbreviation for "per"; the second with a completely different "p" followed by a form of "er" which occurs nowhere else in the "signatures" and has an undeciphered mark over it; the third has another completely different "p" which could be another legal abbreviation for "per" with two other letters added as if the writer thought he had made a mistake. They were clearly written by three different clerks, who also used three different spellings of the Christian name "William".

Some scholars have pointed out similarities between some of the individual "signatures", particularly in the two capital letters, W and S. They have pointed to the use of a long "Italianate" letter "s" in the middle of the name – at least in those cases where the "s" actually got written. They have noted that the "signatures" all appear to have been abbreviated or truncated in some way, with the three copies of the name on the will appearing to have been first written in a shortened form before someone added on the endings – looking like "ere" – afterwards. Yet if each of the four clerks involved in the writing – three for the first three signatures and one for the will – were copying from a specimen of Shakspere's name which someone had written for him to carry with him, that is just what would be expected: there would be similarities in the general form, but drastic differences in the detail – like the name "William" being written in a variety of spellings, and the "W"s all different. If the copy of the surname was abbreviated (as apparently it was), the ending would probably have been transcribed in different forms at the whim of the individual clerk (as it obviously was). The clerks could not have thought when they were writing those "sworn names" that one day they would be collected together and scrutinised. They did not know they were dealing with someone who later would have his identity stolen, so that their casual efforts at writing Shakspere's name for him might be called on as evidence for him being able to write when what they do tell us – and the clerks knew – is that he could not even write his name.

If the reader wants to know the tests "experts" should have applied to verify if the "sworn names" were all signatures of one person, they can look at David Ellen (1997) – though, in this case, that would be like using a DNA test to check if Marilyn Monroe was a man. (Dr Audrey Giles demonstrated some of the methods for BBC TV in 2002 when showing that Ireland's Sir Roger Casement did write the disputed "Black Diaries", but no one would waste time using such methods in this instance.)

If the reader wants to see how orthodox scholars can get into a mess when they select "experts" who will tell them what they want to hear, they should look at the discussion in *OCS* of a three-page handwritten scene which was added to a muddled play called *Sir Thomas More*. That book says that this scene "is generally agreed" to be in the handwriting of Shakespeare, meaning Shakspere. The only "expert" they quote is Hamilton (1985). Yet Hamilton's "proof" that this Addition (as it is known) was handwritten by Shakspere depends on two claims nobody else believes, including *OCS*. One is that Shakspere wrote his own will; the other is that the handwriting in his will is the same as in the Addition in *Sir Thomas More*. Writers will often imply (e.g. Ackroyd, Greenblatt, Wood) that everyone accepts that the Addition was handwritten by Shakspere; because of that, and the way the various claims about it impact on the problems of the "signatures", this canard is examined further in Appendix E.

The trouble with the discussions of Shakspere's "signatures" by orthodox scholars is very simple: if they were to accept the evidence that all were not written by the same person they would have to cease to be orthodox scholars. Yet here we have only looked at one impossibility: that of accepting they were all written by the same hand. The other impossibility, that of accepting they were all made by one of the most literate men of his age, is even worse for the orthodox theory.

Because of the different spellings of Shakspere's name in the six forms that people want to identify as his signature, it has been dinned into large numbers of students by their mentors that "Shakespeare could not spell his own name," a claim that rivals the "upstart crow" insult as the best known "fact" about Shakespeare. Yet, whoever the great writer was, the confident and gratuitous use he made of such a wide range of words in his works – from "viol-de-gamboys" to "praemunire" to "honorificabilitudinitatibus" – and the consistency of the use of "Shakespeare" for his works makes it hard to think he would have had a problem spelling his own name. The research of W. W. Greg has shown that literary men developed regular signatures early.

Now, though they hardly affect the question whether Shakspere could write, it is necessary to look at two pieces of "evidence" put forward in an effort to show he could at least read, that being a much more widely spread ability than writing. Neither appears valid. The first relies on him being a player and assumes a player had to be able to read to learn a part. Yet, even today, when the oral/aural tradition of learning that existed in Elizabethan times has been very much weakened, actors often learn parts by ear, while dyslexic actors learn major roles that way. If Shakspere had played major roles, reading would have been an advantage, but the failure of anyone to notice him in any part, let alone a prestigious one, indicates he never did.

The second piece of evidence used in arguing that Shakspere could read is the existence of a letter Richard Quiney of Stratford wrote in 1598, intending to send it to Shakspere to request a loan. It is the only letter known to have been addressed to Shakspere, and it is said to "prove" Richard Quiney knew he could read. Yet that cannot be so. The letter was never sent, and the business matters referred to in it were carried out by other means. What the letter might therefore prove is that Quiney thought, at the time he wrote it, that Shakspere could read – for it was not the type of letter he would have wanted Shakspere to get some third party to read to him. The fact that Quiney then decided not to send the letter after expending time and effort writing it, suggests he learnt that Shakspere could not read. That is consistent, of course, with the total lack of correspondence sent or received by Shakspere in all his fifty-two years, and the fact that he could not even write his name.

To try to get round the serious problem of Shakspere being illiterate, it has been proposed that Richard Quiney's ability to write should be accepted as evidence that any Stratford boy (or even girl) could have done so. Yet it is known that Quiney could have learnt from members of his family who were literate – his father could read Latin – while none of Shakspere's relatives were. A claim that Quiney's literacy guarantees Shakspere's literacy would imply that everyone in Stratford was literate.

Another such error is to suppose, as some do, that people like the family of the Stratford Town Clerk, Thomas Greene, and the literate Quineys would not have consorted with Shakspere if he had been illiterate: but that is to misunderstand society at the time.

There are scholars who have tried to say that the educational impediments faced by Shakspere were shared by some well known later British writers. The four examples most used have been the poets Thomas Chatterton of Bristol and Robert Burns of Ayr in Scotland, and two writers, George Meredith and Charles Dickens of Portsmouth. Yet these were all from literate families, and their biographies clearly show the sources of their education. The strangest case was made by Brown (1949) who tried to show Shakspere's problems were no worse than those of Dickens: one might think that plausible, coming from a top scholar, until one realised that Dickens's elder sister won a scholarship to London's Royal Academy of Music at age thirteen, his father was a reporter on *The Mirror of Parliament*, his grandfather ran a music business and his mother opened a school.

Recently, with growing scepticism about the supposed literacy of Shakspere, some have resurrected a neglected piece of information that has been neglected for good reason. It is the name of William's brother, Gilbert Shakspere, written where a signature could have been when he witnessed a Stratford lease in March 1610. It read "Gilbart Shakesper" in a good Italianate (or italic) script. Some now say this shows brother Gilbert was literate. But a single copy of someone's name with nothing for comparison cannot be taken as their autograph signature. If it could, then it would have been better for the orthodox case if a single version of William Shakspere's "signature" had been found rather than six very different ones. It is not surprising most scholars treat this supposed Gilbert "signature" as irrelevant; and it is just as proper, as pointed out earlier, to ignore claims that two laboriously-written copies of the name of William's daughter Susanna – made after her marriage to Dr John Hall – show she was literate. Greer (2008) stated: *"Susanna could certainly read an English text by the time she was ten"*, for which there is no evidence; then, eighty pages later in her book, she wrote:

> Until at least the mid-1590s Shakespeare [meaning Shakspere] was certainly not a wealthy man, and no attention would have been paid to providing Judith with an education.

Yet the girls were only twenty-one months apart in age; and Shakspere clearly educated neither.

Finally, an entry in the accounts of the sixth Earl of Rutland in 1613 (mentioned in Chapter 6) has been claimed to show Shakspere could write. This reads:

> To Mr Shakespeare in gold, about my Lord's impreso, xlivs; To Richard Burbage for painting and making it, xlivs.

Some doubt this referred to our Shakspere at all as he was living in Stratford at the time, and the task of making a device for a shield for forty-four shillings would hardly have enticed him miles away. If he had been Shakespeare, his level of skill would not have been needed for an *impresa*; if he was not, it is not clear what skills he would have provided. Indeed, the phrase "about my Lord's impreso" could mean anything, possibly simply "management of". Oddly, this record is frequently said to show Burbage was an artist and, from that, a portrait of a man in Dulwich College gets passed off, without evidence, as being his self-portrait. The Shakspere myth is infectious.

Note on a seventh "signature"

There is a 1568 book, *Archaianomia* (classical Greek for "old law"), in which can be made out the name "*W Shakspere*" hidden in the decorative printed frieze of the title page. In 1992, more than fifty years after he had first seen that name in the book, Giles Dawson, as Director of the Folger Library in Washington that owns it, set out to persuade the "Shakespeare" community that this was a genuine signature of William Shakspere of Stratford. He referred to it as a "*seventh signature for Shakespeare*". The history of the scholarship surrounding it is odd.

J. Q. Adams, former Director of the Folger, stated (see *SDL*):

> At the end of several months' investigation, Dr Tate [Folger's Chief of Research] reported that, after applying all the tests known to him, he could discover no evidence that the signature was not contemporary with the poet, and hence what it purported to be, namely a genuine signature of some person named "William Shakespeare" [*sic*]; and that after comparing its individual letters with those of the dramatist's, acknowledged it to be in all likelihood from the same hand.

What Dr Tate actually wrote was:

> No chemical tests of ink and paper have been made and it is impossible to determine the age of ink by any known test. ... It is apparent that the evidence is inconclusive. It is exceedingly difficult to make a statement proving or disproving the authenticity of this signature on the basis of the materials to hand.

Further evidence for there being something fishy about this "signature" is a passage handwritten inside the book which states: "Mr Wm Shakspeare lived at No 1 Little Crown St." The address has not been located, and house numbering did not come in until the 1700s. Yet, in an article Dawson wrote on the "Shakespeare signatures", he concluded this "seventh" was certainly his (meaning Shakspere's), even though it is quite different from all the others that he believes are Shakspere's; it is much better written and is not in the Secretary Script. The best bet is that it is a "genuine" forgery, possibly one of those by Ireland or Collier.

Chapter 11

The Will and Wealth of William Shakspere

The last will and testament of William Shakspere reveals much about our subject, though it could have told more. It was drawn up as a draft in January 1616, suggesting he was unwell at the time. He swore to the correctness of its amended contents on 25th March (which was then New Year's Day) but it was not written out as a fair copy before he died around 23rd April (see *EKC*).

When the will was discovered in 1747 by the Reverend Joseph Greene, schoolmaster and curate at Stratford, he naturally thought he had found the first personal document to come to light that had been composed by the great writer William Shakespeare – and he was bitterly disappointed. He noted that the language of the will:

> appears to me so dull and irregular, so absolutely void of the least particle of the spirit which animated our great poet, that it must lessen his character as a writer to imagine the least sentence of it his production.

It seems he would not have been surprised had someone told him his fellow townsman Shakspere was never Shakespeare. Some scholars were even moved to suggest, perhaps to hope, it might be a forgery, especially given the nature of the "signatures" on it; but we know it is not. It is very much what one would have expected from Shakspere. The bequests made in the will, the value of the estate deduced from it and the identification of the handwriting of the body of the will as that of someone who worked in the office of Francis Collins of Warwick, the solicitor named in the will who had worked for him before, all point to it being genuinely Shakspere's.

There are some quite interesting features to the will, not least being the famous bequest of the "second-best bed" to Shakspere's wife Anne (the former Anne Hathaway). And an odd game was tried with the will almost two centuries after its discovery when, in 1937, the identity of the second overseer of the will, Thomas Russell, was transferred to a man who, it was thought, would strengthen the Shakspere myth. This trick, welcomed by most biographers, is discussed at the end of the chapter.

The form of the will fits exactly with Shakspere's family pride, ninety-nine percent of the estate going to his immediate relatives. The bequests he made outside the family, including the £10 he left to the Stratford poor, came to about one-percent of his estate. The main beneficiaries, and joint executors of his will, were his favourite daughter, Susanna, and her husband, Dr John Hall. They were his residuary legatees, and would get everything remaining when expenses and all other bequests had been paid out. One can estimate – by taking his share in local tithes, the land he had bought around Stratford, the seven or eight houses he owned, including New Place and the Blackfriars Gatehouse in London, and the cash he must have had in hand – that they were left with a residuary legacy worth over £1500 (nearly £1 million today). And that takes no account of the gift of land worth over £300 (nearly £200,000 today) he had given Susanna as a dowry on her marriage nine years earlier. There is reason to believe Shakspere had already sold his shares in the Globe and Blackfriars Theatres, but, if he had not, his total estate would have to be revalued upwards by a considerable sum. There were various redistributions of Globe shares in the 1600s and it is not clear what Shakspere held at the end.

The size of Shakspere's estate poses problems for the orthodox theory that he had no power to publish works he might have written. It may be the belief that he was powerless that led Stephen Greenblatt to write of *King Lear* in "Around the Globe", Summer 2008:

> If *King Lear* is any indication, [Shakespeare] shared with his contemporaries a fear of retirement and dread of dependence upon children.

He then must have realised that the man he thought was Shakespeare was one of the richest men in Stratford when *Lear* was written and growing richer. This would explain Greenblatt's sudden change of tack:

> Once again, there is no obvious, easy relation between what Shakespeare wrote and the circumstances of his life,

though he meant, of course, " the circumstances of *Shakspere*'s life".

Shakspere did, though, have a major problem in 1616 over his younger daughter, the thirty-one year old Judith. She had married Thomas Quiney in February 1616 before the will was signed, and this new son-in-law was almost immediately indicted for "fornication" – sexual intercourse outside marriage – with a lady who died while giving birth to their child. That threat hanging over Quiney is thought to be the reason for the haste with which he had rushed Judith to the altar. It may also be why Shakspere amended the will drafted in the January so that Quiney could only get a small benefit from it if Judith should die prematurely. Of the £300 he left her, he made half provisional on her living a specified number of years, but he also left her a very personal item in his silver and gilt bowl, which demonstrated his affection.

William's grand-daughter, Elizabeth Hall, who was eight years old in 1616, would have been treated as a minor whose main benefit from the will would come through her parents. However, she too got a personal gift: her grandfather's silver plate which must have been worth more than the £15 he left between his three nephews, sons of his sister Joan, one of whose names he could not even remember.

To his widowed sister Joan, his only surviving sibling, Shakspere left £20 plus the right to live almost rent free for life in the Henley Street house that she already occupied (now the site of the "Shakespeare Birthplace"). She was also left his "wearing apparel" which, for a man of his substance, could well have been worth more than the £20 cash. She would have needed all he left her, because her husband, the Stratford hatter William Hart, had died only a week before her last surviving brother William.

To the Stratford boy William Walker, his godson of eight years' standing, Shakspere left just 20s (or £1).

The family bequest that has caused most speculation is that to his wife, Anne. Squeezed between two lines of the draft will as an afterthought, he left her his "second-best bed with the furniture", those last three words meaning the furnishings for the bed itself. That late addition is most frequently taken to be a derisory provision for an unloved wife or a hint of some problem of which we are otherwise ignorant, but neither of those is necessarily true. It may be she was already provided for, perhaps with a sum of money given beforehand or by an agreement for her to live as a "pensioner" with the Halls in New Place for the rest of her days: we will likely never know.

It has been said that Shakspere's arrangement with Trustees when he bought the Blackfriars Gatehouse in 1613 was designed to ensure his wife could not benefit from it, but an earlier similar arrangement had been made to ensure the individual assets in the Globe went to his family, not the other sharers. John Hall and Susanna inherited the Gatehouse, and soon disposed of it. It is not clear Anne benefited from anything but "the bed", which could have been quite valuable. (It has been suggested Shakspere did not want his wife buried with him, but that is just based on the wording on a poor anonymous Stratford gravestone that could

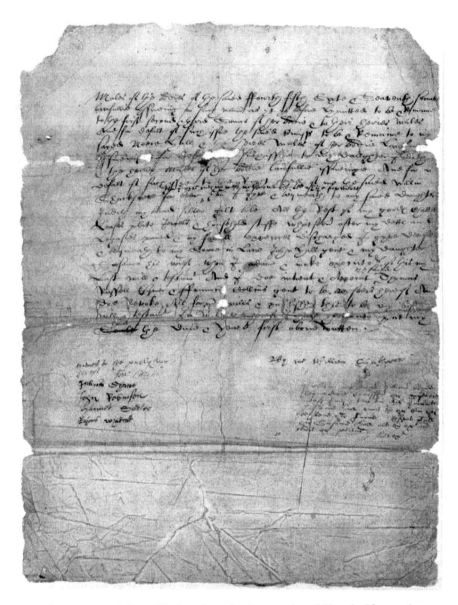

8. Last page of the will showing the interpolated line half-way down which says, "Item I gyve vnto my wief my second best bed with the furniture". See detail below:

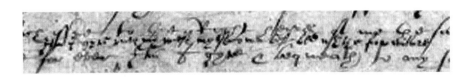

have been anyone's, though probably not his – see Chapter 13.)

Perhaps in the hope of making Shakspere more suited to be Shakespeare, some have tried to claim that wife Anne had a right in law to one-third of her husband's estate. Yet Lawrence Stone showed that the "one-third" provision only applied in London, Wales and York, and, anyway, unless Shakspere's will was invalid, Anne could have had no rights to any of the estate he identified in it – apart from "the bed". This is consistent with the finding of Schoenbaum that other Stratford wills made substantial separate provision for wives, including that of the Francis Collins who drew up Shakspere's. Since there is no evidence that Anne finished up destitute or was an unloved mother, it is best to assume she was provided for outside the will and that "the bed", probably hers anyway, had been overlooked.

Eight of Shakspere's close friends or colleagues were each given 26s..8d (or two marks) to buy rings as mementoes. Five of these were Stratford men and the other three were Richard Burbage, Henry Condell and John Heminges who each had two features in common with Shakspere that distinguished them from the mere players of the Lord Chamberlain's Men or the King's Men: they had all been sharers in the Globe theatre from the beginning as well as sharers in the troupe of players.

Only one proper legacy remains to be mentioned: the very personal gift of Shakspere's sword to a Thomas Combe. It is a bequest that at once quashes stories made up years later about animosity between Shakspere and the local Combe family of Stratford. These seem only to have been invented as part of a trick to pass off on Shakespeare some pathetic and unoriginal rhyming epitaphs about the Combe brothers, John and Thomas, and so link him to Shakspere. Shakspere had earlier been left a bequest in John Combe's will, and he now left his sword to Combe's nephew.

In sum, as we have mentioned, Shakspere's total estate – the bequests, residue and expenses – had to be worth over £2000, well over £1 million today.

Finally, three matters arise or have arisen from the will that affect the myth that Shakspere was Shakespeare. First is the question of memory. It is clear that, just as he forgot the bequest to his wife when his will was drafted in January 1616, Shakspere forgot those to his closest surviving colleagues from the King's Men which also had to be added between the lines in minuscule writing. And he had forgotten the forename of his nephew Thomas Hart, his sister Joan's son, so it had to be substituted with a line in the final document. His failures of memory here are consistent with his failure to recall the crucial evidence he should have given in the Belott–Mountjoy case in 1612, four years earlier (see Chapter 8). Those failures may not seem to amount to much, but they are all we know of

Shakspere's memory and, like Joseph Greene's comment on the will itself, they are not what would be expected from the author Shakespeare.

Second is the problem that the will contained no mention of books, though some people try to brush this away. If Shakspere had been Shakespeare, the books he must have owned and regularly used would have had a face value of several hundred pounds, a good proportion of his total estate and as "collectors' items" their value must have been much higher. If he had had Shakespeare's library, it would have been a treasured possession and a prominent feature in his home. Of course, given the mixture of houses and other property Shakspere owned and the attenuated mention they get in the will, there must have been a separate inventory, and a full list of books could have been included there. But, as with his property, it seems impossible some of his most important books would not have been mentioned in the body of the will, possibly as bequests to selected individuals. Oddly, among thousands of probate records retrieved from that time, his have never been found.

If Shakspere had had books to leave, they must have gone mainly to the literate Dr Hall, but there is no evidence any did. When Hall died in 1635, he left all the books he owned to Thomas Nash, his son-in-law, with the instruction to do with them what he would. Had some of them been Shakespeare's, he would surely have noted them as prime items and probably willed at least some to his wife and daughter as personal heirlooms. Books used by other Elizabethan writers have come down to us, and can be found in collections, but none of Shakespeare's numerous tomes have come through Shakspere's family. Books will naturally have been left by the real Shakespeare, but he and they are yet to be identified.

The seriousness of the problem of the missing books is illustrated by the attempts made to get round it, such as claims that people did not bother about such things, or that Shakespeare did not use as many books as scholars have calculated, or he read the books he needed to use without buying or owning them. This is dealt with more fully in Chapter 15.

A third matter, one created artificially from the will, is the use made of a name in it to help in passing off Shakspere as Shakespeare. This is the name of one of the two people who received payments under the will for their services, rather than bequests such as Shakspere made to his friends. The first of these was Francis Collins who received £13..6s..8d (20 marks) for his work as the solicitor who drew it up and, as first overseer, was charged with ensuring the will's provisions were carried out. The second person who received such a payment was a Thomas Russell, Esquire. He received £5, a fairly standard sum for the minor task of second overseer. It is this second man's identity that has become a part of the myth-making; and this is how it started.

It was in 1937, 190 years after the will was discovered, that Professor Lesley Hotson published a book *I, William Shakespeare* in which he claimed to have identified that second overseer as a Thomas Russell who lived at Alderminster, five miles from Stratford. In 1603, this man had become stepfather to Leonard Digges, one of the three friends whom Jonson got to write make-weight dedications for the Shakespeare First Folio (see Chapter 13). Because of that connection, this claim has become almost an article of orthodox faith. Hotson said he had concluded this man was the second overseer because only someone who lived locally to the testator – Shakspere in this case – would have been asked to act in that minor role. A man could not be expected to travel any distance just to back up the first overseer in checking the administration of a fairly uncomplicated will. Indeed, another Thomas Russell, Esq., identified as second overseer by Lee (1916), was ruled out because he lived in London. The trouble is that it is clear Hotson knew he was setting a false trail, partly because he tried to strengthen it with two others.

One of these was to assert that this Russell introduced Shakspere to his stepson Leonard Digges when he visited Stratford as a teenager, and that was why he wrote a dedication to Shakespeare for the "First Folio" of his plays in 1623. Yet, as we shall see in Chapter 13, Digges was just a minor pawn in Jonson's machinations over that publication. Also, as we shall see below, it is unlikely he would have written a dedication for Shakespeare at all if he had thought he was connected to his stepfather.

Hotson's second ploy was his repeated claim that Russell and Shakspere were close friends: he referred to them in the book forty-six times as friends, and sometimes "special" or "acknowledged" or "faithful" or "intimate" friends, but he had no evidence. He invented "affection" between them, and eight times referred to "Shakespeare's Russell" – really meaning "Shakspere's". As readers will guess, there is no hint among all the records we have of this Russell that he even knew Shakspere. He was not just an Esquire, but a scion of an aristocratic family and his close friends would not have included the trader and moneylender Shakspere, even if they had been neighbours instead of living five miles apart – when they were both in Warwickshire.

Now, when Hotson wrote, for future scholars to repeat, that the Russell he "identified" as second overseer of Shakspere's will lived at Alderminster near Stratford, he knew he was being economical with the truth. At least seven (and possibly eleven) years before Shakspere died, this Russell left Alderminster to live at Rushock near Droitwich in Worcestershire, where he had married Anne Digges in 1603. This was twenty-five miles from Stratford direct, thirty miles by road and track: a three-day excursion at least in Elizabethan times (see Mountfield, 1976). Thus the very criterion Hotson claimed to have used to identify

Shakspere's second overseer, namely that he was someone living close to Stratford, was not met by his Russell. Moreover, if this man, who did not live near Stratford, had actually been the second overseer, he must have been named in the will as being of Rushock in Worcestershire, just as he was named as being "of Rushock" in his mother's will in 1608, and as the solicitor Francis Collins was named as being from "the borough of Warwick" in Shakspere's. The reason scholars seem to have missed this trickery was not because Hotson did not mention where this Russell really lived, he just concealed the information in an appendix with the title "Thomas Russell and John Hanford" which implied it was not relevant to the main matter in the book – although it was fundamental. In that appendix, he showed he was aware of what he was doing, when he turned the arguments he had used in the body of the book upside down. Having claimed Shakspere would only have used someone local to be the mundane second overseer of his will, and then pretended the Thomas Russell he had picked was a local man, he now admitted in that appendix that his chosen Russell actually lived a prohibitive distance away at Rushock. Then Hotson claimed it was precisely that great distance that proved he was a such a close friend of Shakspere. Of course, any scholar who realised Hotson's Russell lived at Rushock, far from Stratford, would have known he was not the one named in the will: he would have been inappropriate, his place of residence would been written in the will, and his fee and expenses plus legacy as a special friend would have been more than £5.

To help shore up his invention, Hotson tried to say that Russell was of good character and hence ideal as second overseer. Yet it is known that his stepsons, Sir Dudley and Leonard Digges, detested Russell, who had worked hard to deprive them of their inheritance of £12,000 from their father. Indeed, when their mother died, they had her buried as Anne Digges wife of Thomas Digges, with no indication she had been married to Russell and died as his widow. Hotson knew she was not with Russell when he was ill and making his will. He knew Russell had failed in his duties as first overseer in the case of the will of a John Hanford. He knew Russell had faced a court case, charged with obtaining money from a Mr Bamfield – £150, or £90,000 today – by pretending to be married to Anne Digges when he was not. And that is by no means all. If Shakspere had known Russell of Rushock – and there is no evidence he ever did – he would hardly have foisted him on his heirs as even second overseer to his will, wherever he lived.

The fact that Russell of Rushock cannot be linked to Shakspere, means the other Hotson fantasies about how that man introduced Shakspere to a network of aristocrats and establishments, from the Earl of Essex to the Virginia Company, evaporate. Though they never had corroborative evidence or credibility, those fictions Hotson created are still quoted as if they were hard facts. But the book was a real *tour de fraude* in which he span a web of confusion, drawing in some 500 irrelevant characters, from Queen Elizabeth to Tycho Brahe, Giordano Bruno to Cardinal Archduke Albert, in order to distract his readers' attention from the black hole which was at its core.

Note

For the misuse made of Thomas Russell of Rushock to invent illness and infidelity for Shakspere (and Shakespeare) through a poem, *Willobie his Avisa*, see Appendix H.

Chapter 12

What did Shakspere
Look Like?

In 2006, London's National Portrait Gallery (NPG) mounted an exhibition entitled *Searching for Shakespeare*. They displayed some dozen portraits, and among them one might have hoped to find a true representation of William Shakespeare the author or William Shakspere of Stratford or both. The exhibition pre-publicity said that only two Shakespeare portraits are authentic: the face on a "Shakespeare" bust in Holy Trinity Church, Stratford (Figure 11) and the portrait provided by the twenty-two-year old Martin Droeshout for Ben Jonson to put at the front of the Shakespeare First Folio (Figure 9). Yet those two cannot be said to be sufficiently similar to authenticate each other, and their moustaches are from different periods of fashion. The other portraits exhibited were all acknowledged to have no evidence to support their identification with Shakspere or Shakespeare, although – known misrepresentations that they are – they are regularly preferred to the two so-called "authenticated" portraits when it comes to selling Shakespeare. Actually, that may not be so odd: the supposed "authentic" ones look more like fakes than the others.

The prestigious handbook of the exhibition, also titled *Searching for Shakespeare* and costing £35, began its final paragraph on its final page with: "We will probably never know what Shakespeare looked like." This is an admission that none of the portraits exhibited could be relied on as authentic, though almost all of them have, at some time, been used to promote the Shakspere myth. Yet the NPG failed to exhibit the one portrait which had the best chance of being authentic, though it is almost never included in orthodox works because it undermines their cause. We will look at that below.

Let us first discuss why the two portraits normally talked of as being the most authentic are not authentic at all. Neither is a portrait of William Shakspere of Stratford. Neither represents the person behind

9. The Droeshout "portrait" – original version from the First Folio

10. The Droeshout "portrait" – as amended in subsequent printings

the pseudonym Shakespeare, and it is fairly obvious they were only ever intended to provide icons to please the faithful, just as the figures of Christ and his disciples in Da Vinci's *Last Supper* were only fictions based on people the artist knew. Yet all is not hopeless. Once the fictional portraits are out of the way, it may be realised that we know what both William Shakespeare and William Shakspere looked like.

We start with the First Folio "portrait". On the three-hundredth anniversary of Shakspere's death in 1916, the then Director of the National Portrait Gallery, Lionel Cust, gave his view that the apprentice Martin Droeshout began by finding a suitable picture to copy and changed it to make it fit with the image of a writer. That is kinder than another suggestion that it was done from a drawing-instruction manual.

Now Droeshout was, as all kinds of scholars have pointed out, a man of small reputation and less skill, and did a poor job. He gave the figure an artistic hairstyle (though with different lengths on the two sides of the head), and shading on the portrait so it seemed the light was coming from two directions at once. That last mistake was too much and the etching used for printing the portrait was changed more than once during the First Folio print run from that of Figure 9 to that of 10, where the light is from above and to the right side of the head. As a result, one now rarely sees exactly what Droeshout's original looked like. Various minor errors can be ignored, but an obvious major one was that the figure was given a doublet with two left sleeves (what one sees for the right sleeve is just the back view of the left one). Because of this, the portrait was used in the nineteenth century by the London tailors Moses to advertise how they would *not* dress their customers. Some have said the oddities of the portrait were to warn people it was a fraud, but Jonson's verse "praising" it would have done that, as we shall see below.

It is no wonder "portraits" that are known to be unconnected to Shakespeare are preferred for advertising his works. It is also no wonder many scholars have believed Jonson wrote his poem for the Droeshout "portrait" and had it printed next to it without even seeing it, a view that fits with it being plagiarised from a poem Malherbe wrote for a portrait of Montaigne – see Lee (1916).

Cust's view found support in 1988 from an American computer-imaging expert at AT&T, Dr Lillian Schwarz. She showed that the face of Queen Elizabeth's "Armada Portrait" of 1588 – the most reproduced picture of the age – had a facial shape close to that of Droeshout's final product; it was readily available and would have provided a suitable template to which he could add masculine features. She did not say that Elizabeth was Shakespeare, a thought that quite shook some orthodox scholars, or even that Drocshout had copied it exactly, but she showed its use would explain the appearance of his "portrait".

The use of the odd Droeshout "portrait" merely to give people something to glance at while they read Jonson's praise of both it and the author of the First Folio should be enough to make one wonder about the reliability of the rest of the introductory material in that book. The portrait really tells us that someone felt a deception was needed, and those orthodox scholars who try to browbeat readers by demanding how anyone can believe the editor or editors of the First Folio would have stooped to such a deception have a real nerve: the experts who mounted the exhibition *Searching for Shakespeare* in the NPG obviously felt, like Cust, that they had.

When we look at the second "authenticated" portrait, the face on the present Stratford bust, we find that it is no more reliable than the Droeshout portrait, and for similar reasons. And the insults about the face on the bust – that it is like a "bladder" or a "self-satisfied pork butcher" – are as irrelevant to the appearance of Shakespeare or Shakspere as the Droeshout portrait.

In the 1740s, the 1623 Stratford bust was reported to be badly damaged – *"much impaired and decayed"* – with great damage to the face caused by mould. Also, significantly as we shall see, the right hand was reported as being broken. The town decided to hold fund-raising events – with a gala production of *Othello* – and called for contributions towards its restoration. The work on it started in 1747, ending in 1749, and it could not merely have been cosmetic as is often claimed.

The instruction to the first repairers may have been *"that the monument shall become as like as possible to what it was when first erected"*, but the money raised, the time taken, the description of the damage and much else, tell us something drastic happened. One cannot sculpt a new face from badly decayed stone and get one like a bladder. One cannot resculpt a broken stone hand to produce a new stone hand. (The damage could have been made good by the use of cement or plaster, but it was not.)

It is not clear if all the changes that have been made to the original bust actually occurred in the period 1747 to 1749, because there were three other dates in the eighteenth and nineteenth centuries when repairs were reported. However, it seems clear that the original bust made at the Janssen works in London around 1623 was removed at some time and replaced with one carved from Cotswold free-stone, a cheap material that would not have been worth the expense of carrying to London to make the original Monument (see Brill, 1968). That 1747 occasion would have been the chance for major changes to be made to the bust, for it seems never to have been in as bad a decayed state again, so it is assumed that that was when the major change occurred.

The serious ways in which the bust was transformed are shown by comparing the sketch of the original made in 1653 for Sir William Dug-

11. The Stratford Monument as it is today.

12. Detail of Hollar's engraving of Sir William Dugdale's sketch of the
original Monument in his *The Antiquities of Warwickshire*, 1656.
By permission of the Bodleian Library, University of Oxford,
shelfmark: Gough Warwick 22.

dale's book *The Antiquities of Warwickshire* (1656) – Figure 12 – with a photograph of the present one shown in Figure 11 above. Claims by some partisans that the Dugdale sketch is unreliable are now discounted: it may not be perfect, but, as we will discuss, its major features cannot be disputed. Indeed, the difficulty of dismissing that sketch has led some to suggest the original was not made for Shakspere but for his father John: but that would raise far more questions than it could answer. It is seen that the hands of the original bust were holding a sack-like object: this has been thought to be a woolsack because of the way the corners had been tied to provide ears for easier lifting, though it could be for corn. The clothes and appearance are those of a plain man – a Puritan, Greer has suggested. The face was lean rather than fat, the beard unkempt compared with its replacement, the moustache right for the period, while that for the replacement is more "Charles II".

It would have been an obvious change, at a time of growing interest in celebrating Shakspere as a writer, to alter the bust so the hands could hold a pen and a sheet of paper: those were the iconic symbols used for writers. However, the question is raised why a cushion was used on which to rest the paper when a flat surface would have been easier to make and more usual as a writing surface? May be it was felt that losing the sack completely would be too much of a change; it was bound to have been noticed by locals even when the bust was decayed. The introduction of the pen and paper was a risk, but they were probably felt to be imperative.

The idea of giving the Stratford bust a pen may have come from the rogue artist George Vertue when, in 1727, he made a drawing of it without even seeing it. He had the Monument's proportions all wrong and his drawing for the head of the bust was a copy of the totally unauthentic "Chandos portrait" now owned by the NPG. To the bust he added, possibly because he thought it would automatically have had one, a pen. This man Vertue may be held up by some orthodox scholars as a model draughtsman but he was nothing of the sort. He sold Pope a miniature portrait of James I to represent "Shakespeare" in his edition of the plays in 1725. And he made another out-of-proportion sketch of the bust when he saw it for real in Stratford in 1737. He gave it a pen again when its right hand was definitely broken so it could not possibly have held one, even if it had not been holding a sack. It is probable that, as Vertue's previous drawing for which he had invented a pen was already published (replete with its other errors), he felt he had to continue the deception or look foolish. It seems quite likely that the two pen-holding drawings based only on Vertue's imagination could have helped inspire those who changed the Stratford Monument in various ways a decade later and replaced the genuine bust of Shakspere with one of an imagined Shakespeare with his iconic symbols.

The face of the bust was altered in 1747 and acquired then its domed "genius" head. It seems clear that those who produced the new bust thought they had no need to worry about its exact appearance. Just as, in 1741, those who raised the almost aristocratic statue of "Shakespeare" in Westminster Abbey knew they need only produce an icon to be worshipped by the faithful, so those who changed the Stratford bust in 1747 knew they could by now ignore the appearance of the original. And this has to be regretted.

This loss of the original bust by decay (helped by man) meant Stratford lost what had to be at least a passable likeness of Shakspere. For, while those who had produced the First Folio might have got away with a fake portrait of Shakespeare that met the need of readers who had no idea what he looked like, the same did not apply to those who raised the Stratford Monument. In 1623 there were still living in Stratford a number of close relatives of Shakspere (a sister, two daughters, two sons-in-law, two nephews, and a grand-daughter), five men who had been beneficiaries in his will, and close acquaintances like Town Clerk Thomas Greene and his wife, who lived in New Place for nine years. Even those who could not read the English part of the inscription on the Monument would have known whether the original bust looked like Shakspere or not, and whether it represented him in his proper occupation or not. And those who ordered the bust would not have wanted locals raising awkward questions about the monument when a visitor tried to follow up the hints in the First Folio that the author Shakespeare was a Stratford man. We must be thankful we still have the sketches of it.

If the appearance of the 1623 bust had to be such as would satisfy Stratford residents, there is a question over the basic errors in the Monument's inscription which existed whether or not Shakspere was Shakespeare. Though we will discuss them more fully in the next chapter, it is worth noting here some of the simpler ones that must have attracted the scepticism of the literate. The subject of the inscription was said to be *"within"* the Monument (which he could not have been) and that it was his *"tombe"*. The reference to *"passengers"* (meaning travellers) going by the Monument *"so fast"* could not have been written by someone who knew where it was to be placed (virtually in a corner); and the inscription gave no information of the sort one would have expected about Shakspere, not even a Christian name. Some would have noticed the Monument's subject was named as neither Shakspere nor Shakespeare; that words in the inscription were misspelt; and the punctuation was incompetent. Locals may have shrugged off some of those errors as what one might expect when strangers erected a monument with no real knowledge of either person or location. And some educated locals may have been persuaded to turn a blind eye to the more scholarly discrepancies in the inscription, and the obvious omissions. Those who commissioned the Monument would have known a man, the poet Sir Fulke Greville, who could put pressure on any Stratford citizen who might cause ripples: he was the Recorder of Stratford, and, as a former Chancellor of the Exchequer, would have been well known to the Herbert brothers, the Earls of Pembroke and Montgomery, who both had a major hand in the First Folio, and probably in the Monument.

Returning to the original Dugdale sketch of the bust, one must not be surprised there have been attempts to conceal and discredit it. It is not what the orthodox would want a bust of Shakespeare to look like. It gives quite the wrong message with its sack of goods in its hands, with corners designed for easy lifting, rather than a pen and paper. And, though some may criticise Dugdale, no one can seriously believe this scholar could have omitted, and others would not have noticed he had omitted, the iconic Shakespeare pen if had it been there. A symbolic pen and paper on a monument for any writer at that time was exactly what Dugdale would have expected to see, and he obviously did not.

As we said above, the clear evidence is that the bust was drastically changed in 1747 to make it very different from Dugdale's sketch, although that sketch was verified more than once. A slightly different drawing of the Shakspere bust from Dugdale's was included in the first Shakespeare biography (Nicholas Rowe, 1709), but it had all the salient features. It is known that Rowe's researcher, top actor Thomas Betterton, had scoured Stratford for information on Shakspere, and may have provided Rowe's sketch of the Monument. Even if Rowe had copied Dugdale's sketch, Betterton would have known to warn him if it made the blatant error of omitting a pen. Just as important is what Dr William Thomas did when he issued a new edition of Dugdale's book in 1730. Firstly, he corrected a number of the book's engravings where he found discrepancies between them and the original monuments (all of which errors seem to have occurred when Dugdale relied on other people's work). Secondly, this Thomas, who lived twenty miles from Stratford, left Dugdale's "Shakespeare" engraving as it was, even though, if those who doubt it were correct, it contained the most important errors of any of them. There were other confirmations of Dugdale's drawing, but one can only prove something so many times.

A heated exchange of correspondence took place between orthodox scholars in the *Times Literary Supplement* in 2006 on the authenticity of the present bust. This led one Shakespearean Professor to protest that it should not be doubted because

> the absence of a pen in Dugdale and the 'woolsack' canard have been used ... as supposed evidence that ... someone else wrote the plays.

This led another orthodox scholar to object to such anti-scholarship, saying,

> I would be more worried that, by distorting the evidence, we might perpetuate the myths attached to his [Shakespeare's] biography.

So should everyone.

The Dugdale sketch of the Monument, as confirmed by others, may hold one thing more for us. We know that the "portraits" usually talked of as "Shakespeare's" or "Shakspere's" are nothing like the face on Dugdale's sketch. Yet one claimed portrait of Shakspere that has recently attracted valid interest is different. This is the so-called "Sanders" portrait (see Figure 13). Forensic tests have shown this portrait is consistent with Shakspere's dates. The date on the painting is 1603, the year Shakspere was appointed a Groom of the Chamber by James I. It has none of the aristocratic adornments of most of the spurious portraits. The Canadian family who own the "Sanders" portrait claim to have traced its provenance to a member of Shakspere's acting troupe. The features, though of a younger man, are similar to those in Dugdale's 1656 sketch of the original Stratford Monument, though no one seems to have checked the portrait against it. The most frequently raised criticism is that the sitter looks younger than Shakspere's thirty-nine years in 1603, but flattery by artists is not unknown. (The portrait has a full description in Nolen, 2002.)

Sadly there are no contemporary descriptions of Shakspere or Shakespeare to compare with his supposed portraits or the original Stratford bust. Some writers repeat John Aubrey's anecdote that Shakspere was *"a handsome well-shaped man"*, which is hardly helpful even if reliable. Ben Jonson, in conversation with William Drummond (1619) and in writing (1641), did make comments about Shakespeare, but only about his writings, not his physical appearance. Jonson's comments on other writers, e.g. Drayton, Marston and Sidney, leave one feeling that he had actually seen them in person, but he left no hint that he had ever met either Shakspere the actor or the man behind the pseudonym "Shakespeare".

Duncan-Jones (2001) proposed a possible likeness for Shakspere on the basis of the trivial joke about him and Richard Burbage we mentioned in Chapter 6. For this, somebody had clearly invented a story about Shakspere beating Burbage to the bed of a willing female so they could get in the punch line, *"William the Conqueror was before Richard the Third"*. Duncan-Jones said that the joke – which had to be explained to the man who recorded it because he did not know Shakspere was named William – might mean Shakspere resembled Burbage and hence resembled a

13. The Sanders portrait of ?William Shakspere, 1603.
With thanks to the owner, Lloyd Sullivan.

painting in Dulwich College that has been claimed without evidence to be a self-portrait of Burbage. That may seem a step too far, as do insults aginst Shakspere and Shakespeare that have been invented from this tortured witticism, but we will rebut the latter in Appendix H.

The best portrait we have for Shakspere, unless the "Sanders" portrait is found to be his, is the sketch of the original Stratford bust although, for obvious reasons, no one has thought to use either of those for selling the works of the writer Shakespeare. It is likely that a picture which does properly represent Shakespeare already exists, since all the candidates with a real chance of being the true author – whether Bacon or Marlowe or someone else – seem to have left portraits of themselves. The question of who that might be is left for discussion in Chapter 16, but once there is a consensus – aye, there's the rub – the search for the real portrait should be over.

Chapter 13

The Theft of Shakspere's Identity

Stage 1: The First Folio and the Stratford Monument

T he following account of the first steps that led to the creation of the Shakspere myth introduces little that is not well known to the Shakespeare community, even if it does not seem to reach the general public.

For a start, contrary to the simplistic story in most biographies, we do not know who it was that took the decision to publish Shakespeare's collected plays in November 1623 in a large and prestigious "folio" edition. Whoever it was – and it may have been more than one person – not only had to have the resources to risk in backing such an ambitious project, but they also must have had the power to stem, if not stop entirely, the unofficial, piratical publication of the plays for almost twenty years. He/they were holding on to, or had access to, up to nineteen Shakespeare plays that had never been published when the First Folio project was put in hand in 1621, and three of those nineteen – *All's Well That Ends Well*, *Coriolanus* and *Timon of Athens* – had never before been performed or otherwise made known to the public. Simple?

One group of people, and we do not know who they were either, did manage to break the embargo on publication of the unpublished plays when they got *Troilus and Cressida* printed in 1609. These "pirates" wrote – anonymously, of course – of how they had got round those who were obstructing publication. They boasted that the play had escaped from its *"proud possessors"*, whoever they were. It is certain that the plays were not being held by an acting company or theatre managers or an impresario like Philip Henslowe: such people would not have been referred to as proud possessors, and no such people were recorded as paying Shakespeare for his plays. The evidence is that plays held by people in this walk of life tended to disappear, not be protectively hoarded away. In what may roughly be thought of as "the Shakespeare years" – 1590 to 1610 – when it seems the majority of Shakespeare's plays became known (though they

112

may have been written earlier), some eighty-five percent of the twelve-hundred or so plays performed were lost to posterity. Of the 180 that were saved, thirty-seven were Shakespeare's, and – *pace* the modern nonsense about a play *Cardenio* (see later) – there is no evidence that any of his disappeared. Just as odd is the fact that, of the other plays that survived, some forty had been falsely published as being by Shakespeare, seemingly to increase their sales, but indicating that the man using the pseudonym Shakespeare could be relied on not to reveal himself by protesting in the way other writers would do at such misuse of their names. Simple?

Whoever held on to the unpublished plays must have done so because they were in powerful positions, rather than by any legal right, since there was no straightforward legal redress against those printing plays without permission if the author himself made no objection. If nobody could block Jonson and others from publishing plays they had already sold, it had to be people with real power and influence who could block attempts to print without the permission of the silent Shakespeare. When William Jaggard and Thomas Pavier – two men who were "not too fussy" about how they published as Schoenbaum put it – proposed printing a set of Shakespeare plays in 1619, they were blocked. It seems that, after the third Earl of Pembroke became Lord Chamberlain in 1615, there was a stop on the publication of all plays that had been performed by the King's Men (including those already published as Quartos), and this "stop" naturally caught Shakespeare's. Only *Othello* seems to have squeezed through the net, being published in 1622 after the censor, Master of the Revels, Sir George Buck, had a mental breakdown.

All the evidence points us to the Herbert family. It has been well argued by Ogburn that the only person with power to block Jaggard and Pavier was William Herbert, third Earl of Pembroke, who had clung on to the post of Lord Chamberlain which was central to his family's control of the theatres. It is also consistent with him and his brother, Philip Herbert, being the dedicatees of the First Folio. Moreover, their desire for control would explain why Sir Henry Herbert, a relative of Pembroke, paid £150 per annum to become the effective Master of the Revels in 1622. His appointment was just in time to ensure that, during the publication of the First Folio, there would be no unwanted censorship from that quarter for plays such as *Richard II*, *Henry VIII* or *Macbeth* which might have attracted the nit-picking attention of someone less perceptive of where his interests lay. It is consistent also with Jonson receiving a substantial addition of £100 to his pension from William Herbert while he was working in the Pembroke's London home, putting the plays together.

Yet the "grand possessors" who held the Shakespeare plays must have faced a serious dilemma, which would explain why they delayed the official publication so long and why it possibly only took place when their hand was forced by the threat of Jaggard and Paviers's rogue publication. They knew that, if they published a full collection of Shakespeare's great plays, a burst of curiosity about their author was bound to follow: for, whatever may be said to the contrary, it is obvious that the name Shakespeare was a pseudonym. There was simply nobody of that name operating in the literary circles of England. It was as early as 1598, some twenty years before the First Folio project started, that two writers of literary standing, Joseph Hall and John Marston, the one to become a bishop, the other an Anglican minister, went public on the question of who the real writer behind the pseudonym was (see Gibson, 1962), though they were not the first to raise the matter.

Hall and Marston each published a book that gave to the author of *Venus and Adonis* and *The Rape of Lucrece* the sobriquet "Labeo", and did so unequivocally. This name was taken from a Roman lawyer-writer and may have been a hint at the person they favoured as author. However, Marston went further than Hall and used for this Labeo the slogan *Mediocria Firma* – "the middle ground is firmest" – which was the personal motto of Francis Bacon. Marston's allusions not only confirmed Hall's identification of Shakespeare as a pseudonym, but pointed to Bacon as the writer behind it. Of course, Hall and Marston might have been in error in hinting at Bacon, but their efforts were obviously not welcome. The most powerful man in England at that time regarding publication was the Archbishop of Canterbury, John Whitgift, a former tutor and present friend of Bacon; and he not only recalled the offending books – Hall's *Biting Satires*, and Marston's *Pygmalion's Image* – but ordered the burning of the most specific one, Marston's. Wisely, for his protection, Marston had written his book under a pseudonym – "W. Kinsayder" – or he might have suffered personally. Some scholars have suggested that Hall and Marston provided the strongest evidence for Bacon being Shakespeare. That may or may not be so, but for our purposes what they certainly showed was that Shakespeare was not thought to be the actual name of a real person, and also that there was interest, indeed curiosity, about who it was the pseudonym was hiding, for it seems these two writers worked quite independently. (The case of "Labeo" is discussed further in Appendix H.)

The problem faced by the "proud possessors" was how to deflect that curiosity: to deter people from searching for the author, as it looked almost certain some would. We may not know the details behind their need for secrecy until the true author is known, but it seems they solved their problem of protecting the identity of the real Shakespeare – possibly better than they could have hoped – when they decided to use a decoy, someone to provide an alternative identity for the writer using the pseudonym, and so distract the curious from pursuing the real

Shakespeare. This decoy technique was not new; it had been used in Roman times, and even in the Old Testament. What was needed was someone who could be relied on not to complain about the theft of his identity, and who could reasonably be passed off as Shakespeare by clever presentation – at least to the generality of readers. The substitute chosen was our William Shakspere: he would have looked a good candidate as decoy for several reasons; he was around at about the time the works by "Shakespeare" were becoming public; he had been associated with the theatre (though almost invisible in his activities); his name was similar to Shakespeare; and he was dead.

The man chosen to manage the deception would have to produce written material with appropriate hints about Shakespeare as part of an introduction to the First Folio plays. And, for that purpose, there was an equally obvious choice: Ben Jonson. This skilled, indeed cunning, writer had successfully published his own works in 1616. He had few scruples about writing ambiguous material (see Dutton, 1985), and he was always in need of money. He was a pensioner of the most powerful man in the theatre, a man who would be the senior of the First Folio's two dedicatees, those being William Herbert and his younger brother Philip, the Earls of Pembroke and Montgomery respectively, who must have supported the publication even if they did not provide all the financial backing.

We mentioned in the previous chapter how Jonson wrote a spoof verse for the spoof portrait of Shakespeare that accompanied the First Folio. His advice to the reader to ignore the portrait was almost blatant, and when he said of the artist's representation of Shakespeare "he hath hit his face", he would have known his readers could, if they were sharp, understand that the word "hit" had a long usage for "hid", as in the works Chaucer and others.

> This Figure, that thou here seest put,
> It was for gentle Shakespeare cut;
> Wherein the Graver had a strife
> With Nature, to out-do the life:
> O, could he but have drawn his wit
> As well in brass, as he hath hit
> His face, the Print would then surpass
> All that was ever writ in brass.
> But, since he cannot, Reader, look
> Not on his Picture, but his Book.

Similarly, Jonson would have known that the phrase "*It was for gentle Shakespeare cut*" had two possible meanings, and the one "It was as a stand-in for gentle Shakespeare" made most sense. Finally, as Droeshout actually worked on copper, the double use of "brass" in the poem stresses its meaning of insolence.

To the Reader.

This Figure, that thou here feeſt put,
  It vvas for gentle Shakeſpeare cut;
Wherein the Grauer had a ſtrife
  with Nature, to out-doo the life :
O, could he but haue dravvne his vvit
  As vvell in braſſe, as he hath hit
His face ; the Print vvould then ſurpaſſe
  All, that vvas euer vvrit in braſſe.
But, ſince he cannot, Reader, looke
  Not on his Picture, but his Booke.

                            B. I.

14. Ben Jonson's "To the Reader" from the First Folio, 1623.

One thing that is uncertain about the publication of the First Folio is when the decision to use Shakspere's identity for Shakespeare was taken. One hint might be the way Jonson treated Shakspere in the 1616 folio of his owns works, giving him a high position in the lists of players and the clear name "Shakespeare". Another clue might be found in a curious section near the beginning of a poem Francis Beaumont wrote to Ben Jonson (as Mr. B. I.) seemingly late in 1615; it suggests he was aware of an intention to make out that Shakespeare was someone with no learning.

> *here I would let slip*
> *(If I had any in me) scholarship,*
> *And from all learning keep these lines as clear*
> *As Shakespeare's best are, which our heirs shall hear*
> *Preachers apt to their auditors to show*
> *How far sometimes a mortal man may go*
> *By the dim light of nature, 'tis to me*
> *An help to write of nothing: . . .*

This appears to warn Jonson that any pretence that Shakespeare had gone far "by the dim light of nature" – that is, without any learning – would encourage Beaumont to write no more. It seems unlikely he would have written those words unless he knew Jonson was to be involved in the dumbing down of Shakespeare, acting as one of the "*preachers apt … to show how far, etc*". The lines may even indicate that Shakspere had already been earmarked as a decoy. He was, as we have said, a pretty obvious choice to put before the reading public, and he was in poor health at the time Beaumont was writing or he would not have had his will drafted in January 1616. Actually Beaumont seemed to hint at Shakspere directly when, just after the above lines, he wrote of there being a choice between two men, one of them a "fallen sharer", which described Shakspere, the sick former partner in the Globe. Some Shakespeare scholars have corrupted Beaumont's words by adding, subtracting and changing them around – or just reporting them selectively – in an effort to reverse their meaning and make it seem Beaumont actually thought Shakespeare was unlearned, when he was really expressing concern that Jonson might make him out to be so. Those who invert the meaning of this poem never seem to be rebuked for it.

The view here of Beaumont's poem is based only on what he actually wrote; and he obviously thought he had to give a warning to Jonson, a colleague who would write an elegy for him when he died in March 1616. This was an honour Jonson did not extend to Shakspere – as the supposed Shakespeare – when he died a month later!

Even if the decision to pass off Shakspere as Shakespeare in the First Folio was taken early, it must have been late in the day, possibly when the printing was nearly finished, that it was realised an appropriate memorial for Shakspere was needed in Stratford to give credence to the hints that were soon to be published about him. If readers of the First Folio had gone to Stratford and found nothing there to commemorate William Shakspere, with at least some suggestion that he was a writer, suspicion must have been aroused. It is likely the Monument was only made at the last moment because, despite its cost, including transport from London, those who paid for it did not have time to get the crude errors in its inscription put right (see below).

Now it was as early as 1770, while he was preparing a new edition of Shakespeare's plays, that the scholar George Steevens deduced that Jonson was the mastermind behind the introduction to the First Folio, and that it included various deceptions. Malone confirmed this in 1800, and his colleague Professor James Boswell, working on his papers in 1821, noted there was "something fishy" about the First Folio. Of course, orthodox scholars generally were silent on those findings, which had been so smothered during the nineteenth century that, in 1907, Castelain, an editor of Jonson's *Discoveries*, could write of Jonson's role in the First Folio and think it was an original discovery. (A pithy summary of the arguments is given in Greg (1954), but it omits the obvious conclusions.)

The major deception contained in the First Folio – after the use of Shakspere as a decoy, that is – was perhaps Jonson's misuse of the names of Henry Condell and John Heminges, two of Shakspere's close fellows in the King's Men. Of course, orthodox scholars will tell their readers that these two men "wrote" parts of the First Folio introduction and put their names to them, but as we shall see, the evidence says they did not.

We may never know if Jonson had their permission to print their names at the bottom of the dedication of the First Folio which he had written for the two Herbert brothers, William and Philip, as well as on the tongue-in-cheek appeal he had written *"To The Great Variety of Readers"*. Yet it is hard to think that these two players would have wanted to be credited with the falsehoods and light-hearted inaccuracies and sly insults that Jonson seemed unable to avoid slipping into such pieces. They do not appear to have been paid for doing work on the First Folio as Jonson was, nor would they have been able themselves to write the material that appeared over their printed names: that was all Jonson, containing material he had either already written or was going to write in the future.

For example, the text showed easy familiarity with Jonson's *Bartholomew Fair,* and also with his unpublished translation of a piece by Pliny. In an epitaph Jonson wrote for Lord Henry de la Warr (or Delaware), we can see the line *"If, passenger, thou canst but read"* which has echoes in the appeal to the readers of the First Folio and on the Stratford Monument; the first has the phrase *"to him that can but spell"* and the second *"Stay passenger"* and *"read if thou canst"*. There exist many more such parallels, and they have long been used to expose Jonson's role in the First Folio.

If Heminges and Condell had done the actual writing and had thought this expensive Folio was all about their fellow Shakspere, they must have ensured there was a good portrait of him – as there were of Jonson and Bacon, say, in their books – not a poor spoof that would attract centuries of derision; and they could hardly have avoided saying something about him as a player (as Cuthbert Burbage would later) or as a theatre manager or as a founding shareholder of the Globe, and so on. In fact – and it is the same for the Stratford Monument – there are no personal details in the First Folio introduction that would have indicated it was actually Shakspere who was being written about as Shakespeare. These two players, if they had been writing something to the Herbert brothers, would have done it seriously and formally, not convolutedly and frivolously and, in effect, insultingly (as Jonson was given to do, and did, and on occasion went to prison for it). Similarly, they would not have treated "the Readers" disrespectfully by saying, *"Whatever you do, buy"*: that was pure Jonson: he had made a similar appeal to readers in the 1616 folio edition of his own works.

Heminges and Condell would hardly have written to readers who had paid around 20 shillings (some £600 in today's money) for the First Folio, as though they might include *"those that can but spell"*, telling them to *"judge your six-penorth* [six pennyworth]". In this appeal to the readers and in the dedication to the Herbert brothers, they would hardly have apologised twice for the author being unable to edit his own plays through some reason, possibly death, when they knew that was untrue if Shakespeare was Shakspere. And they would not have insultingly repeated three times to the Herbert brothers that what they were offering them were "trifles" when they were anything but. The orthodox Gibson (1962) identified three particular false claims Jonson foisted on Heminges and Condell:

(1) That the Folio, unlike the previously printed Quartos, was perfect in its text.
(2) That it was wholly based on Shakespeare's own original handwritten manuscripts.
(3) That the plays had been provided by Shakespeare with hardly a correction.

They would hardly have demeaned themselves to write such stuff, knowing it was deceitful. And if they had done, as many biographers still claim (at least in public), their value as witnesses for anything else would be destroyed.

The truth is that Heminges and Condell are not known to have written anything, and there is no evidence they could write or had been to school. Nothing is really known about Condell's upbringing, but Heminges was apprenticed to a grocer at the age of twelve, hardly an indication of an educated background. The only "evidence" ever put forward for the two men being able to write is actually the claim that they edited the First Folio and that they wrote (and signed) the "epistle" and "dedication" that were clearly Jonson's. What happened is perfectly clear – their names were simply printed beneath them. In 1613, Heminges should have signed his name – if he was able to write – alongside those of the other trustees, William Johnson and John Jackson, on the two deeds for Shakspere's purchase of the Blackfriars Gatehouse, but he did not. *EKC* notes that he had been written off as "old and stuttering" in that year, ten years before the First Folio appeared, while Condell had disappeared from the acting troupe before 1620.

The only purpose the names Heminges and Condell served in Jonson's deception was to create the impression it was they, members of the King's Men and former friends of Shakspere, who had collected and edited the plays themselves. Yet, in 1623, they would have had no right to claim to represent their former acting troupe, at least not without acknowledging their erstwhile colleagues, of whom some still held important and active positions in the King's Men, including at least one of Richard Burbage's relatives. One half of all those who had acted in Shakspere's troupe were still alive in 1623, and later, when the King's Men were really associated with a dedication, no fewer than eleven of the company's members had

TO THE MOST NOBLE
AND
INCOMPARABLE PAIRE
OF BRETHREN.

WILLIAM
Earle of Pembroke, &c. Lord Chamberlaine to the
Kings most Excellent Maiesty.

AND

PHILIP
Earle of Montgomery, &c. Gentleman of his Maiesties
Bed-Chamber. Both Knights of the most Noble Order
of the Garter, and our singular good
LORDS.

Right Honourable,

Hilst we studie to be thankful in our particular, for the many fauors we haue receiued from your L.L we are falne vpon the ill fortune, to mingle two the most diuerse things that can bee, feare, and rashnesse ; rashnesse in the enterprize, and feare of the successe. For, when we valew the places your H.H sustaine, we cannot but know their dignity greater, then to descend to the reading of these trifles: and, vvhile we name them trifles, we haue depriu'd our selues of the defence of our Dedication. But since your L.L. haue beene pleas'd to thinke these trifles some-thing, heeretofore ; and haue prosequuted both them, and their Authour liuing, vvith so much fauour : we hope, that (they out-liuing him, and he not hauing the fate, common with some, to be exequutor to his owne writings) you will vse the like indulgence toward them, you haue done

A2 *vnto*

The Epistle Dedicatorie.

vnto their parent. There is a great difference, vvhether any Booke choose his Patrones, or finde them : This hath done both. For, so much were your L L. likings of the seuerall parts, vvhen they were acted, as before they vvere published, the Volume ask'd to be yours. We haue but collected them, and done an office to the dead, to procure his Orphanes, Guardians; vvithout ambition either of selfe-profit, or fame : onely to keepe the memory of so worthy a Friend, & Fellow aliue, as was our SHAKESPEARE, *by humble offer of his playes, to your most noble patronage. Wherein, as we haue iustly obserued, no man to come neere your L.L. but vvith a kind of religious addresse, it hath bin the height of our care, vvho are the Presenters, to make the present worthy of your H.H. by the perfection. But, there we must also craue our abilities to be considerd, my Lords. We cannot go beyond our owne powers. Country hands reach foorth milke, creame, fruites, or what they haue : and many Nations (we haue heard) that had not gummes & incense, obtained their requests with a leauened Cake. It vvas no fault to approch their Gods, by what meanes they could : And the most, though meanest, of things are made more precious, when they are dedicated to Temples. In that name therefore, we most humbly consecrate to your H.H. these remaines of your seruant* Shakespeare; *that what delight is in them, may be euer your L.L. the reputation his, & the faults ours, if any be committed, by a payre so carefull to shew their gratitude both to the liuing, and the dead, as is*

Your Lordshippes most bounden,

IOHN HEMINGE.
HENRY CONDELL.

15. The Dedication over the names of John Heminges and Henry Condell from the First Folio, 1623.

their names put on it. It is worth observing that, if Heminges and Condell had been acting for the King's Men, their obvious dedicatee would have been their patron, King James, who had employed them generously over many years and financed them when the plague closed the theatres. They would hardly have let the only reference to him be an off-hand mention in a poor couplet at the end of Jonson's elegy – "*And make those flights upon the banks of Thames,/ That so did take Eliza, and our James*": that was dismissive and over-familiar, and put him in second place to the dead predecessor whom he had reasons to hate.

Another major problem for those who claim Heminges and Condell edited the First Folio on behalf of the King's Men is that the valuable handwritten manuscripts, from which at least eighteen of the First Folio plays must have been typeset, disappeared when the project was complete. If they had been representing the interests of their company and the company owned the manuscripts (as is so frequently claimed), they would have had a duty to preserve them, if only to be sold for profit. That would still be the case if, as shown by the evidence and contrary to what Heminges and Condell are supposed to have said – see *OCS* – some of the manuscripts used were copies made by professional scriveners like Ralph Crane. It seems obvious the manuscripts were not collected by Heminges and Condell and that the obvious reason for their disappearance was that at least some could have given away Shakespeare's identity.

Finally, contained in all this evidence which shows that Heminges and Condell had nothing to do with the First Folio, is the fact that, if John Heminges had seen what Jonson had craftily passed off as his work, he must not only have noticed his name misspelt twice in two different ways in it, but have then left it misspelt for posterity.

One can just imagine the pleasure the naturally sardonic Jonson must have had in passing off the unlearned Heminges and Condell as the editors of the great First Folio in order to strengthen the hoax of passing off the unlearned Shakspere as Shakespeare! Indeed, he could not forbear a shot at "grocer" Heminges when he wrote in the dedication "*We cannot go beyond our powers. Country hands reach forth milk, cream, fruits or what they have*", as though that is what the respectful players would have written to senior Lords of the realm.

If the First Folio introduction had been a true document instead of a Jonson spoof, there would have been no shortage of good poets – professional and amateur – ready to write commendations and elegies for William Shakespeare. There would have been no need for Jonson to bring in his three friends, Leonard Digges, Hugh Holland and James Mabbe, whom we noted earlier as being classed as "nonentities". Of course, when Jonson produced the folio of his own works in 1616, he attracted a dozen top writers – like George Chapman, Francis Beaumont, Lord Buckhurst

– to write dedications for him. The three Jonson chose for Shakespeare satisfied his need for men who, like Droeshout with his "portrait", would ask no questions. They were basically translators with no reputation to lose as poets, and Mabbe's elegy was based on one he had translated. Digges obviously knew nothing about Shakespeare's work or he would not have dumbed him down in another poem, published in 1640, where he praised him for the way he wrote his plays without having or using scholarship! Such lasting fame as attaches to those three minor elegists derives solely from their being invited by Ben Jonson, at his moment of need, to write for the First Folio.

The hints that were included in that book's introduction to imply the author Shakespeare was our William Shakspere all show how cleverly ambiguous Jonson could be. The first hints are references to "Shakespeare" over the printed names of Heminges and Condell in the dedication to the Herbert brothers: it is implied that Condell and Heminges had themselves collected the plays *"only to keep the memory of so worthy a friend and fellow alive as was our Shakespeare"* and then they *"most humbly consecrate to your Highnesses these remains of your servant Shakespeare"*. Nothing in those statements actually says the name "Shakespeare" was intended to indicate Shakspere the player-manager. The writer Shakespeare would have been as much a fellow of the Lord Chamberlain's and King's Men – albeit a clandestine one – as Dekker was of the Admiral's Men for whom he wrote. However, in the appeal to the readers, there is the statement: *"It has been a thing, we confess, worthy to have been wished, that the author himself had lived to have set forth and oversee his own writings,"* which cannot have applied to Shakspere: he would have had more free time after 1610 to publish plays than Jonson had had when he published his plays and poems in 1616. Shakspere was rich enough to have employed assistance (even Jonson himself) to help prepare the First Folio for publication (if it had been his), while he also could have called on his son-in-law Dr John Hall, who was literate and a future author.

Jonson's dedicatory poem in the First Folio contains his oft-quoted reference to *"Sweet Swan of Avon"*: this is usually said to be definite evidence that Shakspere was Shakespeare though it was nothing of the sort. Nobody had ever referred to Shakspere as sweet or as a swan, or referred to him in connection with a river Avon. Nobody had ever made biographical references to Shakespeare such as those, and he never mentioned the river Avon in his works. The person who best fitted that phrase, and who would have been well known in literary circles to fit it, was the Countess of Pembroke, mother of the two dedicatees of the plays. This lady was born Mary Sidney, the sister of the poet Philip Sidney; she was an author in her own right, patron of poets and playwrights; she decorated her dresses with the symbol of the swan, and lived in Wilton

House in Wiltshire where the River Avon flowing past it was more famous at the time than the river in Warwickshire. Not only that, but the phrase about the Avon in Jonson's poem is followed by one about the writer's *"flights along the Thames"* which echoed lines the poets Daniel and Drayton wrote about Mary Sidney and London's river. This analysis should make it clear Jonson was using an ambiguous phrase which did not clearly identify his subject as William Shakspere.

Another possible hint about Shakspere in the First Folio occurred in the poem by Leonard Digges where, writing as if to Shakespeare, he referred to *"thy Stratford moniment"*. Now that name "Stratford" by itself was ambiguous. There are a dozen Stratfords in England: it simply means "street ford", and Stratford-upon-Avon would hardly have been the first to occur to any reader. Two of those Stratfords are on the better-known Wiltshire Avon where the family home of the two dedicatees of the First Folio was situated; while just outside London, not far from the book-stalls around St Paul's churchyard, was Stratford-le-Bow with its famous church, and the oldest stone bridge in the country. It is most unlikely Digges would have seen the monument at Stratford-upon-Avon, and he probably wrote just what Jonson told him.

One can easily see in Jonson's lines a warning to the educated reader. Having "praised" the Droeshout portrait with a plagiarised poem, he uses words plagiarising another early poem in his dedication to Shakespeare. When he writes *"While I confess thy writings to be such, / As neither Man, nor Muse can praise too much,"* he is using a poem written to Spenser by an unknown "Ignoto" where it says: *"I here pronounce this workmanship is such, / As that no pen can set it forth too much."* In the same Ignoto stanza are the words *"To free my mind from envies touch,"* which Jonson echoes with *"To draw no envy (Shakespeare) on thy name."* He is blatantly saying the thing is a fraud, as he also does with his lines: *"These are, as some infamous bawd or whore, / Should praise a matron.",* and *"Or crafty malice, might pretend this praise, / And thine to ruin, where it seemed to raise."*

Nothing in the introductory material of the First Folio told the reader Shakespeare was an actor. For a hint in that direction, some look to the most minor elegy from the least known contributor: he who used the initials I.M., James Mabbe. He included the two lines:

> *We wondered (Shake-speare) that thou went'st so soon*
> *From the world's-stage to the Grave's Tiring-room.*

There would have been no reason for a purchaser of the First Folio to take that as other than a good metaphor for the death of a theatre dramatist, especially since it described leaving the "world's-stage" not a theatre stage. If it was a hint about Shakspere, it was hardly a glaringly obvious one. He was no world-shaking actor; he retired from acting long before he died; and his age at his death, 52 years, was no less than the average life-span of his theatre contemporaries. And, if he had been Shakespeare, he had had time to get his works into print.

Those who have never doubted Shakspere was Shakespeare may well think the hints involving Stratford and Avon and so forth in the First Folio were unambiguous references to Shakspere, but that is with hindsight and conditioning. Most theatre-goers in 1623 were unlikely to have heard of Shakspere the actor-businessman or even of Stratford-upon-Avon. The hints were subtle and ambiguous: they would have provoked no reaction from those who knew Shakspere and knew he could not write. Jonson would only have been worrying about those whose curiosity might lead them to try to work out who Shakespeare was, and how to give them something to nudge them in the direction of Shakspere. It is hardly surprising that it was well after the First Folio was published that someone recorded visiting Stratford-upon-Avon and noting a monument in the church that was supposed to be for Shakespeare the writer. Or that it was very much longer before the town itself realised who it was supposed to have harboured. For, and the same applied to the Monument, every opportunity in the First Folio for an unambiguous statement about Shakspere being Shakespeare had been carefully avoided.

Orthodox scholars rarely mention that there are ambiguities in Jonson's lines, some we may never fully understand until we are sure who Shakespeare was. But of all the ambiguous statements in Jonson's dedicatory poem to Shakespeare, probably the cleverest, and certainly the one which has most harmed Shakespeare scholarship, is the line:

Though thou hadst small Latin and less Greek.

This was for a long time taken to mean that Shakespeare was an unlearned man and could therefore have been Shakspere. It was to lead Milton to write a sonnet to Shakespeare as if he had been a country bumpkin – *"Fancy's child, warbled his native woodnotes wild"*. It was to lead others to write books "proving" Shakespeare's works demonstrated a lack of learning and scholarship and knowledge of languages, and, on occasions, even to dumb down the plays to fit the myth that they were by an unlearned Shakspere. Yet today we all should know, just as the erudite Jonson must have known, that Shakespeare used sources in more languages than Jonson himself could manage – Latin, Italian, French, Spanish, English, and Greek – while his other learning and knowledge was phenomenal. So scholars have had to look at that line again. The words "Though thou hadst small Latin" can mean "Although you had only small Latin", but they can equally mean "Even if you had small Latin", just as Psalm 23's "Though I walk through the valley of the shadow of death" means "Even if I walk etc.". Jonson knew, of course, that only the second meaning fitted Shakespeare, for he could not have written his plays if he only had "small Latin and less Greek". As with his other ambiguous hints about Shakspere being Shakespeare, Jonson clearly designed this one, as he did others, so he could meet any challenge to its correctness by claiming it had been misunderstood, just as, when he wrote, pretending to be Heminges and Condell, *"he was a happy imitator of nature"*, he knew that had a range of interpretations.

That Ben Jonson knew "Shakespeare" was a pseudonym is obvious from sources other than the First Folio. He wrote some three hundred and fifty epigrams, many for writers with personal comments included about them. Yet he wrote none for Shakespeare, and he wrote nothing personal about him until he did it for pay in his First Folio spoof in 1623. He wrote numerous commendatory poems for the literary works of his rivals as well as his friends, but nothing for Shakespeare – until the First Folio. According to orthodox scholars, Jonson is supposed to have been a personal friend of Shakespeare for nearly twenty years; yet that is hardly consistent with the record of Jonson's conversations with the Scottish poet William Drummond (1619) or with what Jonson wrote in his own book *Discoveries* published in 1641. In those conversations and that book, Jonson discussed many English poets that he obviously knew, and left reminiscences of them and their characteristics, but for the great Shakespeare he left nothing that he had not derived from his writings or that he did not admit was second or third hand, and then only about him as a writer. Even when he wrote of Shakespeare and used the oft-quoted phrase *"I loved the man ... (this side idolatry)"* he virtually told us in the same breath (as discussed in Appendix H) that was simply to give force to his criticism of Shakespeare's work, and was written as no more than a conventional way of saying "I liked his work but ...". Jonson's comments about Shakespeare were no more personal than when Dryden (born 1631) wrote, *"I admire [Jonson] but I love Shakespeare"*, and they were much less sincere.

Jonson's stage-management of the First Folio deception is shown by the way he tried to deal, in one blow, with two of the biggest problems for the theory that Shakespeare was Shakspere, namely the failure of anyone to write an elegy for him on his death (which is discussed later) and the absence of a burial for him in Westminster Abbey. Given those problems, it is natural that orthodox scholars quote with (misplaced) relief an apparent elegy which had the title

> On Mr Wm Shakespeare
> he died in April 1616

and opened with a plea for Chaucer, Spenser and Beaumont – poets already buried in Westminster Abbey – to move over in their graves so

126

Shakespeare could be buried alongside them. This was first published in 1633 in a collection of poems by John Donne, and, as it had no name on it, was initially thought to be his. Then, in 1640, it was published again, but this time over the initials "W.B." Later still, a manuscript copy of the poem was discovered with the name William Basse written on it, with the result that it was credited to that very minor poet. The poem is naturally seized on as showing someone did write an elegy to Shakspere, though it was accepted that it was only written shortly before the First Folio came out, partly because the date – April 1616 – would not have been necessary if the poem had been written at the time of death and partly because Jonson effectively replied to it in his 1623 dedicatory poem to Shakespeare as though he expected it to be fresh in at least some people's minds. He used the poem's proposal for Shakespeare to have a burial at Westminster as an opportunity to pretend it was better he should not have been, and did it with the aid of the clever line *"Thou art a moniment without a tombe"*, which everyone quotes but no one understands.

The hope some scholars had that the "Basse" poem – with its impractical proposal for disinterment – might be claimed to be evidence for Shakspere being Shakespeare disappeared with the discovery – see Lee (1916) – that the earliest manuscript version of the poem was in the handwriting of another W.B., the poet William Browne, and was dated by the British Museum as after 1620. This poet was not only a close colleague of Ben Jonson, but, like him, worked in the library of their joint patron the Earl of Pembroke. As a result, the poem, and Jonson's riposte to it, are most easily seen as a necessary and clever ruse to cover up the absence of elegies and a state burial. It seems clear that Browne's poem was circulated in manuscript copies around the time the First Folio appeared, but it is not known how Basse's name got associated with it. It may have been another decoy, for it would have undermined Jonson's First Folio deception if it had become known his colleague Browne was the author of this late "elegy". Basse is not known to have written as late as 1620 and he may have been content for his name to be so used, since he moved in circles connected to the Herberts.

Sometimes, in spite of all the research done on the First Folio introduction, orthodox biographers may still imply there is nothing amiss with it, though the problems are hardly a secret. It was orthodox scholars who, around 1800, most clearly exposed Jonson as the man behind that introduction, but its problems had been noted earlier. Doubt had been publicly cast on Jonson's veracity as early as 1640. In that year, a collection of Shakespeare's poems, mixed with the work of others (including the W.B. poem discussed above), was published by a John Benson who is normally said to be a publisher or bookseller, though the name appears to be a play on Ben Johnson, Jonson's original name. The front page of

Benson's collection, whoever he was, mocked both the Droeshout portrait and words that Jonson used in his dedicatory poem.

Just as Ben Jonson used the initials B.I. and introduced his own First Folio with an address "To the Reader", so John Benson's mocking address "To the Reader" had the initials I.B. Benson included a re-working of Droeshout's supposed portrait of Shakespeare, giving it a more patrician face, a sardonic smile, patrician clothes, a laurel shoot in its hand (to indicate a poet), and one right sleeve instead of two left ones. The figure was drawn facing left (instead of right as Droeshout's was), a normal convention at the time for implying the existence of an error or deception; and, under his mock portrait he put the mocking words:

> This shadow is renowned Shakespear's? Soule of the age
> The applause? delight? the wonder of the Stage.

That, together with the changes to the "portrait", is a pretty explicit expression of scepticism, and it was published while one of the dedicatees of the First Folio (Philip Herbert, by then Earl of Pembroke and Montgomery and Lord Chamberlain) was still alive and in a position to do harm if he thought someone was wrongly criticising Jonson. It is not clear how Benson got away with issuing the first public challenge to the authorship of the First Folio and its editorship, even if he did wait until after Jonson had died to do it.

It has been claimed that, at the time, the query sign – "?" – that Benson employed in his parody was often used where the exclamation mark – "!" – might be normal, but that looks like another invention. As Benson obviously knew what he was doing, and it went well beyond replacing exclamation marks with queries, it is unlikely his swopping the two signs was accidental. Moreover, following up on suggestions that the two signs were often interchanged, it has been found, for example, that, in the original printing of the Sonnets, nowhere among the dozens of "?" signs were any used for other than a question, or for a sentence with a question word, like "how" or "why", or for a rhetorical statement that could take a query sign rather than an exclamation mark. One claim made was that the two signs were freely interchanged in the play *Hamlet*. Yet a quick run-through of that play echoed exactly what had been found in the Sonnets. It seems Benson did know exactly what he was doing, and that was to challenge correctly Jonson's veracity.

There is actual evidence of an earlier private challenge than Benson's public one. In a copy of the expensive First Folio, now in Glasgow University library, someone, most probably its initial purchaser, left a telling note in the introductory section. Underneath the name "William Shakespeare" where it appeared at the top in the list of actors of the plays, there are the handwritten words *"leass for making"*. Now, in that phrase, "making" was the contraction for "playmaking" and the word "leass" meant deceit (see Crystal's *Shakespeare's Words*, 2002). Thus the owner of that First Folio (deduced as probably a lawyer and knowledgeable theatre-goer from other annotations to the text) was saying he knew that hints in the First Folio about the actor Shakspere being Shakespeare were a deceit. A recent orthodox biography claimed the perfectly clear word "leass" was actually "least" or "ceast" or "less", which may reflect the problem some people have in accepting that there is actually real evidence that Shakspere was not Shakespeare.

To complement the above discussion on the First Folio, we can look in more detail at the Monument in Holy Trinity Church, Stratford, which was clearly an integral part of the plan to steal Shakspere's identity. As pointed out above, some apparent memorial to Shakespeare in Stratford was necessary if questions were not to be raised when people who had spotted the hints in the First Folio went there making enquiries. It did not need to say anything specific or even accurate, or to give much information. As long as inquisitive visitors found some suitably impressive icon with hints about Shakespeare, the rest could be left to their imaginations. Indeed, it would not have been wise for real information about Shakespeare's plays and poems to have been included on the Monument for fear of raising questions among the locals, who had known Shakspere as an illiterate businessman and not a writer. Yet the ambiguity of the inscription may have contributed to the delay – over a century in fact – before Stratford really took on board the status the town was supposed to have as the birthplace of England's greatest writer.

The actual decision on the nature of the Monument seems likely to have been Jonson's, given he was already so involved and that the insolence and ambiguity in its inscription were typical of him. There is clearly no chance that anyone from Stratford erected it, as is sometimes wistfully claimed. A London firm of masons was appointed to make the Monument – Gerhard Janssen's according to Dugdale – and it was they who cut the bland inscription for it, with more errors than useful information, and much unchecked punctuation. It reads:

JUDICIO PYLIUM, GENIO SOCRATEM, ARTE MARONEM
TERRA TEGIT, POPULUS MÆRET, OLYMPUS HABET

STAY PASSENGER, WHY GOEST THOU BY SO FAST,
READ IF THOUT CANST, WHOM ENVIOUS DEATH HAS PLAST
WITH IN THIS MONUMENT SHAKSPEARE: WITH WHOME,
QUICK NATURE DIDE WHOSE NAME, DOTH DECK THIS TOMBE,

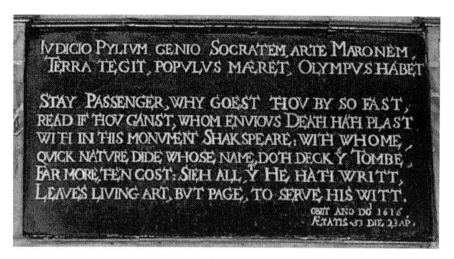

16. The inscription on the Stratford Monument.

FAR MORE THEN COST: SIEH ALL, THAT HE HATH WRITT,
LEAVES LIVING ART, BUT PAGE, TO SERVE HIS WITT.
OBIIT ANO DO[1] 1616
ÆTATIS 53 DIE 23AP

Many writers today will say the inscription clearly identified Shakspere as Shakespeare, but again they work with hindsight. And they forget that, when it was erected, the bust portrayed a dealer, not a writer – see Chapter 12. Very few, if any, of those who saw the Monument initially would have known of the First Folio, with its hints that Shakspere might be Shakespeare. To those who were able to read the inscription but had not seen those hints it would have had all the characteristics of the sort of picture-puzzle in which one does not see the face until it is pointed out. Even those who could read English might not have understood the Latin allusions, while the well educated could easily have been distracted from taking the Monument seriously simply because of the errors in the inscription. Twice it wrongly indicates that the person commemorated was buried within the Monument, which he was not; the letters SIEH had been cut instead of SITH (meaning "since"); the punctuation was a mess even for that period; the position of the Monument in the building meant that no passenger (traveller) could go by it fast as the words in the first line in English imply. The invitation, *"Read if thou canst"*, echoes, as we have pointed out, Jonson's sarcasm to the First Folio readers where he wrote, *"From the most able, to him that can but spell. There you are numbered. We had rather you were weighed."*

The normal formalities for an epitaph to William Shakspere identifying him as husband, father, brother, grandfather, local landowner, second biggest house owner, theatre manager, player and sharer, citizen of Stratford, greatly loved, sadly missed, were all deliberately omitted; and the name written as "Shakspeare" was misspelt, whomever it was supposed to be for. The only words that might have pointed even vaguely to the Monument being for Shakespeare are (with modern spelling but original punctuation): "since all, that he hath writ, leaves living art, but page, to serve his wit.", and those, to the educated, would at the most have been poorly written, conventional flattery of the sort used for deceased writers all the time, even minor ones. If the educated readers were local, they would probably have wondered what the misspelt illiterate Shakspere had been getting up to in London: to them, what he "hath writ" would have meant a blank "page".

If one thinks what could have been written by someone intending to honour Shakspere and Shakespeare in one monument, it will be clear why most orthodox biographers no more spell out the Stratford inscription than they present their readers with all the copies of his supposed "signatures". Indeed, they are more likely to quote the doggerel verse from an otherwise unmarked stone in the church floor.

If some local Stratford people could read and understand the two-line Latin inscription, they would certainly have known it did not apply to Shakspere, and neither were they likely to have associated it with Shakespeare. Translated it reads:

A Nestor in Judgement, A Socrates in Genius, A Virgil in Art, Earth Covers Him, People Mourn Him, Olympus Holds Him.

As Olympus was the heaven to which statesmen went, while Mount Parnassus was reserved for poets, the readers would be puzzled already. If they realised the word "*Maronem*" was just a clever way of saying the person commemorated had the characteristics of Virgil (full name Publius Vergilius Maro), that would hardly have pointed them to Shakespeare, whose works echoed the spirit of Ovid. If they realised "*Pylium*" was another code, this time to indicate Nestor, a judge, statesman and warrior, that would not have said Shakespeare or Shakspere to them. And the Socrates reference has particularly caused scholars trouble because, with Nestor and Virgil, it seems to point to someone more like Francis Bacon in his role as lawyer, teacher, poet and philosopher than to the Shakespeare of the plays and poems. It is generally admitted the great poet-playwright would have better been likened to Plato, Sophocles and Ovid. The whole ensemble – Monument and inscription – looks like another Jonson fantasy. All types of scholars have studied the Monument and its inscription to find clues to some meaningful message, but what they really tell is that the Monument was designed, not as a memorial to Shakspere, but as part of the scheme to steal his identity.

It is likely, of course, that there was originally a conventional gravestone cut for Shakspere when he died. It is hard to believe that the heirs he had so enriched would have left him to lie without a properly marked grave. Yet, if such a genuine stone did exist, whether in the church or the graveyard outside, it would have had to be removed to avoid it conflicting with the deception being perpetrated with the aid of the 1623 Monument.

The anonymous stone in the church floor with the line *"And curst be he that moves my bones"*, which is usually referred to as being for Shakspere and composed by Shakespeare, is just a pathetic distraction – see Chapter 5. It was small, it was set in the floor with no name, no date, just four crudely cut lines of unoriginal doggerel verse. It could not have been a stone provided by his rich heirs for one of the richest men in Stratford. It was replaced at some time by a stone with better lettering but with the same unconvincing wording. The fact that it is close to the gravestones of members of Shakspere's family bearing proper inscriptions bought with the wealth he left them should point up that there is a real problem, which actually includes doubts about them not all being in their original positions. There is certainly no good reason to believe that any of Shakspere's bones lie beneath that crude stone, especially given the report of Washington Irving, who was told by the Stratford sexton in 1816 that excavation had shown there was nothing there.

Though the facts related here about the deceptions in both the First Folio and the Stratford Monument were analysed by orthodox scholars two centuries ago, they appear to be unknown to most current orthodox writers. Gibson, in his 1962 book *The Shakespeare Claimants*, did admit the deception concerning the names of Heminges and Condell, but felt he could get away with saying that it:

> does not conform to an ideal ethical standard; but it is a trick that has long been common in the publishing trade.

Yet that is nonsense. Without the deceptive use of those two names, there would have been no Shakspere myth. There would have been no monument in London to Condell and Heminges as the saviours of Shakespeare's plays, if it had been known their role was exactly the same as that of their friend Shakspere – namely, to have their identities used, almost certainly without their permission.

Although the orthodox Stratfordian Gibson, writing in 1962, felt he could say "these points [i.e. the Heminges and Condell scams] are conceded by Statfordians", and claimed they could not possibly matter because Stratfordians had discovered them, whenever the deceptions perpetrated in 1623 are alluded to, orthodox scholars try to ridicule the idea that such deceptions would have been possible, and to scoff at the notion that any author (or any author's family) would have wished to maintain his anonymity. Such scholars are effectively denying knowledge of the nature of the age, with its plots, conspiracies, denunciations, and a tradition of anonymous authorship which is spelled out clearly in Mullan's *Anonymity*. The theft of Shakspere's identity would have been a much less demanding exercise than most of the plots that were scattered through the reign of James I. It is sometimes forgotten, for example, when one reads of how James's Scottish favourite at court, Robert Kerr, was replaced with the handsome Englishman, George Villiers, who then went on to become the Duke of Buckingham, that Villiers had been chosen to be Kerr's substitute and the plot to install him was managed by the First Folio dedicatee and Jonson's patron, William Herbert, Third Earl of Pembroke.

It should be clear that no reliance can be put on the introduction to the First Folio or on the Stratford Monument for support of the claim that our William Shakspere was the real person behind the pseudonym Shakespeare. Rather, the deceptions involved in both of those – given the effort that went into them – should be enough by themselves to destroy faith in the orthodox theory; and it has to be interesting how few orthodox biographies now rely on them as a prime reason for believing Shakspere was Shakespeare. It seems that it was realisation of the problems with those First Folio deceptions that induced orthodox scholars, who could not let go of their Shakspere myth, to put their effort into alternative strategies for maintaining it.

The expedients involved in those new strategies will be examined in the next chapter. Some people, it seems, thought that the straight forgery or alteration of documents would be a good tactic, but most of their efforts have now been exposed and eliminated, though not all. What has remained is largely the more subtle "forgery" of traditions, anecdotes and "factoids" – things passing as facts.

Chapter 14

The Theft of Shakspere's Identity

Stage 2: Myths and Inventions

Today, if anyone asks to know why they should believe a player-businessman from Stratford wrote the plays of Shakespeare, the most likely reason they will be given is that that was his name, even though, as we have shown, it was not. If anything, the constancy of Shakspere's use of that name and the fact that he never used the name Shakespeare, would, in other circumstances, be treated as good evidence they were two different men. The inquirer may be offered other fictitious reasons for believing Shakspere was Shakespeare: "that no one during his lifetime denied Shakspere was Shakespeare"; "that the dates of Shakespeare's plays fit exactly to Shakspere's working life"; "that the author Shakespeare used the language of Warwickshire in his works"; "that Shakespeare put places and people from around Stratford in his plays"; or "that only a country boy could have written those plays", and so on. Yet, whenever such erroneous inventions are put forward as reasons to believe the player was the writer – and dozens are tried – the fiction that they had the same name is always close to hand. It is unlikely the enquirer will be told that, for the determing events of his life, the player was baptised Shakspere, married Shaxpere, had Shakspere children, and died Shakspere: that would be too inconvenient.

The invented or fictitious reasons for believing the myth that Shakspere was Shakespeare grew up over a long period. They surfaced even before the grave doubts over the First Folio had taken hold, and did so because what was known about Shakspere did not fit Shakespeare. But they became more important afterwards, and are continually augmented, assisted by assumptions, while evidence that contradicts the orthodox theory or the Shakspere myth was and is disguised or buried. It may be this happened because too much had been invested – financially and emotionally – in the Shakspere myth by the late nineteenth century for it to be sacrificed on the altar of ugly facts. As people find it difficult to change their religion, or political affiliation or football team, they can find it difficult to give up the myths they love.

The importance of the name-trick for orthodox scholars was shown by Wells (2007) when, to "prove" Shakspere wrote the plays and poems of Shakespeare, two pages of his book were taken to list people from the reigns of Elizabeth I and James I who had referred to the author of the First Folio plays as Shakespeare: he then claimed that this proved Shakespeare wrote the plays. One can imagine the reaction of English scholars if the same book had spent two pages listing those Victorians who referred to the author of *Silas Marner* and *Middlemarch* as George Eliot, and then claimed that this proved someone called George Eliot wrote them. Yet almost all biographers do that for Shakespeare. No person named George Eliot was writing in Victorian times, and no one named Shakespeare was writing in Elizabethan times: these were pseudonyms. The trouble is that, in Shakespeare's case, people are conditioned.

The "no denial" Myth

The pretence that Shakspere's name was Shakespeare is closely associated with another trick. This one states that, during his lifetime, no one denied Shakspere was the author Shakespeare. This is clearly nonsense; people do not go around denying what has never been claimed to be true, and no one during his lifetime ever hinted that Shakspere wrote the works of Shakespeare. The hints came well after his death. Yet some people seem to be taken in by this argument. The French scholar George Connes actually wrote that he thought the lack of such a denial was the strongest reason for him to believe Shakspere was Shakespeare; yet one can guess that Connes did not think he himself was the President of France because no one had ever denied it.

Shakspere effectively denied it when he failed to describe himself as a poet or playwright or to claim he was Shakespeare when he and his father were applying for a coat of arms in 1596, though it might have saved them embarrassment, delay and probably expense. It was effectively denied when he was not buried in Westminster Abbey, and when no one wrote an elegy for him when he died. Furthermore, the fact that people thought "Shakespeare" was a pseudonym for a hidden writer is as good as a denial. We have mentioned what happened when the writers Joseph Hall and John Marston identified that name as a pseudonym in 1598, and, as discussed in the previous chapter, claimed that it was being used to hide Francis Bacon (who was definitely not our Shakspere).

The real Shakespeare seems to have indicated he was using a pseudonym when he called the first work to carry the name "Shakespeare" – *Venus and Adonis – "the first heir of my invention"*, though it was by no means the first work he had written. That view was clearly accepted by the writers T.H. and Thomas Nashe when, within the year, they produced parodies of *Venus and Adonis* – the erotic *Oenone and Paris* and the pornographic *Choice of Valentines* respectively – and accompanied them with mocking dedications, the first with indications of a "hiding" author, the second with a pretence it was for the Earl of Southampton.

In addition, there is a clear indication that John Davies of Hereford, a well connected writer, knew that the name "Shakespeare" was a pseudonym. In an epigram from the early 1600s entitled *To Our English Terence: Mr Will. Shake-speare*, Davies likened Shakespeare to a Roman slave, Terence, whose name was believed at the time to have been used as a cover for the works of aristocratic writers such as Scipio and Laelius. Davies stressed his point when he placed this epigram in the midst of others with titles using obvious pseudonyms (even including "Somebody" and "Nobody"). In the last couplet of the poem, Davies addressed "Shake-speare" as a hidden writer who was not getting the proper honour ("honesty") for his works. It has been suggested that Davies's title meant he thought Shakespeare wrote like Terence, but the poem does not suggest this. He was always likened to Plautus, Seneca, Ovid and Virgil. At the time Davies was writing, the name Terence was not even thought of as belonging to a writer, let alone a serious one. Davies's poem is treated more fully in Appendix H.

There is much to show that the name "Shakespeare" was a pseudonym and that no one suspected it was being used for Shakspere. Perhaps the strongest evidence is what happened in February 1601 during and in the aftermath of the Earl of Essex's rebellion against Elizabeth. Essex, sensing he was vulnerable following his military failures in Ireland, felt he had to save his political position by forcing the Queen's abdication or by abducting her. In an attempt to get popular support for Essex's cause, one of his allies arranged for performances of Shakespeare's play *Richard II* to take place at the Globe as well as other venues in the capital. In the event, it was performed in London at least forty times as a prelude to the rebellion, complete with the scene showing the forced abdication of Richard II (which was normally omitted). The Queen was furious and said, "I am Richard II, know ye not that?".

After Essex was captured, Elizabeth ordered that the author of *Richard II* be found and brought for examination, but without success. So determined was she to discover the author, that she ordered the arrest of a Dr John Hayward who had written a history of Henry IV, which was dedicated to Essex and included details of Richard II's deposition. She was sure he must know who had written the play, if he had not written it himself, and demanded he be put to the rack (almost as good as a death sentence) in order to extract from him a name or a confession. However, no one pointed the finger at Shakspere as the author. He was not arrested. He was not questioned. He was not required to attend a hearing when the Lord Chamberlain's Men (of whom he was a manager) were interrogated as to their reason for putting on the play at the Globe the day before the rebellion. Nobody in the inquiries that followed suggested looking for a man with the name "Shakespeare", showing it was known to be a pseudonym. The fact that Shakspere was never questioned is as good as a signed statement by the Queen's agents – men who were employed precisely to know or to find out such things – that he was not Shakespeare, nor had any connection to him.

John Hayward was saved from physical torture only by the intervention of Attorney General Bacon, but he was still sent to prison and kept there until the death of Elizabeth two years later. If Shakspere had actually been the author Shakespeare and had, as orthodox scholars claim, written *Richard II* under his own name, it is a racing certainty he would not have survived the Essex rebellion unscathed, if at all. Weak attempts by orthodox scholars to deflect attention from the strength of the above evidence – like saying Shakspere was not interviewed because the Queen's agents already knew he was the author, or because the players claimed *Richard II* was an old play, or that Hayward's book was changed into a play for the occasion – speak of desperation rather than conviction. Such excuses are not consistent with the determination of the Queen to find the author and the total failure of her trained agents to produce him. In her reign, writers such as Jonson, Marston, Dekker, Chapman, Kyd and Nashe were sentenced to imprisonment in circumstances much less serious than those surrounding *Richard II*, and Kyd did not survive.

The "dating" Myth

A particularly good example of an invented argument, actually a circular argument, which is often called on to strengthen the case for Shakspere being Shakespeare, is to say that the dates of Shakespeare's works match Shakspere's supposed writing career. This is based on a fallacy: namely choosing the dates of the plays in the first place so that they fitted that invented writing career. The fact that this has persisted may seem incredible; but it started quite simply.

Around 1790, the London lawyer and Shakespeare scholar Edmond Malone set himself to find dates for when individual Shakespeare plays might have been written, as opposed to dates when they were first published or performed which might be, and sometimes were, decades later. Of course, he first took it for granted that Shakespeare was our

Shakspere. He then assumed Shakspere's family commitments after the birth of his twins in 1585 would have kept him in Stratford until at least 1586, a year when the theatres were closed by an outbreak of plague. So Malone could not place Shakspere in London before 1587 without having him behave too badly to his family. Next, Malone assumed Shakspere, with his non-literary and non-theatrical background, would have had to serve an apprenticeship in writing and drama and could not have finished a play for performance before 1589 at the very earliest. So Malone chose 1589 as the date of the first Shakespeare play, as he thought anything earlier would mean Shakspere was not the author and anything later would make it very difficult to fit in the known early plays.

To get a date when Shakespeare finished writing, Malone worked out from the records of his Stratford activities that Shakspere must have left London by 1610 at the latest, so he used that date for Shakespeare's last play. (There is, of course, no evidence Shakspere was in London before 1592 or after 1604, but we will ignore that for now.)

So Malone had invented a "dramatic career" for Shakspere of some twenty-one years – 1589 to 1610 – and Shakespeare's writing of plays would have to fit this, irrespective of the order in which they were written. In this way, Malone had ensured that the dates he gave to the various plays would fit the writing career he had created for Shakspere; so the fact that they did fit (well, almost fit) could be evidence of nothing. That is what a circular argument does. If Malone had assumed Bacon was the author, for example, his method would have given another set of dates entirely.

Now there is much evidence that the real start date of Shakespeare's writing was earlier than 1589, though it is usually avoided in orthodox biographies. For example, *Stow's Annales* for 1615, edited by Edmund Howes, included a list of twenty-seven Elizabethan writers in what it said was the order of their "priorities", i.e. who began writing first.

In this list, Shakespeare came before Marlowe, which puts the date of 1589 that Malone gave for the earliest Shakespeare play at least three years too late, since Marlowe's first play was certainly written by 1587. The list also shows Shakespeare writing before Drayton and Daniel, who were both older than Shakspere. Because that does not fit the orthodox theory, some have tried to say "priorities" referred to the writers' social rank, others that it meant their order of merit as authors. However, since the list correlates best with the dates of birth of the named writers – the first in the list, and first born, was George Gascoigne, born 1534, and the last in the list, and last born, was George Withers, born 1588 – priorities has to mean the order in which they started their writing careers.

The positioning of Shakespeare in the "Stow" list fits with the view of a number of scholars (e.g. Honan and Emrys Jones) that the language of his early plays is old-fashioned for the dates the orthodox put on them.

It equally fits with the early dating of some plays, for instance by Ben Jonson. He put *Titus Andronicus* between 1584 and 1589, and also, in his dedicatory poem in the First Folio, compared Shakespeare's works with those of Lyly, Kyd and Marlowe, who wrote nothing after 1593. On the orthodox dating, Jonson's comparators would have been later writers like Marston, Dekker and Webster. Of course, the evidence that dates the plays earlier than Malone does, has to be rejected by the orthodox, unless they are happy to assume that Shakspere, against the customs and laws of the time, abandoned his new family.

Some might try to support Malone's dating by refering to a note made by a vicar of Stratford, John Ward, in the 1660s when he wrote:

> I have heard that Mr Shakspeare was a natural wit, without any art at all; he frequented the plays all his younger time, but in his elder days lived at Stratford, and supplied the stage with two plays every year, and for it had an allowance so large, that he spent at the rate of £1000 a year.

That, of course, reads like a collage of speculations on what might have happened if Shakspere had been Shakespeare. Yet Shakspere would not have been able to frequent the theatre from Stratford in his younger days; there is no evidence that part of his working life for the theatre could have been spent at Stratford; and there is nothing to suggest his expenditure was anything like the sum mentioned or even that he had an "allowance" such as a pension. Sadly, Ward apparently got nothing – at least nothing he could use – from the members of Shakspere's family still around during his 19 years in Stratford. Indeed, his notes refer to him writing a letter to Shakspere's daughter Judith and awaiting a reply, but he added nothing to them as a result of meeting with her. Ward's diary showed he had a magpie mind, not a researcher's; it contained such gems as

> King James used to say merrily, he had three things no prince ever had – a secretary who could not write, a bishop who could not preach and something else.

and

> Nick Culpepper says that a physician without astrology is like a pudding without fat.

and, one he should have heeded, *"Good scholars seldom take things on trust."*

After laying out his hypothetical framework for dating Shakespeare's plays, Malone assumed that *Henry VI Part 1* was Shakespeare's earliest and gave it the earliest possible date (according to his theory) of 1589/90.

He then assumed *Twelfth Night* was Shakespeare's last play because it was considered the most perfect, and gave it the latest date he thought Shakspere was in London, 1610. However, he then came across "evidence" that fooled him into thinking *The Tempest* was written as late as 1610/11, and he moved *Twelfth Night* firstly to 1612 and then 1614, delaying Shakspere's retirement and creating a period of ten years when he was supposedly working in London without leaving any record. (Another result of his new date for *The Tempest* – which, as the play at the front of the First Folio, was taken to be Shakespeare's earliest – was that it had to be reassessed from being an example of his immature writing to one of his most polished works. That's scholarship!) With his end points "fixed" by speculation and wrong information, Malone juggled the remaining thirty-four Shakespeare plays in the First Folio, plus *Pericles* to fit the twenty-five-year writing career he had created.

No one suggests Malone was trying to deceive anyone: he was just trying to bring some rationale to the chronology of Shakespeare's work on the assumption it was Shakspere's. He admitted he had to guess the order for the plays, having minimal evidence to support their dating, and most orthodox scholars will concede that is what he did – though some will only do it privately, or at least cautiously. The orthodox Wilson (1993) put the matter colourfully but accurately when he wrote:

> Shakespeare's plays can be likened to beautiful, individually shaped beads dropped from a unique necklace of which the connecting thread has been lost. Even to this day there is no general consensus on the exact sequence in which they should be rethreaded, let alone the nearest year in which each was written.

There are few, if any, of the plays for which there is hope of dating them from definite evidence. More than that, the idea that the plays could be dated from their form, quality and style was early undermined when *Twelfth Night*, originally dated at 1610, then 1612, then 1614, was found to have been performed in the Middle Temple of the Inns of Court in 1601. And all that told us was that 1601 was the *latest* date by which the play must have been ready – its *terminus ad quem* for Latin scholars – though it could have been written well before then. Orthodox scholars insist on pushing it to the latest date, 1601, even though Feste's song in it, "*O Mistress mine ...*", was included in a collection of songs published by Thomas Morley in 1599, pushing the play's latest date for writing to 1598. It is a real puzzle that orthodox scholars will, if possible, assume the plays were written just before they were published or performed, dating them as late as they can to try to fit Shakspere as author. Yet Marlowe's *Tamburlaine*, for example, appeared about four years, his *Dr Faustus* sixteen years and his *The Jew of Malta* forty years, after writing. There is evidence that dating Shakespeare's plays to precisely when they were first known is as unreasonable as it would be for Marlowe's.

For the dating of any of the plays, hard evidence is not going to go down well with the orthodox if it clashes with the assumed career of Shakspere. Although, as we mentioned, Jonson put *Titus Andronicus* before 1589, the normal orthodox chronology puts it as late as 1592/3, which even ignores its playing history as spelled out on the title page of its 1594 Quarto edition: three different companies are named as having held the play for acting before 1594 and that fits a pre-1589 date, not 1592/3. Similarly, although *Hamlet* is now put at 1601 in modern orthodox chronology, there was a definite reference (by Thomas Nashe) to a play of that name in 1589, and an almost definite reference to Shakespeare's *Hamlet* in 1596 by Thomas Lodge. It is possible to date *Hamlet* early and still keep it within Malone's scheme – he originally dated it at 1596 – but that now means other plays must be shifted and may have to be moved outside the writing career invented for Shakspere.

Various scholars, including orthodox ones, have wanted to date some Shakespeare works well before 1589 on the basis of serious evidence – Hotson (1949), Brown (1949), Alexander (1951) for example – but such views are generally pushed aside as spoiling the Shakspere myth, and kept away from the general reader. Ten Shakespeare plays have been put forward by different orthodox authors as being his earliest, which causes problems when it comes to juggling them around to fit within Malone's dates; and the situation gets worse when it is realised that Shakespeare had a habit of revising his plays, some seriously, so what was published may not be his first version.

The fact that Malone's dating of the plays was fallacious would not automatically mean Shakspere could not have written them, but the apparent inevitability of some of the earlier dates can make things very awkward. In addition to that problem, there are features of some orthodox dates and attributions of late plays – like *The Tempest* and *The Two Noble Kinsmen* – which, often unnoticed, could be fatal to the Shakspere myth if they were true: these will be discussed in Appendix F, along with the dating of the early plays and the Sonnets.

There are problems with the orthodox dating of specific plays, like that for *The Merchant of Venice*, for example. In 1594, the Queen's physician, Dr Lopez, was executed on a charge of plotting to poison her which was seemingly fabricated by some powerful faction. Much was made at the time of him being a *"Jewish doctor, worse than Judas himself"*. So, if *The Merchant* did make its case for the fairer treatment of Jews in 1597 (as the orthodox dating has it), the author risked the wrath of some powerful people best avoided by being anonymous, which does not fit the author being our Shakspere. But, if the play is moved to before 1594 to avoid that problem – and no facts say it was later – it puts more pressure on his supposed start date.

Finally, we must consider *Measure for Measure* and *All's Well that Ends Well*. Although both plays depend on the "bed trick", with a man duped into sleeping with the "wrong" woman, the orthodox dates oddly have Shakespeare iterating the trick within twelve months.

If the problems of dating the *writing* of the plays is left to one side, the known dating of their *publication* is, all by itself, extremely awkward for the theory that Shakspere was a businessman and was also writing plays as a jobbing author of a company of players or a playhouse. If five specific dates are used to define any proposed dramatic career for Shakspere – namely 1585 (the birth of his twins); 1593 (the first use of "Shakespeare"), 1603 (accession of James I), 1616 (Shakspere's death) and 1623 (the First Folio) – the distribution of dates of publication of Shakespeare's works comes out as follows:

1585–1593: none printed.
1593–1603: 15 plays printed (16 if *Edward III* was Shakespeare's as many claim) plus 2 major poems.
1603–1616: 3 printed (including *Pericles*) plus the Sonnets.
1616–1623: 1 printed.
1623   First Folio printed with 36 plays, of which 18 were "never before printed" (including 3 never before heard of).

That table – which omits two debatable "Shakespeare" poems, *The Phoenix and the Turtle* and *A Lover's Complaint* – argues all by itself for a relationship between the writer and the plays which does not fit the hard-nosed Shakspere. The explanation often given by the orthodox, namely that Shakspere could not publish his own plays – though other writers could and did – just stresses how difficult their case is.

The "Greene's *Groatsworth*" Myth

If the orthodox method of dating Shakespeare's plays fails to help the Shakspere myth, then one of the most frequently quoted pieces of fallacious "evidence" used to support it is positively harmful to the cause of Shakespeare scholarship. This is the interpretation most orthodox scholars put on a section of a tract known as Greene's *Groatsworth*, which was mentioned in Chapter 6. As was said there, this tract was probably not by Greene, did not refer to Shakspere, and did not, as is frequently claimed, attack Shakespeare as a plagiarising "upstart crow".

Given Shakespeare has three times as many original quotable quotes in the *Oxford Dictionary of Quotations* as all his rivals put together, one would think that such an attempt to dumb him down relative to his rivals just to try to fit him to the Shakspere myth would explode more than just that myth. The *Groatsworth's* problems have often been pointed out, even by some orthodox scholars, but they are still largely ignored. This collage of scraps attributed to Greene is discussed more fully in Appendix C; there it will become clear its best use is as a litmus test for those biographies that try to use it to brand Shakespeare as a plagiarist.

The "Shakespeare spoke Warwickshire" Myth

Another twist in the theft of Shakspere's identity relies on a serious fallacy about the language in Shakespeare's works. It is obvious that our William Shakspere would have been immersed in the speech of Warwickshire for the first twenty years of his life at least, so that his speech must have been formed accordingly: he would have spoken "Warwickshire". Because of this and by ignoring the facts, most orthodox scholars have simply assumed that the writings of Shakespeare reflect this speech, its accent as well as its dialect. They then expect readers of their biographies to accept simply that Shakespeare spoke "Warwickshire", and, in a typical circular argument, to believe this is proof that he was Shakspere. Sadly for the orthodox case, the opposite is true. Shakespeare's language tells us unequivocally that he was not from Warwickshire.

Kokeritz (1953), after a major investigation designed to prove Shakespeare's works reflected a Warwickshire accent, was forced to admit failure: the accent in the plays just did not fit with the author being William Shakspere from Stratford, and no research since has challenged that finding. Kokeritz, who must have been bitterly disappointed, chose to argue that one should not expect Shakespeare, whoever he was, to have written with any particular regional dialect or accent, which was an awful cop-out: his whole research was based on that expectation (which would have been absolutely valid if Shakespeare had been Shakspere). What is clear is that Shakespeare made much use of dialect words (and accents) from different English regions in his works, but he used virtually nothing unique to Warwickshire. As the *OCS* put it:

> It is somewhat strange that Shakespeare did not, in fact, exploit his Warwickshire accent, since he was happy enough to represent, in phonetic spelling, the non-standard English of French and Welsh speakers, and the national dialects of Scotland and Ireland.

This is only strange, of course, if one thinks he was Shakspere.

Kokeritz's result was confirmed by Crystal (2005) in his book, *Pronouncing Shakespeare*, where, in discussing putting on plays at

"Shakespeare's Globe" in their original pronunciation, the Warwickshire accent did not figure once (nor did it figure in the programmes for his two productions at the Globe – *Romeo and Juliet* and *Troilus and Cressida*).

Brook (1976) carried out a review of Shakespeare's language that confirmed Kokeritz's findings and concluded that the author's colloquial language was mainly based on London and the area to the southwest. Even so, there were other regions – like Yorkshire, East Anglia, Scotland and Ireland – that contributed substantially to Shakespeare's vocabulary, though not Warwickshire. This is totally consistent with the surprise of Appleton Morgan (1900) in not finding a single Warwickshire word among the 60,000 in *Venus and Adonis*, the first work published under the pseudonym Shakespeare. Brook and Kokeritz were not the first to show there was a major problem with Shakespeare having the wrong accent and dialect to be Shakspere, but they were the most thorough.

The serious research done on Shakespeare's language does not stop some insisting he used a Warwickshire accent and dialect. One recent biographer said "*Shakespeare spoke with a Warwickshire accent*", another that "*his debt to Stratford is peculiar and profound*". They generally rely on a claim by Onions (1911) that he had found twenty-four Warwickshire words in the plays. Even if this were true, these would only make up some two percent of all Shakespeare's dialect words, but it is in fact a considerable over-estimate – and the claim was omitted when Onions's book was revised in 1986. For example, the word "mobled" in *Hamlet*, referring to Queen Gertrude running down the corridor in disarray, was said by Onions to be a Warwickshire dialect word meaning "muffled": yet it is actually a Herefordshire word meaning "in disarray". Brook identified only seven of Onions's selected words as being used in Warwickshire, but even two of those – "ballow" and "batler" – have since turned out to be misreadings of the texts of the plays, and four of the other five are too common in other counties to locate them anywhere specific. For example, the word "tarre" meaning "to urge on" is found in Warwickshire, but it had been used by the London-born Spenser before Shakespeare. One only has to refer to the *Oxford Dictionary of Dialects* – and not limit oneself to looking at words used in Warwickshire – to get a clear picture. Of all the regions of Britain, Warwickshire is one of those that had the least influence on Shakespeare's language, and that alone should destroy the Shakspere myth.

Writers on Shakespeare may be still found to assume Warwickshire provided most of his dialect words. In 1938, Fripp – a keen Warwickshire man – claimed all the oddly spelt words in the First Folio such as "kisse" and "sonne" were from Warwickshire, though they could be found all over the country. A typical problem here is the word "breeze" in *Antony and Cleopatra*. Shakespeare wrote of the Queen in her ship: "*The breeze upon her like a cow in June, hoists sails and flies.*" It is often said "breeze" was a Warwickshire word meaning "gadfly", an insect known to torment cattle. In this sense, it is actually old Anglo-Saxon and too widely known in England to identify the writer's origin. Moreover, both in this quotation and when it occurs in *Troilus and Cressida*, the use of "breeze" for a brisk wind is more appropriate than its use for a gadfly. There is a similar problem when phrases like *"rough hew"* (from *Hamlet*, meaning the first stage in carving of wood or stone) and *"golden lads and girls"* (from *Cymbeline*, possibly referring to dandelions) are occasionally claimed for Warwickshire, though they are not specific to that county. Similarly, as we shall see below, *"Cotsall"* was wrongly put in the *English Oxford Dictionary* as a Warwickshire dialect word simply because Shakespeare used it: the "Fripp effect" can fool the greatest.

Two other counties have been named as providing some of Shakespeare's dialect words because anecdotes say Shakspere stayed there: Gloucestershire and Lancashire. Yet there is only one dialect word specific to the first of those counties ("keech" – a lump of fat – in *Henry VIII*) and only one (and that shared with Yorkshire) for the second ("slough" – pronounced "sluff" – a skin – in *Hamlet*).

Now the fact that Shakespeare's language was not Shakspere's undermines another poor effort to "prove" Shakespeare was Shakspere. This is the reinterpretation of Sonnet 145 by Gurr (1971) – using the Fripp effect – to make it into a poem Shakspere wrote to his wife around 1582 when he was courting her. The last two lines of that Sonnet are:

> *I hate, from hate away she threw*
> *And saved my life, saying not you.*

Gurr claimed that, in old Warwickshire (which Shakespeare did not speak), "hath" and "hate" had the same pronunciation so that "hate away" is turned into a pun by Shakspere/Shakespeare on his wife's name, Hathaway. Suddenly it would become necessary to think of this Sonnet, previously thought of as the worst in the sequence, the one voted most likely to be rejected as not being Shakespeare's, as the most important he ever wrote. In a 1926 review by Robertson of the Sonnets which scholars identified as ripe for rejection, No. 145 came top. Today, though, if an orthodox biographer finds space to quote only one Sonnet, it has to be this one, hoping to link Shakespeare to Shakspere by claiming it is obviously Shakspere's tribute to his bride (though what she was supposed to like about the litany of hate that runs through it is not explained). Even the *OCS* approved this interpretation, though it had rejected its very basis by admitting Shakespeare did not use the Warwickshire language. The dire quality of the Sonnet is usually blamed on the supposed youth of its writer but, if Shakspere had been Shakespeare, he would not have been just any young man: he would have been a genius of a young man, at least as able as, say, Brooke, Byron, Keats and Shelley who all had excellent poetry published by the time they were eighteen.

Gurr's interpretation requires one to forget not only that Shakespeare did not speak "Warwickshire", but also the doubts about the authorship of this Sonnet. The reasons for rejecting it are strong, and not just because it is a terrible poem. Sonnet 145 has lines of eight syllables while all the rest have ten. The twelve lines of its introduction are oddly divided into five, three and four lines, while Shakespeare's all have four, four, and four. It is not at the start of the sequence as one might expect, but at the end among a number of Sonnets, several having a theme of hate, which seem to be make-weights added by Thorpe to fill the normal blank pages found at the end of a quarto. If he has fooled some scholars into including John Ford's *A Funeral Elegy* in editions of Shakespeare's works by adding the initials WS to the poem and to its dedication, he has fooled a few more with this Sonnet 145.

It seems a little superfluous to point out (see Chapter 3) that "hate" and "hath" were not pronounced the same even in Warwickshire. In truth, different scholars, in using this Sonnet to "prove" Shakespeare was Shakspere, give different Warwickshire sounds for "hate" and for "hath"; but, remarkably, when they guess their supposed old Warwickshire sound of "hate", they always guess exactly the same sound for "hath".

The "Shakespeare knew Stratford" Myth

We now go to Shakspere's home town. It was pointed out in the discussion of Shakspere's time as a lodger with the Mountjoys (see Chapter 8) how that occasion had been used to create five stories to help the Shakspere myth, none of which stood up. Many more inventions have been attempted in relation to Stratford-upon-Avon. These have depended on various matters in the plays – places, people, etc. – picked out to suggest the plays were written by a man from Stratford, or even that they could only have been written by Shakspere.

The prime claim in this category relies on two place names that appear in two related lines of *The Taming of the Shrew*:

"Am I not Christopher Sly, old Sly's son of Burton Heath?"

and, two lines later,

"Ask Marion Hacket, the fat ale-wife of Wincot."

The trick here is to claim that Shakespeare's Burton Heath was actually

Barton-on-the-Heath, fifteen miles from Stratford, where Shakspere's uncle Lambert lived, the one who foreclosed on the mortgage on his mother's property (see Chapter 4). Sometimes, to try to reinforce this identification, biographers will write "Barton" when they quote those lines instead of Shakespeare's "Burton". It has actually been claimed that this is the strongest evidence for Shakspere being Shakespeare because no one else but he would have thought of that little village where his delinquent uncle lived. Yet normally no one would actually think that changing Burton Heath to Barton-on-the-Heath was a proper way for a scholar to make up evidence, especially when it needs one to accept that Shakspere, writing as the brilliant Shakespeare, forgot what the actual name of the village was. It will not surprise any reader who has followed us so far to know that there are a number of Burton Heaths in England, waiting to be tested to see which of them Shakespeare actually meant, but we will leave the choice of the obvious one until we have dealt with the second place-name referred to above.

The folly about Burton Heath is usually compounded by claiming "Wincot" in the second of the two lines above was a village five miles south west of Stratford, which actually does not exist. There is a Wincot Farm there, but it has no building where a Marion Hacket could have lived, no record of any Hacket ever having lived there and no ale-house has been identified anywhere near it in spite of excavations. (There are some mulberry trees there that the owner jokingly told this writer were brought down from Stratford and planted by "Shakespeare" himself, but that is not the same – or perhaps it is.)

The Wincot that Shakespeare referred to (see *SCDL* – or visit it) is actually thirty miles away from Stratford, a full three-days' round trip. It lies on Watling Street, the old Roman Road from Canterbury, via London and Shrewsbury into Wales, one of the ten best roads in the country at the time. (Today, north of London, it is officially the "A5".)

Whoever Shakespeare was, it is clear he "walked" that road which cuts through a good deal of the terrain of the Wars of the Roses. It was the route taken by Henry IV's troops to fight Hotspur and his allies at Shrewsbury; it was the route followed by the Princes back to London in *Richard III*; and there are dozens of references to places on or near it in the plays. Shakespeare's true Wincot – spelt Wilnecote, but pronounced Wincot to this day – adjoins the town of Tamworth (Staffordshire) where Richard III passed on his way to Bosworth Field. Hacket and Hackett are local names, there being many more of them in Tamworth and Wincot than there are within twenty miles of Wincot Farm. There were five inns or ale-houses in Wincot village in Elizabethan times and, sadly, the one that has been identified as occupied by Hackets was converted into a mill and later demolished. The fact that Shakespeare saw, and possibly stayed at, this Wincot on Watling Street should not surprise anyone. Some writers excitedly report that, in 1591, a "Hacket" was baptised in the parish of Quinton, the one next door to that containing Wincot Farm, but that can change nothing written here – all it proves is that the baby was not born at Wincot Farm.

Now, if one looks at the stretch of the Watling Street near Wincot, it turns out that Burton is a common prefix in the names of places (such as Burton Hargreaves) and in those of geographical features (such as Burton Fields). South from Wincot, at about half-a-mile from Dunsmore Heath where Shakespeare records the 13th Earl of Oxford mustering Henry VI's troops, lies Bourton Heath. In the local dialect, Bourton would be heard as Burton, and its identification as the place associated with Wincot fits neatly among the places near the Watling Street that the real Shakespeare would have visited in familiarising himself with the terrain of the Wars of the Roses – and none of them has anything to do with Stratford.

There are so many places mentioned by Shakespeare along Watling Street, besides Wincot, Dunsmore Heath and B[o]urton Heath – like Barnet, St Albans, Stoney Stratford, Hinckley, Tamworth, Atherstone, Shrewsbury and others – that one orthodox scholar tried to claim it was Shakspere's most direct route to London from Stratford when, of course, it was nothing of the sort.

The most spectacular nonsense resulting from orthodox attempts to uproot places named in Shakespeare's works and transport them to the vicinity of Stratford is the statement, still in books today, that a place-name "Cotsall" was an old name for the Cotswolds, which it was not. When the *Oxford English Dictionary* stated that Cotsall first appeared for the Cotswolds in Shakespeare's First Folio in 1623, they did not realise they had been misled. Shakespeare referred to this place twice: in *The Merry Wives of Windsor* when a character said a greyhound had been *"outrun on Cotsall"*, and in *Henry IV Part 2* where *"Will Squele, a Cotsall man"* was linked to *"John Doit of Staffordshire"*. No reference book has identified Cotsall as a name for the Cotswolds, and inquiries made there found no one who had heard of them being called that. But a number of Cotswolders were pleased to point out that "Cotsall" was where the Albrighton Hunt still met across Codsall Woods, and the place where a hare would have tried to outrun a greyhound. It is in John Doit's county of Staffordshire, close to Boscobel House, a hospitable venue where a researching Shakespeare could easily have stayed on his way along Watling Street, which passes close by on its way to the site of Henry IV's battle at Shrewsbury. It has long been spelled as Codsall, but it is always pronounced as "Cotsall".

Another misidentification about a place in Shakespeare being near Stratford is the claim that the forest called Arden in *As You Like It* was

Shakspere's "local" forest and identifies him as the author. Yet everyone knows the play was set in France. It was based on a story set near Bordeaux where there was an Arden (the Celtic name for forest) along the Dordogne. The play makes it clear that it was not set in an English forest by its reference to an exiled Duke with *"merry men"* in the forest *"like Old Robin Hood of England"*. (Some productions of the play leave out that reference: it does give the game away.) Today, those who do admit Arden was in France prefer to say it was the "Ardennes" (pronounced "Arden") on the French–Belgium border, possibly because that is nearer England, but it does not change anything.

Two quite funny Stratford inventions occurred in a quite recent biography. One involved claiming that whenever Warwickshire is mentioned in the plays – such as when Falstaff passes through along Watling Street on his way to the battle of Shrewsbury, or when the Earl of Warwick says *"In Warwickshire I have true hearted friends"* – it indicates the author was from there. The other was a claim that when Helena, disguised as a pilgrim in *All's Well that Ends Well*, says to an inquisitive Florentine she is going to *"Saint Jacques le Grand"* – meaning St James of Compostella in Spain, the best known Christian shrine in Europe at the time – Shakespeare was really thinking of the little church of St James the Great at Snittering near Stratford.

The last location to be looked at in this review of the Shakspere place-names fallacy is in another quotation – *"By'r Lady, I think 'a be but goodman Puff of Barson."* – from *Henry IV Part 2*. To link that to Shakspere, it has been assumed *Barson* was Barcheston, a smart little village off the beaten track ten miles south of Stratford. There is good evidence this village was pronounced as "Barston" in the sixteenthth century (see Britton, 2001, and graves in the floor of the church). There is weaker evidence from a single use of the name on a tomb in the church that it was called "Barson". There is now no memory of it being pronounced anything but Barcheston. The history of the village makes it unlikely there would have been a goodman (or yeoman) Puff for Shakespeare to meet from Barcheston, as one reason for knowing it was called "Barston" is a court case where the yeomen of the area protested at being driven from their parish by sheep enclosures in the early 1500s. And they may all have disappeared by around 1550, killed off by a serious outbreak of cholera. No: the likely place for Shakespeare's goodman Puff is a large village not far from Watling Street, close to where Richard III's body would have passed on its way from Bosworth to Leicester. In the past, it was spelt Balson; now it is Barleston; but its pronunciation in the Leicestershire dialect was and still is, especially with the older folk, Barson.

No places mentioned in the plays would have been counted "near to Stratford" in 1600. Those claimed to be so, all turn out to lie around the route that the author Shakespeare would have taken if he had travelled the locations of the six plays covered by the titles *Henry IV*, *Henry VI* and *Richard III*. He would have gone out of London along Watling Street through Barnet and St Alban's, past Dunsmore Heath, Bourton Heath, Stoney Stratford, and Hinckley, Atherstone, Tamworth and Wincot, Sutton Coldfield and Cotsall to Shrewsbury and on to Ludlow (where the two Princes were lodged in *Richard III*), then down the valley of the Severn through Bridgnorth (where Prince Hal stopped), to Gloucester, Berkeley Castle and Bristol, and back through Cirencester and Chertsey (all eighteen places being in the Shakespeare plays). He would have found Woncot (short for Woodmancote) in Gloucestershire, that is not (as is frequently said) a misspelling of Wincot. (It was a William Visor of Woncot who was mentioned in *Henry IV Part 2* and that village is the home of the Visors still.)

Other arguments that try to fit Shakespeare to Shakspere's home town fare no better than those about locations and the Warwickshire dialect. For example, it has been claimed that the *dramatis personæ* of the plays include fourteen names found in Stratford records around Shakspere's time and these have been said to be evidence that he was the author. It will not do. Of those fourteen names, only four are not actual names of historical figures that Shakespeare would have taken from his sources. For example, the name Pace in *Henry VIII* was said to be from Stratford but he was Dr Pace, the Dean of St Paul's. Also a Stratford name, Bardell, was mistakenly written as Bardolfe on one occasion and then claimed to have given rise to Bardolph in *Henry IV*; yet that name came from Lord Bardolph who fought against Henry IV. Of the four names that were not historical, three were so common – Bates, Court, Curtiss – they could have been found anywhere in England. We are left with one odd name in a play that is similar to one from Stratford: Fluellen. He is the Welsh soldier in *Henry V*, who forced the character Pistol to eat a leek. However, "Fluellen" is not only a common variant of the Welsh name Llewellyn but it is the Welsh name of a flower related to the leek: there is thus no need to wonder why Shakespeare picked it for his leek-wielding Welshman, particularly when the plays show whoever wrote them had a good knowledge of Wales.

Even Shakspere's purchase of New Place in Stratford in 1597 has been called on to link him to a play. In *Henry IV, Part 2*, a passage compares the drawing up of a political plot with planning the building of a house:

> ... When we mean to build,
> We first survey the plot, then draw the model:
> And when we see the figure of the house,
> Then we must rate the cost of the erection;

Encouraged by the fact that the orthodox guess for the date of *Henry IV, Part 2* is 1597/98 (which is by no means certain), Murray (1936) claimed that a man might have written those lines if he were buying a house that needed repair, but this sounds like desperation.

It is sometimes claimed Shakespeare must have been Shakspere because he used a Stratford-born London printer, Richard Field, to print his *Venus and Adonis* in 1593 and his *Rape of Lucrece* in 1594. In support, it will be said that, because John Shakspere was appointed to value Richard's father Henry Field's estate when he died in 1592, they must have been friends. Yet such an appointment would relate to debts, not friendship: solvent estates were not independently valued. Anyway, since John had sued Henry in 1556 for eighteen quarters of grain, worth £20,000 today, their families might well not have been on speaking terms. Of course, if Field had been some second-rate printer nobody but a friend would chose, and Shakespeare had used him regularly, that might have suggested a connection of some sort. But Field was one of the best London printers, a natural choice for prestigious poems whether he was known to the author or not; and he has not been found to be used by Shakespeare again, nor among the dozens of other printers used for Shakespeare plays in quartos or the First Folio. This suggests he had no connection with Shakespeare and is consistent with there being no indication that Field sent news home about Stratford's rich businessman Shakspere being the famous Shakespeare; and he lived to 1624.

An odd claim has been made about Field based on an event in *Cymbeline*. This is Imogen's use of the sobriquet "*Richard du Champ*" for the headless corpse of the rich Cloten, a boor whom she hated. It has been said that this was Shakspere, as Shakespeare, honouring Richard Field. Yet it looks anything but flattering, especially when it is noted – as Shakespeare would have known and Field's French wife would have pointed out – that "*Richard du Champ*" translates as "Bucolic Moneybags". When Field wanted such a mock pseudonym for himself he chose "*Ricardo del Campo*" which does translate as "Richard of the Field", and – with a French wife – he would hardly have used that if "*Richard du Champ*" had been acceptable.

Another person from the Stratford area called upon to aid the Shakspere myth has been a Kathleen Hamlett, a spinster of unknown age, who accidentally drowned not far away in 1579. Her identity has been treated nearly as badly as Shakspere's by some orthodox biographers. To try to link Shakespeare to Stratford, it has been claimed her death gave him the idea for Ophelia's drowning in *Hamlet*. Some biographers will even tell their readers that she was the subject of a Coroner's report that contained all the details Shakespeare used for Ophelia's death, including it being the suicide of a love-lorn maiden whose parents used the same legal arguments about her death as those joked about by the gravediggers in *Hamlet*. Regrettably for Shakespeare scholarship, that story is rarely corrected even though the "Coroner's report" that is quoted was simply faked in the 1920s to help the Shakspere myth. It suddenly appeared in biographies complete with all the relevant points from Shakespeare's play. The actual Coroner's report on Kathleen Hamlett's death still exists (see Fripp, 1938): her age is not given, the verdict was that she died by accident – "*per infortunato*" – and there were no legal arguments. To add to this foolishness, it is sometimes said this is where Shakespeare got the name "Hamlet" for his play, though his source was historical. Adding further insult to injury, Shakspere's son is sometimes said to have really been "Hamlet", though he was baptised "Hamnet", buried "Hamnet" and named after Shakspere's neighbour, Hamnet Sadler. Possibly to help this flummery, somebody has altered to "Hamlett" Sadler's first name as a beneficiary in Shakspere's will, though his signature as witness had to be left as Hamnet Sadler.

A comedic Shakespeare character used to provide false evidence for the orthodox theory is the very Welsh schoolmaster Hugh Evans in *The Merry Wives of Windsor*. Some will assert his inclusion in the play showed Shakspere remembering one of his own teachers from Stratford, a Thomas Jenkins. However, in spite of Jenkins being a Welsh name, the records show this teacher – who was too late to have taught Shakspere – was the London-born son of a Londoner and educated at Oxford University.

Another Stratford schoolmaster who has been called on to help with the Shakspere myth, twice, is an Alexander Aspinall, who was not appointed until 1582 and could not have taught Shakspere even if he had gone to school. First, he is claimed to be the model for the pedant Holofernes in *Love's Labour's Lost*, though nothing is known of his nature; second, it is claimed Shakspere (as Shakespeare) wrote a poem to go to Aspinall's "mistress" with a present of gloves:

The gift is small, | The thought is all, | Alexander Aspinall.

That is recognised as the worst doggerel attributed to Shakespeare, even worse than a supposed epitaph for an Elias James and the verse on Shakspere's supposed grave stone.

A man often libelled in support of Shakspere's candidacy is Sir Thomas Lucy, the Justice of the Peace from Charlecote, near Stratford. He figures in many Shakspere anecdotes, though none have any foundation but repetition. An attempt to give them substance has involved a claim that he was caricatured as Justice Shallow of Gloucester (why there?) in *The Merry Wives of Windsor*. The link depends on Shallow having a coat of arms with twelve "luces" (a luce being a pike) while Sir Thomas's had three luces. Today, even orthodox scholars recognise there was a Justice who was identified by twelve luces on his arms (that was what arms were for) and might have been mocked by any playwright, and that was William Gardiner of Southwark who tried to get the south bank theatres closed (see Chapter 7).

From what has been outlined above of the attempts to invent evidence to link Shakespeare to Stratford, readers should now know enough to be aware that, if they should come across other such efforts, they will simply be deceptions produced on the assumption that no one will bother to check them. For example, a book recently published in Canada included an invention that was said to prove Shakespeare must have been from Stratford. This was that a backward swirl of water which occurs under the town's Clopton Bridge is similar to one described in Shakespeare's second narrative poem, *The Rape of Lucrece*, and therefore must have been seen by the author standing on that bridge. Yet such backward swirls are so common that there is probably no river in the world that does not show this phenomenon where the flowing water meets an obstruction: indeed, swirls of the type described by Shakespeare are used in the ultrasonic detection of minor obstructions to blood flow in arteries.

Just one more before one loses the will to live. There is a line in *Twelfth Night* where Viola is told her brother may have escaped a shipwreck *"like Arion on the dolphin's back"*, and it is claimed that reflects William Shakspere's memory of an occasion in 1575 at age eleven when he was taken most improbably (and expensively) to a Royal entertainment at Kenilworth near Warwick in which the classical scene with Arion was acted out. The only certainty is that Shakespeare knew the original story of Arion. Yet one biographer managed to get four pages of padding on that entertainment, none relevant to Shakspere or Shakespeare.

The "son of John Shakspere" Myth

A line of inquiry obvious for orthodox scholars wanting to show Shakspere was Shakespeare has been to search the plays for something linking them to his father's trades. Their reward has been a single item in *The Merry Wives of Windsor* where a man had *"a great round beard like a glover's paring knife"*. That is said to be a technical reference only someone in the gloving trade would know. Yet glover's workshops, where people could watch as they used their paring knives, were plentiful then, with a dozen in a small town like Stratford and scores in London. It would have been far easier for Shakespeare, whoever he was, to see a glover's paring knife than for Shakspere to have known the real technical terms in dozens of other activities referred to in the plays (and discussed in the next chapter).

Actually, other writers used gloving terms more abstruse than this one of Shakespeare's. Thomas Nashe mentioned how "Glover's balls" were made of human hair during the plague, while Middleton referred to someone putting their fingers into a glove's "sockets" which was a specialist term that could not be learnt by just looking: and nobody claims they were glovers' sons. There is another reference in a play that has been said to be a technical term only a glover would use, but which really argues against the author being technically involved with leather. This is in *Romeo and Juliet* where it is said conscience can stretch like the fine kids' leather, cheveril, *"from an inch narrow to an ell broad"*. A glover would have baulked at such a statement, knowing no leather would have stretched a tenth of that without tearing.

The pressure to link Shakespeare to John Shakspere's trades has been such that the mention of a leather apron in one play, dog's leather in another, leather harness in a third and so forth have all been claimed to show an author involved with glove making.

A link between Shakespeare and Shakspere has been sought through references to sheep and wool in the plays because John Shakspere was a known "brogger" or wool-trader. The plays certainly have more references to sheep and wool than to gloving, but only one of them might connect to brogging, and that is unconvincing. This is where, in *The Winter's Tale*, a shepherd refers to the price of a *"tod"* of wool (28 pounds weight), and asks *"fifteen hundred shorn, what comes the wool to?"* The problem here is that, while a shepherd or sheep owner might know and be interested in the weight of wool to be got from a sheep, a trader would be unlikely to care how many sheep of a particular kind had to be shorn to get a tod. So that does not point to a brogger, and nor do the other wool and sheep references in Shakespeare, which point more to shepherds and sheep owners.

An anecdote from John Aubrey about Shakspere being apprenticed to his father as a butcher has been discredited because John Shakspere would have needed a licence for that trade, and there was already a licensed butcher in Stratford. That has not stopped some taking the references in Shakespeare's plays to the blood from wounds coagulating and turning black, and turning them into evidence for Aubrey's butcher anecdote being correct and for Shakspere being Shakespeare. Yet the plays have over six-hundred references and allusions to blood in many different contexts suggesting wide reading and wide experience beyond anything that could be attributed to a butcher's apprentice – which it is pretty certain Shakspere was not.

The absence of genuine technical references in the plays to gloving and wool-trading becomes more significant when it is noted how many there are, for example, to carpentry and to wheel-wrighting. Nothing about Shakspere, if he was writer Shakespeare, explains why he would have been ready with more specifics on these latter two activities than he was on gloving, which he would have known at first hand.

The scarcity of technical gloving references has to be compared, for example, with the scores on medicine, and treatment of illness. Many articles have been written on Shakespeare's knowledge in this area, one even suggesting the plays could make a text book for a student of sixteenth-century medicine. Yet nobody has claimed Shakespeare was the son of a physician. Some have claimed Shakspere would have got medical knowledge from his son-in-law Dr John Hall, but most, if not all, of Shakespeare's medical allusions were in works written before Hall came into Shakspere's life. In the next chapter, it will be seen that there are dozens of allusions to subjects in the plays that pose problems for the orthodox theory, and contrast sharply with the absence of the sort of allusions that would have been expected from Shakspere.

In looking for other possible links to John Shakspere, a reference in *Romeo and Juliet* to an *"agate stone on the fore-finger of an alderman"* is sometimes said to show Shakspere using the fact of his father being a Stratford alderman in his writing as Shakespeare, even though it was no secret that aldermen had official rings. Yet that quoted phrase actually harms the orthodox theory: for when Shakespeare made a similar reference in the later play *Henry IV Part 1* it was corrected to an *"alderman's thumb ring"*, suggesting he had learnt in the meantime how aldermen actually wore their rings.

The "Shakespeare was an actor" Myth

One claim that is made about Shakespeare, a fairly obvious one to try, is that his work showed an actor writing. Of course, that cannot be justified simply by his ability to write plays to be acted: all successful dramatists have to do that and most have not been professional actors (and most actors do not become playwrights). One might seek in this context for signs of empathy with professional actors, though the opposite seems to be the case. References in the plays to actors tend to be uniformly pejorative, and allusions to acting generally unfavourable. It is strange, for instance, that Sonnet 110 is often claimed to be an actor speaking because of the lines:

> *Alas, 'tis true I have gone here and there*
> *And made myself a motley to the view,*
> *Gor'd my own thoughts, sold cheap what is most dear*

Yet that is a negative allusion to acting, and is only being used by

155

Shakespeare as a metaphor for regretting he has made himself foolish ("motley" indicating a clown) and distorted his true thoughts ("goring" meaning to insert patches into a costume). Similarly, the oft-quoted opening of Sonnet 23 is not helpful:

> *As an unperfect actor on the stage,*
> *Who with his fear is put beside his part,*

That is an allusion anyone who performed in a school play would have grasped. The references to the acting troupe in *Hamlet* are hardly complimentary, while the treatment of the "rough acting" in *Love's Labour's Lost* and *Midsummer Night's Dream* does not help the claim that the writer was an actor with Shakspere's background. There have been suggestions that Shakespeare's remarks *"One man in his time plays many parts"* and *"Thus play I in one person many people"* are an actor speaking, but they are factual statements, not profound acting metaphors. (Barrel-scraping comes to mind.) All this does not prove Shakespeare was not an actor, but it does contradict those, and there are many, who like to say his plays show he was. Few writers use acting or playing metaphors, and that is as true of those like Nathan Field, Anthony Munday, Thomas Heywood or Ben Jonson who all began their careers as actors. Shakespeare outdoes his rivals with his multitude of uncommon metaphors and allusions, but, among them, his acting metaphors are not what one would expect from a professional actor, and we will return to this subject.

The "Shakespeare was a country boy" Myth

Some writers have tried to support the orthodox theory by trying to show Shakespeare's works somehow fit better to an author of Shakspere's background than to one from a city or a country estate or a more affluent household. Yet that seems to be wishful thinking. It is difficult to reconcile the country-town Shakspere with Shakespeare's failure to be business-like over his works or with his dismissal of money, wealth and gold from first to last, from *A Comedy of Errors* to *Cymbeline*.

When one looks at Shakespeare's numerous references to flowers and animals, it is obvious that the unorthodox Shakespeare candidates like Bacon, William Stanley and others, had opportunities for learning about country matters at least as good as Shakspere's, and better in respect of books, tutors and time. Bacon's philosophic and other writings, for instance, mention almost all the plants in Shakespeare. Lord Burghley's gardener, John Gerard, author of *Herbal, or General History of Plants* (1597) would have been known to most of them. Mary Sidney had a variety of flower and herb gardens under her charge. What is difficult is to believe that Shakspere would have picked up the horticultural knowledge of Shakespeare simply by walking the fields around Stratford. This point is made plain by looking at Ophelia's garland in *Hamlet*: each of the four flowers in it – nettles, crow-flowers, daisies and long-purples – had connotations relevant to the love sickness that led to her suicide – spurned love, virginity, unfaithfulness and a phallic symbol respectively. And the problem is worse when one notes that, prior to her suicide, Ophelia distributed rue, fennel, columbine, rosemary and pansies in the Court, and referred to withered violets, all flowers associated with her forlorn state. The reality is that every time a point in the plays is said to represent the knowledge of a man from a country town – as with mention of the red spot in the flower of the cowslip (*Cymbeline*) or a hint of the bawdy name for long-purples (*Hamlet*) – simple consideration of what all people brought up in a largely rural England would have known shows the argument to be wishful thinking. The knowledge of plants that is demonstrated in Shakespeare's works is sophisticated rather than bucolic, and does not help Shakspere's candidacy.

The most troubling anomaly for a writer trying to present Shakespeare as the son of a craftsman from a country town is the way his representation of crowds in his plays always leaves one feeling they are gullible and self-seeking. Even in *Coriolanus*, where the main character is obnoxious, a working-class theatre-goer would leave a performance of it feeling ashamed of his confrères as represented on the stage for the way they treated the "hero". One orthodox writer, seemingly unintentionally, exposed the serious confusion over Shakespeare's treatment of the common people, including not only crowds but individuals like Dogberry in *Much Ado About Nothing*. Because they are treated by Shakespeare in a way quite contrary to what would be expected from a man of Shakspere's background, Patterson (1989) concluded that either he (meaning Shakspere as Shakespeare) did not understand what he was doing or we (the readers or audience) must have mistaken what he intended. She explained it quite concisely:

> Common sense suggests that a popular dramatist, himself the son of a country Glover, and whose livelihood depended on the huge and socially diverse audiences for the London public theatre, was unlikely to have unquestionably adopted an anti-popular myth as his own.

That ignores the obvious answer – Shakespeare was not the son of a country glover. Instead, Patterson attempted to say we are all wrong about how we see his common people treated in *Coriolanus, Julius Caesar*, and several other plays. Yet Shakespeare is too consistent for anyone to think it is accidental: try as he will to be even-handed, the political attitudes at the core of his philosophy do not fit him as a small-town craftsman's son.

On the title page of *Venus and Adonis*, for instance, Shakespeare quoted Ovid's Latin tag "*Vilia miretur vulgus*" which actually translates, though some pretend otherwise, as "Let the common people admire vile things". Also, in the dedications of both that poem and *The Rape of Lucrece* to the Earl of Southampton, Shakespeare has been noted as giving the impression of being disrespectful – a risk if the author was the non-pseudonymous Shakspere. He also did something that would have been an actual insult at the time (and still is in some societies): he starts his dedication of the first, *Venus and Adonis*, with the address "Right Honourable". He then not only omits that title for *The Rape of Lucrece*, but highlights the fact by calling his dedication "*this pamphlet without beginning*".

An added difficulty with *Venus and Adonis* is how Shakspere could have got away with not only writing a poem which was openly talked of as pornographic at the time (and parodied as such), but also dedicating it to one of the Queen's favourites, who was a ward of Lord Burghley. Even if Lord Burghley and the Queen did not protest, there were others, like Gabriel Harvey, who would have delighted in taking a "country bumpkin Shakspere" to task.

There is a further problem in claiming that the plays point to an author with Shakspere's background, and that is their very nature. Of the thirty-seven plays – thirty-six in the First Folio plus *Pericles* – only three have no King, Emperor, Prince or Duke among their main characters; while only one – *The Merry Wives of Windsor* – is vaguely plebeian, and that has a knightly theme. Some will say all playwrights at the time used such royal or aristocratic characters, but that only passes for fact until someone goes through their works (see Dutton and Howard, 2006). Even some orthodox scholars have allowed that, while others wrote for the generality of playgoers, Shakespeare seems to have written for the aristocracy. Indeed, the fact that he did so, concentrating as it were on "celebrity" with idealised or fantastical situations rather than the ordinary, has been put forward as a reason why his plays have continued to be popular.

In keeping with his choice of "upper class" subjects, is Shakespeare's trick of having characters disguise themselves but always as someone of lower caste – like the Duke of Kent as a fool in *King Lear*, the Duke as a Friar in *Measure for Measure*, Celia as a country wife in *As You Like It*. The trick is always completed when the people disguised return to their "proper" status. The only case of someone dressing upwards into a higher caste instead of downwards is Christopher Sly in *The Taming of the Shrew*, but that was a trick played on him when he was drunk, not his own doing.

Coupled with the above errors about Shakespeare writing as a countryman is the frequent assertion that he did not understand court etiquette or use it properly in his plays. Yet Byrne (1934), the oft-quoted expert in this area, said of his treatment of this subject that *"Many of the Elizabethan writers are too true to be good"* while *"Shakespeare is topical only in his superfluity – in an aside, a simile, an image, a flourish, a jest."* She shows how Shakespeare, in his self-confidence, used court etiquette as he needed it, not pedantically.

In *Hamlet*, he makes Ophelia behave very properly, and wait to be summoned to the Queen's presence because it enhances the dramatic effect, but he has Hamlet ignore the niceties and rush in on the Queen for exactly the same reason. It has been said by the pedantic that no one who understood court practice would have written the hilarious scene in *Richard II* where the Duke of Aumerle and his parents, one tumbling after the other, rush in on Henry IV, unimpeded by guards or ushers. Shakespeare clearly knew that proper practice was often honoured more in the breach than the observance, as when a muddy and armed Earl of Essex barged into the Queen's dressing room in the middle of her toilette. As Byrne put it, *"When it suits him to do so Shakespeare keeps close to contemporary practice."* However, in her article, it seems she felt forced to suggest Shakespeare was initially ignorant of court practice and, being Shakspere, increased his knowledge with time. That conclusion, which appears to be directed to placating the orthodox, is totally contradicted by the evidence she presents. She shows that Shakespeare used or abused court practice as it suited his purpose. Just take the scene in *Romeo and Juliet* where Capulet breaks the tension surrounding Juliet's intended wedding to Paris by stopping to organise dry logs for the fire: of this Byrne says it could not have been based on Elizabethan practice. In an English house, she says, Capulet would have had minions for that purpose. Yet the way Shakespeare uses that simple moment of light relief to accentuate the pressure which is on Juliet and her family is stage genius. Anyone who has followed commentators like David Starkey and Alison Plowden would know that Queen Elizabeth kept a sword by her, swore like a man, told her Parliament that she would survive "if turned out in her shift", and took the initiative to put out a fire during a meeting with Privy Councillors; they should have had no difficulty with the Capulet scene.

Another problem with the claim that Shakespeare wrote as a country boy is his political sophistication as it was particularly spelled out by the renowned essayist William Hazlitt in the early nineteenth century, and has since been echoed by many scholar-politicians, even the orthodox. Hazlitt argued that studying *Coriolanus* alone would obviate the need for reading some of the standard political text books, and another dozen plays extend what is, in effect, Shakespeare's political teaching. Hazlitt's view has been confirmed by Headlam Wells in the new edition of his book *Shakespeare's Politics*. Some, realising Shakespeare was thoroughly informed on court practice, suggest Shakspere would have become familiar with the court and politics while acting in plays there. This is moonshine, like claiming a cathedral choirboy would become familiar with the life and work of a bishop.

Nearly half the history plays (*Henry VI, Parts 1, 2 and 3* and *Richard III*) had been written, even on the orthodox dating, before he could have had much if any experience of acting. Shapiro (2010) claimed Shakspere acted at Court "scores" of times. Yet the most any company acted there between 1588 and 1592 when that tetralogy was complete was on four occasions. Acting at Court would not explain how he came to understand the conflicts of private and public functions, of personal wishes and public demands, as found in, say, Prince Hal (an aspect not in Byrne's remit).

Given Shakespeare wrote on social matters in a manner totally unexpected from a country boy, it is futile to try to prove he was a man from a country town (and possibly Shakspere) by quoting, say, his knowledge of flowers or of the shape of a glover's paring knife. Whether Shakespeare had been a country-town boy, yeoman-farmer's boy, or son of a big estate, he would have known the country, but his attitudes and knowledge seem very much to derive from somewhere other than where Shakspere grew up.

Miscellaneous Myths

A recent and complex attempt to forge a link between Shakspere and Shakespeare indicates how the process of fabrication carries on. This starts with the discredited anecdote (see Chapter 7), that the birth of poet-laureate Sir William Davenant in 1606 was the result of adultery between his mother Jane and Shakspere. She was then twenty-eight and he forty-two. Now, because the date generally guessed for the play *Antony and Cleopatra* by the orthodox is also 1606, and the ages of the lovers Cleopatra and Antony at the time of the play's action were twenty-eight and forty-three, it has been claimed that Shakespeare must have written the play to celebrate the "success" of his fictional adulterous liaison with Jane Davenant. Speculative, indeed nonsensical, as all that is, one must expect to see it used in future to "prove" Shakespeare was Shakspere and Davenant was his bastard son.

Some earlier stratgems designed to fit Shakspere up as Shakespeare have been discussed previously, like changing Aubrey's notes to "prove" Shakspere could write, or claiming Thomas Russell of Rushock was second overseer of Shakspere's will, or the five inventions related to the Belott-v-Mountjoy case. We will not go over those here, but we will consider two of the many epitaphs that have been fathered on Shakespeare.

As seems usual, these were attributed to Shakespeare or had his name written onto them as pure conjecture or just for mischief. It is reported, for example, and regularly repeated that there was an epitaph on the Stratford tomb of John Combe that, attributed to Shakespeare, insulted him as a moneylender. If this were true, then it would be good evidence that Shakespeare was not Combe's moneylending friend, William Shakspere, who left his sword to Combe's nephew and was himself left a legacy by Combe. However, it was just a common piece of doggerel that was used for many usurers – see *EKC*.

Another such epitaph that a few orthodox biographers have tried to use as evidence for Shakspere being Shakespeare is a handwritten copy of an epitaph to an Elias James to which the name "Wm Shakespeare" has been added. No one pretends that name is in Shakspere's handwriting, and Malone, who found the epitaph, judged it to be "un-Shakespearean". Schoenbaum rated it "dismayingly pedestrian". Most scholars put it aside as another obvious misattribution, especially since no epitaphs that are reliably Shakespeare's have ever been found. Yet Honan (1998) suggested that the poor quality of the epitaph might have been because Shakespeare *"knew when to write less than brilliant verse"*, which echoes claims that Shakespeare wrote a tatty verse for a tatty gravestone in Stratford's church so the sexton could understand it. The enthusiasm for this epitaph went orbital – for some – when Professor Hotson found an Elias James had lived in London near Blackfriar's Theatre, who, having died in 1610, acquired a posthumous brother-in-law in 1613 named John Jackson, the same (common) name as a trustee for Shakspere's purchase of the Blackfriar's Gatehouse. Yet there is no evidence this James was the James of the epitaph; no evidence he ever knew his brother-in-law; no evidence that the brother-in-law was "Shakspere's Jackson". But there is plenty of evidence that the epitaph was not written by Shakespeare. It might surprise one to learn that this epitaph has been said to be the most likely of all such items to have been by Shakespeare – if one did not know just how pathetic is the evidence for all the others. Put it down to more desperation.

Finally in this chapter we examine the use of some Sonnets as evidence for Shakspere being Shakespeare, besides No. 145 discussed above. First in this context are three so-called "Will" Sonnets, Nos. 135, 136 and 143, which are used to imply the author's name was Will because, between them, they repeat the word "will" or "Will" twenty-two times. Yet, Lee (1916) carefully showed these Sonnets, un-Shakespearean in style and content, were probably among those the publisher Thorpe added as make-weights, like Sonnet No. 145 which followed them. Lee showed they were poor examples of a bawdy poetry that punned on the word "will" in its then sense of the female, as well as the male, sex organ, with other senses of "will" mixed in. Lee's analysis is universally approved but does not stop some biographers talking as if these Sonnets were evidence for "Will" Shakspere being Shakespeare. Also, in Elizabeth's time, Will was a regular nickname for a poet, being used, for example, for both Sir Philip Sidney and Edward de Vere, Seventeenth Earl of Oxford; so it could not identify a particular poet if it identified one at all.

The second point about the Sonnets here is that, although they have been claimed to be autobiographical and show us what Shakespeare was like, the temptation to see in them what one wants to see is often too strong. Some scholars will assume they were by Shakspere and then interpret them and manipulate them (and their dates) to fit him as the writer, ignoring whatever is inconvenient and using their results to support the Shakspere myth. Other scholars, with different Shakespeare candidates to support, will do exactly the same thing. However, a neutral analysis of the Sonnets seems to show an author who liked both sexes, gave advice on marriage to a young person, had fluent command of legal terms, disliked being forced by his/her social position to dissemble, may have been physically lame, was self-regarded as old and of superior class, and did not oversee the Sonnets' publication. That may not look like Shakspere, but some orthodox scholars have recently decided the Sonnets should not be treated as autobiographical: some hope. An attempt to date the Sonnets later than they were is looked at in Appendix F.

In an attempt to connect Shakspere to Shakespeare, the Sonnets are sometimes linked to an odd poem, *Willobie his Avisa*, mentioned in Chapter 11. This was called an *"insubstantial witness"* by Brown and *"elusive"* by Schoenbaum and is ignored by most biographers, but it is used by some to insult Shakspere falsely: so see Appendix H.

In this chapter, we have reviewed and dismissed "evidence" that has been invented or distorted to try to get people to believe Shakspere was Shakespeare. Such evidence is also frequently used as padding in biographies, but it goes way beyond simple speculation and could make a good research study in itself.

Chapter 15

How do we know Shakspere was not Shakespeare?

Particularly in the previous two chapters, but also elsewhere, we have shown how numerous attempts have been made to distort, invent or forge "evidence" to help prove that William Shakspere was the writer Shakespeare. It just does not work. But, as a London judge said in 1964 of scholars who had given evidence to try to block a bequest to the Francis Bacon Society, it was not that they thought their evidence proved Shakspere was Shakespeare, but that they saw no reason to doubt it. (The judge, Mr Justice Wilberforce, ruled that the bequest – made to help clarify who the author actually was – should stand.)

We know there is a "vertiginous" gap between that which one would expect to find if Shakspere were Shakespeare and the great nothing that has actually been found, but it should be no surprise there is also cumulative, even categoric, evidence that he never was. Readers will judge for themselves whether the evidence presented here can simply be dismissed, as some claim, as the product of snobbery or prejudice.

The theory that Shakspere was Shakespeare will be seen to come up against items of evidence which each, on the balance of probabilities, reduces its chance of being correct but, when put together, make it appear wholly untenable. For example, just contrast the Warwickshire-man Michael Drayton with Shakspere: he got his coat of arms easily – not Shakspere; had several patrons – not Shakspere; was in Shakspere's son-in-law's notes as a writer – not Shakspere; died broke - not Shakspere; as a poet, was made Esquire of the Bath (one of the highest orders of chivalry) – as a player, Shakspere was made Groom of the Chamber.

Yet there are pieces of evidence which are so strong that each by itself can be considered enough to prove William Shakspere of Stratford could not possibly have been the writer Shakespeare. Most scholars will be aware of some if not all of these defining pieces of evidence, but they tend to get swept under the carpet. Here we begin with nine of them.

Some Defining Evidence that Shakspere was not Shakespeare

• Take for instance the case when the Queen ordered the arrest of the author of the play *Richard II*, and her agents could not find him. Shakspere was not questioned over the matter at all, not even when other members of his acting troupe were. The Queen went as far as ordering that the author of a book on Henry IV, John Hayward, be put to the rack to extract from him the identity of the writer Shakespeare, so desperate was she, but the man behind that pseudonym was not uncovered. It is impossible that he was Shakspere writing openly, as orthodox scholars claim. A member of Parliament, Peter Wentworth, was sent to the Tower by Elizabeth simply for raising the question of her successor, and died there in 1596. It does not need much imagination to guess what might have happened to Shakspere if he had been the author of *Richard II*. In a dangerous age, it was pseudonymous writers like Shakespeare who were safest from arrest and other detriment (see pp. 136–7).

• As we have already discussed in Chapter 14, the accent and dialect in Shakespeare's works were not from Stratford-upon-Avon. Yet, as Shakspere was born and raised there, learning his language from his family and fellows for over twenty years, the local language would have been a fundamental part of what he spoke and wrote. The language of the works of Shakespeare is hard evidence he was not Shakspere.

• When, in 1635, Cuthbert Burbage made petition to the Lord Chamberlain, Philip Herbert, a dedicatee of the First Folio, it involved a matter of financial importance to the Globe. In aid of his petition, he called on the name, among others, of the dead William Shakspere [*sic*] whom he described as a "player". He would have had to name him as "Shakespeare" and remind Herbert of his wonderful plays, if that was who he was: that is how things were done. This statement is so damning that one scholar tried to dismiss Burbage as *"a pizzle-pated old boy"*; yet there is no evidence he was at all infirm and, anyway, the petition was not his alone. In another case, Cuthbert Burbage referred to *"those deserving men Shakspere, Heminges, Condell, Phillips and others"*, "men" in this case meaning players. This is all solid testimony Shakspere was not Shakespeare.

• Dr John Hall, William Shakspere's son-in-law, wrote short pieces on hundreds of his patients with a view to publication. Most were post-1616, but not all, and he would have had time to include Shakespeare. He particularly noted those who contributed to literature, such as a man who published a French dictionary, the Countess of Northampton (a patron of writers), and Michael Drayton. Yet he left no record of his supposedly much more famous father-in-law – and he cannot have been prevented by his Puritanical views, as some have suggested, since he wrote about others involved with the arts. There was much Hall would have been expected to do if his father-in-law was Shakespeare – about his books, his manuscripts, his publications, his fame, etc. – and the fact Hall did nothing is as good as sworn testimony that he was not. Hall could easily have produced an authoritative and saleable biography of Shakespeare if the latter had been Shakspere, for he would have known the details of his life and work if anybody did.

• When the scholar Henry Peacham wrote his 1622 book *The Complete Gentleman*, he named the seven greatest deceased writers of the Elizabethan era. He was steeped in literary knowledge as his father had been before him, and his list would have been reliable. The seven he gave were Edward, Earl of Oxford, Lord Buckhurst, Lord Paget, Sir Philip Sidney, Sir Edward Dyer, Edmund Spenser and Samuel Daniel. The order of these seven may have been determined by social precedence but it is obvious all classes were included on merit. It is equally obvious the list does not include the name Shakespeare, which indicates either that the writer behind the pseudonym was still alive when Peacham compiled the list, or that his real name was unknown, or that he was one of the named seven. Whichever alternative was correct, Peacham has unequivocally informed us that William Shakspere was not Shakespeare.

• As we have pointed out at length, William Shakspere would have been bound to name himself as the playwright-poet Shakespeare in his quest for his coat of arms if he could have done so; and, if he had, he would have ensured that when his father died in 1601 he would have had the title "Gent." or "Gentleman". That he did not claim to be a poet using the name Shakespeare even when insulted as an "undeserving person" by the College of Heralds because he was a player, clearly indicates he was not Shakespeare.

• The Shakspere Coat of Arms was used prominently on the ambiguous Stratford Monument to identify it firmly as being meant for William Shakspere. That was perfectly legal. Yet it was omitted from the First Folio when, by its use, Jonson would have ensured the author was unambiguously identified as the unlikely Shakspere, and that indicates that he knew that it would be illegal, which is good evidence Shakespeare was not Shakspere.

• The analysis of the so-called "signatures" of William Shakspere given in Chapter 10 has proved beyond doubt what is well known from much other evidence: he could not write, and so could not have been Shakespeare.

• In 1598, the literary Londoners and future clerics, Joseph Hall and John Marston (a colleague of Jonson's), identified the name "Shakespeare" as a pseudonym, but not for Shakspere. Their conclusion had been preempted by, *inter alia*, the author of *Oenone and Paris* in 1593. It was confirmed by, *inter alia*, John Benson (with his scornful comments in 1640 on Jonson's dedicatory poem and the portrait he used in the First Folio), and by the original purchaser of what is now the Glasgow University copy of the First Folio (who indicated it was a deception used to pass off the player named as "William Shakespeare" in the list of players in the First Folio as a playwright or play maker).

Readers may decide those nine are enough but they might easily make up that number to ten (or more) by identifying for themselves other items of evidence from earlier in this book which they see as comparable obstacles to the theory that Shakspere was Shakespeare. The deceptions used by Jonson in the First Folio to pass off Shakspere as Shakespeare come in that category, with nonentities being used to draw the portrait and write additional elegies instead of volunteer celebrities.

Then there are the areas of expertise or knowledge identified by Spurgeon and others in Shakespeare's works, for which there is no evidence they were possessed by, or even could have been possessed by, Shakspere: some may think that "*vertiginous*" gap – Schoenbaum's word for the difference between what we know of Shakspere and what we deduce for Shakespeare – is enough on its own to tell us that Shakspere did not write the plays. One might also think that the way Shakspere used his own name and never used Shakespeare (or Shake-speare), and vice-versa, would convince any jury they were two men, not one.

The Missing Evidence of Authorship

To distract attention from the mis-match between Shakspere and the writer Shakespeare, and the absence of records of an actual person named Shakespeare writing around 1600, orthodox writers often try to claim "more is known about Shakespeare" than about any other writer of the time except Jonson, when they mean "known about Shakspere". Yet the records in our Appendix I show that what was found about Shakspere in the great searches *c.* 1900 (and earlier) make it more difficult to believe he was Shakespeare, not less. As Professor Trevor Roper put it,

> [Shakspere] has been subjected to the greatest battery of organised research that has ever been directed on a single person.

Dozens of man and woman-years were spent turning over every available archive, library, diary, commentary and location that might have yielded something to show Shakspere of Stratford was a writer. Yet, in all the documents and detail discovered about him, not a thing was found to show he could write, let alone that he was Shakespeare. That by itself should deal the myth a fatal blow. For those who undertook that prodigious search, it was not just like looking for a black cat in a dark room, but for one that simply was not there. Trevor Roper noted that one-percent of the effort expended on Shakspere would have yielded a substantial literary biography for any minor writer of the time, though it yielded a great nothing for Shakspere and the hidden Shakespeare.

To clarify the really serious problem disclosed in that previous paragraph, Price (2000) identified ten headings, indicated in bold below, under which a professional poet-playwright, as Shakspere has been deemed to be, might have left something behind for biographers to use; the stuff they depend on, like letters, manuscripts (MSS), diary entries, etc. Then she took Shakespeare's twenty-four nearest rivals as comparators for Shakspere. Of course, one would not expect to find all twenty-four rivals left something under all ten headings, but on average they left something under six, and all left us enough to be sure they were writers writing under their own names. But nothing was found for Shakspere.

(i) **Evidence of Education.** There was none for Shakspere. Orthodox scholars say he "must" have gone to school but there is no evidence he or any of his brothers did, and none that he or they could write, not even their names (see Chapters 4 and 10). Someone said there is no evidence for Jonson's education either, but they cannot have looked. Of course, we know Shakespeare was educated but that does not help with Shakspere.

(ii) **Evidence of Correspondence.** None for Shakspere or someone named Shakespeare. We have no letters written by him on matters literary or anything else, and the only letter known to have been written to him was in his role as a moneylender and was not sent (see Chapter 10).

(iii) **Evidence of Payment for Writing.** None for Shakspere. Some will say Shakespeare must have been paid by Southampton for the poems dedicated to him, but there is no evidence for such payment to any one named either Shakespeare or Shakspere.

(iv) **Evidence of having a Patron.** None for Shakspere. *Venus and Adonis* and *The Rape of Lucrece* were dedicated to Southampton, but there is no evidence he supported or even knew Shakspere, or was patron to a person with the name Shakespeare.

(v) **Evidence of MSS in the writer's own handwriting.** None for Shakspere. Some say a minor passage in the play *Sir Thomas More* is in Shakspere's writing, but it is not – see Appendix E. Some say that minor passage might have been handwritten by its author and that the author might be Shakespeare but, even if both those "mights" could be removed, it would not tell us who "Shakespeare" was or anything about

Shakspere.

(vi) Evidence of the writer receiving, sending or keeping handwritten accounts, receipts, etc. relevant to him as a writer. There is none for Shakspere or anyone named Shakespeare. This is not the same as correspondence. It could be any document relevant to the writer as a writer. Fifteen of the twenty-four rivals, 62%, had separate documents under this heading indicating they were writers.

(vii) Evidence of commendatory verses, etc. composed for the writer's individual literary works at the time of writing, or similar material that he had written for others. None for Shakspere or Shakespeare. No one wrote poems for a Shakespeare work before it was published so that they could be bound in with the work, as happened for others who wrote under their own names. For Shakespeare, praise written for his work was always after the event, not at the time of publication, and even then it was about the work and never for him personally. Nothing was written by Shakespeare (or Shakspere) to praise or support the work of anyone else. Yet 83% of Shakespeare's rivals had an entry under this heading.

(viii) Evidence of the writer being identified as a writer during his lifetime. Nothing identified Shakspere of Stratford as a writer during his lifetime. Things were written showing it was known someone was writing as Shakespeare but not that he was a known person. It was the same with George Eliot: people wrote of the books written under that name as if her books were by a man – until Marian Evans was unmasked. Things written about the works of a disembodied "Shakespeare" cannot be said to be written for a man Shakspere of Stratford. Yet *all* twenty-four rivals had an entry under this heading.

(ix) Evidence of books the writer had bought, borrowed, been given or had written in. None for Shakspere or a person named Shakespeare. Ten of the twenty-four rivals, that is 40% of them, had entries under this heading. Someone at some time wrote "W Shakspere" in a careful hand on the title page of a book, *Archaianomia*, but it cannot be shown to have been owned by, read by or used by our Shakspere or Shakespeare (see Chapter 10).

(x) Evidence that the writer's death had been noted in writing as that of a writer within twelve months of his death. None for Shakspere or Shakespeare. Of the twenty-four rivals, 40% have an entry here. A poem supposedly written by William Basse, one that mentioned the date of Shakspere's death, is naturally quoted by orthodox scholars as an elegy to him: yet it has been shown to be a scam written after 1620 (see Chapter 13).

Some scholars try to escape the problems posed by Price's analysis, by insisting that anyone who ever wrote about works written over the name Shakespeare should be taken as referring to a known man Shakespeare. That method was made much of by Professor Alan Nelson on his website. If this were applied to "George Eliot", it would prove a man of that name wrote the novels of Marian Evans. He argued, for example, that a Leonard Digges showed he knew a man Shakespeare because, in a letter he wrote about sonnets, he used the words *"our Will Shakespeare"*. Yet Milton (born 1608) wrote, after 1623, *"What needs my Shakespear for his honoured bones"*, and he did not know him personally. Goldsmith was not saying he knew the very-much-alive Edmund Burke personally when he wrote *"Here lies our good Edmund whose genius was such . . ."*. One finds many such examples that negate Nelson's claim. Digges's letter was a literary exercise, just as Milton's was, and tells us that he knew of Shakespeare's work but nothing else. The idea that Digges knew Shakspere in Stratford has been dealt with elsewhere (see Chapter 11).

Shapiro (2010) tried to use a note in a book, *George a Greene*, which it seems belonged to Sir George Buck, Master of the Revels 1610–1622, to get a link to the man "Shakespeare". It reads *"Written by ——— a minister, who ac the piners* [sic] *part himself. Teste W. Shak^{e}spe^a"*. This is omitted from *SDL*, *OCS*, and Halliday's records of Shakespeare and Shakspere; and gets no comment in *EKC*. Nelson, who had studied this note, did not use it to try to contradict Price. There seems good reason. Many had already handled this book without noting that compressed *W. Shak^{e}spe^a* when, in 1825, it was passed to J. P. Collier, the great Shakespeare forger; and the next person to open the book found it. That might explain why the name is compressed and looks to be in different writing from the original sentence, and it rather undermines Shapiro's fable that it showed Buck knew a man W. Shakespeare. Shapiro also tried out another neglected annotation, this one in a book owned by a Richard Hunt who, after 1620, was vicar of Bishop's Itchington, ten miles from Stratford. This referred to Shakspere as *"our Roscius"*. Shapiro implied this meant he was known to be something in the theatre, but, since Roscius was a Roman actor, it did not imply he was a writer.

Given the great search for material on Shakspere and the variety of his activities, one would expect more to have been found on him under Price's ten headings – if he had been Shakespeare – than on any of his rivals. But quite the opposite. Jonson left something under all ten, and Daniel, Harvey, Nashe and Peele each left something under nine. At the other end of this scale was John Webster, a man thought of as the most elusive major Elizabethan author (apart from Shakespeare); he only scored in three categories, though they clearly identify him as a man writing under his own name. It has been said that Price was too generous to Shakespeare's rivals yet, for Webster, she ruled out as evidence of education his own mention of being born "free" of the Merchant Taylor's Company, which, in his case, implied "free to go to their school". She did the same with a 1598 entry of a "John Webster" at the Inns of Court which perfectly fitted the playwright at age twenty. Orthodox scholars might consider selling their souls to find such things for Shakspere.

One would think the absence of some of the items under Price's headings for both Shakespeare and Shakspere would be sufficient to give orthodox scholars a sense of despair. The accounts and memoranda of the theatre impresario Philip Henslowe – *Henslowe's Diaries* as they are called – consist of hundreds of pages mentioning all aspects of theatre business from 1594 to 1604, including the names of numerous writers in various contexts. They show, for example, twenty payments to Dekker in 1599 alone, but nothing to a Shakespeare or Shakspere. Henslowe's son-in-law, top actor Edward Alleyn, also kept a detailed diary of the theatre, with the same result. Even if they were not friends, the Richard Field who printed Shakespeare's major poems must have known Shakspere in Stratford, but there was no hint from him that he knew either Shakespeare or Shakspere, let alone knew Shakspere in London as a writer.

Orthodox scholars may, of course, try to explain away the missing information under each of Price's headings by inventions and assumed coincidences, but every coincidence that has to be assumed and every invention that has to be created makes it more difficult to believe Shakspere was Shakespeare – and there has to be many of them. One item often picked out as capable of being explained away is the lack of Shakespeare manuscripts (MSS). It will be said that, because the MSS of over four-fifths of plays in Elizabethan times were lost, it would be the same for Shakspere. But not so. Half of Shakespeare's plays were not in print when the First Folio appeared and some not performed, which means some of the MSS for his plays must have been preserved in handwritten form for well over thirty years before they were printed – and then they vanished. People like the First Folio printers, or Ben Jonson, or senior King's Man Cuthbert Burbage (if he had seen them), would have known their value; and yet they vanished, while forty percent of Shakespeare's rivals left at least one MS to be found. The easiest explanation for their disappearance at a time when their commercial value would have been very high, is that they could have given away their author's secret.

In like manner, attempts to explain why no eulogies or elegies were written for Shakspere when he died fail abysmally. Such poems were commonly written at the time of death for the most famous achievers, including writers, and Shakspere would have qualified, had he been Shakespeare. His name would have been kept fresh in the years up to 1616. Nelson has protested at Price's one year cut-off for an elegy as though Shakespeare needed special pleading. Forty percent of his rivals had had elegies written for them within a year of their deaths as would be expected, none has been found written later than a year after the event, yet none was written for Shakspere. Some scholars have tried to say that Shakspere would have had no elegies written for him because, as Shakespeare, he was not yet really famous. Yet more of his plays were put on at Court between 1603 and 1616 than of any other playwright. But no one used Shakspere's death as a commercial excuse for printing new quarto editions of Shakepeare's plays. We will return to this whole scenario when we look further at the silence of Dr Hall and the absence of a burial in Westminster Abbey.

One can liken the explanations given by scholars for why all the Shakespeare evidence is missing to those of a doctor who, having diagnosed a patient with some disease, refuses to accept he may be wrong even when all the tests for it prove negative. One attempt to get rid of what one might call the "Price problem" is the claim that, by adopting Price's technique, one could show no Elizabethan writer was a real person. Any reader who believes that will believe anything.

In addition to Price's ten areas, there are two others that give zero results for Shakspere that are strange considering the stories of friendships claimed for him in orthodox biographies. One is the absence of records of connections between a Shakespeare or a Shakspere and other writers, many of whom are habitually referred to as his friends. There are records of connections between many writers of the time: Bacon, Beaumont, Breton, Browne (William), Camden, Chapman, Daniel, Day, Dekker, Drayton, Field (Nathan), Fletcher (John), Ford, Greene, Greville, Harvey, Heywood, Jonson, Kyd, Lyly, Marlowe, Marston, Massinger, Middleton, Munday, Nashe, Peele, Raleigh, Rowley (Samuel), Rowley (William), Sidney (Mary), Sidney (Philip), Spenser, Watson, Webster, Wilkins. Some of these lived together, some worked together, some had their names on plays together, some quarrelled publicly, some got into trouble together and even went to prison together. Dekker worked with seven of them plus four minor writers. Jonson had acolytes known as "The Sons of Ben".

Biographers regularly write pages about Shakespeare being a close friend of other writers but have no evidence to support the stories. No writer twitted Shakespeare on his menial background as was done with others like Marlowe and Harvey (and could have happened with him, if he had been Shakspere). Other writers do refer to Shakespeare the writer, but never as if they knew him personally. Some may have added to or revised his plays – Middleton with *Timon of Athens* and *Macbeth*, for example, or John Fletcher with *Henry VIII* – but not at the time he was writing and never in personal contact with him. It will be

171

said they "collaborated", meaning worked together, but the evidence says they always worked separately. To supply this lack of connections to Shakespeare the writer, there has even been resort to unfounded anecdotes or inventions. Shapiro (2010), for example, noted that several writers contributed poems to a collection, *The Phoenix and Turtle* in 1601, one of which was doubtfully attributed to Shakespeare; and he claimed that they all must have worked together. Yet that would not hold up, even if nine of the other thirteen poems were not also over pseudonyms, e.g., "Ignoto" and "Vatum Chorus". The poem attributed to Shakespeare does not even fit the theme of the collection and could not have been agreed by the others. Besides which, it is like nothing else he wrote.

One anecdote that frequently turns up, relates Shakspere's death to a drinking bout in Stratford – "a merry meeting" – with Jonson and Drayton. There are good reasons why that story is rejected. It first appeared long after Shakspere's death and has no evidence to support it. Jonson, a heavy drinker, seriously disliked Drayton, who was famously abstemious. Jonson wrote an epigram for his *"friend M. Drayton"* and then, gratuitously and rudely, criticised him in it. And, of course, if Jonson and Drayton had been the cause of Shakspere's death, the claim that no one was in a position to write an elegy for him in 1616, or to alert the Dean of Westminster to the opportunity of burying him in poet's corner, would look even weaker – if that were possible.

Many anecdotes exist about Jonson and Shakspere or Shakespeare, and all are weak. One of these concerns wit contests between them that sound more like half-wit contests. One has Jonson beginning his own epitaph *"Here lies Benjamin Jonson"* which Shakespeare is supposed to have turned into: *"Here lies Benjamin with short hair upon his chin, who while he lived was a slow thing – and now he's buried is no thing"*. One gets a feeling of biographical desperation. The person – Thomas Plume, born 1631 – who reported this particular contest also "reported" a conversation at Stratford between John Shakspere and a Sir John Mennes, although the only Sir John Mennes on record was under two when John Shakspere died.

To Price's blank sheet for Shakespeare and Shakspere one can add the absence of any descriptions of either. Not all his "top" twenty-four rivals had personal descriptions left about them, but a fair number did. In 1619, the Scots poet William Drummond left a record of what Jonson told him about Shakespeare with nothing in it to indicate knowledge of the man himself. Yet Jonson wrote of the physical appearance of other writers, about their relatives, activities, foibles, blemishes and personal problems. When he said of Shakespeare *"I loved the man"* he admitted it was *"to justify my candour"*, the candour of his criticisms: see Appendix H.

Our knowledge of Shakspere, if one wants to think of him as Shakespeare, is insufficient to connect him to any women who might have been the inspiration for characters such as Beatrice (*Much Ado About Nothing*), Cressida (*Troilus and Cressida*), and Olivia (*Twelfth Night*) who hold dominating feminine roles in their respective plays to an extent no other playwright managed. Two-thirds of Shakespeare's remaining plays had parts for women among their three largest roles. There are some female roles that are comparable in terms of length in the plays of rivals – the eponymous heroines of *The Duchess of Malfi* (Webster), *Dido, Queen of Carthage* (Marlowe), *Patient Grissil* (Dekker) and *'Tis Pity She's a Whore* (Ford), for example – but not as demanding or with the same lustre and status, and women do not appear in equivalent supporting roles. Whole books have been written about women Shakspere *must* have known in London, especially candidates for the "Dark Lady" who appears to be a subject in the last twenty or so of the Sonnets, but no evidence to support even one of them has ever been found. O'Connor (1991) admitted the problem when he said:

> ultimately he [meaning Shakspere] has only his family and his neighbours and friends to write about.

Though we know no more about Shakspere's family and friends than we really do about the character of Shakspere himself, O'Connor felt driven to turn Petruchio and Kate in *The Taming of the Shrew* into Shakspere and Anne Hathaway (two people who are largely blanks to us, *pace* Dr Greer). That may seem desperate, but no worse than when someone else felt they had to assume that Shakspere's mother, Mary Arden, was the model for the ambitious and murderous Lady Macbeth.

Some biographies of "Shakespeare" tell their readers there is no problem about him leaving not a "wrack" behind; not a book or a letter; not a note about him in someone's diary; not a reminiscence about his activities as a writer or potential writer from someone who actually knew him; not an elegy for a friend or colleague or rival written over the name Shakespeare or Shakspere. Yet this is escapism. If one treats Price's data simply as a statistical exercise, one would conclude that the chance of Shakspere, if he was Shakespeare, leaving us nothing would be many thousands to one against. Even John Taylor (1580–1653), the "Water Poet" who came nowhere near to being qualified for Price's group of the best twenty-four rivals to Shakespeare, left enough behind (without any great searching) to give us a literary and human biography.

The weight of evidence we have gone through so far may have left some readers needing a pause. However, they might already have guessed that no case as devastating as the one presented here against the candidacy of Shakspere can be made for any of the other serious candidates for Shakespeare. As light relief, one can illustrate this by going back to the court case mentioned in the opening paragraph of this chapter. In it, one orthodox scholar gave evidence that there were distinct differences between the writings of Francis Bacon and those of Shakespeare. Yet this was an admission that Bacon had left written material known to be his for comparison, evidence which is totally absent for Shakspere.

It may surprise readers that there are yet more items of evidence to shake the orthodox theory to the core, even if all are not quite so definitive as the nine with which the chapter began. As we have mentioned, the weakness of the Shakspere myth is thrown into sharp relief by research like that of Spurgeon (1935) on the range of specialised knowledge Shakespeare used in his plays. This encompassed, for instance, his use of original sources in Latin, French, Italian, Spanish and Greek; his use of military and naval technicalities; his ease with history (English and European) and with classical scholarship and mythology; his knowledge of the Bible and of astronomy and astrology, medicine, philosophy and politics; his familiarity with hunting and falconry, with horticulture and even with bias-bowls. To make out that Shakespeare's knowledge and experience in those matters was available to Shakspere requires very special pleading. He might have known something about some of them, but it becomes ever more difficult, as the number of such instances grows, to accept that he could have left us absolutely no trace of his personal familiarity, or even of the sources of his familiarity, with any of them.

Not all the problems posed by Shakespeare's special knowledge can be mentioned here, though some have been touched on earlier, but we can give enough to provide tests not just for Shakspere to meet, but for all other candidates proposed as the writer Shakespeare. And one cannot accept a view that says Shakspere could do anything Shakespeare could do simply "because he was Shakespeare".

Here we treat eight specific problems of specialised knowledge.

1. The Circulation of Blood

The first of our items of special knowledge, usually omitted from biographies, occurs in the opening scene of *Coriolanus* (I.i.125–158) where Shakespeare cleverly wrapped up Dr William Harvey's revolutionary theory of the circulation of the blood within Menenius's exposition of what is known as "the fable of the belly". This may not seem a major matter at first; however, the theory was not fully published until 1628 and it was only revealed partially outside his intimate circle when Harvey gave a lecture to invited guests in 1619, after Shakspere was dead. There is no reliable evidence of when *Coriolanus* was written, but Harvey's closely guarded research would hardly have been accessible to Shakspere. Harvey was physician to royalty and to other senior figures in the aristocracy and government, and may have confided his thoughts to people in that circle, but it was a circle in which Shakspere did not move. The normal response of orthodox biographers to this problem seems to be to ignore it entirely. Schoenbaum simply said

> Coriolanus contains an allusion to the circulation of the blood, although Harvey did not publish his discovery until 1619,

but he gave no suggestion how Shakspere could have known of it. Claims that have been made, that Harvey's theory was not original, will not stand up, as Schoenbaum knew – see Marbi-Ibañez (1965) – and it was clearly Harvey's theory to which Shakespeare referred. Similarly, the idea of someone passing notes of Harvey's theory for Shakspere to use in a play puts us in the realm of fantasy. But Shakespeare was sufficiently briefed on the theory that he was able so to wrap it up in his play that nobody who was not close to Harvey would have realised what they were being told. He even made an off-hand joke about the big toe always going first but being the last to get its blood, which adds to the sense of someone not just knowing, but confidently knowing, the subject.

2. Marlowe's Inquest

Another neglected problem for the theory that Shakspere was Shakespeare is the inclusion in *As You Like It* of a reference to the coroner's report on the death of Marlowe on 30th May 1593. Shakespeare mentioned a dead poet in the play by using the conventional term "dead shepherd", and identified him as Marlowe by quoting his line from *Hero and Leander* – "*Who ever loved who loved not at first sight?*" He followed that quotation with reference to a man being killed by "*a great reckoning in a little room*" (where "little room" was an echo from Marlowe's *Jew of Malta*).

Shakespeare therefore knew that the coroner's report said Marlowe had died during a dispute over a "reckoning" – the adding up of a bill – a fact not known publicly until Professor Hotson found the report in the archives in 1925. Shakespeare was clearly among the few people who knew of that report in the 1590s, but, given the secrecy that surrounded it, such a group would hardly have included Shakspere or anyone who would have talked to him about it. Yet nobody but Shakespeare publicly mentioned the term "reckoning" in connection with Marlowe's death before 1925, while today it is the term most used.

3. Falconry

A third problem often overlooked is Shakespeare's understanding of falconry. In Shakspere's lifetime, this sport was strictly controlled as far as its pursuit by different social classes was concerned, while its technical language was "owned" by the trainers of the birds, the falconers, and not readily learned from books. Much has been written on Shakespeare's knowledge in this field and, for simplicity, it is useful to quote analysis by the staunchly orthodox Ackroyd:

> The language of falconry becomes almost [Shakespeare's] private possession. One book upon his imagery fills no fewer than eight pages with his references to trained hawks and hawking, to the 'check' and the 'quarry', the 'haggard' and the 'jesse'. There are 80 separate technical allusions to the sport in his published writings, whereas there are few in the work of any other dramatist.

Beyond that, articles by Maurice Pope (1991) and others make it clear that the areas of falconry drawn on by Shakespeare were not those accessible to lower levels of society. It is often said that what we read about falconry is Shakspere's experience "probably picked up in his youth". Yet there is no evidence he left home in his youth to work in a family of rank where he would have learnt this subject, and references to it in the plays begin early with *The Taming of the Shrew*.

Shakespeare referred in his works to dozens of birds, but he treated none with the detail and precision he reserved for hawks, and Spurgeon treats falcons as being in a class apart among his "bird" allusions. It might have been expected Shakspere, if he had been Shakespeare, would have rather used allusions to hunting or poaching or possibly fishing. Yet the allusions in the works from, say, fishing that one might have expected if Shakespeare was Shakspere, given the opportunities in the latter's environment, are not there: the ones we do have hardly go beyond the banal, like "angling" for something, or to "bait" something; the references to field sports in the plays concentrate on falconry instead.

4. The Court at Nérac

The play *Love's Labour's Lost* is a fourth real problem for orthodox theory. In it, Shakespeare used historical events from the closed Court of Henry of Navarre at Nérac, and French and English scholars have been convinced his knowledge came direct from that Court, though it was not easy for just anyone to gain access. Whoever wrote the play, if without information at first hand, would have had to spend time close to, or have had detailed reports from, someone who did. The importance of this point is seen from the way it has been made a reason, mainly by historians and Shakespeare scholars in France, for believing the sixth Earl of Derby, William Stanley, was the writer Shakespeare, because he was one of the few people who might have got the necessary information at first hand. This involved such matters as a visit of a French Queen and her ladies in 1578, the Academy set up at the Court and a dispute between Henry of Navarre and the French King over 200,000 crowns (see Lefranc, 1919). Any candidate put forward to be Shakespeare needs to have had the means to get such knowledge, but nothing half-adequate has been suggested for Shakspere – see Greg, 1955.

5. The Law and Classical Scholarship

A fifth problem in this particular list is the way Shakespeare, in poems as well as plays, made use of the law, legal problems and legal terminology. As early as 1780, the lawyer Malone was so puzzled by this aspect of Shakespeare's works that he guessed Shakspere had worked as a legal clerk: his absence from the records meant he could not have had higher legal training but Malone suggested he might have taught law. Shakespeare's knowledge of the law is such a problem for the Shakspere myth that many orthodox biographers do not mention it, while those who do usually adopt the technique of pretending the problem is something quite different from what it really is. Lee (1916), for example, wrote that the

> theory that Shakespeare had been a legal clerk ... rests on no foundation save the circumstance that [he] frequently employed legal phraseology

which is just not so. Lee then tried to say Shakespeare's "law" was no different from, or better than, that of many other Elizabethan writers. Yet there have been some fifty books written on his law as a literary phenomenon and none about his rivals'. A 1993 survey (see Kornstein, 1994) showed Shakespeare was quoted in over eight hundred legal judgements in the USA, while the second most frequently quoted writer was the poet Milton with fifty-seven, and those whom Lee and others say were "better" than Shakespeare came nowhere. Of the play *Measure for Measure*, the orthodox Rossiter (1961) wrote "nobody questions justice is on trial", and similar views have been expressed of *The Merchant of Venice* where topical tensions between equity and contract law were exposed; nobody pays such compliments to Shakespeare's rivals. He did not just know "legal phraseology", he played with it, manipulated it, built on it

177

and created it, and it is unsurprising that there are university studies in "Shakespeare and the Law".

The problem for the Shakspere myth is not really the quantity of Shakespeare's legal usage but its quality, and the fact that, as Grant White (1959) put it, he used his law "as part and parcel of his thought". Keeton (1967), a lawyer who accepted the Shakspere myth, found himself writing things which just did not fit it. The Sonnets, he said,

> are possibly the richest in such [legal] references and the lawyer can only admire the richness of the imagery which these allusions create.

That is the sort of problem Shakespeare's law poses: his Sonnets absorbed from him more legal metaphors and allusions than were in all other sonnet sequences put together, including those of lawyer-poets like John Donne.

After noting that Shakespeare "impresses" with his "accurate use" of legal terms – using legal knowledge "near the surface of [his] inventive brain" – the orthodox Keeton quotes from Sonnet 13 (the legal terms in bold):

So should the beauty which you hold in **lease** */ Find no* **determination** ...

and asks, rather oddly in view of his orthodox stance,

> would he automatically, and so felicitously, have spoken of a lease's determination had he been completely innocent of legal education?

In the end, though, Keeton felt bound to find Shakespeare had no legal education because all attempts to trace any for Shakspere had totally failed. This paralleled Byrne when she felt she had to conclude Shakespeare lacked knowledge of court etiquette, when she had clearly shown he outdid his rivals. The same with *OCS* where, after noting

> Shakespeare's use of legal language and his fascination with the possibilities of law as a source of dramatic material

and noting how the plays related to *"the practice of arguing 'moots' in legal apprenticeships"*, it concluded *"it is unlikely that Shakespeare ever had such training himself"*, although the evidence it gave, and that of so many others, indicates that he must have done, even though Shakspere had none.

In desperation, some orthodox scholars who admit Shakespeare's use of law was exceptional, have sought banal explanations that their readers might swallow. Kornstein said he might have discussed his writings with legal experts. Yet his main and most impressive use of law is in non-legal situations. Romeo, at the high point of the play, sees Juliet apparently dead and says: *"Seal with a righteous kiss, a **dateless bargain** with **engrossing death**"* – three legal terms, and the audience totally gripped. That had to flow from the mind, not have come from a legal consultation. Similarly, in *All's Well that ends Well*, the rogue Paroles, believing himself under threat of death, betrays his Lord with

> For a cardecu [a quart of an écu] he will sell the **fee-simple** of his salvation, the **inheritance** of it, and cut the **entail** from all the **remainder**

Such a crazy use of law in an emotional situation had to be spontaneous.

Shakespeare's running legal jokes on Yorick's skull in *Hamlet* had to be his own. Kornstein mentioned how some writers took guidance from lawyers when writing of court cases; but Shakespeare would, as he did in *The Merchant*, build on the law, augment it and argue with it, not parrot it as others did. To distract his readers, Kornstein told them Shakespeare could not have been legally trained because, in *Henry VI Part 2*, he had a rebel say *"Kill all the lawyers."* But he also had one of the rebels say *"There shall be in England seven half-penny loaves sold for a penny"*, so he was hardly using them to express his own beliefs.

The orthodox Barton (1929) pointed out that Shakespeare must have got some of the law he used from books; but, when he compiled the list of abstruse texts he must have used, he found himself forced to the view that Shakespeare must have been a student at the Inns of Court in order to see them. There was particularly the case of Hales-v-Petit (1553), the arguments of which were so oddly, but carefully, used for the gravediggers' scene in *Hamlet*: this was only available in Norman-French. Shakespeare's attendance at the Inns of Courts' "moots" mentioned in *OCS* and seconded by Barton are consistent with the open acceptance by other orthodox writers like Brown (1949) of Shakespeare's legal training.

Failing to find an explanation of how Shakspere could have got Shakespeare's legal expertise, many orthodox scholars pretend that Robertson (1913) – on whom Shakespeare's brilliant use of law for metaphors, jokes, poetics and drama was wasted – "proved" Jonson and other rivals of Shakespeare used more law more accurately than he, not realising that this was not even the right problem. If an author wrote a play with a court case and numerous legal terms in it, with no literary impact, the bean-counting Robertson would rate it highly. He claimed Jonson outshone Shakespeare when he used a legal dictionary to produce a long string of legal terms – legal "mumbo jumbo" as one lawyer put it. When, for example, someone praised Shakespeare for Mistress

179

Page's exact use of the phrase "fine and recovery" in *The Merry Wives of Windsor*, Robertson thought to trump him with pages of examples where other authors had used the separate terms "fine" (a money payment) and "recovery" (regaining something lost), perhaps not knowing that "fine and recovery" was a phrase with a complex legal meaning all of its own involving a legal fiction or false assumption that the others did not use.

Another book admired by the orthodox is that of Clarkson and Warren (1968), which showed Elizabethan writers using as many legal words in the field of property law as Shakespeare, but reading it would give no idea of his brilliance in this whole area.

In their turn, Robertson and others quote Devecmon (1899), who set out to find errors in Shakespeare's law without even recognising when he was making legal jokes. Sprague (1902), whom the orthodox blank out, crunched each point made by Devecmon (who retracted some himself). One "error" he attributed to Shakespeare is his use of "heir apparent" in *Henry VI Part 2* instead of "heir presumptive", a term which did not exist until 1609. He even saw an "error" in Shylock's bond in *The Merchant* being called a "single bond", though a legal dictionary would have shown it to be exactly right.

Another instance of Shakespeare being accused of legal error treats of when he slotted into the play *King John* a brief analysis of the law as it would later affect the question of Edward IV's legitimacy which arose in *Richard III*. Yet Shakespeare's analysis in that case was exact, and it could not have been made up from general knowledge or found in some easily available source. To explain away such knowledge, Robertson came up with another oft-quoted fabrication: this one was that, in Shakspere's time, ordinary people would pick up law as regular spectators at courts. Yet, in truth, attendances at courts were only substantial for exciting cases, usually when hangings were expected; otherwise they were so sparse that it was often difficult to find any lay persons present to stand in for absent jury members, and officers of the courts had to be pressed into service (see J. Cockburn, 1977). Anyway, the material Shakespeare used was not that of the everyday courts where debt, criminal action, bye laws and such would dominate.

Writers who rely on Robertson and Devecmon and ignore those who have rebutted their claims, will not tell their readers of better references. It is preferable to rely on the professional approach of Sokol and Sokol (2001) for accounts of Shakespeare's brilliant legal usage, or N. Cockburn (1998).

Shakespeare's legal usage becomes a worse problem for the orthodox theory when it is noted he was one of few writers whose plays were performed in the Inns of Court. From 1590 to 1610, only one man who was known not to be a member of the Inns had his plays performed there; and he, George Chapman, had his lodgings in one of them. So the deduction has to be, given everything else, that Shakespeare was a member, and that rules out Shakspere.

One might ask, in respect of Shakespeare's plays being accepted at the Inns of Court, how the officers could have known he was a member if he was using a pseudonym; yet the plays carried their own message. Lawyers who attended the first performance of *Twelfth Night* in Middle Temple Hall in 1601, for example, would have spotted within minutes that the author could run off legal jokes an ordinary audience, and possibly the players themselves, would have missed. For example, in the third scene, Sir Toby Belch says of Olivia *"Let her except before excepted"* which echoes an abstruse Latin legal tag. John Bayley, in editing *Troilus and Cressida*, asked who one might think the play was written for, if it was not the Inns of Court? There are other plays, too, that ask that question.

Robertson also used his bean-counting method to "prove" Shakespeare had less classical scholarship than his rivals. This again depended on preferring quantity to quality. Burton (1621), writing under a pseudonym, criticised those who "lard their lean books with the fat of others' works". He would have despised Robertson for praising those who, in his phrase, were "stealing from Homer". One follower of Robertson criticised the lack of conventional classical allusions in Shakespeare's *Venus and Adonis* – only three references to Venus, thirteen to Adonis, and seven to others: yet it was not suggested how including more would have improved the poem. However, in his poetic narrative of *The Rape of Lucrece*, where the story, plot and drama needed them, Shakespeare put nineteen references to Lucrece, twenty-five to Tarquin, thirty-two to Collatine, and sixty-seven references to thirty-seven other classical figures or events – but only used them when they had a specific purpose. Shakespeare used so many fields of knowledge for his allusions and metaphors – see Spurgeon – and used them so ingeniously, that just counting the numbers is not going to explain the splendour of his works.

A proper analysis of Shakespeare's classical scholarship that should discourage those who would dumb him down to fit Shakspere, was given by Highet (1949) who, while not doubting he was Shakspere, identified him as a "classically educated poet" and even said of him that he "has rendered ... better than his sources, the essence of the Roman republic."

6. Italy

A sixth and totally different problem for the Shakspere myth is that Shakespeare somehow had the knowledge and confidence to write nine comedies based wholly or partly on Italy – *The Two Gentlemen of Verona*,

The Comedy of Errors, The Taming of the Shrew, All's Well that Ends Well, The Merchant of Venice, Much Ado About Nothing, Twelfth Night, The Tempest, and *The Winter's Tale* – and even some orthodox scholars think he had written the first two by 1590, though that implies he already knew local details of his Italian settings of a sort that others, like Marlowe, could not manage for any of their plays. Oddly, this phenomenon, Shakespeare's love affair with Italy, does not get mentioned in some orthodox biographies at all: one cannot fit a long period in Italy into Shakspere's career, nor find a record of a group in which he could have been kept safe on the journey and supported financially for so long, nor find some intimate friend he could have tapped to get the varied, detailed and arcane knowledge used in the plays. In *The Taming of the Shrew*, Shakespeare identified the inland town Bergamo one hundred miles from the sea as a centre of sail-making. This was said to show his ignorance and that he could not have been to Italy, but, at the end of the twentieth century, it was realised the town had been the centre for the flax industry, and sails were made there. It is unlikely he would have thrown that minor matter so casually into a play without being certain of it. Yet that was the sort of thing he did with his knowledge of Italy. For instance, he put a sycamore wood for Romeo to walk in outside the west wall of Verona – it is still there today – but one could not imagine dropping such a minor but accurate detail into a play unless it was from personal knowledge. He knew Juliet could go to see a priest after evening mass in Verona even though all other towns in Italy only had mass in the morning. And there is much more.

It is often claimed Shakspere would have got Shakespeare's detailed knowledge of Italy by talking to some of the fewer than a hundred Italians then living in London; yet this stretches credulity. The plays are located from Sicily to Milan, and almost all refer to local detail a writer could only use if he could visualise it on the instant, and see that it fitted what he was writing. Shakespeare's knowledge had to be personal or closely passed on by an intimate friend. A person often named as giving Shakspere such knowledge is John Florio, a tutor in the Earl of Southampton's household: but he was born in England and never visited Italy. Another candidate, Emilia Lanier, is spoken of as a Venetian and the source of the local detail in *The Merchant of Venice* and *Othello*. Yet she was English born and bred. It has been said Shakspere knew an Italian restaurateur in Elizabethan London, Paolo Marcus Lucchese, and, as Shakespeare, put him in *Othello* as "Marcus Lucchese". Yet the original name in the play was Marcus Luccicos – a Greek name for a Greek – and the substitution was made by Edward Capell in the eighteenth century to help the Shakspere myth (just as he put Sir John Somerville in *Henry VI Part 3* to help turn Shakespeare into a relative of the Catholic Ardens). There is, of course, no evidence Shakspere knew Florio, Lanier or Lucchese, and this collection of inventions underlines how serious the "Italian question" is for the theory that Shakspere was Shakespeare.

Shakespeare's knowledge of Italy, and the way he used it – and misused it to turn it into jokes – has convinced Italian scholars that he had been there, or had absorbed it from some very intimate, well-travelled proxy. Yet some orthodox scholars have trawled the "Italian" plays to catch him out in errors that someone who had been to Italy would not have made. Lee (1916) denied Shakespeare's direct knowledge of Italy by saying that, in *The Tempest*, Prospero was put on an ocean-going boat at Milan: yet the play says he was put on that boat only when he reached the sea. Such attempts at dumbing down the author's Italian knowledge have made the problem for the orthodox theory worse through the discovery that Shakespeare was often right when the references available in England were wrong – see, for example, Grillo (1949) and Praz (1954). The way orthodox scholars have dealt with this problem is very revealing. Some wave it away. Some ignore it. Some simply say that Shakspere never went to Italy and leave it there. But Chambers, in *EKC*, said he would have believed Shakespeare visited Italy before writing his Italian plays if it were not certain he (meaning Shakspere) had not been there. Finally, Shapiro (2010) told of a man who had written in convincing detail on China, finding his information "in the British Library, and from films, newspapers and the internet" and implied Shakspere could have done just the same with Italy!

In a recent interview about a new play on Shakespeare, its author gave three "facts" which, he imagined, showed Shakespeare's ignorance, and so fitted him to be Shakspere. These were 1) a journey from Milan to Verona by boat in *The Two Gentlemen of Verona*; 2) a sea-coast for Bohemia in *The Winter's Tale*, and 3) a wrong route to Roussillon in *All's Well that Ends Well*. Yet sixteenth-century records show a route by canal and river from Milan to Verona, a sixteenth-century map shows Bohemia had a sea-coast on the Adriatic (mentioned by Robert Greene in his novella *Pandosta*); and the French Roussillon in *All's Well* was not, as the orthodox claim, the region near the Pyrenees south-west of Marseilles which only became French in 1659 but a small town to its north with a chateau. Shakespeare ignorant?

Some "errors" do occur in the Italian plays and are quoted to show Shakespeare did not know Italy but, as Italian writers have noted, these occur in the comedic scenes. For example, one comedy character warns passengers on a river boat to hurry lest they miss the tide. (That may actually reflect him seeing one of the surges of current, then common at Verona, that helped speed boats down the Adige.) It is sad that, in rejecting Shakespeare's obvious knowledge of Italy, some scholars miss entirely the significance of the Italian plays.

Just as the detail in Shakespeare's Italian plays is revealing, it is equally clear he selected for the only comedy he set in England – *The Merry Wives of Windsor* – a location he knew in the way he knew, say, Verona or Venice, and drew on his knowledge fluently. The play includes much that indicates he had stayed in Windsor, talked to its denizens, walked its streets, and knew its stories and myths. He made passing reference to German visitors of 1592, one of them there to seek the Order of the Garter. He knew the routes they had taken; and the quarto edition of the play used an anagram of one of their names – Momplegard – possibly as a precaution against royal anger. He described easily the route from Mistress Ford's house to the ditch into which Falstaff was tumbled. And so on. Of course, no evidence has been found for Shakspere staying at Windsor, or how he might have learnt details of a Garter candidate whom it was necessary to disguise to avoid censure. Moreover, whoever wrote the play had to get away with parodying Dr Caius, the Queen's physician, and, given the Tudors' Welsh roots, get away with insults like calling Huw Evans "a Welsh devil", "a Welsh fairy", "a Welsh goat" and "a Welsh flannel".

It is sometimes claimed writers would include local details in their plays without having close knowledge of the location, but that seems not to be true for the sort of details Shakespeare left us. Marlowe, for instance, had not one piece of local knowledge in his play *The Jew of Malta*; and though some writers quote in contradiction his reference to the "roads of Malta" that is a nautical term, not a Maltese one.

7. Cambridge University

Another problem for the Shakspere myth, the seventh in this particular set, arose in 1923 when Boas's research on Shakespeare and the universities showed he had knowledge peculiar to Cambridge. His findings have been extended by others – see, for example, N. Cockburn (1998) – and are consistent with a tract *Polimanteia* published in 1595 by a Cambridge man, William Clerke, who had worked out Shakespeare was a university poet. There were telling references in the three "Parnassus" plays of 1601 by Cambridge students. In the second of these (titled *The Return from Parnassus Part 1*) fulsome praise was lavished on Shakespeare as a poet and playwright along with disgust at the theft of his plays. It seems the authors of the play laid claim to him. In *The Return from Parnassus Part 2*, actors (seemingly the Lord Chamberlain's Men) were insulted. A speech given to the comedian William Kempe (making him out to be uneducated) judges Shakespeare superior to most of the "University men" and to Ben Jonson. Clearly he was not seen as one of the players – those were treated with scorn – and treatment of him as "our fellow

Shakespeare" in Kempe's speech would again fit a man believed to be a Cambridge writer. (As people wrongly claim Shakspere was personally insulted in those plays, they are discussed further in Appendix H.)

There are links to Cambridge through Shakespeare's *Richard III* which clearly used a source play, *Ricardus Tertius*, unknown outside that university until much later. In *The Merry Wives of Windsor*, there is Cambridge-specific knowledge in Dr Caius's hatred of the Welsh, whom he barred from his College. Also a play, *Laelius*, again only known in Cambridge until much later, was used for *Twelfth Night*.

The way Shakespeare used "Cambridge" knowledge for his plays shows he either studied at Cambridge or had close association with that university. Contrary to what some say, his familiarity with Cambridge was not part of the author's general knowledge, as there is nothing comparable in his plays specific to Oxford University. For example, when King Lear complains to his daughter Regan saying, *"'Tis not in thee ... to scant my sizes"*, that phrase is Cambridge jargon for "to reduce my rations" – an undergraduate punishment. Nothing similarly specific is taken from Oxford. Then the word "keeping", with the Cambridge meaning of "lodging", occurs in a number of plays. Boas clearly intended his research to show how wide Shakespeare's knowledge was, but he found it necessary to disguise the obvious conclusion from it, and it seems orthodox biographers dropped reference to it when its serious implications for the Shakspere myth were realised.

8. Music

As an eighth problem, one might ask how Shakspere would have gained Shakespeare's familiarity with music without some trace of musicality being found among those with whom he lived and grew up? All the plays except *The Comedy of Errors* had music written in. Almost all the plays contain musical metaphors, with none of the common errors creeping in, and there are over a hundred songs between them. Twenty-six musical instruments are mentioned in the plays and over a hundred musical terms. The placing of the music in the plays is recognised as amazingly apt. Yet nothing known about Shakspere would lead one to expect any of that. More is written in *OCS* about Shakespeare and his brilliant use of music than about any comparable matter, including his dramatic poetry or his use of English – and very, very much more than about his supposed knowledge of gloving and wool-dealing; yet there is no hint of how Shakspere would have attained the perfection in this field that he would have needed early, if he had been Shakespeare. No musicians, music, or instruments have been found having any connection with Shakspere or with anyone he knew in Stratford or London. When it is said that "more is known about Shakspere etcetera", it is never the "more" that relates to Shakespeare's knowledge shown in the plays, such as in the use of music.

Shakespeare's Vocabulary

The extent of the English vocabulary used in Shakespeare's plays would be difficult to explain away for Shakspere, even if he had gone to school. A conservative count – with "dog", "dogs" and "dog's", for example, taken as one word – shows some 20,000 words in the plays and poems, double the number used by his nearest rival, Milton – and Milton had Shakespeare to draw on. If Shakspere had written as Shakespeare, he would have needed most of that vocabulary by the late 1580s. Yet even grammar-school boys did not learn English. In the sixteenth century, they would have been taught Latin, the language of law, church and medicine. English was not considered a language for scholars or scholarship until Shakespeare and others showed otherwise. There was not even an English dictionary until 1604, and that was a pathetic effort compared with Dr Johnson's 1755 masterpiece.

Shakespeare's vocabulary is such a nuisance to the Shakspere myth that an odd attempt has been made to demean it. It is to say that an average person today who counted the words they recognised in a dictionary would find his/her vocabulary was larger than Shakespeare's (and, of course, every other writer's). This is comparing two different things: words an average person may recognise and those – habitually less than 3,000 – they may use in their writing. Shapiro (2010) wrote "most of us use at least 50,000 words", which is eight times as many as the prolific Charles Dickens used, and he comes third in vocabulary after Shakespeare and Milton. This use of the fallacy of not comparing like with like stresses the threat Shakespeare's vocabulary poses to the Shakspere myth.

A related problem is how Shakepere could have come by a knowledge of rhetoric from anachrony to zeugma, classical grammar, and foreign idiom, – so that, in writing as Shakespeare, his works could have been used as a text book on the subject, as Rhodes (2004) put it. Shakespeare would have built on what he had learnt, not created from scratch his extraordinary use of language, and the route to such usage would normally have been through a good tutor. Ben Jonson, for example, who did go to grammar school, wrote heart-felt tributes to the personal efforts of his teacher William Camden who – as one of the great scholars of the period – took pride in having prepared his pupil for his writing career. No one has traced anything similar, or at all, for Shakspere.

Bias-bowls

Another problem for the Shakspere myth is created by references to the game of bias-bowls in Shakespeare's works. This game, using bowls weighted to bend their trajectory, was played by those with private bowling greens. Ordinary bowls – or boules – was outlawed for various reasons. The game occurs nineteen times in the plays, more than all other references to games put together, whereas only one other author mentions it. No one has even hinted how Shakspere could have known the game. There is no evidence for him being a guest at grand houses, the only places he could have played it, and certainly not by the time he used it for a metaphor in *The Taming of the Shrew*.

Shakespeare's Failure to protect his Copyrights

To treat of a mysterious matter, we look at Shakespeare's invisibility when it came to protecting his work. No other author suffered from piratical publishing of his plays in the way he did. No other author's name was misused as his was to increase the sales of books that were not his, or to hide the identities of other writers who wished to remain anonymous. Yet he never once complained at this treatment. It seems impossible our litigious Shakspere, working for a commercial theatre and acting troupe, would be so supine, letting himself be robbed of his works, his rights and his name in that way. On the other hand, one can easily see how the invisible Shakespeare fits the findings of Pollard (1920) and Sheavyn (1967) that it was only people with good reason to protect their anonymity who did not protect their works, and whose pseudonyms were therefore free for the taking. The business-man Shakspere would have objected and tried to save his property just as other and lesser writers than Shakespeare did. The facts and logic – and Pollard, and Patterson (1968) – destroy that oft-repeated invention that Shakespeare had no rights in his work, as does the knowledge that Jonson, Beaumont and Fletcher and others published works they had already sold for performance. Writers published their own works, stopped them being published, had agreements with publishers, and got paid for them while working for an acting company: Shakespeare must have done those things if he had been Shakspere, and the fact that he didn't is evidence he wasn't.

Shakespeare's failure to protest when his works and name were stolen has proved a real problem for the orthodox theory. How real, is shown by the prominence given by many orthodox biographers to the one occasion when there was the merest hint that he might have been "offended" by the misuse of his name. In reality, the way that hint arose makes it look

187

more like an invention by another author to help strengthen his own protest, than anything Shakespeare did.

The occasion was in 1612, when a revised edition was published of a collection of poems known as *The Passionate Pilgrim*, first issued in 1599. This collection contained works by various poets, but the publisher chose, for its selling potential, to use the name William Shakespeare for the author of them all. When that new edition came out, it contained two poems by Thomas Heywood that were not in the first. This had included poems by Marlowe, Barnfield and Griffin, some anonymous ones, and a quarter by Shakespeare. Heywood complained sharply at his poems being published under another poet's name and suggested he knew that poet was "offended", though his message was confused because he seemed unsure how to refer to Shakespeare. It is doubtful Shakespeare would have suddenly spoken out in this case when he had kept silent for years over the misuse of his name for the first edition, and there is no evidence that he did. He never complained. When Heywood protested in 1612, his two pirated works were removed from the collection, an indication that Shakespeare could also have successfully protested if he was willing to expose his identity. Strangely, one biographer got so excited over Heywood's hint of Shakespeare being offended that he claimed it showed he "could get angry"; another excited biographer claimed "Shakespeare was enraged by this piracy"; and yet another came up with an invention that he had written to protest on his own behalf. Shakespeare, in these situations, always remained silent, and the ecstacy of the orthodox over this hint that he did not in this case, shows that it is not a trivial matter.

Dr John Hall, as Executor, and the Puzzle of the Missing Books

We now return to the role of Dr John Hall who, we saw, left no information about his supposedly-famous father-in-law and wrote no biography. Here we get three mysteries for the price of one. The first is that Hall and his wife, executors to Shakspere's will, apparently showed no interest in retrieving for the estate the valuable manuscripts of Shakespeare's works that must have been used in the printing of the First Folio in 1623. Coupled with this is the fact that Hall and his wife apparently never had a copy of the First Folio, or benefitted from it in any way. Indeed, in spite of inquiries being made in Stratford in the seventeenth century, there is no indication that anybody in the town possessed or heard of any book written by Shakspere or Shakespeare.

The second additional problem related to Hall is his failure to make known or even hint at books being left by Shakspere. If his father-in-law had been Shakespeare, his library would have been a major part of his assets. Books Ben Jonson is known to have owned still survive – as do books owned by other writers. Shakespeare had clearly used two bibles in writing his works, the "Bishops'" Bible and the "Geneva" Bible. As Ackroyd pointed out, there is hardly any significant character in the plays who does not use a biblical quotation, and those were drawn from forty-three of the sixty-nine biblical books. Yet no Bible passed down through Shakspere's family. A Bible was a major purchase for an ordinary family, and Shakspere's copies would have been well thumbed and annotated, if he was Shakespeare, as well as being used to record family anniversaries. They might have been expected to be treasured even if all his other books were thrown away.

The evidence that Shakspere owned no books has four legs:

(a)   no books were left in his will;

(b)   none has been identified or even mentioned as being passed down to or by John Hall or has come to light with evidence that it was Shakspere's;

(c)   when Shakspere was assessed for sums of around £5 for taxes in London, these were never large enough to cover the value of even a few of the books he must have owned if he had been Shakespeare, some of which, individually, would have been worth over £1;

(d)   the sheer weight of those books would have discouraged Shakspere from moving lodgings as often as he did, and from commuting to Stratford with them at those times, like in 1596–98, when it is claimed he was doing business in both Stratford and London, while busily writing plays.

That the missing books pose a major problem for the orthodox theory is shown by the nature of the attempts made to get round it. It has been said, for example, that it was common for books not to be mentioned in wills, and one biographer claimed there was no more chance of people mentioning their books in a will than mentioning their dogs. Yet much less impressive collections than Shakspere would have had – if he had been Shakespeare – were included in the contemporary Stratford wills of John Bretchgirdle, John Brownsword and John Marshall, besides that of John Hall himself (whose own father had earlier left him named books when he died). John Hall's will was also totally dismissive of the books which he left to his son-in-law, Thomas Nash; he instructed him to do with them as he would, clearly indicating they were not Shakespeare's large and valuable collection. Book collections like Shakespeare's did not just disappear.

The problem of the sheer number of books – over five hundred – that scholars such as Bullough, Gillespie, Muir and Miola and others have identified through many years of diligent research as being used by Shakespeare in writing his plays, and the absence of any trace of them being owned by Shakspere, has led to the invention of odd explanations beyond the one attempted above. These are based largely on the idea that Shakespeare did not need actually to own the necessary books that scholars have identified. (This is a commonly used ploy: if the facts do not fit the Shakspere myth, change them.)

Perhaps the most popular of the "explanations" is that Shakspere, if he had been Shakespeare, would have read the books he needed in the London print shop of the Stratford man Richard Field. That ignores the evidence that the Field and Shakspere families might well not have been on speaking terms and the lack of evidence for Shakspere ever associating with Field, and the fact that printers were not in the business of stocking books for people to borrow like a lending library but of moving them on in pristine condition to publishers. There is also the insuperable problem that an analysis of Field's records shows he only printed three of the books that Shakespeare used – see Kirkwood (1931). To get over this, David Kathman put up a list of Field's books on a web site and argued that Shakespeare must have read those and not the sources identified from the texts of the plays. The best is silence.

As an alternative to Shakspere using Field's print shop as a library, it has been recently proposed that acting troupes kept libraries for their dramatists to use. But Shakespeare obviously knew the books he was referring to well, and drew on a number (as many as forty) in respect of individual plays, quite a few in languages other than English. It is difficult to imagine a troupe of actors providing the capital, the space and the security that a valuable collection like the one Shakespeare used would have needed, and the only reason for suggesting that this might have happened is the problem that Shakspere had no books of his own.

Then there is the idea, see Bate (2008), that Shakespeare only really needed a permanent collection of some forty books, though the ones Bate identified would not have been cheap or light to transport, nor sufficient for the purpose, given that the poet picked and chose from them as he wrote.

Finally, it has been proposed that Shakspere's method was to visit booksellers' stalls around St Paul's Cathedral and read the books he found in situ, presumably separating their folded pages with his paper knife in front of the bemused stall-holders – the mechanical cutting of pages came in much later. The books had no indexes or proper tables of contents, so he would have had to scour them, rain or shine, to find what he wanted, or might use. No writer who has employed a fraction of the number of books Shakespeare did would think they could use that method, and its very proposal shows the problem posed by the missing books.

Lack of Contemporay Family or Local Stories

The third Hall-related piece of evidence against the claim for Shakspere being Shakespeare is that, among all the relevant anecdotes collected from around Stratford, not one is traced to John Hall or any other member of the Shakspere family, or to the various local people who must have known John Hall and Shakspere well. The Rev. John Ward, referred to above, was not the only notable to visit Stratford and come away with no useful information on Shakspere before his last surviving daughter died in 1662. A particular case is the silence that followed the visit of a Dr James Cooke to Susanna Hall in 1642 to look at her late husband's books; for though he subsequently wrote (and published) about her husband, he seems to have learnt nothing about her supposedly famous father.

Miscellaneous Puzzles

Why did the rich Shakspere, if he had been the education-applauding writer who wrote superior parts for females in most of his plays, not educate his two daughters instead of leaving one of them unable even to write her own name, while the other only wrote hers with difficulty (if she did)? Why did he leave no mention of, or bequest to, the Stratford Grammar School, if it had given him the education that was the foundation of his great career as a poet-playwright? Why, if he was Shakespeare, did Shakspere's name not figure in the Bishop of Worcester's list of scholars with potential to go into the church? Why, if Shakspere was Shakespeare, did William Camden not include him in at least one of the many revisions of his book, *Britannia*, where he listed the worthies of Stratford-upon-Avon, or note his death in 1616, as he did Burbage's in 1619?

Camden's omissions are serious testimony that Shakspere was not Shakespeare. He was well up in theatrical affairs and a party, as a herald, to the Shakspere application for a coat of arms; yet, whenever he mentioned Shakespeare, he did not mention Stratford, and vice-versa.

Why did the prolific letter writers of the age – John Chamberlain and Henry Wotton in particular, who both wrote about the theatre – never associate the Globe-sharer Shakspere with the writer Shakespeare, not even in their accounts of the Globe burning down as a result of an action in the play *Henry VIII* that took place on the instruction of the author? Why did they only mention Shakespeare's works and not the real man? Why did the 1615 edition of Stow's *Annales* list Shakespeare as writing before Marlowe, when it seems certain that Shakspere, if he was Shakespeare, could only have begun writing quite a bit later? And so on.

Why did no one mark his Death publicly?

There is, though, one other piece of evidence, partly covered earlier, which has to run the silent testimony of John Hall very close for its deadliness to the orthodox theory, and that is the total silence and lack of reaction that greeted the death of Shakspere in 1616. Besides having no eulogies and elegies written for him, there was no move to have him buried in Westminster Abbey. It is sometimes claimed that the tributes came over seven years later in the First Folio in 1623, though on that occasion Jonson was paid to write and had to recruit nonentities to join in with him, which was hardly an outburst of spontaneous grief. We have seen that even the supposed elegy by William Basse – actually written by William Browne – was part of the 1623 First Folio scam, probably written in the form it was to help disguise the mystery of why the decoy Shakspere was not buried in the Abbey. If he had been Shakespeare he was famous enough. Some scholars will say he had been forgotten, though his plays were regularly commanded by the King to be performed at Court and new editions of his already published plays were regularly issued in the quarto format.

The claim that Shakspere's death went unnoticed because he died in Stratford, and not because he was not the famous Shakespeare, simply does not stand up. Dr John Hall could easily have let his London contacts know, including his patient, the poet Michael Drayton, who in turn had contacts in the Inns of Court where he had substantial patronage.

John Hall would have told his patients, the Earl and Countess of Northampton, about his famous father-in-law (if he had been Shakespeare) and they again had their London contacts. The Reverend John Rogers, vicar of Stratford in 1616, could have written to the Dean of Westminster. The Town Clerk of Stratford, Thomas Greene, who called Shakspere "coz", had offices in Stratford and in London. Fulke Greville, the poet who was the Recorder of Stratford, was also the Chancellor of the Exchequer in 1616. The Stratford carrier Greenway was always available for taking messages up to London, and, if the matter was as important as the death of Shakespeare would have been, there is no reason to believe a rider could not have been found to take the news to London rapidly.

As Shakspere's heir, John Hall would not have been short of a few shillings to honour his wife's father as he would have deserved, if the latter had been Shakespeare. Brief letters bearing the news of the great Shakespeare's death sent to Ben Jonson, Richard Burbage, Thomas Greene, Michael Drayton, William Camden, Fulke Greville and the Master of the Revels (Sir George Buck) and others would have had the news around the capital in short order. (One might think of much more important names than these, like George Carew – first Baron Clopton, that place being near Stratford – Southampton, Pembroke, the Dean of Westminster and King James himself.) Arrangements for a burial in Westminster Abbey would have been absolutely natural. A reason put forward is that Shakespeare would have been refused burial by the Dean of Westminster because he had already buried the much lesser writer Francis Beaumont there in early March 1616; it is hardly impressive.

It has to be remembered that, in respect of the lack of elegies and an appropriate burial, Shakspere was a man who would have been known in many roles to many people if he had been Shakespeare, and greatly famous. One can easily identify dozens of poets, professional and amateur, major and minor, who would have been eager to write elegies for Shakespeare, if he had been a real person. The curious incident of these "dogs who did nothing in the night" – to paraphrase Sherlock Holmes – is another piece of compelling testimony that Shakspere was not Shakespeare. The poems of forty-three elegists were published on the death of Ben Jonson. The odds against Shakspere having no elegies, if he had been Shakespeare, would be enormous.

Bad as the lack of elegies or an Abbey burial are for the theory that Shakspere was Shakespeare, there is also the absence of any mention of his death in the diaries of people who kept such complete and interesting records that they have since been published. And nobody descended on Shakspere's home to seek mementoes or memorabilia or unpublished manuscripts as somebody did, for example, on the sudden death of Robert Greene in 1592. In fact, there was no mention of anyone visiting Stratford in pursuit of "Shakespeare" until well after the appearance of the First Folio and many years after Shakspere's death. No one capitalised on Shakspere's death by bringing out special editions of previously published Quartos of Shakespeare's works. How many negative results must a theory yield before it is realised it might be wrong?

Shakespeare's Insults to the Great and Good

Very different evidence against the orthodox theory is how Shakespeare got away with insults to the great and good that could have been fatal had he been Shakspere writing under his own name as claimed.

We have noted his insults to the Queen's physician, Dr Caius, and to her Welsh origins in *The Merry Wives of Windsor*; his insolence in the dedications to *Venus and Adonis* and *The Rape of Lucrece*; the risk of dedicating such quasi-pornographic poems to a noble ward of Lord Burghley; but worse were his jibes against the great Lord Burghley himself, and he the Queen's first minister. One example from *Hamlet* will suffice. There is no doubt the Danish King's first minister, Polonius, was based on Burghley. Polonius's oft-quoted advice to his son, Laertes, telling him, among other things, "neither a borrower nor a lender be" is known to paraphrase Burghley's advice to his son, Thomas. Burghley liked it to be known he was born in 1521 during the Church Convocation known as the Diet of Worms, where Luther resisted the Emperor's efforts to make him recant his "heresies". After Hamlet had killed Polonius with a sword thrust through the "arras", he told the King:

> A certain convocation of politic worms are e'en at him.
> Your worm is your only emperor for diet.

Nothing could have been more designed to attract attention at the highest level to Shakespeare's careless insults. Yet nothing happened to Shakspere like the ire that descended on Jonson and others in such situations and actually landed them in prison. (Shapiro has claimed that the quotation could not have referred to Burghley because he was dead when *Hamlet* was written. That would be weak even if the play was not known before Burghley's death in 1598, but Malone himself had dated it as 1596.)

The Staging of the Plays

Over two hundred years ago, Charles Lamb wrote:

> I cannot help being of the opinion that the plays of Shakespeare are less calculated for performance on the stage [than for reading].

Dr Johnson had had the same thought earlier, and Lamb was seconded by the critic William Hazlitt. Other scholars have since discussed whether the plays were not actually written more as literary works to be read rather than acted – "for the page not the stage" – most recently by John Bayley and Lukas Erne in the magazine *Around the Globe*. This is not to deny they are wonderful in performance; of course they are. But the normal length of a play for the theatres in Shakespeare's time was, for good reason, well short of three hours. The conveniences we take for granted in theatres today just did not exist for spectators then. As an actor, and even more as a manager and sharer in the Globe theatre, Shakspere would have known what the defining conditions were and have written accordingly.

It is clear that Shakespeare did not have commercial considerations in mind when he regularly wrote plays that exceeded the maximum playable length. Well over a third could not have been produced for a normal performance without serious cutting. *Hamlet*, even without an interval, runs over four hours. It is often said, as though it explains away the problem of length, that Shakespeare's longer plays were written for the indoor Blackfriars theatre. Yet there is no evidence Shakespeare's plays were ever put on at that theatre, which the King's men only opened in 1610, while some longer plays – *Henry V, The Winter's Tale* and *Pericles* for example – were certainly put on at the Globe, and would have been too long for either theatre. The question, though, is not simply one of length.

The author was clearly determined, at the cost of time and effort in revising his plays, to produce poetry in them at least as wonderful in reading as in performance. They have far more quotable quotations than all his rivals put together and contain dozens of long speeches that are used as stand-alone poetry. Shakespeare clearly extended to his plays the theme in the Sonnets that a writer's poetry promises immortality. All this makes it hard to believe that Shakespeare's plays were written by a man working as a jobbing writer for a troupe of players in the commercial theatre.

Reconciling Dates

Another feature that does not fit with Shakespeare being Shakspere is the need to make earlier the dates of the writing of at least some of the first plays. As more scholars realise they must locate Shakspere in London well before 1587 in order to fit in with the plays and the evidence of Stow's *Annales* (1615), they come up against the serious question of him abandoning his wife, possibly even while she was pregnant with the twins and in breach of both the mores of the time and the requirements of ecclesiastical law. These problems by themselves suggest that Shakspere was probably not the author; they may not be as conclusive as many of the others, but Gilvary's *Dating Shakespeare's Plays* (2010) suggests otherwise.

Coded Messages?

In broaching our last item here, it is hoped readers have noticed we have studiously avoided the supposed coded messages, hidden anagrams and arcane allusions which some find in Shakespeare's works and elsewhere, and give such fun to scholars, professional and amateur, of all denominations. Yet one writer left a quasi-cryptic message so blatant that to ignore it would be perverse.

It has been noted how, in 1622, a Henry Peacham effectively identified "Shakespeare" as someone who had been hidden by a pseudonym or was still alive. Ten years before that, in 1612, he had published a book full of symbolism with a cryptic comment on that pseudonym. The title of the book was *Minerva Britanna*, where "Minerva" was the Roman name for the muse Pallas Athena, the Spear-Shaker: it can thus be interpreted as "Britain's Spear-Shaker". The picture on the front cover was of a theatre arch with its curtain drawn back enough to reveal a hand holding a pen that had written in Latin (upside down to the reader) "MENTE VIDEBOR" or "I shall be seen by the mind!" – which either indicated a hidden writer or was nonsense. The picture surround was a laurel wreath, the poet's crown. Two other Latin phrases, one either side of the stage, read *"Vivitur in genio"* or "One lives in one's genius", and *"Caetera mortis erunt"* or "All else will be wiped out by death", which are major messages of Shakespeare's Sonnets. Above the book's title is the phrase: *"Ut aliis me consumo"* or "Thus I am used up for others," an echo of John Davies's epigram of two years earlier on *"Our English Terence, Mr Will. Shakespeare"*, which also indicated a hidden dramatist benefitting others, not himself.

There are debates about the exact translations of those phrases, but not their meanings, and, even if Peacham's fondness for illusions and allusions were not known, one would have to "read" the picture as saying there was a hidden writer, that he was associated with the term "spear-shaker", and had thoughts echoing Shakespeare's. Whatever arguments there may be on the detail of Peacham's message, he had just added to the pile of evidence that the name "Shakespeare" was a pseudonym for an unidentified poet-dramatist.

(It is worth remembering that, well before Peacham and Davies wrote, someone had experimented with writing different forms of the name "Shakespeare" – none of which were Shakspere – on a document known as the Northumberland Manuscript which referred to Shakespeare's works: this is discussed in the next chapter.)

We have now shown that much is known about Shakespeare that tells us he could not have been Shakspere, and much is known about Shakspere that shows he could not have been Shakespeare. So the only obstacle to admitting Shakspere was not Shakespeare seems to be the emotional and other capital that has been invested in that belief for so long. Yet, as the mis-selling of the Shakspere myth is known to have depended for its existence on the deliberate deceptions included in the First Folio, backed up by the Stratford Monument, focussing on these alone should make it easy to believe Shakspere was not Shakespeare.

Summary

To complete this section, and as a quick reference for the reader, we briefly give some of the strong reasons for being certain William Shakspere was not Shakespeare.

1.   Most serious scholars even among the orthodox acknowledge that it is impossible to reconcile what is actually known about William Shakspere of Stratford with what the works of Shakespeare reveal about their author. The intensive search for something that would identify William Shakspere as someone who could write, let alone be a writer, has been a total failure. That, by itself, should remove him as a "candidate" for being Shakespeare.

2.   From his cradle to his grave, William Shakspere never used the name Shakespeare for himself (or for his children); and he never called himself a poet or playwright, even when that would have helped secure the family coat of arms to give his father the title "Gentleman" before he died. It is impossible to believe Shakspere could have written under the name Shakespeare, so close to his own, and then failed to use it even when it would have been to his and his family's advantage. This consistent use by Shakspere matches that of the writer "Shakespeare" who regularly used that name and never Shakspere.

3.   Not one of William Shakspere's friends, colleagues, acquaintances, relatives, fellow actors, fellow theatre sharers, managers, supposed fellow playwrights, fellow pupils or schoolmasters (if he had any) has been identified as the source of any reference to him or any anecdote about him as Shakespeare, or as a poet or playwright. Even when it would have advantaged Cuthbert Burbage financially in two legal disputes to use that name and those terms for him, he only referred to him as the player or man Shakspere. (The use of the names of Heminges and Condell, and the hints that Shakspere of Stratford was Shakespeare in the First Folio were clearly part of the deception.) There is no evidence anyone from Stratford who knew Shakspere in London reported home on his fame. During his lifetime no one in Stratford noted him as being famous and no one is known to have reported his death to anyone in London, and no one owned a copy of any of his works. And, when he was on his way to being famous after 1623, no visitor to Stratford got useful information on Shakspere as a writer from surviving friends and family.

4.   The mysterious nature and distribution of the dates of the publication of Shakespeare's plays cannot be reconciled with him being the theatre-sharer, player-sharer and businessman Shakspere. There is a similar problem with the identification of dates before 1589 for some of the plays, and the fact that Shakespeare wrote the first ever tetralogy

before 1592, when it seems impossible to get Shakspere into London much before 1589, even if he could write.

5.   William Camden, Jonson's tutor and a member of the College of Arms, knew of both Shakspere and Shakespeare. He wrote of the worthies of Stratford, but never mentioned Shakespeare when he wrote of Stratford, or Stratford when he wrote of Shakespeare, and did not take any note of Shakspere's death.

6.   The deceptions in the First Folio would not have been needed if Shakspere had really been Shakespeare, and are as good as a signal that he was not. Shakspere's coat of arms would have graced that book if it had been his, and the conventional pen and paper would have graced the original Stratford bust. Yet the original bust in Stratford Church, which did have the Shakspere coat of arms, showed a trader, not a writer or learned man, while the inscription below it was clearly made to be ambiguous.

7.   Nobody doubts William Shakspere would have been steeped in the accent and dialect of Warwickshire, and the absence of those from the works of Shakespeare (who did use dialects and accents from elsewhere) shows he was not Shakespeare. And their absence is consistent with the lack of other Stratford-related features in the works.

8.   It is impossible to reconcile the litigious William Shakspere, working for a profit-making acting company, with the writer Shakespeare who was known among writers and publishers as the man least likely to protest if his works were published piratically or his name was put on other people's works.

9.   There is no evidence of literacy for William Shakspere or any of his ancestors, siblings or children. There is no evidence that he, or any of his brothers, qualified to go to school or could have qualified: quite the opposite. The conclusion from the way William Shakspere's name was written for him so differently in form and spelling on legal documents in the places where a literate man would have written his regular signature is that he could not write. The only evidence available on Shakspere's intellectual abilities indicates he did not have a good memory, and not just when he was approaching his death.

10.   It is near impossible to believe the actor-manager Shakspere would have written plays too long to be performed without cutting, or plays and sonnets derogatory about actors.

11.   There are major areas of specialist knowledge demonstrated in the plays which even individually must make it impossible to accept Shakspere as the writer Shakespeare. In particular these relate to the following matters:

(a)   William Harvey's theory of the circulation of the blood;
(b)   Cambridge University jargon and events;
(c)   the Inns of Court;
(d)   the law, its language and abstruse cases;
(e)   the inquest into Marlowe's death;
(f)   Italy;
(g)   the Court at Nérac;
(h)   Latin, French, Italian, Spanish and Greek;
(g)   English vocabulary, usage and rhetoric;
(h)   falconry;
(i)   bias-bowls;
(j)   music.

To this list may be added many other items, many identified by Spurgeon, the cumulative effect of which also is to eliminate Shakspere as a Shakespeare candidate.

12.   Nobody doubts the writer Shakespeare knew the third Earl of Southampton, but decades of research have found nothing to link William Shakspere to the Earl or to anyone or anything connected to him. There is also no evidence of links between Shakspere and the others it is claimed he must have met if he had been Shakespeare.

13.   No known professional playwright of the time had anything like the range of business activities of Shakspere, or the geographical range of his commuting between London and Stratford and touring as an actor-manager during the time he was supposed to be writing. None had the high level of earnings from other activities that he did which would have made a writing career into a difficult secondary occupation if he were Shakespeare, especially with the apparent absence of any income from it.

14.   Though Dr John Hall wrote summaries of the lives of his patients, he wrote nothing about his father-in-law. Dr James Cooke who visited Susanna Hall, Shakspere's daughter, to see Dr Hall's books, wrote about her husband but not her supposedly famous father. Hall himself showed no interest in Shakespeare's manuscripts or books, nor did any family member, and Shakspere was not mentioned as a writer on any family gravestone. Moreover, while Shakespeare must have possessed and regularly used hundreds of books, the evidence is that Shakspere owned none in Stratford or London.

15.   The failure to find evidence for a real writer named Shakespeare is consistent with different people, including the writer himself, identifying the name as a pseudonym and with the fact that no one was called to task or punished for the insults to the great and good or other political matters in Shakespeare's plays, and with the failure of the Queen's agents to identify the author of *Richard II*.

16.   Shakespeare's name was so famous that it (or just his initials) were those most often stolen to increase the sales of others' works, yet not one elegy or eulogy was written for him when Shakspere died in 1616, nor was Shakspere buried in Westminster Abbey. Shakespeare wrote no dedications, eulogies or elegies for anyone and, in turn, nobody of note, except Jonson for pay in 1623, wrote poems for the publication of his famous works.

17.   Here we mention a paradoxical point. If *The Tempest* did use the "Strachey letter" as is claimed, and if *The Two Noble Kinsmen* was a working collaboration of Fletcher and Shakespeare, those "facts" – generally insisted on by orthodox scholars – would rule out Shakspere as a candidate; but, as shown in Appendix F, the claims do not stand up.

The main task of this book is now complete. The "evidence" and inventions relating to the myth that William Shakspere of Stratford was the writer Shakespeare, and the efforts made to show he could have been that writer, have been sifted, and it has been shown they are dust: hard evidence shows he was not Shakespeare. As a result, his real identity can be restored to him; and, with what is really known about him, and about the world in which he grew up, lived and worked, an attempt has been made to give a fair picture of the sort of life he would have had. Yet it would leave a gap in Shakspere's story if we did not ask who might have been hidden behind his identity for nearly 400 years. That will occupy our next chapter, while the final one will look at why ending the Shakspere myth and restoring his true identity is so important.

Note

For readers who would look further at how orthodox writers deal with the problems for the Shakspere myth identified in this book, it seems impossible to find good references. Those that deal with the problems of the Shakespeare myth concentrate on picking holes in the cases for other Shakespeare candidates (which are minor compared with the chasms in the case for Shakspere) in the apparent hope that such distractions improve the case for Shakspere being Shakespeare.

Chapter 16

Who could have been writing as Shakespeare?

It has been known for over 400 years that, one day, there would be a serious search for the real writer who had been hidden behind Shakspere's identity. Some today claim that search was a peculiar nineteenth-century idea, but Joseph Hall and John Marston tried to identify the pseudonymous Shakespeare as early as 1598, well before Shakspere was used as a cover for him. And, though they were not the first to see it was a pseudonym, they got into trouble for it. Ben Jonson must have forseen the search when he mocked the fake "Shakespeare portrait" in the First Folio in 1623. John Benson, whoever he was, knew it in 1640 when he poked fun at that portrait, asking *This shadow is renowned Shakespear?*" It must have been suspected by Dryden and others who noticed the satire Ben Jonson put in his elegy in the First Folio.

In 1769, the year actor David Garrick organised a Shakspere bicentenary celebration in Stratford (five years late), his surgeon friend Herbert Lawrence wrote a pamphlet *The Life and Adventures of Common Sense* which mocked the tales of the Stratford man – "*a person from the Playhouse*", "*profligate*", "*Deer-stealer*", "*a Thief from the Time he was first capable of distinguishing any Thing*" – and mocked the idea that he was Shakespeare. That tells us Lawrence doubted the myths about Shakspere whom his friend Garrick was celebrating, although he warned against spreading his doubts and harming a national legend.

Then, in 1786, *The Story of the Learned Pig* appeared anonymously, wrapping up within a fantasy of a reincarnated soul, a tale of a playhouse horse-holder "*father'd with many spurious pieces. 'Hamlet', 'Othello' ...*" The suspicions are very clear. Charles Dickens raised funds for the "Shakespeare Birthplace" in Stratford, but said in 1847, "*I tremble every day lest something should turn up*". In 1932, orthodox scholar Allardyce Nicoll published documents seeming to show a James Wilmot of Warwickshire had doubts about Shakspere in 1785 and thought Bacon was Shakespeare.

If Wilmot did, he would not have been the first; but in 2002, physicist John Rollett discovered the story was a clever work of fiction.

Yet, however long the search may have been contemplated, it poses a major problem. The very sublimity of Shakespeare's dramatic and poetic output, and the knowledge it uses, can make it seem futile to look for a real person to take on his mantle. Indeed, it is not hard to see why some give up and stick with the Shakspere myth. As nothing of a literary nature is known about him, he can act as a blank sheet on which any invention can be written, which explains why there are hundreds of different works of fiction which are passed off as biographies of him.

The learning, knowledge, abilities, experiences, opportunities and resources Shakespeare must have had, combine to form an authorial template that looks almost too demanding for any non-mythical person to match. The way orthodox scholars seek to be exempt from showing how William Shakspere could fit the template, filling awkward gaps with assumptions and inventions, is understandable. Yet, comforting as that is, it is not scholarship.

It is no wonder the search for the real Shakespeare has lead to so many candidates being examined and rejected. This is how lateral thinking works, or should, in the arts as well as the sciences. (When it was realised Newton's classical theory of relativity was flawed, many new ones were tried and rejected before Einstein's was published. Yet nobody thought Newton's had to be taken as correct until the real correct one was found.) Most candidates put forward to be Shakespeare – not claimants, as some pejoratively call them – will be eliminated fairly rapidly, though hardly any suffer the problems of Shakspere's candidacy. All will have something to recommend them – even if it be only that they could write – but, when they are found to fail on some crucial point or points, they must be eliminated, but on the facts, not prejudice.

Potential Shakespeare candidates split into two groups: a majority who will prove to be impossible candidates, and a minority who are possible but must be examined in detail. It is from the latter group the real Shakespeare can be expected to emerge, or at least the most probable Shakespeare candidate, but it should not be expected to be straightforward. The efforts made at the time to protect the true writer may prevent us identifying him beyond all doubt; but we can hope to identify someone as highly probable. (When someone wrote attacking George III under the name "Junius" in 1769, he was not identified from among the dozen or so suspects until 1962 in spite of the punishments meted out to printers and others at the time. The real search for "Shakespeare" has not gone on that long. But at least we have candidates, which is not the case for many of the various anonymous writers who published in his time.)

We will see first how some of the marginal Shakespeare candidates can be eliminated. For example, someone suggested that the vastly intelligent Cardinal Thomas Wolsey, with his knowledge of history and politics and the early Tudors, might have written the works of Shakespeare: but that was before it was known, for example, that many books Shakespeare used in his writing did not exist before Wolsey died in 1530. There are other reasons for eliminating Wolsey as a candidate, but this one will suffice.

A second very marginal candidate is Roger Manners, Fifth Earl of Rutland (1576–1612). He was a precocious youth but, even if the orthodox play datings were right, he would have had to produce at least the first Shakespeare tetralogy – three parts of *Henry VI* and *Richard III* – before he was sixteen in 1592. The Manners candidacy cannot be sustained, though that perfunctory dismissal does not detract from the fact that it was almost certainly he who, after his embassy to Denmark in 1603, provided the information for major changes of names and details that Shakespeare made in *Hamlet* in early 1604.

To have an idea of how elimination works for candidates who face less obvious problems than Wolsey and Manners, we look at two of the more promising "impossible" Shakespeares: the commoner, Edward Dyer (1543–1607), who was knighted in 1594, and the anything-but-common Queen Elizabeth I (1533–1603).

Dyer has been put forward as a candidate in two ways: to be Shakespeare and to be one of a group of poet-playwrights who jointly worked under that pseudonym. (Of course, if there had been a group producing Shakespeare's works, it seems certain that – just as Canaletto was master of his studio in Venice – it would have had a "master" who ensured the works kept a common style and personality, and who would take the title "Shakespeare". We leave that theory aside here.) Dyer attracted attention because he was rated highly among the top ten Elizabethan poets. He was a good linguist and knew the law as part of his training for the diplomatic service. In his travels for the Government, he could have picked up most, if not all, of the information he might have needed to write the plays that Shakespeare set in France, Italy, Vienna (for *Measure for Measure*) and Bohemia (for *The Winter's Tale*). Interest in him as a candidate was encouraged by the lines in Sonnet 111 that contained the words:

Thence comes it that my name receives a brand
... like to the Dyer's hand,

that letter D there being one of the rare gratuitous capitals in the first printing of the Sonnets in 1609. However, Dyer is eliminated as a Shakespeare candidate by two serious drawbacks. First, he was an Oxford University man which does not fit with Shakespeare using so much jargon and knowledge specific to Cambridge, and none specific to Oxford. Second, he published lyric poetry from early maturity to near retirement very different from Shakespeare's. There were also crucial periods in Dyer's life when literary writing would have been very difficult. Moreover, sycophancy and caution were main features in his character, which traits seem alien to Shakespeare.

The thought of Queen Elizabeth being Shakespeare is often treated as nonsense by orthodox scholars. Yet it cannot be entirely ridiculous to think of the best-educated, best-informed Englishwoman of her time as a rival to William Shakspere for the mantle of Shakespeare. She could work in seven languages, translating straight from French, say, into Latin; she had some of the best tutors in England, all from Cambridge. She wrote poems that were used to teach poetry in her own day; and had access to all the information she needed, with secretaries at her call; her speeches were models of rhetoric, persuasion, and political manipulation; she had a ready wit, used language that would not have been out of place in a man, enjoyed music and dance and theatre; and her authorship could account for Shakespeare's interest in the triumph of the Tudor dynasty, the status of women in the plays and various feminine features that are recognised in "his" writings. The claim that Droeshout used a painting of her as a basis of his First Folio "portrait" – see Chapter 12 – is not evidence for her being Shakespeare, though almost every Shakespeare biographer carefully fails to mention it. There is also a puzzle about Sonnet 76, where it is possible to read a message that Elizabeth was the writer. Line 5, – *"Why write I still all one, ever the same"* – seems to echo the Queen's personal motto, *"Semper Eadem"* (Ever the Same). It is easy to imagine her using that, and the phrase "I still all one" which might indicate the writer as the top person. The Sonnet then continues at line 7 with the statement *"every word doth almost tell my name"* which points the reader to look at those clues two lines before. (There are other ways of reading that Sonnet, but they are not automatically right.)

However interesting all that might be, two reasons eliminate Elizabeth from the list of candidates. The first is that she would never have ordered Dr John Hayward to be put to the rack in 1601 to get him to confess to writing the play *Richard II* if she herself had been Shakespeare. There is no record of her personally ordering the use of gratuitous cruelty, rather the opposite. The second reason is that major revisions to *Hamlet* definitely took place after she was dead. (The fact that orthodox dating puts some Shakespeare plays later than 1604 – even if it were right – could not eliminate her a second time.)

Now we turn to two examples of candidates who, it seems, can be dismissed as "impossible" though both have had enthusiastic support: William Stanley, Sixth Earl of Derby (1561–1643), and Christopher Marlowe (1564–?1593), a commoner who did not even achieve the status of "Gentleman". The first has been championed mainly by French scholars – historians and Shakespeare experts – for reasons that will become obvious. The second has a long history of being associated with Shakespeare's works, particularly his earliest ones, and cannot be dismissed as trivially as is often pretended.

The known career of William Stanley, Lord Derby, satisfies a fair number of the criteria to be a Shakespeare candidate. He was intellectually brilliant, matriculating for university at age eleven; he studied at the Inns of Court; he lived through the time Shakespeare appears to have been writing; he was reported as writing "comedies" for his own troupe of players (Lord Derby's Men), a term used then for all plays other than tragedies; he travelled Europe to most locations relevant to the plays, and was closely associated with people who would have shared their experiences of other travels with him; he could probably have accessed all Shakespeare's sources (though we do not know the contents of his library as it was lost during the English Civil War); and the History plays give the Stanley family more prominence than the facts would support.

The prime virtue of Stanley as a candidate, the one that triggered great French enthusiasm – see Lefranc (1919) and later editions – relates to *Love's Labour's Lost*, one of the earlier plays. He was not only in Navarre in 1583, where he might have obtained the peculiar information needed for that play, but he was there with his pedantic tutor Richard Lloyd who wrote the playlet *The Nine Worthies* that Holofernes produced in Act V of the play, and would have made a good model for Holofernes himself.

It is, however, a serious point against Stanley, as was explained above for Dyer, that he was an Oxford University man. It is also unhelpful that his initials were WS, those of Shakespeare: pseudonyms are not chosen to hint at the writer's identity. The case for Derby is weakened by his having left no literary output that is identifiably his own during the thirty years he lived after Shakespeare stopped writing. (There was no reason for *everything* an aristocrat wrote to be anonymous.) Also, it is difficult to believe that, if he had been Shakespeare, he would have taken no interest in getting his works ready for publication when he was in a position to do so. That is damaging enough for the idea that Shakespeare was William Shakspere; but it is even more so for the idea that he was Derby, a man who continued to run his own players until 1618.

Letters exist referring to Derby writing plays, but the contexts suggest it was just for his own troupe. We have no idea what they might have been, but nothing points to his writing at the quality of Shakespeare. Unless something turns up to indicate Derby was a significant Elizabethan writer, the problems with his candidacy must deter one from giving it further consideration.

The second of our two well-supported "impossibles", Marlowe, was long thought to have had at least a collaborating hand in some of Shakespeare's early plays. In fact the play that appeared as *Henry VI Part 3* in the First Folio was printed as Marlowe's with the title *The True Tragedy of Richard Duke of York* as late as 1931. Marlowe went to Cambridge University, and would have known the jargon and information Shakespeare used from there, but it is not clear that he would have had legal training. At one time, he was largely credited with establishing blank verse in iambic pentameter in the English drama (though he did not invent it) and was talked of as the mentor of Shakespeare, but those views have lost their certainty with the realisation that the latter, whoever he was, seems to have written earlier than Marlowe did. Marlowe did travel in Europe but, as it was largely as a Government agent, his itineraries are not known and cannot be used to show how he might have got the ready knowledge Shakespeare had of Italy, France, etc. Yet there is one piece of evidence for him that is quite intriguing.

Around 1900, research by a Dr Mendenhall led him to propose a test for whether two pieces of writing were by the same person. It involved working out the distribution of the word lengths in the two pieces by counting the numbers of one letter, two letter, three letter words and so on and then comparing the frequencies with which they occurred in the two sets. He had found that the distributions in different samples of writing by the same person would all match each other within a very small margin of error. The method was developed as a forensic test like fingerprints, and was widely approved as valid. In addition, Mendenhall found no two writers who produced the same distribution.

Our interest is in this second finding because, when the method was applied to Shakespeare and Marlowe, their writings were found to have word length distributions that were virtually indistinguishable (see Michell, 2000). A review of Mendenhall's method, though, suggests it would work best in showing that two sets of handwriting in the same genre of manuscript were definitely not by the same person. When two sets of writing match in terms of their word length distributions, corroboration is needed to show they come from the same person, and, in the case of Shakespeare and Marlowe, strong reasons exist for believing they did not.

One reason for rejecting Marlowe lies in the styles of the two writers. Similarities they may have, but there are crucial differences. For example, Marlowe lacked the inescapable humour that intrudes, often quite surprisingly, in the plays of his rival: one would look hard in Marlowe for the equivalent of the promise of the disguised Kent to King Lear: "*to fear judgement; to fight when I cannot choose; and eat no fish.*" He also lacked his rival's effortless ability to turn an unforgettable phrase. He lacked the gift to make his characters such as Barabas and Faustus sympathetic to their audience in the way Shakespeare does with, say, Shylock, Richard III,

Macbeth and Othello; and he lacked his rival's seemingly unavoidable attention to trivial detail. Those points stand out, particularly when reading the two sets of plays, and one might almost dismiss Marlowe by comparing just *The Merchant of Venice* and *The Jew of Malta*: but another difficulty for Marlowe's candidacy seems absolutely definitive.

In early May 1593, Marlowe's colleague Thomas Kyd, with whom he shared lodgings, was investigated by the Privy Council. Atheistic papers had been found in his lodgings for which he blamed Marlowe. As a result, a warrant was issued for the latter's arrest on 18th May and he found himself facing execution on charges of atheism and blasphemy. Called for questioning on 20th May, he found he had also to answer charges laid against him by a rogue, Richard Baines, of sodomy and counterfeiting. Unless he was stupid, he would at once have thought of getting out of the country. To avoid pursuit, he would have known he had to fake his own death. Then, in the port of Deptford, Kent, on Saturday 1st June, an inquest was held on a body identified as Marlowe's. The only persons to identify the body were three shady friends of Marlowe who had been hastily called to Deptford, and only they gave evidence (which nobody now credits) of how he died. There is no difficulty believing he had cleverly avoided an unpleasant end.

But Marlowe escaping and not dying does not help the theory he was Shakespeare. That theory assumes he was so determined to continue writing abroad for the English stage that he invented for himself the pseudonym Shakespeare that first appeared on the dedication of *Venus and Adonis*. That is unlikely. There were good careers for Marlowe abroad with his great range of skills, and he would hardly have wanted to write plays with no reward or recognition so they could be performed in a country that had forced him into exile. His character was not as black as painted by some detractors, but he gave no sign of being stupidly altruistic either. Also, if Marlowe had thought of taking a pseudonym, he was too late for "Shakespeare". That was already spoken for. *Venus and Adonis* was registered a month to the day before Marlowe knew he was to be arrested and it must have been printed ready for distribution before 20 May, the day he was first sure of his mortal peril. Moreover, since all Marlowe's plays were published late, he might have published "Shakespeare's" as his without giving away his secret, (if he had written them, that is, and if he wanted nothing for them). Dead or alive, he must be excluded as a Shakespeare candidate.

Because, in spite of the evidence, a range of scholars insist on "proving" Marlowe died at Deptford to remove him as a Shakespeare candidate – which illustrates how distortions occur in this area – the case is discussed further in Appendix G. But the reader has only to note that, when the unbiased and cautious Dean and Chapter of Westminster

Abbey approved a memorial window to Marlowe in 1993, his dates were given as "1564–?1593".

Having seen how "impossibles" may be eliminated, we note that three candidates can be identified as serious "possibles": one is the commoner Francis Bacon (1561–1626), who was elevated to the peerage by James I as Viscount St Albans; another is the commoner Mary Sidney (1561–1621) who married into the peerage as Mary Herbert, Countess of Pembroke; and the third is Edward de Vere (1550–1604), who was born into the peerage and became, at the age of twelve, the seventeenth Earl of Oxford. Contrary to suggestions by some inverted snobs, these are not selected as "Shakespeare" candidates on the basis of their nobility, any more than Marlowe and Shakspere are rejected because they were commoners. Among other things, all three wrote works of a quality comparable with Shakespeare's and have not failed the type of tests that have eliminated other candidates. Bacon had no title until he was knighted on merit at the age of forty-three, after being an elected Member of Parliament continuously from the age of nineteen. Mary Sidney was the sister of the commoner poet-soldier Philip Sidney who was knighted in 1581. She had no title until, as a feisty fifteen-year-old beauty, wit and scholar, she married Henry Herbert, Second Earl of Pembroke, and became his Countess. Only Edward de Vere was born an aristocrat.

Francis Bacon (1561–1626)

Bacon was the very first person to be written of as Shakespeare, a full twenty-five years before the hints about the virtually unknown Shakspere appeared in the First Folio. The reaction of Bacon's friend Archbishop Whitgift to this revelation (if that was what it was) was consistent with Bacon objecting to his loss of anonymity, and that would make him an intriguing candidate even if his ability, learning, knowledge, writings and philosophical viewpoints did not demand his further examination. His intellectual resources and experience were, beyond question, adequate for him to be Shakespeare, whose philosophical thought he echoed at many points. He was a Cambridge University man, an Inns of Court man, and a patient of William Harvey with a chance of being privy to his theory of the circulation of the blood (see the previous chapter).

It seems he owned a document, called the "Northumberland Manuscript" from the house in which it was found in 1867: the front sheet had references relevant to Bacon, others to the author Shakespeare, and there were fifteen attempts at writing that pseudonym in various forms (none being Shakspere). It contained sixteen of Bacon's writings and had held manuscripts of *Richard II* and *Richard III*.

Francis Bacon's travels did not cover all the places from which Shakespeare seems to have taken special knowledge, but that gap can be mitigated by his closeness to his brilliant but exiled elder brother, Anthony Bacon (1558–1601): he seems to have gone everywhere mentioned in Shakespeare, was in frequent, if clandestine, contact with brother Francis, and has been considered by some to be a Shakespeare candidate in his own right.

The normal arguments put forward for disqualifying Bacon's candidacy are not strong, depending more on rhetoric than evidence. It has been asked how he could have written his great historical and philosophical works, the tracts he produced as a ghost writer for other people, and his masques for the Inns of Court revels, as well as the works that appeared as Shakespeare's. Yet even with all that output, he would not have written in total as much as, say, Charles Dickens (who used the same type of quill pen), or Dr Johnson (who also used the same type of unrefined paper). Bacon did not start writing his philosophical works in earnest until 1605, while it seems Shakespeare's works were written before then – see Appendix F. And it is at least as easy to believe Bacon wrote both the "Bacon" works and the "Shakespeare" works as to believe there were two different men living in London at precisely the same time who could both produce unique writings that changed the world. (Those works actually show echoes of each other which are worthy of investigation.)

Another typical argument against Bacon's candidacy is that Shakespeare's writings are not in the style of his known works. Yet writers adopt different styles for different subjects. Cecil Day Lewis, the Poet Laureate who wrote detective stories as "Nicholas Blake", had two very different styles. Bacon is known to have written for the Gray's Inn Revels. He is known to have been a poet in his younger days according to Stow's *Annales* of 1615 and there are references to him as a hidden poet in his later days. He was seen by literary contemporaries (Hall and Marston) as capable of writing Shakespeare's two erotic poems, though they differed in style from his poetic versions of the Psalms.

The impartial enquirer must find it odd that the case for Bacon being Shakespeare is often attacked without reference to the serious evidence supporting it (of which there is much – see N. Cockburn, 1998 and Dawkins, 2004). It is often called "The Bacon Heresy", as though the Shakspere myth were a religious faith – which to some extent it is – and adverse comments are made on those, and even on the names of those, who support it. Orthodox writers will mention one who died in an asylum as though that affects the arguments. Some will claim the case for Bacon being Shakespeare rests only on a variety of hidden messages supposed to exist in the plays, though those are secondary matters, while the case for Shakspere hangs wholly on hints in the First Folio.

(Aficionados of every Shakespeare candidate have trawled the works for cryptic clues to help their case. One day, something unambiguous may be found which identifies the writer, but so far it has not: only signals that the name Shakespeare was a pseudonym.) Yet it must be of interest that "honorificabilitudinitatibus", the longest word in Latin, occurs in *Love's Labour's Lost*, in a puzzle composed by Bacon and, in reduced form, on the Northumberland Manuscript he once owned. It occurs nowhere else relevant, and it is excluded from Shakespeare glossaries.

One can collect many arguments that can apply to Bacon's candidacy. He would, for instance, have needed total anonymity to write as Shakespeare while aspiring to high public office. It was he who used his position to save John Hayward from torture over the play *Richard II*. It was he who, when he died, received tributes which referred to him as a poet, likened him to the spear-shaker Minerva, and compared him with Nestor and Virgil who were both named on the Stratford Monument. However, there are also questions. For example, it is difficult to believe that this man, if he had been Shakespeare, would have let his plays go to press unedited in 1623 when he lived on to 1626. He was still capable then, for he was writing a life of Henry VII, and it is difficult to believe he would have paid Jonson and others to translate his philosophical works into Latin and not have used them (if he was Shakespeare) to get his plays into polished condition.

There are no absolute bars to accepting Bacon as Shakespeare. The mantle might be made to fit him, and the next stage lies in impartial assessment of possible negative factors, like how his known character fits with the psychology of the man revealed by the Shakespeare plays and poems. Yet, if a straight choice had to be made whether Shakespeare's works were written by Bacon or Shakspere, the vote would have to go to Bacon. It is not a straight choice though, as the same discussion must be applied to the other "possible" candidates. (A good overview of the case for Bacon is given in Michell [2000] in addition to the references given above.)

Mary Sidney (1561–1621)

The Countess of Pembroke, Mary Herbert – normally referred to as an author by her maiden name of Mary Sidney – has to be worthy of being a candidate for Shakespeare. She spoke all the languages needed by Shakespeare, and Welsh and Hebrew besides. She translated quite a number of literary and other writings into English and could write rapidly, producing, according to Gabriel Harvey, *"more in a month than [Thomas] Nashe could write in a year"*. She edited and published works by her brother Philip who introduced the sonnet craze into England (though his collection entitled *Astrophel and Stella* was only published four years after his death in 1586). And today, whereas it used to be said some works published under her name could not have been written by a woman and were more likely her brother's, questions are raised whether it was not the other way round, and that she published some of her own work under her brother's name. If the use of a pseudonym by some other writers is easily explained, the need is more obvious for a female and it is interesting that what is known as Philip Sidney's *Arcadia* was called on its title page "*The Countess of Pembroke's Arcadia*".

One of the works she translated from the French into her own blank verse, *Marc-Antoine*, was a major source for Shakespeare's *Antony and Cleopatra*. She ran a school for poets and was patron to some – including Drayton, Daniel, Heywood and William Browne (the latter being responsible for one of the items associated with the First Folio deception). And the first four printed plays of Shakespeare were all performed by a troupe of actors (Pembroke's Men) sponsored by her and her husband. It was her secretary, John Davies of Hereford, who wrote the epigram to Shakespeare entitled *To Our English Terence*, indicating that he thought (or knew) the name was a pseudonym, and it seems it was his poem, *A Lover's Complaint*, that was bound in with Shakespeare's Sonnets in 1609, perhaps having been gathered up by accident.

The candidacy of Mary Sidney must be considered greatly strengthened by the fact that the First Folio was published two years after her death, so making her the only candidate for the authorship to provide an obvious trigger for its publication. Jonson would have been more likely to have referred to her as "*My Beloved*" in his dedication than Shakspere, while his phrase "*Sweet Swan of Avon*" (coupled with "*flights along the Thames*" that echo poems written about Mary Sidney) could be more justly used for her. Her home being on the Wiltshire Avon, the swan was a common motif in Mary Sidney's dress. Indeed, with Jonson's reference to Shakespeare as a "swan" and a "constellation" in the same section of his poem, one is directed to the constellation Cygnus (Latin for swan) and the French word-play on "Sidney" as "Cygne". Also, all who were truly concerned with editing and funding the First Folio seem to have been associated with her, not least her two sons, the Earls of Pembroke and Montgomery respectively, to whom it was dedicated.

Some have cavalierly dismissed Mary Sidney's candidature without giving any reason. Recently Professor Stanley Wells did it cheaply with, "*Of course not!*" As a woman, she could not have matriculated at Cambridge University or registered at the Inns of Court. Yet she was named in a book, *Polimanteia*, in 1595 among Cambridge poets – the only lady to be included – and seems to have had associations with the Inns of Court, two points that do not seem to have been fully investigated in terms of

211

her candidacy to be Shakespeare. There is a problem in that she did not travel in Italy until 1606, when all the plays set there had already been written. However, she had two brothers, Philip (1554–86) and Robert (1563–1626), both writers, who between them visited all the places in Shakespeare's plays before 1584, and could have regaled Mary with their experiences. They both worked with Mary in establishing what was known as the "Wilton Circle" of literary men of experience, many from Cambridge and the Inns of Court. There seems to be little she could not have known, and some things she might have known better than other candidates – like Wales, the game of bowls (with the use of bias described in Shakespeare), medicines, and gardening, all of which show specialist knowledge when they appear in Shakespeare's plays (though herbalism was also known to Oxford and Bacon). If she were Shakespeare, that could explain the sense of the woman's hand some have detected in the works, as in a gentler attitude towards suffering animals like baited bears than male authors generally show. It would help explain the oddity that, in no fewer than ten Shakespeare plays, boy actors had to carry the longest or second longest role as women. Also, she knew Hebrew, and that would explain how the four names, Shylock, Jessica, Tubal and Cush, got into *The Merchant of Venice* when they only came together in Genesis, Chapters 10 and 11, of the untranslated Hebrew version of the Bible.

There are two side issues with Mary Sidney. One of these is based on an account of a visit of a Classics Master from Eton, William Cory, to the home of the Pembrokes at Wilton in 1865. He reported being told that Mary had written to her younger son, Philip Herbert, in 1603 to tell King James, *"We have the man Shakespeare here"*, to entice him there for the Christmas festivities. Unfortunately, though Cory believed the letter still existed, neither he nor anyone else left a report of having seen it. That story has raised many queries but, even if the letter were found, it is unlikely that one could deduce its meaning with certainty. For one thing, Philip and William Herbert were both so keen to fix their interest with James that their mother would have known they needed no encouragement to invite him to Wilton, which he had already visited once since his accession the previous March.

The second side issue is the interest in Shakespeare that has long existed at Wilton. For example, when a statue was erected to "him" in Westminster Abbey in 1741, the Herbert family had a replica made, but with the quotation on it taken from *Macbeth* and the subject's finger pointing at the word "shadows" and not from *The Tempest*, with the finger pointing at "temples" as in the original. The replica was originally placed in a building called "Shakespeare's House", and has given much joy to cryptographic fans.

In her book *Sweet Swan of Avon* (2006), Robin Williams opened the gate for some serious attention to be paid to Mary Sidney's candidacy, and her thesis that the bulk of the Sonnets were written to a man by a woman might remove more problems than it causes. If it should turn out that the greatest poet and playwright was a woman, there would be unmodified rapture in some quarters, but it must be the hard evidence that decides. For a good overview, again see Michell, 2000.

Edward de Vere (1550–1604) – "Oxford"

Our third "possible" candidate for the Shakespeare mantle, Edward de Vere, we will call "Oxford", in keeping with general usage. He was regularly praised as a top playwright and poet – in 1589 by George Puttenham, in 1598 by Frances Meres, and posthumously in 1622 by Henry Peacham – though, as an aristocrat, his plays would hardly have been printed over his own name. Some of his early poems did carry his name, and some are in print today, but no poems were published in his name after 1593, the year *Venus and Adonis* appeared apparently as the "first heir" of the "invention" of the pseudonym "Shakespeare".

There is a marked similarity between some of Oxford's poetry and that of Shakespeare's – enough to confuse some orthodox scholars – but the similarities between the character of the writer Shakespeare (as it is read from the plays) and that of the man Oxford (as read from his biographies and known writings) go further than that: indeed, it was those similarities that led to his choice as a candidate in the first place.

In the early twentieth century, a Thomas Looney carefully worked through Shakespeare's plays and poems to build up a profile of the writer behind them. Profile in hand, he looked for possible "suspects" by trawling all the biographies of Elizabethans he could find (though, by limiting his search to men, he missed Mary Sidney). Without having heard of Oxford before, Looney found he fitted his "Shakespeare profile" in terms of his knowledge, character, manner of thought, behaviour, misbehaviour, experiences, resources and written output. On that basis, he published his book *Shakespeare Identified* in 1920.

Later, the psychologist Sigmund Freud did a comparative analysis between the personality he had earlier identified from Shakespeare's plays and sonnets and that of Oxford. He supported Looney's finding, though he did not publish his conclusions in England while he lived because his other books were threatened with being blacklisted.

Strangely, in his 2001 book *Shakespeare in Psychoanalysis*, Armstrong took exception to Freud's statement (see 1966 reference), "The name 'William Shakespeare' is very probably a pseudonym." Though this writer had more references to Freud in his book than to anyone else – it

213

seems the book might not have been written without Freud's work – he demanded, "Why does he now wish to repudiate the Stratford man, whose mind he had so convincingly penetrated in 1900?" That is an incredible question from a scholar, to ask why Freud discovered – like everyone else – that the information available on Shakspere (much found after 1900) did not at all match the Shakespeare personality he had penetrated in the plays and poems. Armstrong tried to psychoanalyse Freud out of his change of mind, but it was like someone philosophising about why a car won't go when it has simply run out of fuel. The mind Freud had penetrated was never Shakspere's, and he now thought it was Oxford's.

Of course, Looney's profiling is now standard procedure, but there are still orthodox scholars who think they have licence to make fun of it and couple their mistaken sarcasm about the technique with sneering at Mr Looney's name – which says much more about them than it does about him. (In fact, the name is Manx and is pronounced "loney", but it provides a test of the worth of scholars if they think – and there are too many of them – that the pronunciation of a man's name affects the value of his scholarship.)

Oxford matriculated at the University of Cambridge, knew William Harvey and was enrolled at the Inns of Court. He had travelled widely and, in Italy from Milan to Messina, he somehow visited the towns in Shakespeare's plays. He was on terms with William Stanley, Earl of Derby (who went everywhere relevant) and Philip Herbert, Earl of Montgomery (dedicatee of the First Folio); both became his sons-in-law. He was the likeliest person to have created Polonius in *Hamlet*, an obvious parody of his father-in-law and resented guardian Lord Burghley, although the latter's foibles were well known to both Bacon and Mary Sidney.

Those who object to Oxford's candidacy will claim that some Shakespeare works were written after he died in June 1604. Those who believe Oxford was Shakespeare hold the view that that cannot be so, while the orthodox insistence on the late dating of the plays (see Chapter 15 and Appendix F) seems often to reflect a wish to eliminate Oxford from contention. The play on which the orthodox place most weight for this purpose, namely *The Tempest*, is unsuitable and, if it eliminated Oxford, it would also eliminate Shakspere. A more crucial play appears to be *King Lear*, usually dated 1605, though that needs more work. The orthodox date ignores the possibility that Shakespeare used original documents as sources and the fact that the play had multiple versions, the earliest around 1590 (see Appendix F).

If nothing is found that Shakespeare really wrote after 1604, Oxford's "early" death actually has advantages for his candidacy. He fits the term "ever-living poet" in Thorpe's 1609 dedication of the Sonnets since, at the time, that phrase was rarely if ever used for an author who was still alive. Some have asserted that that term never meant immortal, yet Shakespeare himself refers to *"The ever-living man of memory, Henry V"* in *Henry VI, Part* 1.

Oxford fits the statements in the introduction to the First Folio that indicate the author was not able to edit and publish his own plays. His death would explain why, for example, when *Macbeth* was shortened *c.* 1606 (if that date is correct), the author was clearly not around to manage the adaptation properly: if he had been, we would not be left with a fragment showing every sign of amateur hacking. Oddly, the fact that Bacon started his philosophic writing around 1605, that Shakspere left no trace of working in London after 1604, and Mary Sidney began a distracting love affair around 1606, means those three also could have ended their careers as Shakespeare by 1604/5 – if they had had one!

One quite perverse argument advanced against Oxford being Shakespeare is that both were mentioned as top writers by Meres in 1598. Yet it is easy to see why Meres would have mentioned separately works Oxford wrote early under his own name and works he wrote later pseudonymously as Shakespeare (if he did). What is much more interesting is that Henry Peacham placed Oxford at the head of his 1622 list of the top-rank Elizabethan writers who were dead, and did not mention Shakespeare at all, indicating he knew the latter was a pseudonym, whether for Oxford or someone else – or was alive in 1622.

Attempts to discredit Oxford as a candidate by reference to his private life are puerile. Great works may be written by great scoundrels who, as Shakespeare showed in his plays, can be very intriguing people. One writer nonsensically implied Oxford could not have been Shakespeare because he was a paedophile, although his paedophilia was only an allegation by enemies, hardly a fact. The same writer oddly suggested that Shakspere's candidature to be Shakespeare is helped by him being guilty of marital infidelity – for which the evidence only exists in anecdotes and circular arguments.

Professor Alan Nelson, writing in the *ODNB*, stated that

> Claims by literary and historical amateurs beginning with J. Thomas Looney in 1920 and embraced by Oxford's otherwise worthy biographer B. M. Ward, that Oxford wrote the poems and plays attributed by contemporaries to William Shakespeare, are without merit.

This is the Professor Nelson who claimed there is evidence that Shakspere went to school, was paid to write, knew the Earl of Southampton, and had tributes paid at his death, and believes all contemporaries who mentioned Shakespeare thought they were writing of the player Shakspere.

Readable accounts of the Oxford case are Ogburn (1984) and Whalen

(1994) while essays in Malim (2004) give additional information.

Our conclusion has to be that there are definitely three good candidates for being the writer Shakespeare. The positive features of their cases tend to speak for themselves (and we have only given a selection here), but attention is needed to see if it is possible to eliminate any of them. The orthodox arguments against them are usually easily answered, being directed at peripheral, or even misrepresented, features of the supporting cases, but that does not mean that the candidates should not be looked on with a sceptical eye, even if the chance for any one of them being Shakespeare is infinitely greater than that for William Shakspere.

Attempts have been made to eliminate these candidates by computer comparison of their written work against Shakespeare's. The trouble is that the relevant work for the correct candidate is in the plays and sonnets. It is no use entering Bacon's philosophical works, or Mary Sidney's translations or her *Psalms of David*, or Oxford's juvenile poetry into a computer and being surprised when it finds them different from Shakespeare's. If the wrong thing is put into the computer, the wrong answer comes out, and that is so even if the programs used are reliable, which is not always the case. Of course, one cannot make comparisons with the ordinary writings Shakspere left, because he did not write. (Perhaps orthodox computer buffs have not picked up that comparing Shakspere's nothing with Shakespeare's works cannot give a better fit than Bacon's or Sidney's or Oxford's something.)

There must, though, be two more words of caution. First, the true Shakespeare may yet be unidentified as a candidate. James and Rubenstein (2004) have recently proposed Sir Henry Neville (1564–1615), a man well travelled and educated, known to Southampton and to other writers, and named on the "Northumberland Manuscript"; more work is being done to test him against the Shakespeare template. The second is that we have spent no time on the "group theories" which propose that a school of writers produced the works of "Shakespeare": those theories have problems all their own, not least the strong feeling of a single voice across Shakespeare's works (other than where additions were clearly made).

Finally, we would stress here that pursuit of the real "author", good fun though it may be, was not the purpose of this book. That was to give back to William Shakspere his real identity. If, in doing that, the search for the real Shakespeare is opened up to all scholars and aficianados, free from acrimony, that is a consummation greatly to be wished.

Chapter 17

Does the Theft of Shakspere's Identity really matter?

No one seriously denies that the appreciation and understanding of works of art, music or literature are affected, or even determined, by one's knowledge of their creator. This applies also to Shakespeare. His great works must reflect his learning, ability, experiences and cast of mind. We expect to find, and do, that Shakespeare biographers and critics, orthodox and unorthodox, whoever they believe he was, interpret his works in terms of their individual personal images of the author. Sadly, because orthodox scholars insist that the author was William Shakspere of Stratford, though he in no way matches the author revealed by the works, most biographies of our greatest writer and discussions of his plays and poems are bound to be distorted. It is no use arguing – however cleverly – that the works can be analysed without considering the author: it simply does not happen.

The orthodox interpretation of Shakespeare's works and what they reveal are bound to be affected by the assumptions that are made to get them to fit Shakspere and the circular arguments to which they give rise. To appreciate that situation, one need only imagine how the study of George Eliot's works would have been distorted if the authorship claims made for Joseph Liggens of Warwickshire had been pursued as an orthodox theory.

Most damaging to Shakespeare scholarship have been inventions resulting from the misuse of the 1592 tract known as Greene's *Groatsworth*, with Shakespeare being branded as an "upstart crow" guilty of stealing other writers' "feathers": such invention has pervaded thought in this area like a virus. As a result, the bulk of commentators – journalistic as well as literary – believe that Shakespeare was an unlearned plagiarist who was attacked by his peers. Yet the text of the *Groatsworth* is available for anyone to read and to see that this view of it is mistaken: it would have been left to gather dust long ago but for constant repetitions of inventions based on it, designed, not to illuminate Shakespeare, but to protect the myth that he was Shakspere. It is amazing, even scary, that a recent orthodox biographer could tell his readers that the *Groatsworth's* general meaning *"is clear – Shakespeare is a devious, importunate and bumptious literary thief"*, and be praised by orthodox reviewers for his scholarship. Can the defence of the quasi-religious Shakspere myth really merit such a travesty? It should be obvious, without anything more, that if the greatest dramatic writer the world has ever produced must be blackguarded, degraded and dumbed down to fit the orthodox theory, then that theory has to be wrong. The damage to scholarship has to be great when a top orthodox Shakespearean (or Shaksperean) can say *"There can be no doubt that [Shake-scene] refers to Shakespeare"*, when there are much better interpretations. There is a logical problem known as "the fallacy of limited alternatives" and here is a good example – pick the answer you want and ignore all the other possibilities.

The theft of William Shakspere's identity to cover the real author of the First Folio led Alexander Pope to believe he should criticise Shakespeare for writing for money, whereas he was never paid. John Dryden earlier was led to criticise Shakespeare for not understanding dramatic structures because of his lack of education, when what he was doing was writing beyond anything that had gone before him. A Dr Farmer, penning his *Essay on the Learning of Shakespeare* in 1767, felt he had to show how Shakespeare, because he was Shakspere, wrote his great works with no language but English, no classical scholarship, and no extraordinary knowledge of any kind. To this day, there are people who – carefully treading the footsteps of Farmer – think the authorship claim for William Shakspere is best proved by the "fact" that Shakespeare had "Small Latin and less Greek", when it is obvious he had much Latin (and much else) and quite enough Greek.

The belief that Shakspere was Shakespeare makes it necessary to deny or dumb down the peculiar and extensive knowledge contained in the plays such as we have demonstrated in Chapter 15. There are biographies of "Shakespeare", apparently driven by the Shakspere myth, without discussion of his Italian knowledge, or his legal knowledge and usage, or his knowledge of languages and especially English, and so on.

Students of Literature, English, and the Elizabethan Stage have to accept and pass on many odd things about the author Shakespeare, besides his lack of learning and his stealing of other people's works and belonging to a non-existent family of Stratford Shakespeares. They will be told his great works were edited by two people who wrote nothing of their own; that he was not famous enough to be noticed as a writer at his death; that he had a poor anonymous gravestone with a worse verse; and so on. They will be asked to believe he had no rights in plays he wrote, although

Jonson and others had rights in theirs even after they had sold them. It will be claimed the very nature of Shakespeare's plays was changed with the King's Mens' purchase of Blackfriars Theatre in 1608, when they did not open there until 1611. There is no evidence any of his works played there first, or that he wrote any after 1608 – see Nicoll. Indeed, one has the impression that authors of books on Elizabethan theatre, education, publishing, or writing, feel that they must consider carefully how what they write may affect the Shakspere myth.

Students will be told that "experts" have validated, as being the signatures of Shakespeare, copies of the name Shakspere that they would immediately see (if they got the chance, as here) are not spelt or written alike twice together, and are not "Shakespeare". They will find they cannot read about the third Earl of Southampton or Richard Burbage without the myths created around Shakspere intruding. They may wonder at Ben Jonson's entry in the *ODNB* (2004), when they find it allots one-third of a sentence to his contribution to the First Folio, though it may be the only thing some know about him.

They will be asked to accept a fallacious method for dating Shakespeare's works so that they fit to a fictitious writing career of an actor-businessman, even though basic, firsthand evidence, like Jonson's on *Titus Andronicus* or Nashe's on *Hamlet* or Pudsey's on *Othello*, point to it being fiction. They will find that reference books repeat the conventional dating with no warning that it is, at best, highly speculative.

They will be faced with the invention or distortion of evidence, such as the changes made to phrases in Aubrey's diaries so that they say Shakspere could write when they clearly say the opposite; or giving wrong locations, or even wrong names, to places in the plays (e.g. reading Barton-on-the-Heath for Burton Heath); or by insisting that the obvious meaning of a sonnet cannot possibly be right if it does not fit Shakspere: for example, someone claimed that the first line of Sonnet 125, *"Were't aught to me I bore the canopy"* – which might imply someone of rank – must mean "Were't aught to me I bore not the canopy".

An unpleasant consequence of the attempts to pretend Shakspere was Shakespeare has been the insults that have been levelled at one or both of them, often inspired by misuse of Greene's *Groatsworth*, and are still included to pad out biographies from time to time and help justify the theft of Shakspere's identity. (So that readers can see the nature and effect of those insults, a few cases are looked at in Appendix H.)

If a student (or even scholar) should query the claim that William Shakspere was Shakespeare, he or she must expect to be told that only a snob would doubt it. This, of course, should never be an adequate response to any academic question, but such insults are common currency in this area in default of something better. Students may well be challenged: do

219

they think a grammar-school boy could not have written Shakespeare's works? – but not be asked what the facts are that are giving them problems. They may well know that people like Robert Burns, Abraham Lincoln, Charles Dickens, and Ben Jonson, all from unprivileged backgrounds, are accepted unquestioningly for their great achievements because of the abundant evidence to show these achievements were theirs, but not realise that all such evidence is missing for Shakspere having written the works of Shakespeare.

Another frequent attempt to put down inquisitive students in respect of the Shakespeare authorship question rests on demanding if they can possibly believe men like Heminges, Condell and Jonson would have lied in the First Folio, or that the deceptions identified in the First Folio would really have been followed by a centuries-long conspiracy. The word "conspiracy" is often used in this context to intimidate the doubter; but what name can one give to the steady production of inventions and unfounded assumptions that have for years sustained the myth that Shakspere was Shakespeare? Students will not be told it was orthodox scholars who uncovered and spelled out the deceptions in the First Folio in the 1770s, not "heretics" as they are often called, and that the movement to expose the Shakspere myth only really burgeoned after that. Heminges and Condell were almost certainly unaware that their names were being misused, and no one, however much they may protest, can believe Jonson was above a little plotting. He was a fascinating character, but more Faust than George Washington. No one is surprised to learn that he, a supposed Catholic, had dinner on Monday 1st November 1605 with the man – Lord Monteagle – who would expose the Gunpowder Plot on Thursday 4th November, and that he remained unscathed while the plotters were arrested and tortured. In the *ODNB* (2004), Professor Peter Holland's article on "William Shakespeare" implies it is normal for those who disagree with the orthodox theory to be mad or become so, and says of them *"All distort evidence for their own ends."* Yet, as pointed out in Chapter 3, his 78-column article uses the name "Shakespeare" every time there is a reference to a member of the Stratford family whose baptismal name was Shakspere, without warning readers of the alteration. If none of the editors noticed what he had done, it may simply be because the practice had been going on so long.

It is not good if students get to feel it is possible to conduct a major area of scholarship on the basis of invention and concealment, sustained by fear of disadvantage induced in those who would challenge orthodoxy. It is no accident that most of those who have actively challenged orthodox Shakespeare scholarship have not been working in departments of English or History in American or English universities, and have rarely had their material published through the standard routes.

The trouble is that the culture of the Shakspere myth can cause one to be suspicious even when such a reaction may not be warranted. For example, what would students, aware of the authorship controversy, make of what happened in relation to Shakespeare in a splendid monograph of 2007 titled *Anonymity* which covered anonymous and pseudonymous authorship since the invention of the printing press? If they knew that some forty Elizabethan plays – such as *Locrine, Arden of Faversham, Sir John Oldcastle,* and *Thomas, Lord Cromwell* – were published under the name "Shakespeare", though they were not by the author of the First Folio, they might wonder that the book found no room to comment on this situation, which may be unique in the field of publishing. Even more puzzling would be that the book moved on to discuss the searches made to uncover various anonymous authors, and gave a detailed account of one in particular. This explained minutely how Francis Bacon managed to persuade Queen Elizabeth not to put a man to the rack to get him to reveal the pseudonymous author of a play that was performed across London to help boost a rebellion by the Earl of Essex in 1601: but *Anonymity* did not name the play – *Richard II* – nor the pseudonym the Queen was trying to penetrate – Shakespeare. If the students were puzzled, it would not be surprising.

May (1980) took up a hypothesis that there was no great tendency to anonymity or pseudonymity in Tudor times, even amongst members of the aristocracy, and reported dozens of published documents to which aristocratic writers had put their names. Yet a count showed that some ninety-five percent of those documents were factual or advisory, or were translations of non-contentious documents, not literary or dramatic. But, while May's analysis did indeed confirm that there was no "stigma of print" – to use his term – in Tudor times in relation to non-contentious writing, it also showed that the advice of Baldassare Castiglioni (1528) that "*the courtier keep close his verses*" was taken very seriously in the reign of Elizabeth. Moreover, it also showed that when the *anonymous* author of *The Art of English Poesie* (thought to be George Puttenham) wrote:

> So as I know very many notable gentlemen in the Court have written commendably and suppressed it again or else suffered it to be published without their own names.

he was simply reporting a well known fact; a fact that was confirmed in turn by Sheavyn (1967). A student interested in the Shakespeare authorship question might be surprised to find that May's conclusion that there was "no stigma of print" in Tudor times has been used to claim it would be strange for Shakespeare, whoever he was, to have used a pseudonym, when the detail of May's investigation – and that of others – actually showed that, for the type of work under discussion here, exactly the opposite would be true for the three candidates discussed in the previous chapter. We have here named many, including Shakespeare, who found themselves at risk for dramatic writings with a hint of political allusion, while revisers of the Bible, say, were only really safe if well away in exile. It is no surprise that anonymity and pseudonymity increased in Tudor times: see Taylor and Mosher (1951).

Another oddity is that almost all orthodoxs works on "Shakespeare" – but also the works of Jonson – omit discussion of the way the latter passed off Heminges and Condell as the editors of the First Folio. It is hardly a new discovery, being known for over 250 years, and it is hardly insignificant for Shakespeare scholarship. Yet it is hidden from most students as though they lived in a community dominated by religious or political forces that put sensitive matters relating to the Shakspere myth on a proscribed list. If civil engineers worked like that, for example, one might have serious worries about driving over bridges.

Without question, the restoration to William Shakspere of his true identity after all these years is not a trivial matter with trivial consequences. Some may see it as a matter of justice. Some may see it as a first step towards getting a consensus on the real identity of the writer of the world's greatest dramatic works. At bottom, though, it is a basic matter of scholarship that will lead to a more coherent understanding of Shakespeare's works.

In conclusion, it is worth noting the ambiguous opening statement of a website sponsored by T. Ross and D. Kathman on behalf of the Shakespeare Birthplace Trust at Stratford-upon-Avon:

> A mass of evidence from his own time shows a man called William Shakespeare wrote the plays and poems of William Shakespeare.

As we have shown, there is no evidence, from the time the Trust is referring to or otherwise, that there was a real person named William Shakespeare who was writing plays and poems. There was a man using the pseudonym William Shakespeare, yes, but that is not the same thing at all. More accurate and fair might be a message that said:

> No evidence from his own time shows that a man named William Shakspere wrote the plays and poems of William Shakespeare.

But it would be even more accurate to add:

> A mass of evidence shows that he did not.

222

Appendix A

The Genuine Catholic Testament of "John Shakspear" and the false claims for John Shakspere's Religion

The story of the valiant attempts to pass off a genuine Catholic testament as if it had belonged to William Shakspere's father, John Shakspere, has to begin with Stratford's very own fraudster, John Jordan (1746–1809) – and the dates are not insignificant. This Jordan can be considered the godfather of the high epoch of Shakspere and Shakespeare forgery and fabrication. He may only have been a wheelwright by trade, but he had the mysterious gift of "finding" Shakspere or Shakespeare artefacts: he found chairs the writer had sat on, poems that he had written but never published, signatures he had mysteriously left in books and on documents. Shakespeare aficionados would pay good money to own Jordan's fakes, for they were specifically designed to satisfy the need that was felt by many lovers of Shakespeare to have something tangible of their hero's that they could treasure when, of course, there could be nothing genuine for them to buy. Jordan was followed in this trade by W. H. Ireland (1777–1835) after they met in Stratford in 1794, and by J. P. Collier (1789–1883). Both of these men may have surpassed him in skill and quantity but not in nerve and ingenuity. (A light-hearted account of how Jordan, Ireland and Collier kept the "Shakespeare market" supplied with their inventions will be found in Schoenbaum, 1970.)

Given Jordan's reputation, it should have been natural for Shakespeare scholars to be suspicious of anything Shakespearean he might offer them. This should have applied particularly to the London lawyer Edmond Malone (1741–1812), a self-made but excellent Shakespeare scholar whom Jordan had already trapped twice by 1789 over Shakspere or Shakespeare artefacts. Yet even so, when he wrote to Malone in that year, sending him the handwritten text of what he claimed was the Catholic testament of John Shakespeare (meaning John Shakspere), so great was Malone's desire to find anything that shed light on the writer Shakespeare that Jordan was given more than a fair hearing. Indeed, even during their transactions over this testament, which would end with his public embarrassment, Malone was lending Jordan money for other Shaksperean projects.

What Stratford's Jordan sent to Malone in London was a set of five pages, copied out by himself, which had every appearance of being part of a six-page statement of Catholic faith – a spiritual will, in effect – bearing a declaration that the person to whom it belonged would keep it with him or her at all times, even to the grave. What was missing from those pages was the first or title page of the statement. The owner's name, written by Jordan at the various places inside the document that were provided for it, was "John Shakspear".

Jordan's story, as Malone later reported it – and we have absolutely no other source – was as follows. The pages Jordan had copied were part of a six-page booklet which, he said, had been found hidden in the roof of one of the houses that John Shakspere had owned in Henley Street, Stratford, the first page having subsequently been lost. The discovery was said by Jordan to have been made in 1757 by a master-builder, Joseph Moseley (since dead), while he was working on the roof of that house, which, at the time, was in the possession of John Shakspere's great-great-great-great grandson Thomas Hart who, Jordan said, had witnessed the finding of the document. That was when Jordan was eleven, and thirty-two years before he sent his copy to Malone. Jordan said that, for some unexplained reason, the leaves passed from Moselely to an Alderman Payton at Shottery near Stratford; and, though he had not found them and did not own them, Payton had kept them ever since.

Jordan told Malone he had tried in 1784 to get the five pages – which he had personally copied out from the originals – published in the *Gentleman's Magazine* in London. He said he had given his own title to the five pages, namely *"The Spiritual Last Will and Testament of John Shakespeare"*, and sent them to the editor together with his account of the provenance of the document and his interpretation of its significance. The editor rejected Jordan's offer as fraudulent and returned the five pages apparently without comment. Jordan was now asking Malone to publish the five pages in his twenty-two-volume edition of the *Complete Works of Shakespeare*, then in preparation. Of course, if this were done, Jordan's claim for them would be authenticated and their value would increase.

Some of the other people who had already seen the incomplete booklet had treated it as another Jordan forgery, including the Stratford schoolmaster, the Reverend Joseph Greene (1712–1790), who had discovered William Shakspere's will in 1747. However, Malone took a totally different view. He decided that the text he was reading was way beyond what anyone in Stratford could have fabricated; he gave his opinion – and this is crucial to the story, though it is usually ignored – he gave his opinion that the pages had been taken originally from a document written by some scholarly priest, possibly as part of an official Catholic publication.

Malone would never know how accurate he had been, as this view was not confirmed until long after his death when various texts came to light of a "Testament of the Soul", originally authored in Latin and Italian by a Cardinal Borromeo about 1580; these, when translated, proved to be similar to the one Jordan had copied. An early, but somewhat different, English translation of Borromeo's text would come to light as late as 1966. It is now quite obvious that an English variant of the Borromeo text had formed the basis of the five pages of the "John Shakspear" testament Jordan had passed to Malone, although they did not correspond word-for-word or even paragraph-for-paragraph with any of the versions which had appeared in print – see *SDL*.

When Malone asked to see the original from which Jordan had copied, it was obtained for him from Payton by the then vicar of Stratford, the Reverend Davenport. What he got were five pages, all stitched together, that were clearly the remnant of a small six-page booklet that had lost the all-important front page. Malone saw that Jordan had made a good copy, and that the name which had been inserted in the spaces provided in the original text of the document was indeed "John Shakspear". His initial reaction was that the original was in a style of handwriting that only existed after John Shakspere had died in 1601, but he did not give up: he compared the writing with a range of scripts from the late Elizabethan era, and took expert advice. As a result, Malone concluded it was possible that the paper, ink and writing could all have been from before 1600, so they could not be used to rule out the testament as being John Shakspere's. He then accepted the story Jordan had written to him, which, he was told, would be backed up by both Thomas Hart and the daughter of the builder Joseph Moseley: namely that the document had been found in John Shakspere's roof in 1757. He decided to publish the five pages as the Catholic Testament of "John Shakespeare", though there was no way he could know what actual title the booklet had carried. If it was genuine, it was an important document of historic and economic value, even though the religion of the Shakspere family had not at that time become the fashionable subject it is today. There were very few real documentary records of the Shakspere family around, and any addition had to be significant.

After Malone's book had been put into print, along with the five pages of the booklet, he became exercised over the missing first page, the absence of which could raise suspicions all by itself. Under Malone's questioning – and he was a lawyer – Jordan panicked. He told Malone he had discovered that Moseley had made a copy of the lost first page and had put on it the date 29 April 1757 when the booklet was found. What he sent to Malone, though, was not a front page copied by Moseley, but one Jordan claimed to have copied from it in his own handwriting. Malone saw at once that the style and language of this page was nothing like the style and language of the five pages he had already had type-set; he judged it to be a low-level fabrication in which Jordan had even included a quotation from *Hamlet*. He decided to go ahead and publish the other five pages – probably because resetting the type would have been too expensive – but, to the spurious front page that he added in for completeness, he joined a statement of his doubts. Malone's view that this page was another Jordan fraud was fully vindicated with the later discovery of a genuine version of the front page taken from the Borromeo testament.

It could well be that Malone started worrying about what he had done even before the supposed John Shakspere testament appeared in print in 1790 complete with the false front page. In his enthusiasm for something new about "Shakespeare", he had again believed Jordan's word about a supposed Shakspere document, although this time more about its provenance than its actual contents. One can easily imagine the questions that Malone would have started to ask himself. If the document was really found in 1757, a decade after the excitement of the discovery of Shakspere's will in 1747, why had it not been made profitably public then? Why was it not displayed at the great celebration of Shakspere's birth in Stratford in 1769? If the document was found in Thomas Hart's house in 1757 and he was there at the time, why had he allowed it to be handed to Alderman Payton who then kept it for thirty-two years? How did the front page become separated from this important document when the pages were stitched together and would have been hidden (if they were hidden) as a complete item? How did that most vital first page get lost even if it was separated? Did it contradict Jordan's claims? If the document was genuine, why had Jordan become involved, instead of it being given at once to a reputable scholar? Why did Jordan forge the first page and put a date on it? Why was the booklet separated from John Shakspere at all if it was his and he had declared to keep it always with him? Why was it not buried rather than hidden in a roof for anti-Catholic agents to find, to the danger of John Shakspere's whole family? These are just some of the obvious questions one might ask, even without knowing Jordan's reputation.

It seems Malone started asking Jordan slightly different questions at different times and got back letters with inconsistent answers, particularly as to how and when Jordan came to see the booklet. Malone concluded that the story about its discovery was false. He found that it had only come to light around 1770, thirteen years after the 1757 date chosen to fit the repairs at Henley Street. He also learned why the Hart family had not owned and kept the booklet: it was not theirs. He thus exonerated Thomas Hart from any fraud and understood why the first page was missing: it would have carried information contradicting Jordan's claim, which was why he fabricated one of his own. I have used some deduction of my own in this paragraph, but only what fits with the evidence, with Malone's investigation, and his documents in the British Library – and with what he did next.

In 1796, at the risk of his hard-won reputation as a Shakespeare scholar (and as a lawyer), Malone published a retraction of his identification of the testament as John Shakspere's. He said he had proof it had nothing to do with William Shakspere's family. He did not, repeat *not*, retract his view that the testament was based on a genuine Catholic text. It was simply that he had found that the story of its provenance was false. It seems he had discovered that the document had belonged to an actual Catholic named John Shakspear (or something similar), the name being not uncommon, and that conclusion was supported about 1820 by Professor James Boswell, Junior, who had worked with Malone and would have known he had been making enquiries about other John Shaksperes or Shakspears before his retraction. Malone did not produce his evidence for his conclusion, probably because to do so could have seriously embarrassed the Harts and the family of the John Shakspear who had signed the testament.

Malone's conclusion that the document was a fraud perpetrated against John Shakspere (as well as himself) has to be trusted. He would not have exposed himself to possible legal action from the document's owners and Jordan, if he had not been sure the retraction was correct, as he had effectively libelled them as fraudsters and had made their potentially valuable document worthless; neither would he have recklessly exposed himself to public ridicule. His findings were consistent with the strange facts in the case, and he was effectively shown to be right when Jordan never raised the matter in the remaining thirteen years of his life; the owners (whoever they were) never came forward and the document quietly disappeared.

What is startling, given all the evidence and logic, is the number of Shakespeare biographers who have talked about that testament as though it was definitely John Shakspere's and that it proved William Shakspere was a Catholic (which could be their real agenda). About half of all new Shakespeare biographies either do not mention it at all, or mention it only to cast doubt on it. Yet some writers suggest there is no reason to doubt its authenticity while others may tell their readers that Malone only rejected the booklet because he made the mistake of believing Jordan had forged it, and did not realise it was a genuine Catholic document – which is the opposite of the truth. Some scholars claim that Jordan was an honest man – "poet", "antiquarian", "draftsman", "Shakespeare sleuth" are some terms applied to him – and deny he was a major fraudster. Some imply Malone was to blame for letting the "testament" disappear, when it was never his to dispose of. Most ignore the silence of the document's owners (whoever they were), as well as Jordan's forging of the missing first page, and may pretend it was the same as the known English translation found in 1966. Some have printed that English language version as though it was the one that Jordan gave to Malone, when it was not.

Some orthodox writers, perhaps not realising Jordan had taken a quotation out of *Hamlet* to put in his fabricated first page, tell readers that that was where Shakespeare had originally found it. Oh dear, the "upstart crow" story gets everywhere! The full text of the real "Testament of the Soul" has a totally different front page from Jordan's, in style and language as well as in content. It has even been suggested, by way of giving Jordan's story verisimilitude, that John Shakspere hid the document in the Henley Street roof when houses were being searched in Stratford after the executions of Edward Arden and Sir John Somerville. However, as that would have put the Shakspere family at serious risk – the roof being an obvious place to search – the probability of that happening, even if the Shaksperes were Catholics, has to be minimal.

The choice for scholars is either to accept the evidence Malone left us after his investigations – backed up as it was by the subsequent acquiescence of Jordan and the owners of the document – or to rely on fabrications. Some will say that, if it were not for Jordan's involvement, everyone would accept the testament as genuinely John Shakspere's. Yet Malone did accept Jordan's story at first and printed the testament. He showed his own scholarship by working out that the text was genuine long before that could be proved. It was only when he made further inquiries that he worked out the details of the fraud against John Shakspere and issued his retraction. Care must be taken not to do a "Jordan" all over again, by using his attempted fraud to pass off the Shakspere as Catholics and libelling Malone and challenging his evidence – without any basis – in the process.

For reasonably accessible reviews of the problem that faced Malone over Jordan's scam, see *EKC* and *SCDL* and Schoenbaum (1970), although none of these fully acknowledges how right Malone's conclusions were. For the most peculiar account, one could go to Sams (1995) who, treating the testament as genuine, totally ignored the part played by Jordan, the actions of Malone, and the missing front page, etcetera, etcetera – rather like celebrating the *Titanic* without mentioning the iceberg.

Appendix B

The "William Shakeshafte" Myth

Not apparently satisfied with taking William Shakspere's identity to give to whoever wrote the works of Shakespeare, some scholars have set about trying to take the identity of a William Shakeshafte of Lancashire to give to our Shakspere in his turn. Indeed, it is quite amazing what a story they have managed to make out of the discovery of a bequest to this man in 1581 in the will of Alexander Hoghton of Hoghton Hall near Preston, one-hundred-and-thirty miles from Stratford (see Honigmann, 1998).

Though Hoghton Hall was a good (or bad) week's journey from Stratford, some scholars have decided that the Shakeshafte who received that bequest was really our William Shakspere: the slight matter of the spelling of his name and the long journey seem no impediments. Nor does it bother them that the story requires Shakspere to have rushed back to Stratford to father a child on Anne Hathaway in the summer of 1582. It looks as though someone saw this claim as a straw waiting to be clutched, in case it might fill a small part of the missing years that are the prominent feature of Shakspere's history. As an added bonus, there are some who have seen it as a chance to help pass Shakspere off as a "schoolmaster in the country" as related in another anecdote, although there is no evidence that the Shakeshafte in Alexander Hoghton's will was a tutor of any kind. Others have seen the story as a way to explain how Shakspere got into acting, in this case by joining the troupe of players sponsored by Lord Strange, who lived at Lathom Hall, a mere three-day round trip from Hoghton. There is no evidence Shakspere ever acted with Lord Strange's Men, or for any of the other fanciful propositions that have come out of the Shakeshafte myth, including its use to prop up the theory that he was a Catholic.

An event used by some to support this Shakeshafte myth is that a Thomas Savage from Rufford, a village not far from Preston, became a trustee in "Shakespeare's" Globe in 1599, eighteen years after our seventeen-year-old Shakspere was supposedly at Hoghton under the name Shakeshafte. It is then said that coincidence meant *"there may be something in [the Shakeshafte myth]"*. But that is nonsense. This Thomas Savage was a rich goldsmith with funds to invest. He was almost certainly two hundred miles away in London when myth says Shakspere was in Lancashire. Most importantly, he was landlord to the Globe-sharer John Heminges, who put him forward as a trustee. Most supporters of the Shakspere myth manage to resist mentioning that link, which explains exactly why Savage became a Globe trustee without any need to involve Shakspere.

Another piece of "evidence" called on to support the Shakeshafte myth is an anecdote, dignified by the name "tradition", that Shakespeare once stayed at Hoghton Hall or somewhere near. There are dozens of such anecdotes about Shakespeare, and all those with a factual content have been tested and eliminated. For example, there was a well attested "tradition" that Shakespeare wrote *Romeo and Juliet* at St Margaret's, a hunting lodge near Titchfield where the Earl of Southampton lived. At least there was, until the "House Detectives" on BBC television in 2000 showed the lodge was built after 1623. In the late eighteenth century, a tradition was reported by Stratford's vicar, Joseph Greene, that there were rhymes written by Shakspere's girls still on the window-panes of New Place in 1675: that would fall today, among other things, on the fact that neither could write. Traditions that Elizabeth, or Cromwell, or Shakespeare "slept here" (or there) abound, but none is acceptable as evidence by itself. Moreover, there are good reasons for knowing Shakspere was not William Shakeshafte.

Most people give up on this myth when they realise Shakeshafte was (and is) a common name in the area of Preston, and there were records, around 1580, of more than one "William Shakeshafte" living near Hoghton. Also they will note that there was no incentive for the young Shakspere to make the hard, risky, costly journey to Hoghton: the only reason ever offered for that journey at all is that, as a Catholic (which he was not), he would have been safer at Hoghton than at Stratford, though Catholics were arrested at Hoghton around 1581, and none at Stratford. Everything supporting the Shakeshafte myth consists of hypotheses propped up by assumptions, but it falls on the facts.

Let us simply look at the size and nature of the bequest that was made to Shakeshafte in 1581. Alexander Hoghton's will provided a basic legacy to all servants at Hoghton Hall equal to *"one whole year's salary"*. On top of this there were special bequests to eleven of his twenty-nine male servants. Not only was William Shakeshafte included among those chosen eleven, but his additional bequest was also the second largest. This must tell us that Shakeshafte was a man who, among a few others, had given specially long or notable service, most likely both. In an attempt to remove this major problem for the Shakeshafte myth, one senior scholar claimed there was no tradition of long service being specially rewarded, and found an "expert" to back him up who also apparently had never heard of long-service awards or pensions for old servants or "grace and favour" housing.

From what is known of the people named in that Hoghton will, it is clear the size of legacy was not just related to length of service, but it is not easy to accept that a newly-appointed, young servant, possibly the newest of the twenty-nine, received the second largest special bequest when eighteen of them did not get one. Even if one sees no problem in this, the will poses an extra conundrum. Shakeshafte's special bequest was in the form of an annuity, with £2 (£1200 today) to be paid at £1 every six months. That is exactly like a pension for an older servant who is not expected to collect it for too many years. It would not be for a seventeen-year old who might have collected his for another thirty-five years. It also indicates it was a bequest for someone local – like old Shakeshafte – who would have been able to collect his money personally. If it had been for someone from far away, it would have been a long-running nuisance for both the executors and the recipient.

However bad all that is for the Shakeshafte myth, it gets worse. The will provided that, if one of the chosen eleven died, his annuity would be divided equally among the remainder, and so on until only one was left. That not only implies the recipients had to be local, so the executors could easily know of their deaths and make adjustments, but also that, as the total amount of the eleven annuities – around £10,000 in today's money – would have had to be paid out every year until the last of the eleven died, it is unlikely they would have included a teenager. Everything points to William Shakeshafte being a mature servant of long standing who lived in the vicinity of Hoghton, and not a teenager from distant Stratford.

It is now worth looking at a gambit that seems to have infected many scholars. This requires three sentences in Alexander Hoghton's will to be reordered to make it seem as if Shakeshafte was a player, when the correct sentence order tells us the precise opposite. Without the legalese and in the proper order, the sentences read:

> I [Alexander Hoghton] give Thomas Hoghton my brother all my musical instruments and play clothes if he decides to keep players.
> If he won't keep players, then I give the same instruments and play

clothes to Sir Thomas Hesketh.
I require Sir Thomas Hesketh to be friendly to Fulke Gyllom and William Shakeshafte and to take them into his service or help them to some good master.

These are almost always rearranged when used in biographies to say something like:

Sir Thomas Hesketh was given Hoghton's musical instruments and play clothes, if Hoghton's brother would not keep players, and asked to take Shakeshafte and Gyllom into his service.

This is then used to imply these two men must have been players. Yet, if the bequests had gone as intended (as one would presume), Shakeshafte and Gyllom would not have gone with the play clothes.

Footnote on Side Issues

Of the story that Shakspere went to Hoghton Hall, the orthodox Wood (2003) wrote a long paragraph which began:

Far-fetched as this theory may seem, there are certainly some curious coincidences in this tale

and finishes:

no convincing evidence has yet been discovered to prove the Lancashire theory.

But coincidences are just coincidences; odd conjunctions with ordinary explanations – like the Lancastrian Thomas Savage being John Heminges's landlord. Another coincidence often quoted is that a reference to a promontory near a tidal river in *Henry VI Part 3* could be one near Preston; or it could equally be one of scores of others across England. Then there was a Protestant teacher from Lancashire, John Cottam, who was at Stratford up to 1580 and had a Catholic Priest for a brother. It is said he inveigled Shakspere to Lancashire because he was a Catholic recusant, which it has been shown he was not. This is all clutching at broken reeds, not evidence. The "curious coincidences" one finds desperately reported fell to pieces when they were examined at a conference in Stratford in June, 2008.

Appendix C

The Misuse of Greene's
Groatsworth

In Chapter 6, we discussed how Shakespeare scholarship has been distorted using inventions derived from what is called Robert Greene's *Groatsworth of wit won with a million of repentance*. It all started around 1770 when a Thomas Tyrwhitt brought to light a collage of oddments in a 44-page tract with the above title. The author was named as playwright Robert Greene (who died before the tract was published at the end of 1592), but its manuscript was in the hand-writing of a Henry Chettle. It seems it was this upcoming Chettle who composed the tract from three oddments by Greene. He published it and he certainly took the blame for it. When Thomas Nashe was accused of writing it, he distanced himself from it, calling it a *"scald, lying, trivial pamphlet"*. With that for a pedigree, one might expect scholars to treat it with caution. Yet most orthodox scholars seem mesmerised by the fantasy forced on it by Tyrwhitt and his successors.

To understand the odd way the *Groatsworth* was (and still is) treated, one must know that, in 1769, the bicentenary of Shakspere's birth had just been celebrated five years late and there was a clamour for information about him. Five editions of Shakespeare's collected plays had already been published in that century – Rowe (1709), Pope (1725), Theobald (1733), Johnson (1765) and Steevens (1766) – and each had been forced to make do with a pathetic account of the supposed author, hardly a biography. To make matters worse, the discovery of Shakspere's will in 1747 had produced total dismay at its content, its appearance and its unbelievably poor "signatures", while George Steevens had shown that the two pieces in the First Folio printed over the printed names of Heminges and Condell were actually written by Jonson. It is true that a pen and paper had been added to the new Stratford bust in 1749, but that hardly helped. The worlds of literature and theatre were ready to lap up the "Shakespeare" fakes and forgeries that Jordan, Ireland and others would produce. Thomas Tyrwhitt who, in 1766, had shown Shakespeare's work was mentioned in Frances Meres's *Palladis Tamia*, apparently saw another big chance to raise his reputation with his discovery of the *Groatsworth*.

In the *Groatsworth*, Tyrwhitt had found a parody on Shakespeare's phrase, *"A tiger's heart wrapped in a woman's hide"*, and an attack on someone whom it had called a *"Shake-scene"* and referred to as an *"upstart crow"*. He saw how it could be passed off as an attack on Shakespeare as if he were both an actor-manager and a newly-arrived, plagiarising writer, a role never attributed to him before. With George Steevens ready to welcome something new to put in his 1773 edition of Shakespeare's plays, Tyrwhitt's fantasia on the *Groatsworth* was injected like a virus into the field of Shakespeare scholarship. It was to dominate the future of the Shakspere myth, giving future writers a quick, if ridiculous, sound bite on Shakespeare as a plagiarising "upstart crow", and it set a precedent for related deceptions that would follow it.

Yet this tract, whatever its origin, says nothing about the genius Shakespeare. By the end of 1592 when the *Groatsworth* appeared, this writer was not only the poet who had his *Venus and Adonis* ready to be published and become a bestseller, and who had written a number of his sonnets (if only for "circulation among his private friends"), but he had also written the first ever tetralogy (three parts of *Henry VI* plus *Richard III*) and quite a bit more. He was a box-office success, a writer of originality who would leave behind more quotable quotations – the "tiger's heart" one included – than all his rivals put together. It is simply not credible that he would have been attacked in a scrappy tract as if he could not write without stealing from his inferiors. Yet, because the *Groatsworth* can be twisted to support the Shakspere myth, the false belief derived from it that, as one writer put it, *"Shakespeare is a devious, importunate and bumptious literary thief"*, has to be adopted by orthodox scholarship.

The part of the tract that has caused most trouble is a sort of open letter within it that was purportedly addressed by Greene to three writer-colleagues. In total this letter was over one hundred lines long and, in the middle, it had a notorious fifteen-line section that started thus:

> Base minded men all three of you, if by my misery you be not warned: for unto none of you (like me) sought those burrs to cleave: those puppets (I mean) that spake from our mouths, those antics garnished in our colours.

Those "puppets that speak from our mouths, those antics [meaning clowns] garnished in our colours" are obviously actors who are using, possibly taking some advantage of, the writers' plays. This may be a general attack on players, but more likely it is aimed at player-managers who have battened on writers they do not treat fairly. Indeed, the odd word "burrs" in the second line would fit as a pun on the Burbages. So the piece is not an attack on a writer, but a writer warning three colleagues against actors. The open letter goes on:

> Is it not strange, that I, to whom they all have been beholding, is it not like that you, to whom they have all been beholding, shall (were ye in the case that I am now) be both at once of them forsaken?

This is the same theme, a warning against players (and managers) who should have been indebted or beholden both to the writers addressed in the letter and to its supposedly destitute author: it cannot be a complaint against a writer. The letter continues:

> Yes, trust them not: for there is an upstart crow, beautified with our feathers, that with his tiger's heart wrapped in a player's hide, supposes he is as well able to bombast out a blank verse as the best of you;

The term "upstart crow", known from Æsop, was also a reference to a puffed-up player showing off in a part written for him, so that he is beautified with the playwright's feathers. That point is reinforced by the parodying of Shakespeare's already famous words – *"Tiger's heart wrapped in a woman's hide"* – words that were used to insult the proud and fierce Queen Margaret in his successful *Henry VI Part 3,* with "woman" replaced by "player". There are orthodox scholars who have tried to point out to their colleagues that one does not take a quotation like that and misquote it to fit one's purpose, unless it is too well known to need explaining. It becomes a compliment to the author, not an insult. At least one such scholar has cautioned that, if the *Groatsworth* really were what most orthodox scholars take it to be – an attack on an upstart Shakespeare – that would imply he did not write *Henry VI Part 3.*

The term "bombast out" in the third line quoted above refers to a proud actor making a great deal of his part, padding it out, and they continue by identifying that actor, that "upstart crow", as someone like Richard Burbage (or possibly Edward Alleyn), a top actor/manager who could do everything, as the line completing the above sentence shows:

> ... and being an absolute Johannes factotum, is in his own conceit the only Shake-scene in the country.

Here the term "Shake-scene" is no play on the name Shakespeare: it echoes nicknames given to characters in contemporary plays, like Shake-bags and Shake-rags, where the slang word "shake" meant "steal" or "seize" (as Shakespeare also used it). The comedic actor Robert Armin used the insult "shake-rags" for his critics – people who stole his "small worth".

That line therefore carries on the theme of someone stealing a scene when he is acting in a part written for him by an author who had not received his just rewards; and there was perpetual and widespread complaint about such thefts in late Elizabethan theatrical tracts, starting with one by Thomas Nashe in a preface to Greene's *Menaphon* in 1589 – which explains in part why it was suggested he had authored the *Groatsworth*.

Following the sections quoted above, the *Groatsworth* letter continued its attacks on actors, with more and more insults directed at players as *"apes"*, *"rude grooms"*, *"buckram gentlemen"*, *"peasants"*, and *"painted monsters"*, and it recommended that the punishment meted out to these players should be to *"let those apes imitate your past excellence"* and *"never more acquaint them with your admired inventions"*. That makes it clear the complaint was not against Shakespeare; for, if those addressed in the open letter did withhold their plays, it would not hurt him, but increase the demand for his work.

It must be a peculiar imagination that sees this open letter which is directed only against actors as an excuse to call the writer Shakespeare an "upstart crow". He was not beautified with the writings of Greene, Peele, Nashe and Marlowe, the writers said to be identified by the *Groatsworth* as having been cheated by the players. (An actor who merited the title of "Shake-scene" because he stole a scene could not have been Shakspere, who was never noticed in any part: and besides, he could not have reached a status in the theatre by 1592 which would justify calling him a "Johannes factotum" or "Jack of all trades".)

Another nonsense that has grown up around the *Groatsworth* concerns a statement issued by its publisher (and writer?) Henry Chettle regretting that *"a letter [in the Groatsworth] written to divers play-makers, is offensively by one or two of them taken"*. He apologised particularly to one of them, but did not identify which. Today, it is regularly asserted that Chettle's particular apology was to Shakespeare, even though it was directed to some or all of the three writers who were addressed in the *Groatsworth*: there is no suggestion that those three included Shakespeare. This fallacy has been pointed out even by orthodox scholars for at least a century, but it is still regularly repeated.

Sadly, the anti-Shakespeare fictions generated via the *Groatsworth* have caused his image to be totally distorted, even by those who admit that he must have written at least as much by 1592 as the three writers who were supposedly warned against him. There is no wonder a top Shakespeare scholar, Smart (1923) – seconded by Schoenbaum – said of the letter in the *Groatsworth* which is so misused by Tyrwhitt's followers:

> This passage from Greene has had such a devastating effect on Shakspearean study, that we cannot but wish it had never been written or discovered.

He could equally have said "never been distorted or lied about". Tyrwhitt's misuse of it has pointed to a false date at which Shakespeare, the writer of the first tetralogy, was supposedly struggling to get started, and a false rule that, if an idea is common to Shakespeare and another writer, the other writer must be given the priority. Thus are most orthodox scholars prepared to libel Shakespeare, to try to fool people into thinking he might have been Shakspere

Yet there is a further fantasy induced by the *Groatsworth*. This comes from a fragment of it where a "player" meets one Roberto – possibly intended to be its putative author Greene, possibly not. The player has a terrible voice, is carrying over £200 worth of play clothes (£120,000 today), knows no Latin, can afford to build a windmill [*sic*], has been an "interpreter" for actors since 1582 (a deduction made from the fragment). He says he is a "country-author" who can write a "moral", but has no up-to-date dramatic material available. He asks Roberto to write him plays and proposes to lodge him in a thieves' den to do it. It should be obvious nothing known about either Shakespeare or Shakspere fits this rigmarole but, while many orthodox scholars either ignore it or treat it as nonsense, some have marvelled at how much it tells us about Shakespeare, and have honed their powers of invention on it. There are others who treat it as death-bed testimony from Greene that Shakespeare was a bad and uneducated character. Never mind.

Despite the damage the *Groatsworth* fantasies have done to Shakespeare scholarship, no orthodox scholars have justified the persisting belief that these fantasies had something to do with Shakespeare, or have explained how, if they are right, other contemporaries failed to note he was a plagiarist. The subsidiary attempt to show that the tract identifies Shakspere as a scene-stealing actor and Johannes factotum in 1592, and then to link him to Shakespeare is even weaker, if possible. Shakspere was never an actor of note.

There have been attempts to back up the misinterpretations of the *Groatsworth* by identifying other relevant insults against Shakspere or Shakespeare: Appendix H shows these have been futile.

Appendix D

Pericles and the Collaboration Theory

As indicated in Chapter 8, our interest in the theory that *Pericles* was a collaborative work is because of the possibility that it may make a link from Shakspere to Shakespeare. In considering that possibility, we make two assumptions that have general support. First, that most, if not all, of the play was written by Shakespeare, even if it was omitted from the First Folio. Second, that *Pericles* was left out in 1623 because its 1609 Quarto text (the only one available) was too poor to be used for the First Folio, even if it was played by the King's Men after 1620. It was not the only such Quarto. That for *Henry V* was so bad the play might not now be in the Shakespeare canon if a good manuscript had not become available.

Now the orthodox stance about the supposed collaboration on this play as it has grown up in the last twenty years can be fairly paraphrased, we hope, thus:

> Shakespeare collaborated on *Pericles* with a writer, George Wilkins, who was also the brothel-owning landlord of Stephen and Maria Belott, whose marriage was negotiated by Shakspere in 1604 when he lodged with the Mountjoys, and this connection implies Shakspere was Shakespeare.

Unorthodox scholars usually see the Belott episode as irrelevant because they "know" Shakspere was not Shakespeare, but as that is at question here, we must look further. To do this, we split that orthodox stance into the six questions which it effectively poses, and for which there seems to be no good discussion available. Orthodox scholars will want a "Yes" for all six questions we pose below, as a "No" to any one ruins their story. But we will see.

1. Was *Pericles* written by two different authors?
2. If yes, did they collaborate on it – that is, work together on it at the same time?
3. If yes, was Shakespeare's collaborator the writer George Wilkins?
4. If yes, was the writer George Wilkins the brothel-keeping George Wilkins?
5. If yes, was the brothel-keeping George Wilkins a friend/associate of Shakspere's?
6. If yes, does that make it more likely Shakspere was Shakespeare?

What we will find is that none of the first five questions can be given a plain "yes". Take, for example, Question 4: there is no evidence that the writer and the brothel-keeper were the same man. The Palmers (1999) gave an account of the writer Wilkins with no hint he was the brothel-keeping Wilkins; M. Eccles investigated the two in 1934 to show they were, but did not publish his results; in 1939 a G. Dickson decided they were not the same man; and R. Prior (1972) finished by asking "*If [the brothel-keeper] was not the dramatist, who else could have been?*" – which is hardly helpful. Yet the brothel scenes in *Pericles* are so bleak, so likely to put anyone off going to a brothel, one cannot imagine them as the result of collaboration with a brothel-keeper. It is no surprise that the assumption that the two Wilkinses were the same man only flourished when the need for links between Shakspere and Shakespeare was getting desperate.

Similarly with Question 5; there is no evidence Shakspere knew, or had cause to know, George Wilkins the brothel-keeper. It can also be argued that Shakspere would not have messed up his evidence in the Belott–Mountjoy case if he had been friends with him, he being a Belott partisan. It is no use saying that if Shakespeare had been Shakspere he might have known Wilkins the brothel-keeper, who might have been Wilkins the writer, and so on: that is using assumptions to justify assumptions. This failure to get a "yes" for those two central questions, the most straightforward, must put one off asking Question 6. Yet the negative answers we get for Questions 1 and 3 are even worse.

The two-author theory, Question 1, arose because the first two Acts in the 1609 Quarto of *Pericles* (and all the other Quarto editions) are judged to be not of Shakespeare's quality or style, while the last three Acts definitely are. So it is assumed the first two were by an inferior writer, which is unlikely. It requires one to believe Shakespeare, a man much given to revising his own work, not only took up two inferior Acts by another writer and added onto them three good ones of his own, but that he did so without bringing them up to standard. In others of his plays where there are two hands – *Macbeth, Timon of Athens, Henry VIII* –

Shakespeare wrote first, the inferior hand added. It is quite clear that the normal assumption of how *Pericles* was created poses a major problem.

Yet there is another major problem. It is well agreed that the printers of the 1609 Quarto used a text pirated by two men who saw the play and somehow split the job of transcribing it from memory between them. It is agreed that one pirate did a good job on the last three acts while the other made a terrible mess of the first two, so verse came out as prose, prose as verse, with parts moved or omitted and words wrongly recalled. But then the two-author theory asks one to believe a weird coincidence, namely that the poor pirate got all the work of the inferior writer to transcribe and the good one got all Shakespeare's. Those two improbabilities have to cast serious doubt on the two-author theory.

There is no wonder some – like Edwards (1952) and Southworth (2000) – have preferred to see the whole play as Shakespeare's with the poor form of the first two Acts arising from the way they were obtained and treated for the Quarto. Indeed, it has been shown the play can be edited and adapted to be played looking like pure Shakespeare.

This analysis for Question 1 not only undermines the idea that *Pericles* had two authors, but in the process suggests that Question 2 might have to be changed, to ask if some second hand did try to improve the play at a later stage.

In respect of Question 3, the reason some think the writer George Wilkins collaborated on *Pericles* is because it is said there are signs of his style in the first two Acts of the play. But, if he did contribute to it, it must have been in the period when he was writing, 1604–1608. The problem then is that Dryden, whose Cambridge tutors would have known, dated the play before "The Moor", a reference to Aaron in *Titus Andronicus*; and Jonson dated that play as before 1589 (see Sams, 1995). So *Pericles* was old, in keeping both with it being registered as a "late" play as opposed to a "new" one and with Jonson's protest that it was a *"mouldy tale"*, and *"stale"* which is acknowledged to mean an out-of-date story: he could not have meant a rotten play, because it was one of Shakespeare's most popular. The orthodox date for *Pericles* of 1607 is odd since it was obviously being played before 1608 – and Shakespeare plays could take decades to get in the record. That it existed before 1604 is known because John Day took two items from it for his *Law Tricks* written before then, one from Act 2 and one from Act 3. All this points to *Pericles* being too early for the writer Wilkins.

There is, however, another good reason for knowing writer Wilkins did not collaborate on the play. In 1608 he published a novel critical of the author(s) of *Pericles*, and titled it *The Painful Adventures of Pericles Prince of Tyre. Being the true History of the Play Pericles as it was recently presented by the worthy and ancient Poet John Gower.* The phrase, "the true

History of the Play Pericles", indicates the critical nature of the novel. Wilkins obviouisly felt the play misrepresented the true story of Pericles, and that its proper source should have been a 1576 story by Lawrence Twine entitled *The Pattern of Painful Adventures that befell unto Prince Apollonius,* rather than Gower's fourteenth-century *Confessio Amantis* and the various oddments (including bits of Twine) that Shakespeare relied on.

This is hardly the action of a collaborator on the play, who would have been able to make all such points during the writing process, nor is it the likely action of a collaborator to plagiarise large sections of a play verbatim to pad out a novel. It is interesting that *EKC* and Bullough (1966) both ruled Wilkins out as a collaborator on the basis of the novel alone.

Moreover, if Wilkins did initiate the play, as the orthodox claim, writing the first forty percent, the two inferior acts onto which Shakespeare is said to have carelessly added three good ones, it is unbelievable he would not have had his name put on the play when it came out in 1609: he had the right, he would have wanted the kudos, he knew who the publishers were, and, even if he had not got his name on the first Quarto by some chance, there was a second one later the same year. Claims that he was prevented by someone from doing so deny the facts regarding the rights of authors – see Patterson (1968).

The above analysis, with none of the first five questions being answered "yes", renders it pointless to ask if the theory about the play being a collaboration made it more likely Shakespeare was Shakspere.

Now we have shown that the theory of Pericles being a collaboration cannot be sustained, let alone a collaboration with a writer Wilkins, it is worth looking at another theory that does fit the facts, including the way *Pericles* was registered by one publisher in 1608, not printed, and then brought out by a second in 1609, and allows for the possibility that writer George Wilkins had his hands on the first two acts. Suppose that, early in 1608 a publisher had a text of Shakespeare's single-authored *Pericles* waiting to be printed, but the pirated transcription of its first two acts was impossibly bad. Shakespeare was not available to help. Another publisher asked the writer Wilkins to try to patch up those two acts even though time was too short for a good job. In the event, the play went to press in 1609 as it is now. While Wilkins was studying the play and trying to improve it, he decided to profit from his efforts by writing a novel about it, knowing Shakespeare would never object. Such an explanation seems to fit all the facts, including the way Wilkins's novel has since been used to improve the first two Acts as well as explaining why he wrote it; and it avoids the various illogicalities that haunt the current orthodox theories.

Appendix E

The Handwriting in
Sir Thomas More

In 1871, a Richard Simpson suggested that there was, in a muddled manuscript of a play called *Sir Thomas More*, an added scene of which Shakespeare was the author. He claimed its style was similar to Shakespeare's. Yet arguments based on style can be most contentious and open to error, such as when John Ford's *A Funeral Elegy* was printed with the collected works of Shakespeare, although non-stylistic facts, called dates, showed its author must have lived near Exeter – as John Ford did. However that may be, it is for non-stylistic reasons that Simpson's proposal has given rise to one of the most eccentric episodes in Shakespeare scholarship, in which attempts have been made to show the added scene in question was not only authored by Shakespeare (working, it is said, in a forlorn effort to avoid the play being banned) but was actually handwritten by William Shakspere.

Now the total *More* manuscript, obviously written and re-written at various times in the 1590s under the direction of Anthony Munday, contains at least seven sets of handwriting of which only two have been definitely identified. Here, though, we are just concerned with the hand that wrote those three pages that contain "The Ill May Day Scene" as it is called; it is referred to as "Addition II", since it was added by a new writer to try to save the play, and there was already an "Addition I" by a different new writer.

Now the urge to show that the writing in this scene was Shakspere's has, since 1920, often become quite frantic. For example, in *SCDL*, the normally calm Schoenbaum wrote:

> Palaeographers [students of old writing] ... have minutely compared the three pages [of Addition II] with the six authenticated signatures [of Shakspere] and concluded that in every instance the same penman wielded the quill.

242

If that were true, Addition II would be the prime evidence for Shakspere being a playwright, and no one would be wasting time on baseless anecdotes or invented evidence to try to show Shakspere might be Shakespeare. The "signatures" would be their exhibit number one; the *Sir Thomas More* Addition II exhibit number two; the demonstration that the writing in both was the same exhibit number three, and the case would be persuasive. But biographers and scholars do not use this argument because what Schoenbaum said was simply untrue, and it seems he knew it. In his *SDL*, he quoted the conclusion of a police handwriting expert in the Royal Canadian Mounted Police (Huber) who, having noted similarities between certain bits of the signatures with certain bits of Addition II, stated *"It is difficult, nevertheless, to reconcile certain salient differences."* And Huber's colleague Ramsey had stressed that, in handwriting recognition, *"what does not fit is more important than what does"*. Of course, students would generally not be aware of this – but they should be.

Most orthodox biographers who do not believe Addition II was authored by Shakespeare, or handwritten by Shakspere, or either – and they may be the majority – keep silent on the matter like Wilson and Shapiro. Few will be as open as Duncan-Jones, who dismissed Addition II, saying

> I have yet to be convinced that [this document has] anything to tell us about Shakespeare.

Wells and Taylor in their 1998 revised edition of Shakespeare's *Complete Works* referred cautiously to

> the author [of Addition II] ... whom many scholars believe to be William Shakespeare

and they would have been at least as accurate if they had replaced the word "believe" with "do not believe", but they included the play just the same.

There are good reasons to believe that Shakespeare, particularly if he had been Shakspere, would never have have wasted his time trying to doctor a play that had already been shredded and patched by inferior writers serving a rival acting company, especially when it was not likely to be published, which it was not.

The arguments advanced in the main book on this subject – Pollard (1923) – are largely circular ones, though he and his collaborators got through a mound of detail. Pollard's literary collaborators, men who thought Shakespeare might be the author of Addition II, firmed up their theory because they were told the handwriting was Shakspere's. The man who thought the handwriting in Addition II might be Shakspere's firmed up his theory because he was told Shakespeare was its author. Their methods were seriously questioned by Bald (1949), Hays (1975) and others but work of these two is rarely quoted.

Sir Edward Maunde Thompson, the supposed expert on palaeography and handwriting in the Pollard book, seemed to think he could show the handwriting of Addition II was the same as in the "signatures" by showing similarities, not matches, between a few odd letters in them. There are, in total, seventy-six letters in the "signatures" and none of them looks like any of the others – none of the letters "a" in the "signatures" match one another, none of the letters "h" match one another, and so on. It follows that when Thompson thought he found similarities between some odd letters in the text and in the "signatures", the exercise was pointless. He found, he said, one letter "a" in the text and one in a "signature" which were similar to each other and were "unique" – that is, there was no example of the form of those two letter "a"s in any other handwriting. However, the two letters were not a match and were later shown not to be unique. He found similarities between letters "p" that he picked out in Addition II and one in a "signature", but it is not clear why he thought that would be useful for judging the two sets of writing to be the same, especially as they looked like printed "p"s rather than cursive "p"s like the others in the "signatures".

Greg, a literary contributor to Pollard (1923), gave his view that

> there was less chance that all the six signatures were by the same hand than that, if they were all accepted as being by the same hand, that hand had written [Addition II].

He admits the "signatures" are all different, and then says that, if one takes all the differently made characters in them (all seventy-six), one can find similarities with some letters in Addition II, even if there are none within the signatures. Greg's logic implies that, if there were more totally different Shakspere "signatures", it would be easier to show he had written Addition II. (Oddly, in this context, and as we have mentioned before, it was Greg who, in his 1932 book *English Literary Autographs*, showed that mature writers of the time – like Shakespeare – developed consistent signatures. And it is no surprise that, in that same book, Greg wrote *"I have avoided the controversial subject of Shakespeare's* [meaning Shakspere's] *handwriting"*, though it was the handwriting which most needed scholarly consideration.)

Hamilton (1985), who is often quoted as being an expert who has shown Addition II to be in Shakspere's hand, assessed Thompson's contribution to Pollard's book as nonsense. He was right to do so. One only has to note that, when Thompson wrote some three hundred words on the letter "i"

244

as it appeared in the "signatures" and in Addition II, he failed to point out that all the "i"s in the "signatures" were undotted, while all those in Addition II carried a dot. After tracking Thompson's work on *Sir Thomas More* over several years, Hamilton concluded the former had talked himself into believing Addition II matched the signatures – *"parleyed himself into it"* was Hamilton's phrase – and had imagined the evidence he needed. Hamilton then (again rightly) rejected the "signatures", as being of no use in identifying the writing in Addition II! Instead he developed a theory (which no one else believes) that Shakspere handwrote his own will. He then claimed the will and Addition II were written by the same writer (which also no one else believes). What he really did was show that both the will and Addition II were in similar forms of the secretary script and each looked as though it was written by a legally trained hand – which at least agrees with the accepted identification of the will as being written by a man in the Warwick office of solicitor Francis Collins, who drew it up.

One of the latest palaeographers to support Thompson, Dawson of the Folger Shakespeare Library in Washington, had earlier showed that people's signatures were not useful for identifying their normal handwriting, a fact even more pertinent given the time lapse between the writing of Addition II and Shakspere's supposed "signatures" and the glaring disparity between the individual signatures which fail comparisons even among themselves. Pollard himself said that trying such a match for Shakspere was *"an almost impossible task"*, though he should have left out the "almost". The contribution of Dawson (1990) was to repeat Thompson's unreliable findings and add to them. He pointed out that all the letter "k"s in the "signatures" and Addition II were badly made, but this meets no criterion for showing they were all badly made by the same hand: the "k" in the Secretary Script is known to have been a particularly difficult letter. Dawson then claimed he had found similarities between the writing in Addition II and the three words "By me William" in the last Shakspere "signature" that Thompson had (correctly) ignored. As we have seen, those three words were just the ones most obviously written by a legal clerk who had slipped up and momentarily forgotten to disguise his writing (see Chapter 10), a fact Thompson may have spotted but did not mention.

There has been an attempt to argue that the writing must be Shakspere's because no known sample of contemporary writing matches that in Addition II. Yet it has been shown that the writing in Shakspere's will and a specimen of writing by the Sixth Earl of Derby both match it better in total than any of the Shakspere "signatures", and there are bound to be many specimens of handwriting that have not been looked at.

One of the scholars who did try proper tests on Addition II and the "signatures" was Tannenbaum (1927). In one test he looked at combinations of letters that occurred in both the "signatures" and Addition II. For example, the combination "spe" occurs six times in Addition II and should occur in the middle of each "signature" (though it is missing from the first one – see Chapter 10). He found the five specimens of "spe" in the "signatures" all differed from each other, and that none of them matched any specimen of "spe" in Addition II. After comparing many such combinations which all failed the test, Tannenbaum concluded the "signatures" and Addition II could not be by the same hand – as is actually blindingly obvious. For some reason, Tannenbaum's findings (which were more extensive than reported here) are rarely quoted, though they totally contradict Schoenbaum's oft-repeated claim (see above), as do many other such findings, including Hamilton's!

This discussion of attempts to show Addition II in *Sir Thomas More* was written by William Shakspere has actually emphasised the incompatibility of his so-called "signatures" and also his inability to write. That has not stopped orthodox scholars repeating for public consumption that *Sir Thomas More* is the only manuscript containing Shakespeare's handwriting, by which they mean Shakspere's.

Simpson originally suggested Addition II was Shakespeare's on the basis of its style. Today, when it is agreed its style is not definitive and that it is improbable that Shakespeare would have taken on such a rewrite for a rival company (or at all), the claim that it was his tends to rest almost solely on the claim that the handwriting was Shakspere's, and that simply will not do. There are other non-stylistic arguments in Pollard for Addition II being Shakespeare's, and those should be examined free from bias and circular arguments, and the nonsense about Shakspere's handwriting, which has done the same sort of damage to Shakespeare scholarship as has Greene's *Groatsworth*.

Appendix F

Problems of Dating and Attribution of Shakespeare's Works

Few students of Shakespeare can be unaware that there are major problems with the dating of some of his works, and that many of those problems result from attempts to fit them to Shakspere. Some of Shakespeare's rivals sold their plays and had the date of sale recorded, but not he. For him, we may know a date for a performance or publication of a work, but those only give a latest date for its writing. The Sonnets, for example, were published as a set in 1609, but most existed fifteen years earlier. *Venus and Adonis*, usually dated to its time of printing, 1593, could have been written before that, but not after.

We will take these dating matters, for simplicity, in three sections: the early plays, the Sonnets, and the supposed late plays. And we will see in that last section there are also problems with the attributions of some plays that impinge on the Shakspere myth.

The Early Plays

It is sad that the dating of the early plays did not get more help from the discovery in the eighteenth century that some were mentioned in Frances Meres's 1598 *Palladis Tamia* (*Wit's Treasury*). This praised Shakespeare as a poet-playwright, noted his *"sugared sonnets"* had circulated *"among his private friends"*, whoever they were, and gave six examples each of what Meres called his comedies and his tragedies, all of which must have been written by 1597. The six comedies were *The Two Gentlemen of Verona*, *The Comedy of Errors*, *Love's Labour's Lost*, *Love's Labour's Won*, *A Midsummer Night's Dream* and *The Merchant of Venice*. (This shows a play called *Love's Labour's Won* existed but it may have had a different title in the First Folio, possibly *The Taming of the Shrew* or *Much Ado About Nothing*: other plays had their titles changed.) The "Tragedies" in Meres's list were *Richard II, Richard III, Henry IV, King John, Titus Andronicus,* and *Romeo and Juliet,* the first four being known today as "Histories". Given there were two parts of *Henry IV,* while three parts of *Henry VI* existed by 1590/1, Meres's list was clearly selective: it seems that well over seventeen Shakespeare plays had been written by 1598, but Meres sadly left no hint of the total number, their dates, or the order of their writing.

Now, as explained earlier, it was around 1790 that the lawyer-scholar Malone decided to fit the dates of all Shakespeare's plays within the time span of a supposed dramatic career of William Shakspere. To do that he needed to exclude evidence about a play's dating if it would push it or, by a knock on effect, push others outside his time frame. And today it seems many scholars find it difficult, even if they do not believe Shakespeare was Shakspere, to break free from a chronology based on Malone's fallacious assumptions, including his doubtful choice of 1589 for the earliest date of a Shakespeare play.

A good example of how an artificial dating of a play could result from Malone's theory is the case of *Love's Labour's Lost.* This play is really not like any other, and some think it was written specifically for the Inns of Court. It used a style known as "euphuism" introduced by Lyly around 1580, and would have been old fashioned by the 1590s. It has a sense of being topical, but only with events that occurred before 1586, and many scholars believe it to be one of Shakespeare's earliest plays. However, on Malone's theory, because all the dates around 1590 in his Shakspere-determined framework were taken for other plays, *Love's Labour's Lost* has got pushed to 1594/5. To try to justify that late date for the play, it is said a "dancing horse" in Act 5 of the play was based on one that was in a London circus from 1591 to 1594. To stress the supposed importance of that horse – "The Monarch"– for the dating, it was portrayed in a theatre programme for *Love's Labour's Lost* in 2007. Yet there were dancing horses in London well before 1590, and there is more on this erroneous dating in the next section.

Malone dated *Romeo and Juliet* as 1595, but gave no reason. The "agreed" date was later moved to 1591 because the play has the line: *"'Tis since the earthquake now eleven years"*, and there was one in England in 1580 so intense that it had a book written about it. Other evidence also fitted 1591. Yet, as the Malone schedule was too full for it there, it was put back to 1595. Today, to justify that shift, the major earthquake is replaced by a local tremor of 1584 which has grown in violence as the orthodox dating has become less secure. To help the new "earthquake" carry the weight of the late dating, a 1593 source has been proposed for the play, but it is ignored by Gillespie and other experts on Shakespeare's sources.

On a par with the previous two plays is *The Comedy of Errors.* In it,

France is said to be *"armed and reverted, making war against her hair/heir"*, which the orthodox will say refers to a rebellion against Henry of Navarre between 1589 and 1594: so they put it at 1594, setting its date as late as seems possible. Yet Henry ceased being heir to the French crown in 1589. Orthodox theory cannot accept such a date so 1594 has been supported by claiming that "globes" mentioned in the play were not made in England before 1592, although foreign ones had arrived in the country by 1577.

One play has seriously split orthodox dating: *King John*. Three orthodox scholars who edited it for publication – Dover Wilson (1936), Honigmann (1954) and Beaurline (1990) – put it at 1590 (as have others). They all noted that two minor works written after 1590 shared material with Shakespeare's play, and each concluded the others took it from *King John*. Each judged *King John* to be earlier in style than the more mature play *Richard III* (dated 1592), while its anti-Catholic content suggested a date just after the 1588 Spanish Armada. In spite of all that, the play is generally given an orthodox date of 1596/7 because 1590 will not fit the Shakspere framework; and also, of course, Shakespeare the "upstart crow" must have borrowed from the minor writers. Besides, at 1597, the play may be made into a memorial for Shakspere's son Hamnet who died in 1596. It is assumed that Shakspere, if he was Shakespeare, would have written something for his son's death as Jonson did for his; and *King John* might be it? Yet no father mourns a son in the play, and the passage, *"Grief fills the room of my absent child"*, often quoted from it, is a mother speaking of a child who is in prison, not dead. In order to link Shakespeare to Shakspere's loss, some will say he only wrote "dark" plays after Hamnet's death; yet the comedies *Much Ado About Nothing, The Merchant of Venice* and the three Falstaff plays are all orthodoxly dated to 1596–98. As *King John* fails to provide a memorial for Shakspere's son, some have tried *The Winter's Tale* for the purpose, though that is orthodoxly dated years after 1596.

The so-called "accepted" dates of other Shakespeare plays are likewise suspect. We mentioned *Titus Andronicus* and *Hamlet* earlier. The date given *Othello* – 1603/4 – is faced with a pre-1600 reference to the play in the "commonplace book" of Edward Pudsey. Then, for *Pericles* there is evidence it was written before 1590 (see Appendix D) though it is usually put at 1607 because it was registered in 1608.

Malone said he put *Coriolanus* at 1608/9 to fill a gap in his chronology. Some have supported that chance date by claiming Camden's *Britain*, written in 1605, was a source for it. Yet Gillespie showed that everything in that book relevant to the play was also in texts by Livy, Plutarch and Philip Sidney. In an effort to save the Malone date of *Coriolanus*, some say Shakspere as Shakespeare put complaints over food shortages in it because Warwickshire men were rioting in 1607/8. Yet those riots were over enclosures, not food.

As Chambers said of all this in *EKC*, *"There is practically no concrete evidence as to date* [of *Coriolanus*] *and attempts to find some have been far-fetched."* And he was being kind.

Though most Shakespeare biographers seem to like Malone's dating fallacy, with only three plays written by 1591, the orthodox Brown (1949) put eight Shakespeare plays at 1592 or earlier, with *Henry VI Part 1* first; Alexander (1951) dated nine plays at 1592 or earlier, with *A Comedy of Errors* first; the *OCS* (2000) had five by 1592 with *The Two Gentlemen of Verona* first; and Holden (2001) had seven by 1592 with *Henry VI Parts 1* and *2* equal first. Actually, among orthodox scholars, ten plays have been proposed for Shakespeare's first: *The Two Gentlemen of Verona, The Taming of the Shrew, Love's Labour's Lost, A Comedy of Errors, Richard II, King John, Titus Andronicus*, all three parts of *Henry VI*, while Sams (1995) suggested *Pericles* at 1588. This hardly adds up to a real consensus, though when an orthodox writer chooses a "first play" it is usually put at 1589/90. Claims that style and word usage confirm the orthodox chronology are misleading. They neither fit the real evidence nor arrive at the same order.

"Shake-speare's Sonnets"

We will leave the orthodox dating of some plays around 1611–1614 until later, and look at the dating of the Sonnets next. Few things are agreed about the Sonnets themselves – were they a literary exercise or biographical? – which if any should be excluded? – who were the individuals they refer to (if any)? – were they printed with agreement or help from the author? – why was the dedication written by the publisher and who was it written to (and why)? All that is really agreed is that the playwright Shakespeare wrote most of the 154 Sonnets, their publisher Thomas Thorpe, was not the most scrupulous of men, and they are a rich vein for scholars to quarry.

Yet, for the dating of the Sonnets, there are five reliable pieces of evidence. Most sonnet sequences were in date order: no one doubts this for Daniel, Drayton, Sidney, Spencer, Watson and others who wrote pre-1595, and it should be assumed so for Shakespeare unless there is sound reason not to. Second, sonnet-writing flourished in England from about 1590 to 1595, and then dropped off seriously. Sonnet expert Lee (1904) judged Shakespeare's were from that period, and so did Rowse (1963), Sams (1995) and many others. Third, the only Shakespeare plays containing sonnets – *Love's Labour's Lost* and *Romeo and Juliet* – are dated before 1595. Fourth, two of the latest Sonnets – Nos 138 and 144 – were published piratically in 1599 in *The Passionate Pilgrim*. Fifth, the last line of No 94 – *Lillies that fester smell far worse than weeds* – was taken for use in the play *Edward III* written before 1594. These locate the Sonnets in time pretty well.

In spite of that evidence, and almost always ignoring it, attempts are now being made to push the later Sonnets well into the 1600s. The chief weapon being used is Sonnet 107 which, it is argued, must be dated to 1603 so it can allude to Queen Elizabeth's death, James's coronation and the release of the Earl of Southampton from the Tower. Yet this poem has been called the "dating Sonnet" because different scholars used the strong but ambiguous allusions in it to date it to almost every year from 1588 to 1600 (see, e.g. *EKC*).

The crucial point for the "1603ers" seems to be the claim that the line in Sonnet 107 – *The mortal moon has her eclipse endured* – can be forced into a blunt statement that Elizabeth – poetically the moon – has died. Yet Shakespeare uses "endure" 76 times in his plays, always fitting the dictionary definition "put up with without giving in" or "remain firm under". For example, "*I shall endure. I shall not yield,*" *Love's Labour's Lost*; "*I could endure anything before,*" *All's Well*; "*We can both endure the winter's cold as well as he,*" *Julius Caesar*. So the "1603ers" not only overturn the dating evidence of the Sonnets, but attribute a meaning to "endure" the very opposite of Shakespeare's. (They mainly also believe Sonnet 145 was his first Sonnet, written for Anne Hathaway in 1582, but stuck in at the end of the sequence between No 144 on hell and No 146 on the triumph of evil – see Chapter 14.)

The Later Plays

Nothing seems odder in orthodox scholarship than its dating of *The Tempest* at 1611 on the basis of a theory which, if true, would prove, by itself, that Shakspere was not Shakespeare. It all began when Malone, seeing that the play referred to the "*Bermoothes*" or Bermudas and thinking those islands were unknown in England until Autumn 1609 when a Sylvester Jourdain reported two Virginia Company ships foundering on them, dated it as 1610/11. Yet they were known in England by 1593 when a ship was wrecked on them, and a part of London was named after them. When Malone's error was realised, scholars had a double problem: his new date had already changed the play, the first in the First Folio, from its critical status as Shakespeare's 'prentice piece to that of one of his most mature, and they would not want to be seen to change that assessment again as well as its date. Then, apparently, around 1920 someone saw that a detailed letter the poet William Stratchey wrote about the wreck of one of Jourdain's ships had arrived in England around Christmas 1610, and it might be passed off as the source of *The Tempest*, so keeping its date as 1611. But there is a major problem.

When Strachey's letter arrived in London, the Virginia Company thought it so commercially sensitive that they kept it secure and it was not made public until 1625. To get over this "slight" difficulty, orthodox scholars have to claim that this highly protected, commercially sensitive, 114-page, handwritten letter was taken from the safe and handed to Shakspere so he could write a play about it in time for a first recorded performance in 1611 – yet *Coriolanus* is first recorded as played in 1669, and nobody uses that to date it.

It should be obvious that, if one could really show Shakespeare did use the Strachey letter for *The Tempest*, that alone would kill off the myth that he was Shakspere. Yet the way the letter was invented as a source should be enought to prepare us for the conclusion of the orthodox Muir (1977):

> The extent of the verbal echoes of [Strachey's and Jourdain's letters in *The Tempest*] has, I think, been exaggerated. There is hardly a shipwreck in history or fiction which does not mention splitting, in which the ship is not lightened of its cargo, in which the passengers do not give themselves up for lost, in which the north winds are not sharp, and in which no one gets to shore by clinging to wreckage.

Muir found more parallels between *The Tempest* and St Paul's shipwreck in two pages of the Bible than in all the 114 pages of Strachey's letter. (And he found nothing in Jourdain's letter.) The relatively few real similarities between the play and Strachey's letter could be found elsewhere: in the Bible, Raleigh's report on a 1596 shipwreck, writings of Erasmus and Richard Hakluyt, and (see Multhropp, 1999) in the plays *Twelfth Night*, *Hamlet*, and *The Comedy of Errors*. Of course, the island in the play was Mediterranean, not Bermudan. No wonder Gillespie, in his *Shakespeare's Books*, could only say that Jourdain and Stratchey's letters "*offer verbal parallels to certain points in* The Tempest" while Miola's *Shakespeare's Reading* said even less. Two editors of *The Tempest*, Kermode (1954) and Lindley (2002) both used the word "nothing" to describe the contribution of Strachey's letter to the play.

Today, those who want *The Tempest* dated at 1611 will often say – in spite of the above evidence – that Kathman (1997) showed Strachey was a source for the play. He certainly claimed 40 parallels between the letter and the play, but checking one against the other (see Nina Green, 2005), most disappear: he even said "trim" in the dress sense was a parallel for "trim" in the nautical sense, that "scamel" was the same as "seamew", and confused taking down the small topmast with taking down the mainmast.

The few actual parallels were present in documents before 1602.

Some orthodox scholars may like the date 1611 for *The Tempest* if it eliminates some unorthodox Shakespeare candidates, and as long as no one notices it removes Shakspere as well, but it is safer to date it around 1600. The subject matter of *The Tempest* would have suited Elizabeth, not James, who might not have enjoyed being reminded of the storms and magic that led him to write his book *Daemonologie* in 1591. The sources needed for the play were all available before 1602, and allusions that appear to have derived from it existed before 1610.

After reviewing the sources really used for *The Tempest*, Moore (1991) went on to find that all sources for Shakespeare's plays existed by 1603. Speed's *History of Great Britain* (1611) was used for *Henry VIII*, but it was for a section written by Fletcher. Moore's findings seem to be confirmed by Bullough's major review, once the effect of Strachey's letter is removed, while Gillespie's view is that the orthodox dating is "archaic". The latest source Shakespeare used may have been Harsnett's *Declaration of Popish Impostures* (1603) for *King Lear*; yet that needs more study. It seems Harsnett's sources were available by 1594, and were included in the *Miracle Book* (1599), and a 1598 report in Spanish that Shakespeare could certainly read. To justify dating *Lear* after 1603, some suggest Shakespeare's inspiration for it was a court case in that year in which a Cordell Annesley stopped her sisters having their father declared mad. Yet that must just be coincidence as a daughter Cordella appeared in two plays in 1594, *King Lear* and *King Leir*, and these were not the earliest versions.

Besides *The Tempest*, another play likely to have been written for Elizabeth, not James, is *Macbeth*. It included storm-raising witches, as well as breaches of Scottish hospitality and deaths that might remind him of the execution of his mother and murder of his father, while the death in 1057 of the real Macbeth, an anointed King, was at the instigation of Edward the Confessor. It is possible the drastic cutting of the play that seems to have taken place around 1606 without input from the author might have taken out material even more sensitive than that we still have. Reasons for dating the writing of *Macbeth* to 1606 look weak beside those for a date in Elizabeth's reign: the play's reference to "equivocation" by a Catholic priest, for example, had sources before 1600 and did not need to reflect, as some claim, its use in the Gunpowder Plot trials that would have discomfited James; and the ship in the play named *The Tiger* that went to Allepo could only have been one that did go there in 1583, not one that did not go there in 1606, a vessel some scholars seem to prefer.

A spurious "proof" that some plays were written later than 1608 involves the claim that Shakespeare's five-act plays, such as *The Winter's Tale*, were written to be played in the indoor Blackfriar's Theatre which the King's Men purchased in that year and opened in 1610. The theory says the acts were arranged to allow the periodic trimming of candles used for lighting, but, Nicoll (1958) – a senior orthodox scholar – and others found that no play of Shakespeare's was first put on at that theatre. In any case, Shakespeare was writing five-act plays before 1600.

Finally, there are three odd plays that affect the attribution of Shakespeare's work and the theory that he was Shakspere. These are *Henry VIII*, *Cardenio*, and *The Two Noble Kinsmen*, plays which are talked of as Shakespeare "collaborations" with the inferior and younger John Fletcher (1579–1625). The dates given to these by the orthodox – 1612, 1613, and 1614 respectively – create problems for the Shakspere myth as there is no record of him working or acting in London after 1604. His deposition of May 1612 in the Belott–Mountjoy case – see Chapter 8 – showed he had no London address by then. If Shakespeare did collaborate – "work with someone" – on those plays after 1611, this would damage the claim he was Shakspere, but logic and hard evidence say he did not.

Firstly, it is hard to think the great Shakespeare (especially if he was Shakspere) worked as a "nonce" writer – Schoenbaum's term – on substandard plays, with an inferior partner, with no hope of reward. Besides, if he had had writing time to spare, he could have tidied up the poor text of *Pericles* that was left out of the First Folio. He could have restored the lost parts of *Macbeth* which, cut by an alien hand, may amount to over a third of the play. Or he could have got his own works ready for publication, as Jonson did.

Of the trio of plays above, Shakespeare clearly had nothing to do with *Cardenio*. The King's Men did put on a play *Cardenno* in 1613. Forty years later, in 1653, a Humphrey Moseley registered three plays for publication: *Henry I* and *Henry II* by Shakespeare and Davenport, and *Cardenio* by Mr Fletcher and Shakespeare [*sic*], but none was published. The very minor writer Robert Davenport is not known to have written anything before 1625 the year James I died, though he is referred to as "Jacobean": perhaps to make it seem he was a writing contemporary of Shakespeare. However, to bolster the *Cardenio* story, *Henry I* and *Henry II* are also referred to today as "lost Shakespeare plays", not lost misattributions to him.

Some will claim Moseley must have had a script of *Cardenio* but, if he did, it did not appear in any Fletcher and Beaumont collection or Shakespeare Folio or anywhere else, suggesting it was not a Fletcher nor a Shakespeare nor even a good play.

In 1727, seventy-four years after Moseley registered those plays, Theobald Lewis claimed to have three scripts of "*Cardenio* by Shakespeare" (no mention of Fletcher). Yet Lewis did not publish the play. Instead, in 1728, he put on a play he said he had adapted from it – *Double Falsehood*. The reviewers judged it poor and nothing like

Shakespeare (and that is the view today). The scripts Lewis claimed to have possessed disappeared, and no play *Cardenio* was even mentioned in his 1733 edition of Shakespeare's works.

Today, detailed notes on Shakespeare's supposed lost play *Cardenio* are being included in collections of his works. An effort has been made to boost Lewis's *Double Falsehood* by saying that some words in it look like Shakespeare inventions, yet the prize exhibit there, "absonant", was known in 1564. Logic says it were best that present Shakespeare fans discard *Cardenio*, just as Lewis and Moseley clearly did before them.

Next, *Henry VIII*. This play was in the First Folio in 1623 though it may mostly be Fletcher's. Laden with pageantry, the play – initially titled *All is True* – covered events leading to the birth of Queen Elizabeth, ending with celebrations for her baptism. It was clearly intended for Elizabeth who, if she had lived to 7 September 1603, would have been the first English monarch to reach three-score-years-and-ten. Malone actually dated it as 1601. However, as a celebration for that occasion, the play and its title would have lost their purpose when she fell ill early in 1603 and died in March and it would have been set aside. It would have not been good to greet James I with it: he had no love for Elizabeth, who had condemned his mother to death and refused to name him as her successor.

It seems quite clear that Fletcher, on becoming principal writer to the King's Men around 1610, took up the fragments of *All is True* which Shakespeare had abruptly set aside in 1603 and completed, revised and added to them. He may have done this for those intending to publish the First Folio, since the change of title to *Henry VIII* would have eased the finished play's acceptance by James, rounding out as it would Shakespeare's series on the English kings. Under such conditions, Fletcher could well have traded away his authorship rights for a consideration, even though he may have done more actual work on the play than did Shakespeare. He may also have enlisted the help of his fellow lodger, Francis Beaumont, an expert in masques, to manage the the play's pageantry. This analysis fits the facts while removing the nonsense about Shakespeare acting as junior to an inferior writer. Indeed, when the scholar James Spedding first detected a second hand in *Henry VIII* in 1850, he said, "*they had worked, not together, but alternately upon distinct parts of it.*" He was clear it was no "collaboration", though few orthodox scholars today admit that. (The word "collaboration" gets used even when someone simply makes a small addition to an extant Shakespeare play, because it enforces the impression that he was writing late. Claims of "collaboration" in Shakespeare's early works are expressed with far less energy and conviction.)

The idea of Fletcher finishing off a work started by Shakespeare is not strange. Before he tackled the completion of *Henry VIII*, he had written

The Woman's Prize or the Tamer Tamed using the characters in *The Taming of the Shrew*. There may also have been an element of that in *The Two Noble Kinsmen*, a play first noted in performance in 1619 but omitted from all editions of Shakespeare's Folio, even though it had a better text than *Pericles* which made it into the last two editions. This alone should tell us it was no Shakespeare collaboration. If it should turn out that some fragments of his were used in *The Kinsmen* by Fletcher (who has been recognised as Jonson's "*Poet Ape*"), this should be no surprise. The two heroes in the play, Palamon and Arcite, are found in Chaucer's *The Knight's Tale* which Shakespeare also used in *A Midsummer Night's Dream*; and he could have had an idea for a play about them at that time, and left behind some drafts which passed to Fletcher with those of *Henry VIII*.

It is true that Shakespeare was named as second author after Fletcher when *The Two Noble Kinsmen* was first entered for printing in 1634 by a John Waterson, but, as Schoenbaum said, "*about this attribution there would be much contention.*" As we know, many plays were wrongly registered as Shakespeare's, and when the registration of the *Kinsmen* was transferred to Humphrey Moseley in 1646 it was as Fletcher's alone. This should be a clear warning: Moseley's reputation was for adding Shakespeare's name on to plays, not taking it off. He registered six plays with Shakespeare's name, and none were published. So when orthodox scholars say there is no reason to doubt the 1634 attribution, they are whistling in the dark. It is the 1646 one they should rely on.

The very title "*The Two Noble Kinsmen*" was typical of Fletcher. A score of his plays had character preceded by adjective: *The Faithful Shepherdess*, *The Mad Lover*, *The Humorous Lieutenant*, etc. Shakespeare had nothing similar. The *Kinsmen* appeared in more than one set of collected works of Beaumont and Fletcher with no mention of Shakespeare. Parts of the play have been claimed for Shakespeare, but Sir William Davenant omitted nearly all of these when he adapted it in 1664 as *The Rivals;* nor did he ever claim that his adapted play was partly Shakespeare's, as he would certainly have done if there had been a chance it was. Harold Bloom spoke for many when he said: "*I have never seen a performance of* The Two Noble Kinsmen, *and don't particularly want to.*"

To preserve the collaboration theory even though it undermines the Shakspere myth, the play is orthodoxly dated as 1614. However, it plagiarises wholesale a 1613 masque of Beaumont's, which suggests it was written after his death in 1616 when he could not complain, or even later when people did not have the original fresh in their memories. Some have peculiarly said Jonson alluded to the *Kinsmen* in his play *Bartholomew Fair*, written by 1614, but he never did, except in their imaginations. There are no good reasons for choosing that date of 1614 (though there are bad ones) and, given Fletcher's output and methods, a date nearer to its first performance in 1619 looks much safer.

Clearly no one in the seventeenth century thought *The Two Noble Kinsmen* was Shakespeare's, and Lee (1916) was even more sceptical about this play than about *Cardenio*! It was only in the commercial years of the late twentieth-century that it was bull-dozed into the collected works of Shakespeare, as was done with John Ford's *The Funeral Elegy*, and is being hinted at with Theobald Lewis's *Double Falsehood*. Duncan-Jones (2000) put it as Fletcher's. Wilson (1993) did not mention it. The *Oxford Dictionary of Quotations* takes none from this play. Many orthodox writers give it a furtive glance, and hurry on. And who can blame them?

The final blow to the claim that *Kinsmen* was a Shakespeare collaboration should be its fate in 1623 when it was not included in the plays for the First Folio. We know (see *EKC*) that the editor(s) planned to put *Troilus and Cressida* at the front of the "Tragedies" but had no copy available. But, to fill the gap, they chose *Timon of Athens* which Shakespeare had apparently abandoned with incomplete speeches, scenes and sequences, and with unnamed characters. The evidence is that Middleton tried to finish it – adding about half as much as Shakespeare had written, but it was still printed in a poor state. In the event, a copy of *Troilus and Cressida* became available and it was inserted in its original position though its page numbers had been used up and the table of contents had been set. Yet the *Kinsmen*, which existed in a good text, must have been preferred over *Timon of Athens* if it had been a Shakespeare collaboration. In effect, this play of Fletcher's was rejected twice for the First Folio and for all the other editions.

To conclude, this Appendix has added to the case for rejecting the basis of the orthodox dating of Shakespeare's works, distorted as it is partly to fit them to Shakspere, partly to rule out other candidates. Some dates may be correct, but they all need reviewing piecemeal and impartially. Similarly, some orthodox claims that Shakespeare was collaborating on plays as late as 1614 are artificial, and actually harm their Shakspere myth. Just the simple fact that orthodox dating says Shakespeare wrote nearly a third of his plays after 1604, though no source he used has been identified as being later than that date, should give one pause for serious thought.

Appendix G

The Disappearance of Marlowe

The reason for including this appendix is that it shows how the problems of the orthodox theory of Shakespeare have affected scholarship in other areas, one of which, unnecessarily, is the issue of the supposed death of Christopher Marlowe.

Now it has to be paradoxical that the main reasons for doubting this man died in Deptford on Thursday 30 May 1593 came out of the official Coroner's Report into his "death". This was uncovered in the archives in 1925 by Professor L. Hotson and, without it, debates about his death would have still centred on the conflicting rumours about its cause – from a street brawl, to the plague, to a fight in a tavern over a homosexual lover. The trouble has arisen because anyone reading this Report with even a mildly critical eye will see straight away that the story it tells is one of deception. It has left us to ponder whether what happened was a cover-up for Marlowe faking his own death and disappearance, or a plot to have him killed openly and get away with it. Those who try to deny this problem by asserting that no one could doubt the verdict of a Coroner's jury must be very trusting of the ability of juries to reach true verdicts when all the evidence before them is false, or they must be very confident of facing down justified scepticism.

First, one must remember that the man with the strongest motive for getting Marlowe out of the way on that Thursday was Marlowe himself. He would have known that, if he was to escape trial for his life the next week with the risk of excruciating torture and death, he needed not only to flee but to convince his prosecutors and persecutors that he was dead so that they would not pursue him as they had other fugitives. The evidence recorded in that Coroner's Report into his "death" fits this purpose exactly.

That evidence clearly shows there was an arrangement for three shady men – Nicholas Skeres, Robert Poley and Ingram Frizer – to meet

Marlowe in Deptford on that Thursday. All four had worked for Thomas Walsingham, Marlowe's patron and probable lover, and were known to each other as Government spies: they were rogues, if not criminals. The choice of Deptford for their meeting was ideal for Marlowe's plan. It was ten miles north from Thomas Walsingham's home at Scadbury where Marlowe was staying. It was a seaport from which boats went to Holland where he had friends. It was a busy town, suffering at the time from the plague, so there would be bodies of dead sailors or other strangers available to be passed off as Marlowe's – though his accomplices would not have been above creating a corpse of their own clandestinely had it been required.

The Report tells how, during the day (Thursday) of 30th May, the four men paraded around the town for about eight hours. This ensured Marlowe was seen alive with the three accomplices wearing the clothes in which a substitute corpse would be dressed. The four then retired to the house of a respectable lady, Eleanor Bull, cousin to the Lord Chamberlain – not a tavern keeper, as is often said. There they would have no stray witnesses. The next day, Friday, the three accomplices informed the local magistrate that they had the body of Marlowe who had been accidentally killed in self-defence. An inquest was called for the Saturday, 1st June when the only people who identified the body as Marlowe's were these three men. None of the sixteen jurors, nor the Queen's personal Coroner (Danby) – who officiated because Deptford came within his jurisdiction – would have known Marlowe to recognise him. Only these three gave evidence, each corroborating the other, of how Marlowe had attacked Frizer who had killed him in self-defence.

They described an improbable (but carefully worked out) pantomime so that Frizer could admit to the killing without being guilty of murder. Few people today, even if they think Marlowe died, believe their story was true (though the jury had no alternative but to accept it in the absence of any cause to doubt it). The feeble cause of the quarrel was said to be the "reckoning", the cost of the day's food, drink and lodging. This was estimated as, at most, 18d for the day (£10 each in today's money), no great sum for any of the four, let alone the fairly wealthy Marlowe.

The cause of death was said by the three witnesses to be a stab wound over the right eye one inch wide and two inches deep. Doctors have since said that such a wound would not normally have been fatal, let alone "instantly" fatal as Frizer *et al.* claimed. Because of this, some writers feel they must rewrite the Report, describing the wound as "*in the eye*" or "*through the eye*" or "*between the eyes*". Yet the form of the wound as reported suggests it was probably made on the body *post mortem*. The jury had no choice but to find that Frizer killed Marlowe in self-defence. He was imprisoned, pending confirmation, and was pardoned within four weeks when the verdict of *se defendendo* was officially accepted. The body was buried without publicity in the local graveyard on 1st June, with Marlowe's name and the cause of death in the register.

The orthodox approach (supported by some with other Shakespeare candidates) is to say that the story the jury heard covered up a plot by "someone" to have Marlowe killed. It has to be guessed who that "someone" was, and the Earl of Essex, Lord Hunsdon (the Lord Chamberlain), Sir Walter Raleigh, Lord Burghley and his son Robert Cecil, the Earl of Northampton, Sir Thomas Walsingham, Robert Poley and even the Privy Council as a body have all been proposed at one time or another.

The supposed motive(s) of this "someone" was fear of being implicated by Marlowe as an atheist, or a sodomite, or a blasphemer, or something else that carried the death penalty. It has been claimed that, whichever one was assumed, it was a strong enough motive to justify Marlowe's murder and to take the peculiar risks in carrying it out almost in public.

Those who favour murder must also provide credible reasons for the extraordinarily elaborate method used which involved three accomplices who paraded the victim round the town and lodged openly in Eleanor Bull's house, whilst taking the risk that Marlow might draw attention by shouting and fighting back. These men then had to risk exposure by an unexpected witness in the inquest and make untrue statements which would be on record in the Coroner's report. All this instead of getting one man to do the job secretly in the dark in a secluded spot before fleeing into the night. It is all assumption piled on assumption.

The efforts to provide a satisfactory explanation have left us with other unevidenced fantasies. For instance, it is claimed Frizer could only have been pardoned if he was backed by someone very powerful. Yet Walsingham had influence, if it had been needed, while Marlowe and the poet Thomas Watson were pardoned quickly in 1589 without assistance when Watson killed a man who attacked them.

Amazingly, some claim that Marlow's murder rather than his escape provides a better explanation of the scenario described in the Coroner's Report. Some even call to their aid the principle of "Occam's Razor", an old but useful guide which states that, of two theories, the one with fewest unfounded assumptions is to be preferred. Of course, if we assume the plot was to allow Marlowe to escape without pursuit, we need assume no more. We can easily work out what was done, who did it, why it was done, how it was done, and why it was done as it was. If it is assumed it was to cover up his murder, we need to make an assumption at every stage as well as having to change the one finding of the inquest that did not depend on the evidence of the conspirators alone: the description of the wound.

To those who would still say what happened is clear from the Coroner's

Report, we quote Honan in his biography, *Christopher Marlowe*, in 2005: *"the 'legal details' tell the 'whole story' about as well as a sieve holds molasses"*, and *he* assumed it was murder.

Though Marlowe cannot be seen as a credible Shakespeare candidate, those who attempt to "prove" he was murdered, even to the point of changing evidence and blackening his character because they do not want him as a rival, show a striking lack of confidence in their own theories. This was clear from the fuss made over Marlowe's dates when they were put on his commemorative window in Westminster Abbey as "1564–?1593": the naturally cautious clerics who approved this only had facts and logic to work on, and apparently did not realise how important it was that it should be believed he was dead so that he could not be Shakespeare.

Appendix H

Supposed Contemporary Insults against Shakespeare and Shakspere

The wide acceptance of Greene's *Groatsworth* as being an attack on both Shakespeare and Shakspere has led scholars of all kinds to look for other attacks or insults against one or both where it is obvious none exists. We have already discussed, for instance, how some scholars wrongly say Ben Jonson in his *Every Man Out of His Humour* made fun of William Shakspere's motto on his coat of arms when he clearly did not (see Chapter 9). Yet they do not give up on Jonson. In his epigram *On Poet-Ape* (published 1616) he wrote:

> *Poor Poet-Ape, that would be thought our chief,*
> *Whose works are e'en the frippery of wit,*
> *From brokerage is become so bold a thief,*
> *As we, the robb'd, leave rage, and pity it.*

It needs little ingenuity to guess how scholars who have swallowed the "upstart crow" myth have seen Shakespeare or Shakspere as the Poet-Ape who pretends to be a poet and steals other men's works. Even Jonson could never have called the poems of Shakespeare the "*frippery of wit*", and the evidence is that he did not. Asquith well identified John Fletcher as Jonson's target. (Obsession has led a few to see Shakespeare or Shakspere also attacked in Jonson's play *The Poetaster* (1601), though the targets – Dekker and Marston – actually identified themselves.)

Out of such supposed insults has come the crazy idea that Shakspere might have published other people's work as his own. For example, an early twentieth-century cartoon by the critic Max Beerbohm showed Shakspere getting plays off Bacon to publish as a front man!

Another poem of the above genre was one supporting Robert Greene's reputation and memory written by "R. B., Gent." (Richard Barnfield?) two years after the *Groatsworth* appeared. It reads:

> *Greene is the pleasing object of an eye;*
> *Greene pleased the eyes of all who looked upon him.*
> *Greene is the ground of every painter's die;*
> *Greene gave the ground to all who wrote upon him.*
> *Nay more, the men that so eclipsed his fame,*
> *Purloined his plumes: can you deny the same?*

With the phrases *"purloined his plumes"* and *"eclipsed [Greene's] fame"*, it is often said its target was Shakespeare. But, as Schoenbaum (1970) pointed out, it is known to have been aimed at Gabriel Harvey who had defamed Greene immediately after his death.

There is one epigram (mentioned in Chapter 14) that is sometimes thought to criticise Shakespeare (or Shakspere) as a play-broker, and always attracts wild speculation. It was published by John Davies of Hereford (1565–1618) as one of two hundred poems in his collection *The Scourge of Folly*. He gave it the title, "To our English Terence, Mr Will. Shake-speare". The date of the collection was 1610, though the poems could have been written years before.

At that time, Terence was thought to have been an educated slave of about 150 BC whose name was put on the comedic works of Roman aristocrats wishing to hide their identities. (Although Terence would later be credited with writing plays of his own, Davies could not know that.) It follows that the poem implies the name "Shake-speare" either hid a play-broker or was a pseudonym. The latter seems more likely: the poem was in Davies's collection among others with obvious pseudonyms in their titles, even "Somebody" and "Nobody", so he could have been mocking "Shakespeare" for hiding from his public, but not accusing the illiterate Shakspere – whom nobody linked to writing until 1623 – of passing as a front man. The full poem reads (modernised):

> *Some say (good Will) which I, in sport, do sing,*
> *Had'st thou not played some Kingly parts in sport,*
> *Thou had'st been a companion for a King;*
> *And been a King among the meaner sort.*
> *Some others rail; but rail as they think fit,*
> *Thou hast no railing, but, a reigning wit:*
> *And honesty thou sow'st, which they do reap;*
> *So to increase their stock which they do keep.*

Some biographers see this as saying Shakspere acted kingly parts. Yet the repetition of "in sport" in the first two lines indicates Davies is writing in jest, and his subject is unlikely to have been a professional player.

This shows how the poem lends itself to a whole range of interpretations. Schoenbaum said it provides questions but no answers. Brown said "*One can scratch away for ever as to the exact meaning of all this.*" Wilson said of the speculation, "*We will probably never know.*"

What the poem stresses is anonymity, the last two lines indicating the author is not reaping the "honesty" (meaning honour) that he sows. As a tutor in noble houses, Davies could have known more than most; yet, if he wrote anything important in those cryptic lines, he has not left us the key. One hopeful biographer wrote:

> the only plausible explanation of this poem is that Davies believed that had Shakespeare [meaning Shakspere] not been an actor he would have been 'a companion for a King' ...

Yet he had clearly fallen into what is known as "the fallacy of limited alternatives": dozens of other explanations have been invented, and the one given seems hardly plausible. Someone in line to be a "companion for a King", a title that technically refers to a count (*comes*) or earl, would hardly have had Shakspere's difficulty in getting himself a coat of arms.

There are two other odd poems by this John Davies which refer to players and have the initials RB and WS in print beside them. They can be interpreted in dozens of ways and are generally ignored but, if they do refer to Shakspere and Burbage – as some assert – the poems most oddly identify both as men who have not been successful!

A parallel to Davies's likening of the name "Shake-speare" to "Terence" is Hall and Marston claiming that Shakespeare was someone they called "Labeo", who, in turn, was identified as Bacon (see Chapters 13 and 14). Hall criticised Labeo on two counts. The first was moral; a future bishop, he objected to the licentious nature of the poems *Venus and Adonis* and *The Rape of Lucrece* saying, "*For shame write better Labeo, or write none.*" Second, Hall scorned his use of a pseudonym.

> *Who list complain of wronged faith and fame,*
> *When he may shift it on another's name.*

Hall's use of the phrase "another's name" and Davies's likening "Shake-speare" to "Terence" could, encouraged by the myth that Shakspere's real name was Shakespeare and the supposed slanders in the *Groatsworth*, add to the idea that the actor is being identified as a front man. Yet there is no evidence Shakspere had anything to do with Shakespeare's works or was credited with them in his life time. The only thing that Hall, Marston and Davies have left us is a clear indication that "Shakespeare" was not the real name of any writer: the rest is unresolved.

In spite of the evidence that Shakspere took no payment from anyone and made no claim to be a writer, some *un*orthodox scholars have speculated that the real Shakespeare was unhappy with him getting credit for his works, and so insulted him in the plays. The main manifestations of Shakespeare's displeasure are said to be in *As You Like It* – when Touchstone makes fun of the countryman William by showing that he is unlearned – and in *Love's Labour's Lost* where the countryman Costard is treated similarly. A third case, that where the boy William is made fun of by his teacher in *The Merry Wives of Windsor*, is sometimes added for good measure. There is no substance to support such fantasies.

Ben Jonson did criticise Shakespeare's work in a way many saw as spiteful at the time. In his book *Discoveries* (1641) and as reported in William Drummond's *Conversations* (1619), Jonson said he wished Shakespeare had blotted out a thousand lines and that he *"wanted art"*; also that he was too fluent, especially with his wit which he put in inappropriate places, and *"it was necessary he should be stopped"*. He scoffed at Shakespeare for writing that *"Caesar did never wrong without just cause"* which did *not* appear in *Julius Caesar* as originally printed (though it makes political sense). He scoffed at Shakespeare giving Bohemia a sea-coast in *The Winter's Tale*, which it did have in the earlier times in which the play was set. Jonson seems to have been wrong in pretty well all his criticisms, but one really should note his admission that it was in order to justify his making them – his actual words were *"for to justify my own candour"* – that he wrote of Shakespeare that he *"loved the man and do honour his memory"*. So much for those who claim that phrase showed Jonson knew Shakespeare. It certainly rang much less genuine than Dryden's later remark *"I admire [Jonson], but I love Shakespeare"*, though Dryden knew only Shakespeare's works. Yet Jonson never wrote or spoke of Shakespeare as a plagiarist or player, and he would not have missed the opportunities to do so if those were true.

Now, in the three-part Cambridge *Parnassus* plays of 1601 (see Chapter 15) there is unstinted praise for the writer Shakespeare in contrast to insults for players. A student Studioso complains – in the manner of the *Groatsworth* – that writers are badly treated by the players who gain fame and fortune at their expense, or, as he puts it:

> *With mouthing words that better wits have framed,*
> *They purchase lands, and now Esquires are named.*

As the play pokes fun at William Kempe in particular as well as other players of the Lord Chamberlain's Men, this is said to refer to Shakspere buying property and getting the title Gentleman. Yet other members of that troupe had actually received their Arms by 1601, which Shakspere had not, and were known as better players than he, so it is unlikely this was directed at him; nor was it directed at Shakespeare, whom the *Parnassus* plays clearly distinguished from the actors and praised immoderately.

Finally we deal with an insult of a personal nature. Shakespeare is often said to have suffered with venereal disease because the writer of the Sonnets frequently complains of the pain arising from his love (or lust) for an unidentified lady to whom some of them were supposedly written, the so-called "dark lady". However, it seems that this idea only grew up during the search for some illness to explain the peculiar Shakspere "signatures" and was then transferred to Shakespeare. By extension, this insult has been used to explain why Shakspere's doctor son-in-law wrote nothing about him as Shakespeare on his death (as if Hall could not write something, even if he did not tell everything).

A trivial joke made up about the players Shakspere and Burbage (see Chapter 12) has been used by some to insult Shakspere (or even Shakespeare) in terms of sexual behaviour. In the 1601 diary note made by law-student John Mannigham it read.

> Upon a time when Burbage played Richard the Third there was a citizen grew so far in liking with him, that before she went from the play she appointed him to come that night unto her by the name of 'Richard the Third'. Shakespeare, overhearing their conclusion, went before, was entertained and at his game ere Burbage came. The message being brought that Richard the Third was at the door, Shakespeare caused return to be made that William the Conqueror was before Richard the Third. Shakespeare's name was William.

Greer (2007) imagined Shakspere's wife Anne being upset by this story. Holden (1999) used it for his theory that Shakespeare was "*a poet with the clap*". It was inventively used by Duncan-Jones to show Shakespeare/ Shakspere glorying "*shamelessly in his transactions with a precocious woman of ... no breeding.*" And O'Connor said it was why Shakspere was insulted as "Prickshafte" in Dekker's *Satiromastix*, which he was not. Of course, the story was a joke or, as Brown (1950) put it, "*a good Inns of Court story*"; yet, given the shortage of personal notes on Shakspere, this nonsense has had to be made the most of.

Sexual insults about Shakespeare and Shakspere have been mysteriously amplified by misuse of a very odd poem we mentioned earlier. This was *Willobie his Avisa*, published in 1594, which has also been misused in an effort to forge a link between Shakespeare and Shakspere. Yet, in reading the account of this particular flummery below, it should be noted that it has been ignored by both Greer in her analyses of Shakspere's marital relations and by Duncan-Jones in discussing his "ungentleness".

In *Avisa*, there is a character W.S. who, in spite of these being common initials, is often said to be obviously Shakespeare or Shakspere. Because in the poem this W.S. had a "contagion" after paying suit to Avisa, this is naturally said to be a sexual disease. Yet the poem clearly says Avisa remained chaste, and that the "disease" was unrequited love. Similarly, when W.S. is said to be Shakspere because he is called an *"old player"*, the poem is clearly referring to an old player in the game of love, not an actor. Then the line *"And Shakespeare paints poor Lucrece' rape"* in the prologue is taken to be a hint that W.S. was Shakespeare, as though he would be called W.S. in the body of the poem having already been named at the beginning. One fruitless use of the poem has been to try to link W.S. through an Oxford undergraduate named Willoughby to the Thomas Russell of Rushock – Shakspere's supposed "intimate" friend. Yet the poem was no undergraduate frippery. It had over three thousand verses, and many more disguised characters than just W.S and Willobie. And its banning in 1599 hinted it had seditious undertones. Avisa in the poem had five suitors with similarities to the Queen's five suitors, and she repeatedly used Elizabeth's motto *"Ever the same"*, which has led to just one interpretation of the poem that makes more sense than the one touched on above. The preface to the poem has the words *"there is something under these false titles and shows that hath been truly done"* and that, together with its banning, should warn the reader (and scholar) it was no trivial piece about Shakspere.

Finally in this strange catalogue, a press notice was recently beamed around the world blaming Shakspere for his local parish Church being in disrepair twenty years after his death. This insult arose from a mistaken 1930s claim that Shakspere had the right to be buried in Stratford's Holy Trinity Church by virtue of his 1605 investment of £440 in the income from some tithes. (That claim, only made to bolster the idea that a poor anonymous stone in the chancel marked his grave, seems to have been one of many inventions by Frith, 1938.) As these tithes belonged wholly to the Corporation, they could confer no "church" privileges and, in any case, Shakspere had only bought a minor share in the income, not in the actual tithes. Later, some would say the investment also made Shakspere a lay rector, a position which carried a duty to maintain the Church. Yet the detailed accounts of Shakspere's investment (see, e.g., *EKC*), make it clear that it did not give him (or others who made such investments) any rights or duties relative to the Church, which levied its own tithes. Readers will guess that no record exists of any investors in Corporation tithe income being named as lay rectors, or required to make repairs, or having a right of burial in the chancel. This has not stopped it being said that Shakspere (and his heirs) had sole responsibility for maintaining the Church – and failed to do it.

Appendix I

William Shakspere – the Recorded Facts

By 1890, some ten facts were known about the life of William Shakspere of Stratford. All else in his supposed biographies was either anecdote or invention or deduced from the works of Shakespeare. Since then, the sifting of millions of documents in the forlorn hope of finding something to relate Shakspere to Shakespeare, or at least show he was a writer, has revealed more about his life than we know of almost any of his peers. Sadly, though, for the orthodox theory, the new discoveries showed no connection between him and the writer Shakespeare. Records now held for William Shakspere, including some other relevant people, are listed below.

Readers need to know, for the dating of the records, that New Year's Day was changed in 1753 from Lady Day (25th March) to the present 1st January. Most writers use the second of these even for Shakspere's lifetime and we will do the same to be consistent. This may cause discrepancies between our dates and those in a few other records but that can be easily checked. These others put the first draft of Shakspere's will as January 1615, as it was prior to New Year's Day on 25 March: here we give it as January 1616.

Entries put in square brackets are almost certain, though they have been deduced. Within the above records, where there is more than one entry on the same matter – as with the four for William Shakspere's case against Addenbrooke in 1608 – only one has been included here unless others add extra relevant information on him.

1552	Father John Shakspere fined for keeping midden in Henley Street
1556	Father John named as Glover
1556	Father John appointed as "Taster of Bread and Ale"
1556	Father John sues Henry Field (later father of Richard) for 4½ tons of barley
[c. 1557	Father John and mother Mary née Arden married]
1558	First daughter Joan baptised as Shakspere
1558	Father John buys Henley Street property
1558	Mother Mary bequeathed father's land at Wilmecote
1560	First daughter Joan buried
1561	Father John made Stratford Chamberlain
1562	Daughter Margaret baptised as Shakspere (dies in infancy)
26 Apr 1564	Son William baptised as Shakspere at Holy Trinity Church, Stratford
4 July 1565	Father John made Stratford Alderman
13 Oct 1567	Brother Gilbert baptised as Shakspere
1568	Father John made Stratford Bailiff
5 Apr 1569	Sister Joan (second of that name) baptised as Shakspere
1569	Father John sues debtor who has purchased wool
1570	Father John charged with usury, fined 40s (£1200 today)
1571	Father John made Deputy Bailiff
28 Sept 1571	Sister Anne baptised as Shakspere
Jan 1572	Father John goes to London on Stratford business
1572	Father John charged with illegal wool dealing at Westminster
1573	Warrant for Father John over debt for £30 (named as whyttawer – a whitener of skins)
11 Mar 1574	Brother Richard baptised as Shakspere
1575	Father John buys two houses (one next to his in Henley Street)
1576	Father John applies for coat of arms
1576	Father John stops attending Council meetings
1578	Father John mortgages wife's house at Wilmecote to relative, Edmund Lambert
1578	Father John excused poor tax
1578	Father John sells part of his property
1578	Father John named as "whyttawer"
1578	Father John sued for £30
1579	Father John sells and mortgages more of his property
4 Apr 1580	Sister Anne buried as Shakspere
3 May 1580	Brother Edmund baptised as Shakspere
1580	Father John fined £20 in Westminster as a pledge for his conduct
Summer 1580	Father John seeks "sureties of peace" against his creditors for fear of death

[August 1582	In Stratford with Anne Hathaway at conception of daughter Susanna]
27 Nov 1582	Licence issued for marriage of William Shaxpere with Anne Whateley
28 Nov 1582	Bond issued to ensure propriety of marriage of William Shagspere and Anne Hathaway
Winter 1582	Father John witness in Chancery suit about his in-law Ardens' estates
26 May 1583	Daughter baptised as Susanna Shakspere
[April 1584	William with his wife, now Anne Shakspere, in Stratford – at conception of twins Hamnet and Judith]
2 Feb 1585	Twins Hamnet and Judith baptised as Shakspere
Jan 1586	Father John issued with order for debt, but has no goods to distrain
Sept 1586	Father John removed as Alderman for 10 years' non-attendance
1588	Father John and mother Mary begin unsuccessful suit against John Lambert for return of Mary's property (William added as plaintiff)
Mar 1592	Father John recorded absent from church "for fear of process for debt"
Sept 1592	ditto (though never fined for absences)
1592	Father John appointed to value assets of Henry Field (father of Richard) on his death
15 Mar 1595	Payment to William (and others) for play for the Queen at Greenwich, Christmas 1594
11 Aug 1596	Son Hamnet buried as Shakspere
20 Oct 1596	Application for coat of arms for Father John renewed (sketch of Arms produced, later marked "No, without right")
before Oct 1596	Recorded living in Bishopsgate, London
Oct 1596	Pursued for 5 shillings London taxes
29 Nov 1596	Writ in Southwark for William and three others to keep peace.
4 May 1597	Purchased New Place, Stratford, nominally for £60
15 Nov 1597	Reported in London for default of 5 shillings taxes
1597	Father John restarts case over lost Wilmecote lands
1598	Recorded living in St Saviour's parish, London
Jan 1598	Richard Quiney asks William about investing in Stratford land
24 Jan 1598	A. Sturley letter to R. Quiney says William interested in tithes
4 Feb 1598	Recorded as owning corn and malt at Stratford at time of shortage (and living at New Place)
1598	Received 10d (£25 today) for load of stone at Stratford
1598	Received 20d for wine to host visiting preacher
1 Oct 1598	Recorded as defaulter on London taxes in Billingsgate

25 Oct 1598	Letter from R. Quiney to William asking for £30 loan, (letter not sent)
30 Oct 1598	Letter from A. Quiney to son R. Quiney asking him to bring William's money
4 Nov 1598	A. Sturley writes to R. Quiney urging pursuit of William's loan
1598	Noted as hoarding 80 bushels (3 tons) of malt, etc. at lean time
1598	Recorded in "Enrolled Subsidy Account" at Stratford
28 Dec 1598	Assists in transfer of timbers to build Globe in Southwark
early 1599	Recorded owing taxes in Billingsgate
21 Feb 1599	William with others becomes lessee/shareholder in Globe
1599	Refused right to join his arms with the Park Hall Arden arms
1599	Recorded as owing taxes in St Helen's Parish, London
1599	Recorded as owing taxes in Clink in Southwark
1599	Recorded hoarding corn and malt at lean time
1600	First of William's nephews (son to Joan Hart) baptised
1600	Sued a John Clayton in Queen's Bench for 1592 loan of £7
6 Oct 1600	Tax arrears of 1 mark (13s.4d) in London
March 1601	Thomas Whittington's will bequeaths to the poor 40 shillings he is owed by Anne Shakspere (William's wife)
1601	Renews application for coat of arms
8 Sept 1601	Father John buried as Shakspeare (with no added "Gent")
1602	Named as player in draft coat of arms
13 Mar 1602	Mannigham records joke about William and Burbage as actors
1602	Referred to as *Generoso* (implying coat of arms now awarded)
1 May 1602	Buys land in Stratford for £320, brother Gilbert standing in at the exchange of contracts
1602	Legal proceedings over New Place deeds
1602	Thomas and Lettice Greene take apartment in New Place
28 Sept 1602	Buys cottage and land in Stratford for £80
1603	Named by James I as Groom of the Chamber
19 Mar 1603	Named as member of newly formed "King's Men"
15 Mar 1604	Issued with red cloth for entry of James I into London
18 Mar 1604	The Greenes' daughter baptised, named after Anne Shakspere
1604	Lodging with Mountjoys, Silver Street, London. (Negotiates marriage settlement for their daughter)
24 Oct 1604	Lessee of cottage at Rowington at 2s.6d per week
July 1604	Sues Mr Rogers (Stratford) for debt of 35s for 20 bushels of malt
1605	Left 30s in will of Augustine Phillips, less than Heminges and Burbage, same as Condell
24 July 1605	Invests £440 in Stratford area tithes

21 Jan 1606	Shown owing Mr Hubaud of Stratford £20
Easter 1606	Daughter Susanna named for non-attendance at church
5 June 1607	Daughter Susanna marries Puritan Dr John Hall as "Shaxspere" – William gives dowry of land
12 Aug 1607	Edward son of brother Edmund buried as Shackspeere in London
31 Dec 1607	Brother Edmund buried in London as Shakespeare
21 Feb 1608	Granddaughter Elizabeth Hall baptised
17 Jan 1608	The Greenes' son baptised, named after William Shakspere
July 1608	Brother Richard fined 1s.0d by Ecclesiastical Court
9 Aug 1608	With others, William took 21 year lease on Blackfriars theatre
1608	Sues Mr Addenbrooke (Stratford) for £6 debt
9 Sept 1608	Mother Mary buried as Shaxspere
16 Oct 1608	Stands Godfather to William Walker of Stratford
1609	Pursues Addenbrooke's surety, Mr Horneby, for £6
6 Apr 1609	Makes payment to poor relief in Southwark
1609	Brother Gilbert summoned to appear at Court of Requests
1610	Legal proceedings confirming ownership of New Place
1610	Completes purchase of 20 acres at Stratford begun in 1602
1611	Legal proceedings over William's tithe holdings
May 1611	Thomas Greene leaves apartment at New Place
1611	Contributed to cost of Stratford Parliamentary Bill
1611	Leases Stratford barn to Robert Johnson for £22
1611	Issues bill over Combe family default on rent
1611	Interest on William's tithes of £60 (£36,000 today)
11 May 1612	Witness in Belott–Mountjoy case: name on testimony in place of mark is "Willm Shakp"
3 Feb 1612	Brother Gilbert buried (Stratford) as Shakspere
28 Jan 1613	John Combe (Stratford) leaves William £5 in will
4 Feb 1613	Brother Richard buried (Stratford) as Shakspeare
10 Mar 1613	Buys Blackfriars Gatehouse for £140: name on purchase in place of mark is "William Shakspar"
11 Mar 1613	Takes mortgage for Blackfriars Gatehouse: name on document in place of mark "Wm Shakper"
31 Mar 1613	Receives 44s (also Burbage) for *impresa* for 6th Earl of Rutland (there is a query over the identities here)
29 June 1613	Globe burnt down
26 Oct 1613	With others, William takes share of new lease on Globe site
30 June 1614	Globe back in business
10 July 1614	Left £5 in will of John Combe
5 Sept 1614	Noted as owning 127 acres of land at Stratford
28 Oct 1614	Given surety against losing tithe income over enclosure
17 Nov 1614	In London with son-in-law John Hall to meet Stratford Town Clerk (Greene) over enclosures
23 Dec 1614	Meets Town Clerk, Thomas Greene in London, and regularly through 1615 in London and Stratford

26 Apr 1615	Launches "friendly" proceedings to obtain deeds of Blackfriars Gatehouse
May 1615	Prematurely mentioned as being dead in case Ostler-v-Heminges (daughter sues Heminges for taking husband's shares in Globe)
1615	Named with respect to land enclosures at Stratford
10 Jan 1616	Will drafted
1616	Noted in Jonson's Folio with actors in *Every Man Out Of His Humour* (1598) and in *Sejanus* (1603)
10 Feb 1616	Daughter Judith marries Thomas Quiney: causes William to change will
Feb/March 1616	Judith becomes pregnant, carrying boy who will be baptised Shaksper Quiney
12 Mar 1616	Thomas Quiney excommunicated for marrying in Lent without licence
24 Mar 1616	Thomas Quiney punished for getting another woman pregnant
25 Mar 1616	Will finalised showing link to Globe shareholders – name "Shakspere" three times on will in place of a mark with first name as "William", "Willm" and "William"
25 April 1616	Burial of William Shakspere Gent

APPENDIX J

THE TRUE SHAKSPERE FAMILY TREE

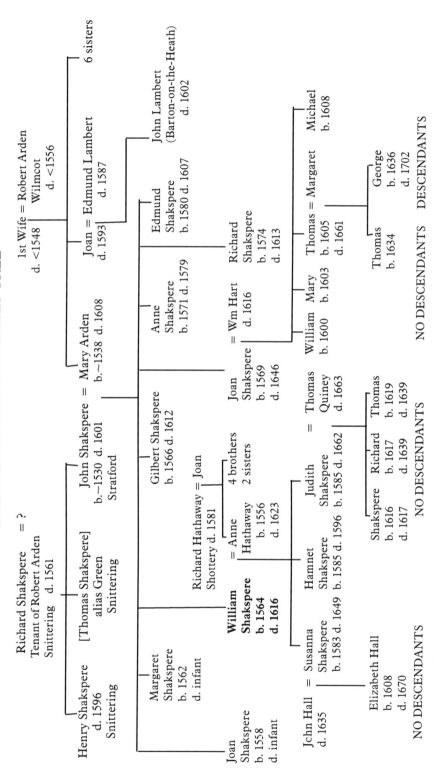

Bibliography

Ackroyd, P. (2006) *Shakespeare*: Chatto and Windus

Adams, J.Q. (1923) *A Life of William Shakespeare*: Constable

Alexander, P. (1951) *William Shakespeare: The Complete Works*: Collins

Anderson, M. (2005) *Shakespeare by another Name: The Life of Edward de Vere*:
    Gotham Books

Armstrong, E.A. (1946) *Shakespeare's Imagination*: Lindsay Drummond

Armstrong, P. (2001) *Shakespeare in Psychoanalysis*: Routledge

Akrigg, G.V.P. (1968) *Shakespeare and the Earl of Southampton*: Hamish Hamilton

Asquith, C. (2005) *Shadowplay*: Public Affairs

Aubrey, J, (circa 1681) *Brief Lives*, Ed. O.L. Dick (1972), Harmondsworth

Bald, R.C. (1949) 'The Booke of Sir Thomas More and its Problems', *Shakespeare
    Survey* 2, CUP

Baldwin, T.W. (1944) *William Shakspere's Small Latine and Lesse Greek*: Illinois UP

Barton, D.P. (1929) *Links between Shakespeare and the Law*: Faber and Gwyer

Bate, J. (2008) *Soul of the Age*: Viking

Bayley, J. (1998) 'A Nature Subdued', *Around the Globe* – No. 7 (Summer):
    Shakespeare's Globe

Beaurline, J. (Ed.) (1990) *King John*: New Cambridge Shakespeare

Bentley, G.E. (1948) 'Shakespeare and the Blackfriars Theatre', *Shakespeare Survey*
    Vol 1, CUP

Binns, J.W. 'Shakespeare's Latin Citations', *Shakespeare Survey* 35, CUP

Bloom, H. (1998) *Shakespeare – The Invention of the Human*: Fourth Estate

Boas, F.S. (1923) *Shakespeare and the Universities*: Shakespeare Head Press

Brill, E. (1968) *Old Cotswold*: David and Charles

Britton, P. (2001) *A Tapestry in Time*: Parish Church of Barcheston

Brown, I. (1949) *Shakespeare*: Collins

Brown, I. and Fearon, G. (1969) *This Shakespeare Industry*: Greenwood Press

Brook, G.L. (1976) *The Language of Shakespeare*: Andre Deutsch

Bryson, Bill (1990) *Mother Tongue*: Penguin

Bullough, G. (1957–75, 8 Vols) *Narrative and Dramatic Sources of Shakespeare*:
    Routledge and Kegan Paul

Burton, R. (1621) *The Anatomy of Melancholy*

Byrne, M.St.C. (1934) *The Social Background*: A Companion to Shakespeare Studies,
    CUP. Ed. Granville-Barker, H. and Harrison, G.B.

Chambers, E.K. (1930) *William Shakespeare: A Study of Facts and Problems*: 2vols, Clarendon Press. **Usually referred to in the text as *EKC*.**

Churchill, R.C. (1958) *Shakespeare and his Betters*: University of Indiana Press

Clarkson, P. and Warren, C. (1968) *The Law of Property in Shakespeare and Elizabethan Drama*: Gordian Press, NY

Cockburn, J.S. Ed. (1977) *Crime in England 1550–1800*: Princeton

Cockburn, N.B. (1998) *The Bacon Shakespeare Question*: Cockburn/Biddles

Connes, G. (1927) *The Shakespeare Mystery*: Palmer

Cox, J. (1985) *Shakespeare in the Public Records* (Ed. Thomas D.) HMSO

Cressy, D. (!987) *Literacy and the Social Order: Reading and Writing in Tudor and Stuart England*: CUP (revised 2006)

Crystal, D. (2005) *Pronouncing Shakespeare*, CUP and

—— (2006) 'Friends, Romans and Westcountrymen', *THES* 6 May

Crystal, D. and Crystal, B. (2002) *Shakespeare's Words*: Penguin

—— (2005) *Shakespeare Miscellany*: CUP

Cust, L. (1916) 'The Fine Arts', in *Shakespeare's England* Vol 2, Ed. Onions, C. T., Clarendon Press

Davies, J.M. and Franforter, A.D. (1995) *Shakespeare Place and Name Directory*: Fitzroy Dearborn

Dawkins, P. (2004) *The Shakespeare Enigma*, Polair, UK

Dawson, G.E. and Kennedy-Skipton, L. (1966) *Elizabethan Handwriting 1500–1650*, Norton, New York

Dawson, G.E. (1990) 'Shakespeare's Handwriting', pp. 119–128, 42 *Shakespeare Survey*, CUP

—— (1992) 'A Seventh Signature for Shakspeare': *Shakespeare Quarterly* 43 John Hopkins UP

DeLuna, B. (1970) *The Queen Declined: An Interpretation of Willobie his Avisa*: Clarendon Press

Devecmon, W.C. (1899) *In re Shakespeare's "Legal Acquirements"*: Kegan Paul

Dictionary of English Dialects (1898, revised 1970) 6 vols. Ed Wright, J.: OUP

Drummond, W. (1619) *Ben Jonson: Conversations with William Drummond*: rptd Bodley Head 1923

Dugdale, W. (1656) *Antiquities of Warwickshire*: Thomas Warren

Duncan-Jones (2001) *Ungentle Shakespeare*: The Arden Shakespeare

Dutton, R. Ed. (1985) *Ben Jonson: Epigrams and The Forest* (p18): Carcanet

Dutton, R. and Howard, J.E. (2006) *A Companion to Shakespeare's Works*, Volume 1: Blackwell

Eccles, M. (1960) *Shakespeare in Warwickshire*: University of Wisconsin Press

Edwards, P. (1952) 'An Approach to the Problems of Pericles', *Shakespeare Survey* 5: CUP

EKC – see Chambers (1930) above

Ellen, D. (1997) *The Scientific Examination of Documents*: Taylor and Francis

Erne, L. (2003) *Shakespeare as Literary Dramatist*: CUP

—— (2004) 'For the Stage and the Page', *Around the Globe* No. 26 (Spring)

Eysenck, H.J. and M.E. (1995) *Mindwatching*: Prion

Foster, D. (2002) 'An Elegy to Error', *Times Higher Education Supplement*, 28 June. (The story of the fantasy on John Ford's *A Funeral Elegy*).

Fripp, E.I. (1938) *Shakespeare: Man and Artist*: OUP (2 vols)

—— (1929) *Shakespeare's Haunts near Stratford*: OUP

Fuller, T. (1662) *The History of the Worthies of England*: London (re-isssue 1952, George Allen and Unwin)

Gibson, H.N. (1962) *The Shakespeare Claimants*: Methuen

Gifford, W. (1816) *The Works of Ben Jonson*: (Reprinted 1875, Bickers and Son)

Gillespie, S. (2001) *Shakespeare's Books*: Athlone Press

Gilvary, K. (Ed.) (2010) *Dating Shakespeare's Plays:* Parapress

Greenblatt, S. (2004) *Shakespeare: Will in the World*: Jonathan Cape

Greer, G. (1986) *Shakespeare*: OUP

—— (2008) *Shakespeare's Wife*: Bloomsbury

Greg, W.W. (1932) *English Literary Autographs 1550–1650*: OUP

—— (1954) *The Shakespeare First Folio*: OUP (Also see Pollard, A.W. and ors)

Grillo, Ernesto (1949) *Shakespeare in Italy*: Glasgow UP

Gurr, A. (1971) 'Shakespeare's First Poem: Sonnet 145', *Essays in Criticism*, 21

Hall, H. (1887) *Society in the Elizabethan Age*: London

Halliday, F.E. (1964) *A Shakespeare Handbook:* Duckworth

Hamilton, C. (1985) *In Search of Shakespeare*: Robert Hale

Harries, F.J. (1919) *Shakespeare and the Welsh*: Fisher Unwin

Harrison, W. (1587) *Description of England* (see in Pritchard, R.E. (1999) *Shakespeare's England*: Sutton Publishing)

Harsnett, S. (1603) *Declaration against egregious popish impostures*: London (Based on interviews with "possessed" individuals in Nottinghamshire published 1599.)

Hays, M.L. (1975) 'Shakespeare's Hand in Sir Thomas More: Some Aspects of the Paleographic Argument', *Shakespeare Studies* VIII

Henslowe, P. (2003) *Henslowe's Diaries*: Ed. Foakes, R.A., CUP

Highet, G. (1949) *The Classical Tradition*: OUP

Holden, A. (1999) *William Shakespeare: His Life and Work*: Little Brown

Holinshed, R. (1587) 2nd Edition *Chronicles* (see Boswell-Stone, W.G. *Shakespeare's Holinshed* (1987))

Holmes, M. (1978) *Shakespeare and Burbage*: Phillimore

Honan, P. (1998) *Shakespeare, A Life*: Clarendon

Honigmann, E.A.J. (1998) *Shakespeare: The Lost Years*: Manchester UP

Hotson, J.L. (1925) *The Death of Christopher Marlowe*: Harvard UP

—— (1937) *I, William Shakespeare...* , Jonathan Cape.

—— (1949) *Shakespeare's Sonnets Dated*: Rupert Hart Davies

Hughes, C. (1916) 'Land Travel', in *Shakespeare's England* Vol I, Ed. Onions, C.T., Clarendon

James I (reproduced 1924) *Daemonoligie*: Bodley Head

James, B. & Rubenstein, W.D. (2005) *The Truth Will Out*: Pearson Education

Jenkinson, Sir H. (1922) 'Elizabethan Handwriting', *The Library*, III

Jones, Emrys (1977) *The Origins of Shakespeare*: OUP

Jonson, B. (1641) *Discoveries (or Timber)*: reprinted by Bodley Head 1923

—— (1984) *Epigrams and the Forest*: Ed. Dutton, R., Carcanet Press (see Dutton)

Kathman, D. various websites

Keeton, G.W. (1930) *Shakespeare and his Legal Problems*: Black

—— (1967) *Shakespeare's Legal and Political Background:* Pitman

Kirkwood, A.E.M. 'Richard Field, Printer, 1589–1624', *The Library*, 4th Ser., XII (1932), ME 59–60

Kökeritz, H. (1953) *Shakespeare's Pronunciation*: Yale U P

Kornstein, D.L. (1994) *Kill all the Lawyers; Shakespeare's Legal Appeal*: Princeton UP

Lawson, J. and Silver, L. (1973) *A Social History of Education in England*: Methuen
Lee, S. (1916) *A Life of William Shakespeare*: Smith, Elder & Co.
—— (Ed.) (1904) *Elizabethan Sonnets*: Constable
Lefranc, A. (1919) *Sous le masque de "William Shakespeare"*: Paris (Translation.
    Cragg, C. (1988) *Under the Mask of "William Shakespeare"*: Martin Books)
—— (1945, 1950) *A la découverte de Shakespeare*: Paris
Leishman, J.B. (1949) *The Three Parnassus Plays (1598–1601)*: Nicholson and Watson,
    London
Looney, J.T. *Shakespeare Identified, Vol. II*: (3rd Edition as "Oxfordian Vistas", 1975
    Kennikat, New York)
McLure, N. (Ed.) (1939) *Letters of John Chamberlain*, American Philosophical Society
McManaway, J.G. (1967) 'John Shakespeare's "Spiritual Testament"', *Shakespeare
    Quarterly*, 17
Malim, R. (Ed.) (2004) *Great Oxford:* Parapress
Malone, E. (1790) *William Shakespeare: Plays and Poems* (see *SCDL*)
—— (1796) *Inquiry into the authenticity of Certain Papers and Instruments Attributed
    to Shakespeare*
Marti-Ibañez, F. (1959) *The Epic of Medicine*: Clarkson N. Potter, Inc.
May, S.W. (1980) 'Tudor Aristocrats and the Stigma of Print', *Renaissance Papers*
Michell, J. (1999) *Who wrote Shakespeare?*: Thames and Hudson
Miles, R. (1986) *Ben Jonson*: Routledge and Kegan Paul
Milward, P. (1973) *Shakespeare's Religious Background*: Sidgwick and Jackson
Miola, R. (2001) *Shakespeare's Reading*: OUP
Morgan, J. Appleton (1900) *A Study of the Warwickshire Dialect*: Shakespeare Press,
    NY
Mountfield, D. (1976) *The Coaching Age*: Hale
Muir, K. (1977) *Sources of Shakespeare's Plays*: Methuen
Mullan, J. (2007) *Anonymity*: Faber
Multhropp, Volker (1999) Undating *The Tempest*: website
Murray, J.M. (1936) *Shakespeare*: Jonathan Cape
Nicholl, C. (2005) *The Lodger: Shakespeare on Silver Street:* Penguin
Nicoll, A. (1958) *Shakespeare Jahrbuch 94*
OCEL or *Oxford Companion to English Literature*: Ed. Drabble (2000)
O'Connor, G. (1991) *William Shakespeare: A Life*: Hodder and Stoughton
OCS or *The Oxford Companion to Shakespeare*: (2001) Ed. Dobson, M. and Wells,
    S.
ODNB or *Oxford Dictionary of National Biography* (2004)
OED or *Oxford English Dictionary*
Ogburn, C. (1984) *The Mystery of William Shakespeare*: Dodd, Mead & Co., NY
Onions, C.T. (1911) *A Shakespeare Glossary*: OUP (revised by Eagleson (1986): OUP)
Oxford Companion to English Literature usually referred to as *OCEL* (see above)
The Oxford Companion to Shakespeare usually referred to as *OCS* (see above)
Palmer, A. and Palmer, V. (1981) *Who's Who in Shakespeare's England*: Harvester Press
Patterson, A. (1989) *Shakespeare and the Popular Voice*: Blackwell
Patterson, L.R. (1968) *Copyright in Historical Perspective*: Vanderbilt UP
Pollard, A.W. (1920) *Shakespeare's Fight with the Pirates*: CUP
—— and ors (1923) *Shakespeare's Hand in the Play of Sir Thomas More*: CUP
Pope, M. (1991) 'Shakespeare's Falconry', *Shakespeare Survey 44*: CUP
Praz, M. (1954) 'Shakespeare's Italy', *Shakespeare Survey 7*: CUP

Price, D. (2001) *Shakespeare's Unorthodox Biography*: Westport, Connecticut
Prior, R. (1972) 'The Life of George Wilkins', *Shakespeare Survey* 25: CUP
Puttenham, George [attributed] (1589) *The Art of English Poesie*
Rhodes, N. (2004) *Shakespeare and the Origins of English*: OUP
Robertson, J.M. (1913) *The Bacon Heresy: A Confutation*: Jenkins
—— (1926) *The Problems of Shakespeare's Sonnets*: Routledge
Rowse, A.L., (1963) *William Shakespeare, A Biography*: Macmillan, London
Sams, E. (1995) *The Real Shakespeare: Retrieving the Early Years*: Yale UP
Schoenbaum, S. (1970) *Shakespeare's Lives*: OUP (2nd Ed. 1991)
SDL (Schoenbaum, S. (1975) *William Shakespeare: A Documentary Life*: OUP)
SCDL (Schoenbaum, S. (1987) *William Shakespeare: A Compact Documentary Life*: OUP)
Schoenbaum, S (1981) *William Shakespeare: Records and Images*: Scolar Press
Shakespeare in the Public Records – see Cox, J.
Shapiro, J. (2005) *1599; A Year in the Life of Shakespeare*: Faber and Faber
—— (2010) *Contested Will: Who Wrote Shakespeare?* Faber and Faber
Simpson R., (1871) 'Are There Any Extant MSS in Shakespeare's Handwriting?' *Notes and Queries*, VIII
Smart, J.S. (1928) *Shakespeare: Truth and Tradition*: rptd (1966): Clarendon Press
Smith, L.P. (1907) *Life and Letters of Sir Henry Wotton*: Kessinger
Smith, Nicols D. (1916) *Authors and Patrons* in "Shakespeare's England" Vol. II, Ed. Onions, C.T.: Clarendon Press
Sokol, M. and B.J. (2000) *Shakespeare's Legal Language: A Dictionary*: Athlone
Southworth, J. (2000) *Shakespeare the Player*: Sutton
Spedding, J. (1850) 'Who wrote *Henry VIII?*' *Gentleman's Magazine* 178, NS 34
Sprague, H.B. (1902) 'Shakespeare's Alleged Blunders in Legal Terminology', *Yale Law Journal*, 11
Spurgeon, C. (1935) *Shakespeare's Imagery and What it Tells Us*: CUP
Stirling, B. (1949) *The Populace in Shakespeare*: AMS Press, NY
Stokes, F.G. (1924) *Who's Who in Shakespeare*: (2nd Edition 1991) Studio Editions
Stone, L. (1967) *The Family, Sex and Marriage*: OUP
Stopes, C.C. (1904) 'The True Story of the Stratford Bust', *Murray's Monthly Review,*
—— (1914) *Shakespeare's Environment*: Bell and Son
—— (1922) *The Life of Henry, Third Earl of Southamton, Shakespeare's Patron*: CUP
Tannenbaum, S.A. (1927) *Problems in Shakespeare's Penmanship*: Century, New York
Taylor, A. and Mosher, F.J. (1951) *The Bibliographical History of Anonyma and Pseudonyma*: U. Chicago P.
Thompson, E.M. (1916) "Handwriting" in *Shakespeare's England* Vol.I Ed. Onions C.T.:Clarendon Press
—— (1916) *Shakespeare's Handwriting: A Study*: OUP [see also Pollard A.W. and ors (1923) above]
Thumm-Kintzel, M. (1909 January) 'Shakespeare Bacon Forschung', *Leipzig Magazine*
Titherley, A.W. (1952) *Shakespeare's Identity – William Stanley, 6th Earl of Derby*: Warren and Son
Twain, M. (1909) *Is Shakespeare Dead?:* Harper
Twine, L. (1594) *The Pattern of Painful Adventures*
Vickers, B. (2007) *Shakespeare, A Lover's Complaint and John Davies of Herefordshire*: CUP

Wells, R. Headlam (2009) *Shakespeare's Politics:* Continuum Press

Wells, S. (2006) *Shakespeare and Co.*: Penguin

—— (2007) *Is it true what they say about Shakespeare?:* Long Barn Books

—— and Taylor, G. (1988) *The Complete Works of William Shakespeare*: OUP

Whalen, R.F. (1994) *Shakespeare, who was he?*: Praeger

White, R. Grant (1859) 'William Shakespeare Attorney at Law and Solicitor in Chancery', *Atlantic Monthly,* July 1859

Wiggins, M. (2001) 'Shakespeare and the Myth Makers', *Around the Globe*, 22 (Winter) London

Williams, R. (2006) *Sweet Swan of Avon*: Wilton Circle Press

Wilson, I. (1993) *Shakespeare – The Evidence*: Headline

Winter, L. (1993) 'Hamlet, Hales and Petit, and the hysteresis of action', *ELH*, 60

Wood, M. (2003) *Searching for Shakespeare*: BBC Books

Worden, Blair, (1992): 'Shakespeare and Politics', *Shakespeare Survey,* 44: CUP

Index

Note: The name of the author – Shakespeare – is treated first, followed by the name of the theatre-businessman from Stratford – Shakspere – in a separate listing. Where convenient, the initials FF have been used for the First Folio. References to illustrations are in **bold** type.